THE WRITINGS
OF
STEPHEN B. LUCE

U.S. NAVAL WAR COLLEGE
HISTORICAL MONOGRAPH SERIES

No. 1

Contents may be cited consistent with conventional research methods. Reprinting in part or whole requires permission of the President, Naval War College.

U.S. Naval War College, Newport, Rhode Island 02840

First Edition

THE WRITINGS
of
STEPHEN B. LUCE

Edited with Commentary by

John D. Hayes
and
John B. Hattendorf

Naval War College Press
Newport, Rhode Island
1975

Library of Congress Cataloging in Publication Data

Luce, Stephen Bleecker, 1827-1917
   The writings of Stephen B. Luce.

  (Historical monograph series; no. 1)
  "Annotated bibliography of Luce's writings": p. 274
  Includes index.
  1. Naval art and science—Collected works.
2. United States. Navy—Collected works. 3. Luce, Stephen Bleecker, 1827-1917—Bibliography. I. Hayes, John Daniel, 1902-
II. Hattendorf, John B. III. Title. IV. Series.
[V17.L8 1977]   359'.00973   76-51419

TABLE OF CONTENTS

Chapter		Page
	Introduction by Vice Admiral Julien J. LeBourgeois	v
	Preface	vii
I	THE MAN: Stephen B. Luce (1827-1917)	1
II	THE NAVAL WAR COLLEGE: An Address Delivered at the United States Naval War College, Narragansett Bay, R.I., June Second, Nineteen Hundred and Three	37
III	THE INTELLECTUAL FOCUS: On the Study of Naval Warfare as a Science	45
IV	TACTICS AND HISTORY: On the Study of Naval History (Grand Tactics)	69
V	LITERARY CRITIC: Three Book Reviews	99
VI	ADMINISTRATIVE REFORM: The Fleet	109
VII	FLEET CONTROL: Naval Strategy	125
VIII	NAVAL BASES: The Navy and Its Needs	147
IX	ANNOTATED BIBLIOGRAPHY OF LUCE'S WRITINGS, On Active Duty: 1862-1888	163
X	ANNOTATED BIBLIOGRAPHY OF LUCE'S WRITINGS, In Retirement: 1889-1911	201
XI	CHRONOLOGY OF LIFE AND WRITINGS	237
	APPENDIX—CATEGORY LISTING OF SIGNIFICANT ARTICLES CITED IN CHAPTERS IX AND X	251
	INDEX	253

ACKNOWLEDGEMENT

The publishing of this monograph was made possible by the generosity of the Naval War College Foundation, Inc. It is this Foundation that so richly deserves the credit of preserving the written works of one of the U.S. Navy's most distinguished officers, Rear Admiral Stephen B. Luce, founding father of the U.S. Naval War College.

INTRODUCTION

Rear Admiral Hayes and Mr. Hattendorf have, through this detailed study of the works of Stephen Bleecker Luce, provided us with an excellent portrait of the man and a timely comment on the intellectual heritage of the U.S. Navy. Here is a look at the individual perhaps most important in bridging the gap between the age of sailing ships and that of steam driven, armored battleships. Indeed, Luce not only contributed directly to the naval service but provided a focus, a direction, and a sounding board for the other great naval thinkers of the day—men like Alfred Thayer Mahan.

While Mahan was the naval strategist, an intellectual who made a most dramatic impact on maritime strategy in his day, Luce was the activist who had the greatest influence on his fellow officers. Rear Adm. Bradley A. Fiske wrote of him, "Luce taught the Navy to think ... he taught the Navy to think about the Navy as a whole ... he saw that a Navy in order to be good must be directed as an entity along a preconceived and definite line of strategy ... "

Luce and his associates were faced with a changing strategic environment in which the challenge was to build a Navy capable of exercising the international potential of the United States. In today's world the U.S. Navy faces a strong competitor and potential new challenges. Luce and the thinkers of his day faced the technological challenge of an industrial revolution and a world steeped in sociological and political change. Luce's experience should therefore provide a useful perspective for the contemporary naval officer concerned with his profession.

How very appropriate, then, that the authors have provided us with a look at Stephen B. Luce, a man who did so much to shape our Navy of the 20th century. It has special significance for the Naval War College for Luce himself once said with reference to the college: "Let officers who have completed their terms of sea service in their respective grades, come here for a two years course of study, not for discussion, but for study." The need for such study still exists. We at the Naval War College, like Luce, must focus our attention and direct our energies to creative thought in dealing with contemporary maritime problems. But the process does not stop there. We must articulate these ideas, and here again we can take a lesson from Luce. He was not only a thinker, but he was an active professional who was able to express his ideas in the forum of the day. He was a man true to his beliefs and committed to his profession; we are deeply indebted to Rear Admiral Hayes and Mr. Hattendorf for sharing the works of this outstanding naval officer with us.

Julien J. LeBourgeois

JULIEN J. LEBOURGEOIS
Vice Admiral, U.S. Navy
President, Naval War College

PREFACE

Stephen B. Luce, certainly one of the U.S. Navy's great officers, is still chiefly known only for having founded the Naval War College and for giving Alfred T. Mahan the chance to write his famous seapower series. As the readers of this volume will soon learn, these were but two of his many far-reaching contributions to his profession. The others were in such fields as education and administration where fame and glory for a military or naval man are seldom gained.

This is a volume of hero worship. The authors believe that the man of whom they have written is a hero in American naval history too long unrecognized. Luce was not the kind of man who was interested in his own fame and fortune. He found complete fulfillment in his career and felt little need to search for other more material rewards. After he retired, several publishers wrote, encouraging him to write his memoirs for publication. Invariably Luce refused. Characteristic of these exchanges must have been that in 1905 with Joseph B. Gilder, founder of *The Critic* and then a literary agent, who had written Luce on this subject. Unfortunately Luce's reply has not been found, but Gilder responded.

> It would be a national loss if the man who could write your letter refusing to be an autobiographist, should refrain from being one! You say you have written yourself out. Is it possible that the articles in which you have done so might be gathered together and printed in book form? I don't believe the Japanese voyage is the only bit of autobiography you have perpetrated in the process of "writing yourself out."[1]

We have taken on the task that Luce himself refused and have gone a step further in attempting to identify all of Luce's published writings.

Stephen B. Luce was not a hero in the popular sense, for although he belonged to the warrior trade, was proud of it, and spent his life preparing men for it, it was only in the preparation for war that he achieved his right to fame: in education, training, and even in those more prosaic seas of endeavor of military management and naval organization. Luce was, above all, a leader who knew how to handle men, even to manage them in the less respected sense of the word.

---

[1] J.B. Gilder (1858-1936) to Luce, 24 October 1905 in the Luce Papers, Naval Historical Foundation Collection, on deposit in the Library of Congress. Hereafter abbreviated as Luce Papers, LC. See bibliography item 126 in chapter X.

Luce was also a prolific writer. He wrote published material for 50 of his 90 years, but he did so for periodicals and magazines. As such he has "joined his fellow magazinists in the limbo of the forgotten ... The magazines are shifting sands."[2]

His prepared writings, however, represent only one side of his literary effort. There are also his letters which portray Luce the man, but the presentation of these must await another time. Luce's letters were not so much chronicles as were those of his respected naval mentor Samuel F. Du Pont,[3] but were letters written to get things done. In them he was "persistent in his demands and prolific with his suggestions,"[4] and whether his letter was five lines or five pages, a recipient or a reader today, as then, would seldom put it down before finishing.

To Luce, writing was a means to an end, a direct vehicle for accomplishing particular purposes. He was an activist, not a contemplative, little interested in ideas for their own sake.

The authors have endeavored to portray this man through his prepared writings and have approached this task from three bearings. They offer:

(1) A brief biographical summary and an essay on Luce.

(2) A half dozen of his most representative and relevant, but not necessarily his best, professional essays, edited in the current form of the discipline.

(3) Abstracts of his prepared articles: periodical essays, book reviews, official reports, and contributions to newspapers with full bibliographical citations to all of Luce's known writings.

This is the means we have chosen to direct military officers, maritime people, historians, and writers, as well as practitioners and students in the areas of management and civil military relations, even naval buffs, to find what we believe to be excellent guidance. Here, too, are some fine yarns, many of which came from the old men-of-warsmen Luce respected and loved.

In the preparation of this volume, we have received the help and support of many, all of whom should be acknowledged. Space considerations, however, allow only a few to be mentioned. Editors will not have it otherwise.

---

[2] Frank L. Mott, *A History of American Magazines*, 5 vols. (Cambridge, Mass.: Harvard University Press, 1966-1968), vol. III, p. 16.

[3] J.D. Hayes, ed. *Samuel Francis Du Pont, a Selection from His Civil War Letters*, 3 vols. (Ithaca, N.Y.: Cornell University Press, 1969).

[4] Donald N. Bigelow, *William Conant Church and the Army and Navy Journal* (New York: Columbia University Press, 1952), p. 209.

To our editor, Comdr. Robert M. Laske, we make the first bow. We shall always be in his debt.

We are also deeply indebted to the late Mrs. Philip R. Alger, that grand lady of Annapolis, Md., whose productive years exceeded those of Luce and whom the senior partner of this writing team regarded as a good friend. From the Army family of Meigs and the Navy family of Rodgers, she was a bridge who attended the actual opening of the Naval War College in 1884. Her clear recollections about it and other happenings of those days in which Stephen B. Luce was involved were an incalculable aid to our efforts. How short are 90 years. She was the widow of Philip R. Alger,[5] editor of the *United States Naval Institute Proceedings* from 1903 until his death in 1912, who we believe to be the outstanding military and maritime editor in the history of American service periodicals. We consider the Alger years to have been the most dynamic in the *Proceedings'* century of publication. He controlled the periodical when Luce so needed it in his fight for line officer direction within the Navy Department.

At the Naval War College, Lt. (jg.) Craig L. Symonds of the Strategy Department faculty has generously offered sound and constructive criticism. Anthony S. Nicolosi, Curator of the Naval Historical Collection, has given staunch support and valuable assistance in a wide variety of ways since the very inception of this project. Both of these scholars have been thoroughly aware of our problems and have been personally most helpful. Professor James E. King, Director, Department of Advanced Research, under whose cognizance this work was undertaken, generously allowed our work to be the first in his newly established department.

Doris Maguire of Centerville, Md., who has unearthed so much new Mahan material, has found for us many Luce letters and leads. David A. Rosenberg of the University of Chicago helped with several difficult research problems.

Many naval officers, historians, and graduate students will join us in our thanks to the Naval History Division, Washington, D.C. In particular, we thank Dr. Dean Allard, Head, Operational Record Section; Mr. W.B. Greenwood, Navy Department Librarian; and Mrs. Agnes Hoover in the Curator's office for their enthusiastic aid.

We thank the librarians who have helped us, notably at Brown University, Providence, R.I., and especially at the Naval War

---

[5] Austin M. Knight, "Professor Philip Rounseville Alger, U.S. Navy—an Appreciation," *United States Naval Institute Proceedings*, vol. XXXVIII, March 1912, pp. 1-5.

College where Luce's own library is part of the collection. The War College librarians not only aided us but put up with us and our clutter blocking their stacks and aisles. We thank the staffs of all the libraries that have helped us: Redwood Library, Newport, R.I.; G.W. Blunt White Library, Mystic Conn.; U.S. Coast Guard Academy Library; U.S. Naval Academy Library; Rice University Library; Navy Department Library; Rhode Island Historical Society Library; Newport Historical Society; the Center for Research Libraries, Chicago, Ill.; Peabody Museum, Salem, Mass.; U.S. Army Military History Research Collection, Carlisle Barracks, Pa.; Marine Corps Historical Office, Washington, D.C.; and the Library of Congress.

The job would never have been done were it not for the editorial, composition, and layout assistance of Miss Leonora Mello, Mrs. Eleanor Silvia, Mrs. Mary DeMenezes, and Mrs. Helen LeBlanc of the Naval War College and our principal typists: Mrs. Sara E. McKee, Mrs. Ruth Saurette and Miss Genevieve Pietraszek of the Naval War College, Mrs. Audrey Amburgey of Manistee, Michigan and Mrs. Vernon Wild of Texas City, Texas.

We thank our families for what they have done for us and which only we can know.

Now we come to the happy, but nevertheless difficult task of sincerely and enthusiastically thanking Vice Adm. Stansfield Turner, USN, and the late Rear Adm. Richard W. Bates, USN (Ret.), President and founder Vice President of the Naval War College Foundation. Without the personal interest of Turner and Bates, the writings of Stephen B. Luce would have still remained unknown.

Finally, we are grateful to the people of the United States whom, like Luce, we have had the honor to serve and who have made all this possible through our active and retired pay.

Stephen B. Luce, it has been a joy to know you; we do not apologize for the rhetoric that you taught us.

JOHN D. HAYES

JOHN B. HATTENDORF

Naval War College
Newport, R.I.
31 August 1973

CHAPTER I

THE MAN: STEPHEN BLEECKER LUCE (1827-1917)

I

Stephen B. Luce was active in the affairs of the United States Navy for 75 of his 90 years. He entered the Navy as a midshipman in 1841, served on active duty through both the Mexican and Civil Wars, and, after his retirement in 1889, continued to advise, to write, and to influence naval men until his death in 1917. Throughout his career he never allowed himself or those to whom he gave counsel to forget that the primary purpose of a navy was to wage war, and regardless of how remote the possibility of war, the professional function of the officers was to study war and to train their men for it. His insight, zeal, and untiring energy helped bring about a transformation in American naval thought.

Luce's most productive years were in the decades of the 1870's and 1880's, an intellectual watershed and material nadir of the American Navy. The contemporary British writer Oscar Wilde noted the situation in his satiric short story "The Canterville Ghost." In this story, Virginia, the American Ambassador's young daughter, advised the 300-year-old ghost of Sir Simon de Canterville that he should leave England and emigrate to America for his self-improvement. The ghost replied to the proposition:

"I don't think I should like America."

"I suppose because we have no ruins and curiosities," said Virginia satirically.

"No ruins! No curiosities!" answered the ghost, "You have your Navy and your manners."[1]

During the Civil War, the American Navy had achieved a remarkable reputation abroad. The battle between the *Monitor* and *Merrimac* had dramatically reinforced the impulse toward

---

[1] The story was published in the collection entitled *Lord Arthur Savile's Crime and Other Stories* which first appeared in 1890. The quotation is from "Stories," *The Works of Oscar Wilde* (London: Collins, n.d.), p. 327. For some recent detailed studies of defense matters in this period, see Kenneth Hagan, *American Gunboat Diplomacy* (Westport, Conn.: Greenwood, 1973); Lane C. Buhl, "Smooth Water Navy," Unpublished Ph.D. Dissertation, Harvard University, Cambridge, Mass., 1969; Stanley Sandler, "A Navy in Decay: Some Strategic Technological Results of Disarmament 1865-69," *Military Affairs*, vol. XXXV, No. 4, December 1971, pp. 138-41; R. Seager II, "Ten Years Before Mahan: the Unofficial Case for the New Navy, 1880-1890," *Mississippi Valley Historical Review*, vol. XL, No. 3, December 1953, pp. 491-512; B.F. Cooling, *Benjamin Franklin Cooling* (Hamden, Conn.: Archon Books, 1973); R.F. Weigley, *The American Way of War* (New York: Macmillan, 1973).

armored steamships among the European navies. In the years after the war, however, a general disarmament and lack of concern in Congress led to retrenchment in naval affairs. In general, the American people turned their eyes and efforts to the development of the heartland. The rich farmlands of the West and the lure of the frontier seemed to offer far more potential than the sea which had been the basis for so much of early American development. The Navy and the merchant marine were neglected. The golden age of American sail which Luce had seen in his youth was gone, and the technological innovation which had been applied during the Civil War had been suspended in naval affairs.

The complex affairs of the 1870's and the 1880's in America gave birth to a variety of elements, each of which had their impact on naval developments. The discovery of rich deposits of gold and silver in Colorado and the Dakotas, the growth of railroads across the continent, the rise of scientific agriculture, and the migration of some 8 million people to the West between 1865 and 1890 led to the disappearance of the American frontier. The outward expansion which for 25 years had absorbed the efforts of America began to move in other directions. Based on more than just a psychological diversion from the land frontier, the stimulus for this new expansion involved the growth of great corporations, the ability to create capital at home and to borrow abroad. It involved the discovery and large-scale exploitation of such natural resources as iron ore, coal, natural gas, copper, gold, silver, and oil. The practical application of science and technology acted as a catalyst to the processes of industry and transportation. This, in turn, was aided by the availability of a relatively cheap labor supply, much of it taken from the rising numbers of immigrants. All these many factors combined to increase the size of cities and factories, to stimulate the growth of the population, to modify social patterns, to widen the American intellectual and political outlook, and to develop American nationalism.

The Navy was very much a part of the general dynamism sweeping the American scene. Many of the factors seen on the broader scale had their impact in naval development. Among other influences, the Navy shared the revived application of technology, the inspiration of industrial techniques of organization and construction, the psychology of expansion, and the broadening of intellectual horizons. While the Navy gave few outward signs of change before the late 1880's, the years after the Civil War were a time of ferment, preparation, and adaptation.

Stephen B. Luce was an important figure in the Navy's

adjustment to the new age. He was able to carry forward some of the spirit of the sailing navy and to infuse it into the newly refurbished fleet. Unlike some of the younger men, he was able to perceive that the individuals who controlled and directed the new technology were far more important than the weapons and machines themselves. This perception provided the basis of his approach and contributed to the growing professionalism of the service. Luce was one of the men who formed a dynamic link between two major periods in our naval history: that of the sail and wooden ship with the navy of steam and steel.

Stephen Bleecker Luce was born in Albany, N.Y., on 25 March 1827, the second son of Vinal and Charlotte Bleecker Luce. The original Luce family came from England and settled in Martha's Vineyard, while his mother was from one of the old Dutch families of New York. When he was 6, his father moved to Washington, D.C., to become a clerk in the Treasury Department.

Stephen was appointed a midshipman in the Navy by President Martin Van Buren in October 1841 at the age of 14. A few weeks later he left his home and dog, Pontius Pilate, to join the line-of-battleship *North Carolina*, then the receiving ship at New York.[2]

His first 6 years at sea, as a midshipman, were spent in two of the finest men-of-war of the day, the frigate *Congress* and line-of-battleship *Columbus*. Two of the very able officers he served under became lifelong friends, David Dixon Porter and Percival Drayton. The *Congress* cruised both the Mediterranean and the South American stations while *Columbus* took the young midshipman around the world, giving him a glimpse of Japan in the first visit that American men-of-war had made to that country.[3] This was followed by 6 months on the California coast during the Mexican War.

Like many other officers in the days before the Naval Academy, Luce received his earliest naval eduation at sea. Although the training was designed as only practical and vocational, the romance and adventure of the sea made a deep impression on Luce's fertile mind. Today, there is little direct evidence which remains to document for us the impact of these early influences, but one small item is striking in its connection with Luce's later career.

---

[2] See his memoir of this experience in a piece he wrote for *Youth's Companion* after retirement, "My First Ship," bibliography item 96.

[3] See "Commodore Biddle's Visit to Japan," bibliography item 126.

Midshipman S.B. Luce, *ca.* 1841

This photograph was taken about the time Luce was assigned to his first ship, the ship of the line, U.S.S. *North Carolina.* In 1892, Luce wrote a memoir of his experiences on board that ship for *Youth's Companion.* After six months on board, Luce was warranted midshipman and assigned to the frigate *Congress* for a cruise to the Mediterranean. During his first cruise he began to collect the songs which eventually became the basis for his book, *Naval Songs,* and to develop a serious interest in history. A painting done from this photograph hangs at the U.S. Naval Academy.

Photo: Newport, R.I., Historical Society

This clue to Luce's development was a rather plain book, an ordinary-looking history of ancient Greece.[4] This small volume had special meaning for a midshipman sailing the Mediterranean among the very ghosts of ancient Greece and Rome. Recognizing a historical interest in a younger friend, one of Luce's shipmates gave him the book so he could better appreciate some of the sights they had seen together. His shipmate inscribed it:

> With this little volume my *Dear* Luce, you can teach yourself the history of one of the most important epochs of the world—when learning was in its infancy—and when education was the monopoly of a class. In giving it to you, I am animated by a sincere wish for your welfare, and with a sincere desire to contribute my all in order to improve you. It would be gratifying to see you an officer in every sense of the word, and to accomplish this end, you must exercise your energy. With a view of leading your mind to a sense of its duties, this book has been presented to you.[5]

The book went with Luce as he sailed around the world in *Congress*. He brought it home, and it remained in his library for the rest of his life. This present from a good friend, in itself, was nothing unusual but the spirit of the gift had a profound effect on Luce's own life. The idea of teaching oneself and training the mind for professional duties stayed with Luce in his later years and marked his approach to education at the Naval War College.

After spending two 3-year cruises at sea, Luce, with a number of his contemporary midshipmen, was sent to the newly established Naval Academy. There he became a member of the second class to be sent to the school. These early classes little expected to follow a finely prescribed curriculum. For the most part, the midshipmen were at Annapolis to review the information which they had learned from their seagoing mathematics professors and to prepare for promotion examinations.[6] Luce spent the months between April 1848 and August 1849 studying for his examinations at Annapolis. As a passed midshipman, he then served, from

---

[4] John Gillies, *The History of Ancient Greece, Its Colonies and Conquests, from the Earliest Accounts Till the Division of the Macedonian Empire in the East, Including the History of Literature Philosophy, and the Fine Arts* (Philadelphia: Wardle, 1835). This inscribed volume is in the Naval Historical Collection, Naval War College, Newport, R.I.

[5] The inscription is signed, "By Your sincere friend, Robert C. Rogers. *Congress*, November 23d. '43."

[6] See Park Benjamin, *The United States Naval Academy* (New York: Putnam, 1900), p. 186. The Naval Academy was established at Annapolis, Md., 10 October 1845. Midshipmen of the 1841 date were promoted to "passed-midshipmen" during the years 1847, 1848, 1849, and 1850.

1849 to 1852, in the sloop-of-war *Vandalia* on the Pacific station. Fortunately, part of his personal journal for this period is preserved among his papers. This ledger-size book gives a good picture of the young officer in Honolulu, San Francisco, and on board ship and also provides an insight into his reading habits: Milton's *Paradise Lost*, Dickens' *Old Curiosity Shop*, works of Shakespeare, and George Grote's 12-volume *History of Greece*. In addition, he read the Bible and knew it well. He became familiar with the writing of Augustin Calmet, a French Biblical scholar, the sailor-poet Falconer, and authors such as Byron, Mommsen, and James Fenimore Cooper. While reading these works, Luce provided for his own liberal arts education through broad reading, travel, and experience. As he became proficient in the practical skills of his profession, Luce developed a sensitive appreciation for the type and quality of men that the naval service required. Understandably, this viewpoint progressed with the scope of his practical experience. In his early years, the young naval officer necessarily dealt with the immediate problems around him: seamanship, gunnery, training, and the education required for officers to lead and to organize men.

Following his tour of duty in *Vandalia* came 4 years in the Coast Survey. For a brief period in 1853 he assisted Lt. James M. Gillis with calculations made from Gillis' observations of Venus and Mars between 1849 and 1852. Luce was then assigned to various survey ships on the Atlantic coast where he continued to gain experience in the scientific aspects of his profession: astronomy, oceanography, cartography, and hydrography. On 7 December 1854, Stephen married a childhood friend, Elisa Henley, daughter of Commodore John C. Henley and a grandniece of Martha Washington.[7]

From 1857 to 1860, Luce served as a lieutenant in the sloop-of-war *Jamestown*, then on the east coast of Central America. By this point in his career he had gained a wide variety of experience from which to draw some sound observations about his profession and to outline the general direction of his future career. In 1858 the 31-year-old officer wrote in his private journal:

> It is my *opinion* . . . that the navy should be re-organized. Let me commence with the officers and enumerate all that I would do. The present system of education for young naval cadets is one which will ultimately be serviceable to the Navy

---

[7]Three children were born of the marriage: John Dandridge Henley Luce (1855-1921), Caroline (1857-1933), and Charlotte (1859-1946).

and highly beneficial to the country generally. Therefore, for the future we entertain no fears at present, but I am sorry to say that there are *now* in our service, men who wear the navy uniform, but who are totally deficient in education, both as officers and gentlemen, men who are not fit to be entrusted with the command of the meanest scow, or to associate with an honest labourer of the lowest order. Let such as these be either dismissed or "laid upon the shelf" never again to do duty in any shape or way. It is such men as these who abuse the little authority granted them, causing greater restrictions placed upon their brother officers, and gaining for the service an unenviable name.... For the younger officers, as I said before the present system of education is good, but it is yet imperfect—it would be a good plan to man a small brig with midshipmen, having some good officer in command. Let them commence and rig her, stow her holds, get the guns on board &c. and perform all the duties of a common sailor, they ought also, at as early an age as is possible be given the charge of the deck, that they may learn to have confidence in themselves.

There is too little attention paid to the crews of our ships. They are *not all* Americans, this is one *very* great fault, they are not allowed enough liberty, and are allow'd too much grog. Let these two very important items be well considered, let a system of punishment be arranged, the present is as absurd as it is useless.

Every ship in the service should have the same internal rules and regulations, the same routine of duty, the same form for station bills, *the same gun exercises* and in fact the same everything, they should differ as little as possible. The English Navy in some respects is a very good pattern. We only seem to copy their uniforms. Will nothing less than a war, effect a change for the better in the Navy?[8]

These words are significant. They express an early perception of many of the problems to which Luce would devote his later career: education, organization, training, and administration. These fields of interest seem unusual when compared to those of other officers at the time, but the choice was very much a product of his own experience.

In the years before the Civil War, he developed a broad

---

[8] S.B. Luce, "Private Journal," *ca.* 1858, Luce Papers, LC.

perspective which encouraged in him a desire for further knowledge of literature and history. He developed an understanding of men and the ways in which they could be sympathetically handled. Even at this early stage of his career, Luce saw that many of the problems which confronted the Navy lay basically in an incomplete system of fleet and shipboard organization. Thus he developed a deep interest in education and training and, at the same time, perceived the need for reform.

Orders to the Naval Academy in 1860, as an instructor in seamanship and gunnery, just before the Civil War, provided his first opportunity to write and to publish. His initial published effort was in the area of practical training: the compilation and revision of textbooks for the Naval Academy.

As part of this work, Luce first revised a small gunnery manual and further saw the need for a text in seamanship. He realized that the books on this important subject which were already in print were inadequate. In recommending to the Commandant of Midshipmen that a seamanship text be prepared, he noted:

> Compared to the Army with their wealth of professional literature, we may be likened to the nomadic tribes of the East who are content with the vague tradition of the past.
>
> Does it seem creditable then, Sir, to this Institution that it should possess no text book on the most important branch taught within its halls?[9]

When this textbook finally did appear a year or so later, it was not an original treatise on seamanship but a compilation from a wide variety of sources.[10]

While Luce was teaching at the Academy, the Civil War broke out, forcing the Luce family to move to Newport, R.I., where the Naval Academy was transferred for the duration of the war. The family remained in Newport during the later periods he was at sea and developed a strong affection for the town. Eventually, in 1880, they settled permanently in Rhode Island.

Luce's service during the Civil War was divided between the Naval Academy and the South Atlantic Blockading Squadron. He participated in the early bockade, the operations at Hatteras Inlet, and the Battle of Port Royal, S.C. His most fruitful activity during

---

[9] Luce to C.P.R. Rodgers, Commandant of Midshipmen, 26 February 1861, Luce Papers, LC.

[10] See the London *Times*, 24 October 1871, p. 6. Here Luce was accused of plagiarizing the seamanship studies of Vice Adm. George S. Nares (1831-1915), British explorer and navigator. No evidence has been found which indicates this accusation was carried further.

this period, however, had nothing to do with the prosecution of the war. In the summer of 1863, he took his first command, the midshipman practice ship *Macedonian,* to Europe, visiting the naval activities at Portsmouth and Plymouth, England, and Cherbourg, France. The French Navy at this time was in the midst of a resurgence. The English met the French challenge, and both nations were developing efficient maritime administrations and excellent training systems. Luce compiled a comprehensive report on European naval training and later used this information as source material in his articles and letters recommending a system which would be appropriate for the United States. Shortly after returning from Europe, Luce was ordered to command the monitor *Nantucket.*

The poor quality of many of the men in the Union Navy at this time was painfully evident to him. The situation was no better than that which he had perceived in 1858. Wartime service in the Navy held few attractions for enlisted men. Blockade duty was arduous and boring, liberty ashore was infrequent, and the grog ration had been stopped in 1862. Even prize money was largely a delusion; only the crews of a few lucky ships received it.

The physical environment for naval officers was somewhat better, and the expansion of the Navy had required them in large numbers. Drawn from both oceangoing ships and river steamers, the Union Navy would have been unable to perform its demanding task without these men, but they did have their limitations.

While in command of *Nantucket,* Luce resolved to search for a remedy. He wrote several articles on naval personnel and training for the *Army and Navy Journal* at this time, and after the war he developed a plan that included an apprentice system for the Navy and a parallel program of maritime schoolships for those aspiring to be officers in the merchant marine. Reform of the merchant training system was his first accomplishment. He based it on the 1862 Morrill Act which established land-grant colleges "to promote the liberal and practical education of the industrial classes in the several pursuits and professions of life." This act was the origin of the agricultural and mechanical arts colleges and many of the country's state universities. Luce expanded on the original concept and extended it to include the knowledge of nautical sciences among young men in the coastal states.

He wrote the bill which both extended the Morrill Act to nautical education and authorized the Secretary of the Navy to loan ships and to detail officers to public marine schools. This bill was enacted into law on 4 January 1874, and by January the following year Luce had personally fitted out the sloop-of-war *St. Marys* and drafted plans, rules, and regulations for her to function as the New York State Maritime School. Comdr. Robert L. Phythian[11] was chosen as the school's first superintendent. Other schools followed in Massachusetts, Pennsylvania, California, Maine, and Texas. To meet the academic needs of these schools, Luce wrote a textbook, *The Young Seaman's Manual*. Taken from *Seamanship*, it provided the information needed in the new curriculum he had designed for merchant marine apprentices.

Once this program was effectively organized, Luce transferred his energies to naval training and education. He spent the years from 1877 to 1883 in schoolships fashioning a naval apprentice program for training afloat. Eventually transferred ashore, it became the naval training system.

It was during this period that Luce produced his volume of *Naval Songs*.[12] He believed that singing was an effective means of instilling traditions of the sea and teaching the type of discipline that stresses dependence on one another.

In the mid-1870's, Luce had established himself well enough in naval circles to receive serious backing in his effort to reform the Navy Department in Washington. While in command of *Hartford* at Norfolk, Va., Luce met Congressman W.C. Whitthorne[13] when the Tennessee Representative was inspecting the Norfolk Navy Yard in February 1876. Whitthorne, a former Confederate general, was chairman of the Naval Affairs Committee in the Democratic controlled 44th (1875-1876) Congress and was the first chairman of that committee. Although from an inland state which did not have a navy yard, Whitthorne became one of the Nation's chief spokesmen for naval preparedness. With other legislators, such as Eugene Hale, Charles Bontelle, Hilary Herbert, and Henry Cabot Lodge, Whitthorne deserves credit for supporting the new American Navy of the 1880's. Luce's meeting with Whitthorne was the beginning of a relationship that was nurtured by 15 years of correspondence. Throughout his letters to Whitthorne, Luce clearly presented his views on the state of the Navy and his ideas on the reforms that were needed. In 1878 Luce advocated

---

[11] Capt. Robert L. Phythian (1835-1917) later served as Superintendent of the Naval Academy 1890-94. Today the school Luce founded is the State University of New York Maritime College, Fort Schuyler, N.Y.

[12] See bibliography items 69 and 116.

[13] Washington Curran Whitthorne (1825-1891), Tennessee Congressman and U.S. Senator.

reforming the Navy Department so that it would more successfully carry out government policy, complement the Army, and adequately represent the Nation. To achieve these goals, he recommended to Whitthorne the establishment of a "mixed commission" made up of Congressmen, Army and Navy officers, as well as other prominent citizens. For a time there seemed promise of success, but in the end the attempt failed. It was to be 30 years before the Moody Board would consider the basic problems behind this recommendation. Nevertheless, Whitthorne continued to listen to Luce's advice while serving in the House of Representatives and, later, the Senate. In this relationship, Luce had found an outlet in Congress for his views.

It was during this same fertile period in Luce's thinking that he came into contact with Col. Emory Upton,[14] then at the Artillery School at Fort Monroe, Va. In 1877 Luce had been giving a considerable amount of thought to establishing an advanced school for naval officers. Some years later he wrote to his friend W.C. Church, "I used to talk to my old and lamented friend Genl. Upton about it a great deal. He was very enthusiastic and urged me on to make a move in regard to it. But I have never seen my way clear till now."[15] The opportunity came for Luce in 1882 with his assignment as the senior member of a commission to study and to make recommendations on the conditions of navy yards and naval stations. It was during the year that he was engaged in this work, that he was first able to closely associate with a Secretary of the Navy and present to him his ideas on naval education, strategy, and administration.

The beginnings of the Naval War College, its conception, and the early steps Luce took to get it established are clouded in some mystery and not a little myth,[16] but on 8 March 1884 Luce finally presented to the Secretary of the Navy a draft of a general order establishing the school. Secretary Chandler appointed Luce

---

[14] Col. Emory Upton (1839-1881) held the rank of brevet major-general during the Civil War. He was the author of *A New System of Infantry Tactics* and *Military Policy of the United States* (Washington: U.S. Govt. Print. Off., 1907).

[15] Luce to W.C. Church, 2 November 1882, Church Papers, LC.

[16] The Luce papers for this period are sketchy at best. Better sources exist in Luce's letters in other collections, especially those of Senator Nelson W. Aldrich (1841-1915) of Rhode Island and William C. Church (1836-1917) founder-editor of the *Army and Navy Journal*. Both collections are in the Library of Congress. Some of Luce's later correspondence relating to this period indicates that he was not clear in his own mind about events back in 1884. See also Ronald Spector, "Professors at War: The Naval War College and The Modern American Navy," unpublished Ph.D. dissertation, Yale University, New Haven, Conn., 1967.

to head a board which would elaborate on the subject and make specific recommendations. The board consisted of Luce, his sympathetic friend, Comdr. W.T. Sampson, and Lt. Comdr. Caspar F. Goodrich.

The report of the board, submitted 13 June 1884, concisely made the argument for establishing an advanced school of naval warfare and went on to consider the curriculum and location. Washington, Annapolis, New York, Newport, and Boston were all mentioned, but only the last two were critically examined. Newport was favored over Boston because in Rhode Island the college could be located close to a promising fleet base where a school of application could be established. At the same time the facility would still be close enough to "the Hub" to ensure that eminent talent from Harvard, the Massachusetts Institute of Technology, and other centers could easily visit the school.

The Naval War College was established by General Order 325 of 6 October 1884, and the first course was presented from 4 to 30 September 1885. The account of the actual opening has become apocryphal, no doubt blending truth with an element of drama. According to at least two accounts, before unlocking the door to the newly acquired building, Luce invoked the blessing of the Father, Son, and Holy Ghost on the former almshouse and made the sign of the cross. Whether truth or legend, the call for divine aid caused some wits in Washington to dub the new institution "Trinity College."

The Naval War College remains the most important single contribution made by Luce. For him all parts of the Navy came together there as a kind of brain for the naval *corpus*. It was not an intellectual refuge against technological innovation, but a place where the burgeoning technology could be effectively harnessed. At an early time, Luce saw the interrelationship between the fields of military and naval power and technology and international politics. While he himself was not equipped to provide the original theories which could tie these diverse elements together, he perceived the need to do so. Aside from his central role in establishing the Naval War College and creating its curriculum, Luce's crucial task was to choose the men who would carry out his program. He chose men for his faculty who he believed could provide the intellectual contribution which he felt the Navy needed. As the individual who could at once develop new and improved theories of naval tactics and contribute to the understanding of practical problems found in controlling a rapidly developing, technically oriented fleet, Luce chose Lt. William

McCarty Little. Eventually Little would be the man who adapted and developed naval war gaming for this purpose. As the theorist and historian who could elucidate on the interrelationship between national power and naval capability, Luce chose Capt. Alfred Thayer Mahan. These men were only two of many, but they were certainly the most successful in solving the problems which Luce had set before them.

The Naval War College was conceived as only part of Luce's larger scheme for the systematic development of the Navy, but in the latter portion of his lifetime, it became the aspect to which he devoted the majority of attention. Even after its establishment, the development of the War College along the lines which Luce had envisioned was not assured. The history of the Naval War College is not only the story of a battle for survival, but also an effort to retain a conception of curricular study which emphasized the development of naval science, intellectual stimulation rather than the mere training of officers in already preconceived ideas. In both these aspects Luce led the effort and advised those who followed him.[17]

A year after its opening, Rear Adm. Stephen B. Luce turned the presidency of the Naval War College over to Capt. Alfred T. Mahan and took command of the North Atlantic Squadron. Although markedly successful in this important command, Luce experienced some disappointment. The War College comprised only the theoretical part of Luce's plan, and it should have been supplemented by a permanent squadron of evolution, a sort of seagoing laboratory where the theoretical work of the college could regularly be tested. Luce tried to make the North Atlantic Squadron fulfill this function, but his hopes were not completely fulfilled.

There were several factors contributing to this: the poor condition of the majority of ships which made them unsuited for such work, unsettled conditions in Caribbean and Canadian waters which kept the squadron scattered, and an unfortunate feud in 1887 with the Secretary over the difficult Canadian fisheries question.

Arising from a difference of interpretation concerning American fishing rights in Canadian waters, Luce's deep interest in international law and politics led him into direct dealings with the

---

[17]See Spector, op. cit. Since many of Luce's ideas were derived from Britain and British experience, it is interesting to compare these developments there in officer education. See the excellent study by Brian Bond, *The Victorian Army and the Staff College, 1854-1914* (London: Methuen, 1972).

Commanding Officer of the Dominion Fisheries Service. The answers which Luce obtained from him regarding the Canadian position on the issue were distributed by Luce to American fishermen. By giving the fishermen the opportunity to understand the Canadian position, Luce believed that he was warning the fishermen and preventing them from getting into trouble with the Canadian authorities. Luce's initiative in the matter was widely reported in the newspapers, but a large segment of public opinion saw Luce's action as an outright recognition of the Canadian claims. Luce was reprimanded for not consulting the State Department on a matter which was under negotiation at the highest levels. Secretary of the Navy W.C. Whitney ordered Luce to withdraw his circulars.

Luce further incurred the wrath of the Secretary when interviewed by a New York journalist shortly after the event. Deeply embarrassed by the situation and still defensive, Luce unwisely referred to the Secretary of the Navy in a quotation from Shakespeare:

" . . . Behold the great image of authority:
A dog's obey'd in office."[18]

Shortly thereafter Luce offered his resignation of the North Atlantic Squadron. In an interview with Secretary Whitney, Luce explained that his intention had only been to protect the well-being of the American fisherman; he had not considered that it might be interpreted in such a way as to compromise the American negotiating position. In refusing Luce's resignation, Secretary Whitney wrote "[I] am satisfied that you should retain your present command. Your handling of the squadron at sea and the practice in tactics and fleet movements which you have given your officers during the last year, are especially to be commended."[19]

The exercises for which the Secretary commended Luce were indeed the high points of his command. It was on these occasions that the squadron was used as a squadron of evolution and first exercised tactically as a fleet. Adapting the theories used on the war gaming boards at the Naval War College, Luce applied them to practical tests with real ships and men. Most importantly for the future development of tactical doctrine, he emphasized coordina-

---

[18]The newspaper clipping containing the quotation from *King Lear*, act IV, scene 6, line 63, may be found in the papers of Secretary W.C. Whitney, LC.

[19]Whitney to Luce, 23 September 1887, Luce Papers, LC. For reports of the squadron exercises see bibliography items 76 and 83.

tion between land and sea forces during amphibious assaults and in attack on coastal fortifications. Using the entire squadron as a single tactical unit, Luce was able to demonstrate in practical terms some of the problems in joint operations. Thus, he succeeded in contributing to a broader perception of fleet control and employment.

Required by law to retire from active service on his 62nd birthday, 25 March 1889, Luce advanced his retirement a month and a half at his own request. On 16 February 1889, without ceremonial fanfare on board *Galena* at Key West, Fla., he simply had his flag hauled down at sunset. By 23 February he was at home in Newport, a distinguished retired officer, ready to devote himself completely to being a writer and adviser on naval affairs. He plunged directly into naval politics with his campaign to preserve the unique character and function of the Naval War College, which had been consolidated with the Torpedo Station on Goat Island in January 1889. His first letter dealing with this problem was mailed to Senator Nelson W. Aldrich of Rhode Island on 4 March 1889, the day the friendly Republican administration of President Benjamin Harrison took office.

"Permit me," he wrote the Senator,
to congratulate you on the success of your efforts to gain Congressional recognition of the College. That is a great point gained. And the appropriating of $100,000 for it is a handsome and substantial evidence of appreciation.

The next important step is to have the site changed from the location designated by Congress[20] to where it was first placed.[21]

On 14 March he mailed a long letter to the new Secretary of the Navy, Benjamin Franklin Tracy, unequivocally stating the problem as it related to the Torpedo Station, the Naval War College, Goat Island, and Coasters Harbor Island. Luce pointed out in the letter that there had been a measure of congressional misconception in understanding the character of the two schools. Those who had supported the consolidation of the Torpedo School on Goat Island with the War College believed that they were schools of the same genre which could be economically combined under one principal and one faculty. Luce, however, pointed out that:

---

[20] The Naval Appropriation Act of 2 March 1889 committed the money for a building at Goat Island, where Secretary Whitney wanted the Naval War College merged with the Torpedo School, instead of Coasters Harbor Island.

[21] Luce to Aldrich, 4 March 1889, Aldrich Papers, LC.

Each one was unique, of its kind, and bore little or no resemblance to any other institution in the land. One had to do with *Materiel* the other with Personnel. One had to do with the *manufacture* of a single implement of war; the other with the intelligent *uses* of all implements of war. The sphere of the one was limited to mechanical appliances and manual training; the other was scientific, and embraced the widest fields of research of the warrior and the statesman.[22]

It is no hyperbole to claim that this letter, in the hands of a sympathetic Secretary of the Navy, was instrumental in saving the Naval War College.

In the letter Luce also stressed the success of James R. Soley's course of lectures in international law, "an indispensable branch of the great study of war." Soley, the previous summer, had delivered one of his Lowell Institute lectures on European neutrality during the American Civil War. When in July 1890 Soley became Assistant Secretary of the Navy, under B.F. Tracy, Luce was spared further worries about the college while his friends were in office. Luce could now turn his attention to other matters such as the Revenue Cutter Service, his duties as Commissioner-General representing the United States at the Columbian Historical Exposition in Madrid, and, later, his official orders to duty as a retired officer, on the faculty of the Naval War College.

In July 1889 Luce published his article "Our Future Navy," one of his most influential articles.[23] In this piece he stressed the great need for battleships in the American fleet. Despite the popular interest for the new steel cruisers that had recently been built, Luce pointed out that the Navy was not yet an effective force for the application of American national power. The fleet needed balance in the form of battleships and cruisers. Each type of ship was designed for separate functions, and they could not effectively do each other's work. In an era of growing American imperialism, this article sparked a great amount of interest and enthusiasm among those who saw the Navy as an essential part of American power. Predating the publication of Mahan's first *Influence of Sea Power* book by 9 months, Luce outlined the course necessary for America to take in order to construct a fleet which could exercise power which Mahan had outlined in historical terms.

In this regard it is important to understand the close relation-

---

[22] Luce to B.F. Tracy, 14 March 1889, Record Group 45, National Archives. Tracy had taken office as Secretary of the Navy on 6 March 1889.

[23] See items 86-87.

ship between Mahan and Luce in the publication of this work and in the similarity of their ideas. In August 1889 Luce wrote to an old friend for help in getting Mahan's book published. The book was a collection of the lectures which Mahan had given at the Naval War College, the first ever offered at the school. Luce explained that "no one has urged Mahan more than I have to have the first series of lectures published..." After searching for a publisher willing to bring out Mahan's work, Luce felt,

> It is desireable now that he should "unload" as it were this large amount of ms. to enable him to relieve his mind of its care &c &c that he may continue this very valuable work and bring his history down to the present time. For you must understand that this is but part of his work. He and his collaborators are yet to develop from the lessons of the past the Science of *Modern* Naval Warfare. In short I am justified in saying that Mahan is doing for Naval Science what Jomini did for Military Science.[24]

Here is Luce, mentor, promoter, and agent for Mahan, helping to make connections that would be important for Mahan's success and encouraging him in a task which that writer found very unpleasant: the search for favor and money. Luce's motives were mixed in all this. He saw clearly the importance of Mahan's work and the need for its publication. He knew as well that success for Mahan in the wider world would justify his own work at the Naval War College and help to ensure its perpetuation. Mahan, after all, was dealing in his "Sea Power" studies with the assignment and direction which Luce had provided. Luce was continually prodding Mahan to bring his work up to date, to make direct analogies between history and contemporary problems, to generalize in a way which would have direct impact on the world of the 1890's. Well acquainted with the substance of Mahan's lectures, Luce wrote his article "Our Future Navy" in such a way that it made the quantitative jump between theory and practice. Using history as his basis, he recommended practical suggestions which would lead to the development of a strong, versatile Navy.

By direct, active, and effective lobbying during the congressional sessions between 1890 and 1893, Luce devoted himself to other maritime problems as well. He helped to prevent the Revenue Cutter Service, later the Coast Guard, from being

---

[24] Luce to J.S. Barnes, 5 August 1889, unsigned draft, Luce Papers, LC. Mahan's manuscript was finally accepted for publication through another connection by Little, Brown, and Co. of Boston in October 1889. The first copies came off the press in May 1890.

amalgamated with the Navy. At the time this union was being advocated by both the Revenue Marine and many officers in the Navy. It had the approval of the Secretaries of the Navy and Treasury. The fact that Luce was able to organize substantial opposition from among the Navy's senior grades that was able to counterbalance the power of those supporting the proposal demonstrated that his influence and leadership were still strong, despite his retirement.

"I am afraid I have stirred up a hornet's nest—unwittingly—or 'Put my foot in it,'" he wrote Soley, "But having put my hand to the Plough, cannot very well turn back—on the subject of Revenue Marine bill."[25]

Luce's opposition to joining the two services stemmed from the dissimilarity between their purpose and the nature of their activities. The function of the Navy, he held, was military; that of the Revenue Marine, civilian. The operating area of the first was the high seas; that of the second, the coastal waters of the United States. In event of amalgamation, some functions would likely be neglected, while others were given preference. The sought after improvement in the Revenue Marine was later achieved through legislation relating to that service itself and reforms within it beginning with the Act of 31 July 1894, requiring that a captain of the Revenue Cutter Service be chief of this division in the Treasury Department in place of a political appointee.[26]

At the height of American public interest in overseas expansion, Luce avidly supported those who wished to obtain American colonial bases. As Commander in Chief of the North Atlantic Squadron nearly a decade before, Luce had made many friends and established numerous contacts in the Caribbean. In 1897 Luce wrote a letter of introduction for the French consul at St. Thomas in the Danish West Indies to Senator Henry Cabot Lodge, in hopes that the two men might discuss ways in which the Danish West Indies could be easily transferred to American control. "The policy of acquiring outlying territory for our protection," Luce wrote Lodge, "once entered into, must continue up to a certain point. The Sandwich Islands coming under the American Flag must be followed by Cuba—peacefully, let us pray; and later by St.

---

[25] Luce to J.R. Soley, 22 September 1890, Luce Papers, LC.

[26] The reforms ended in 1915 with the amalgamation of the Revenue Cutter Service and the Life-Saving Service as the U.S. Coast Guard. See Capt. S.H. Evans, USCG, *The United States Coast Guard, 1790-1915* (Annapolis: United States Naval Institute, 1949). Its first captain-commandant was Ellsworth P. Bertholf (1866-1921), who resigned in 1883 as a U.S. Naval Academy cadet, class of 1886, entered the USRCS, and was a member of the Naval War College class of 1895.

Thomas by purchase, at a very small figure."[27] Nearly a year later, shortly after Dewey's victory at Manila Bay, Luce would recommend that Lodge bring to the attention of President McKinley the opportunity for the United States to seize the Spanish-held Caroline and Ladrone Islands in the Pacific.[28] Luce was no solitary voice in these matters, but it is significant that a leading naval officer was directly encouraging the Government to move along expansionist lines.

Shortly after the turn of the century, Luce once again turned his interest toward the U.S. merchant marine and its people. In 1904-1905, an attempt was made to revive the ailing American merchant marine encouraged to some extent by Winthrop L. Marvin's 1902 book *The American Merchant Marine.* Interest raised by this work resulted in the formation of the Mercantile Marine Commission by Congress with Jacob H. Gallinger, the powerful Republican Senator from New Hampshire, as chairman and Marvin as secretary. Marvin asked Luce's help and invited him to appear before the commission.

As usual, he went to considerable effort to assist the commission. The conference was held in Newport in the summer of 1904, and during its proceedings Luce was able to interest several of the participating active-duty admirals in the problem. Luce, the only retired officer in the group, prepared a letter to Senator Gallinger to be forwarded through the Secretary of the Navy. Capt. Charles S. Sperry, President of the War College, added a strong endorsement, as did the Chief of the Bureau of Navigation. Both the Secretary and Capt. A.T. Mahan testified before the commission.

Luce, in his testimony, read the letter. "A navy" he stated, "may be said to be the offspring of foreign trade... Our own history furnishes a conspicuous example of an extensive commerce giving birth to a navy."[29] He then discussed the contributions

---

[27] Luce to Lodge, 25 June 1897, Luce Papers, LC. The first serious suggestion for American purchase of the Danish West Indies was made in 1865. A treaty was ratified by Denmark in 1867 but never approved by the U.S. Senate. A second treaty was concluded in 1900, but the Danish legislature refused to ratify it. In 1917, after a plebiscite in the islands and at the height of fears that Germany might establish a naval base in the Caribbean, as Luce had hoped, the islands passed to the United States at "a very small figure," $25 million.

[28] Luce to Lodge, 10 May 1898, Luce Papers, LC. The United States acquired Hawaii in July 1898. Guam was taken in 1898, but the remainder of the Ladrone or Marianas Islands with the Caroline Islands were sold to Germany in 1899 by Spain. Following World War I, they were mandated to Japan in 1920. The two island groups are part of the United Nations Trusteeship of the Pacific Islands and have been under the jurisdiction of the United States since World War II.

[29] Luce to J.H. Gallinger, 17 November 1904, Luce Papers, LC.

made by merchant sailors in all our wars. However, he also cautioned that the contest with Spain had proved the merchant marine of 1898 insufficient to provide the reserves needed for even a brief war with a third-rate power. Luce claimed that there was still a need for sailing vessels and that even steamships required sailors, not just men who had acquired the "sea habit." He contrasted the good records of Japanese fishermen and merchant seamen against those of the naval conscripts in Russia. He called attention to the need for schoolships to maintain the competency of merchant marine officers and then ended with a plea for the subsidies necessary for that purpose. His efforts had little immediate effect.

In the same year, 1904, the 77-year-old Luce took on one last major task: the installation of military direction in the Navy Department. Having met with little success toward this goal in earlier years, he vigorously attacked the problem again. Luce's early articles on naval administration had been primarily directed toward this goal. Even in the midst of the Spanish-American War, he had complained to Senator Henry Cabot Lodge that the "Navy Department is not organized for a state of war."[30] In Luce's opinion, the Navy needed centralized direction by professional officers for the efficient conduct of naval operations.

In 1902 and 1903, the annual reports by the Chief of the Bureau of Navigation, Rear Adm. Henry C. Taylor, had pointed out that the Bureau could not efficiently handle both the administration of naval personnel and the formulation of war plans. Secretary of the Navy William H. Moody and President Roosevelt concurred in Taylor's opinion, and both urged the Congress to create a naval general staff similar to that which had been provided for the Army. In April 1904 hearings were held before the House Committee on Naval Affairs to consider a direct link between the General Board and the Secretary. There was a great deal of opposition to this proposal. The Bureau Chiefs feared encroachment on their own departments, while Congressmen feared a decline in civilian control of the military.

In the midst of this rising controversy, Luce took a radical position. He proposed not merely an adviser, but an entirely new office which would have the responsibility for fleet operations. In a letter to Henry Taylor on 25 June 1904, Luce wrote,

> Up to the present time no Secretary has recognized the fact that naval operations should be included among his duties.

---

[30] Luce to H.C. Lodge, 24 May 1898, Luce Papers.

Let this grave oversight be repaired at once by an Executive Order creating under the Bureau of Navigation the Office of "Naval Operations." ... The Office should be placed in charge of an officer of rank and one of recognized qualifications for its duties. His relations with the Secretary will be close and confidential. He will be the Secretary's adviser on all questions of a military nature ... The duties of the office will be such as would have gone to the General Staff had one been created. Thus will the Secretary obtain, under the law, the substance of a General Staff without the empty shadow of the name. There is no such thing as spontaneous generation. Plant the seed now and let it grow.[31]

The seed grew into the Aid for Operations and eventually the Chief of Naval Operations. Its development, however, was slow, and at first even Taylor had his doubts. He promised to bring the suggestion to the attention of Secretary Moody before he left office, but Taylor did have reservations. "If we plant this other seed that you suggest," he wrote Luce, "I am afraid the two plants would not grow together well."[32]

Luce pressed forward and in March 1905 his article "The Department of the Navy" appeared after having been awarded an honorable mention in the Naval Institute Prize Essay contest. On being published, he sent a copy as his latest plea for an improved naval organization to Admiral of the Navy George Dewey. "The time for action has come," he wrote Dewey, "I have a plan of action which I would like to lay before the General Board ... "[33] Appearing before the Board on 31 March, he outlined in detail his proposal and urged the Board to take immediate action in support of an Executive Order that would activate the plan without waiting for Congress. Legislative sanction, he believed, would follow as a matter of course, as it had for the Naval Academy, the Torpedo Station, the War College, and the naval training service. The matter was considered, but no action was taken.

On 9 July 1906 Luce wrote a letter to Mahan which was to eventuate into the latter's last book *Naval Strategy*. In it Luce, after reminding his friend that the Mahan Lectures were still part of the Naval War College curriculum, also wrote:

> I venture to suggest, now, that you should revise these lectures, and bring them up to date, ... showing how the

---

[31] Luce to H.C. Taylor, 25 June 1904, Luce Papers, LC.

[32] H.C. Taylor to Luce, 29 June 1904, Luce Papers, LC.

[33] Luce to Dewey, 24 March 1905, Dewey Papers, LC.

principles you have laid down have been illustrated in actual practice, and pointing how, and where, those principles have been ignored or violated. You have made a great reputation by your work on Sea Power, this last work will be, in effect, the capstone, as it were, of the great monument you have reared, ...

Mahan did so and *Naval Strategy* appeared, after 3 years work, in November 1911, 1 month before Luce published his last essay.[34]

In November 1906, the Annual Report of Secretary Charles J. Bonaparte stated that radical reform of the Navy Department was necessary. However, he soon left it to become Attorney General. In April 1907, during a visit to Washington, Luce gave the new Secretary copies of his articles on naval administration and several papers on naval efficiency, all with little apparent effect. When Luce returned to Washington 3 weeks later, he found that Secretary Victor Metcalf intended to rely on the Congress which, he felt, would certainly take up the matter at the next session.

Luce was not to be put off. In early October he took advantage of a general order soliciting "suggestions to improve the efficiency of the Navy" to again propose that an office of "Naval Operation" be established which would supervise the military operations of the fleet. Again, no action was taken as politicians and bureaucrats thwarted the reformers. However, the climate improved in December 1907 as the Navy reentered the public spotlight. The Great White Fleet started its well-known cruise around the world, and the hearts of the Nation sailed with it.

With the Navy in the forefront, *McClure's Magazine* published an article in January 1908 entitled "The Needs of the Navy" by Henry Reuterdahl, an American editor for *Jane's Fighting Ships*. Written with the encouragement of Comdr. William S. Sims, the outspoken Inspector of Target Practice and recently appointed naval aide to President Roosevelt, the article summarized many of Sims' opinions on naval problems. Repercussions were heard in all quarters. In February the Senate reacted with an investigation into the problems brought to light by Reuterdahl and Sims.

Luce quickly saw that much of the trouble to which these men pointed could have been avoided if the Navy had had more effective central direction. In the spring Luce took up correspondence with Sims. Here was an opportunity to transmit his views to the President through a sympathetic naval aide. The

---

[34] See also Luce to Mahan, 15 July 1907, both in Luce Papers, LC; W.D. Puleston, *Mahan* (London: Jonathan Cape, 1939), pp. 97, 268, 290-291; and item 148.

Senate committee abruptly ended its investigation without recommendations, and it seemed essential to procure Presidential action. While the Senate committee was falling into inaction, Sims and his predecessor as naval aide, Comdr. Albert L. Key,[35] brought to the President's attention some serious design faults in the battleship *North Dakota,* then under construction. The President appointed a commission at the Naval War College to investigate the matter. This conference in Newport gave Luce and Sims the opportunity to talk at length about the basic problems of naval administration. In the midst of the conference, Luce wrote directly to the President and suggested the establishment of a commission to consider and to report upon the reorganization of the Navy Department. Within 2 days the President replied that he would carefully consider Luce's "very interesting suggestion."

In October 1908 Luce published his article "The Fleet" in the widely read *North American Review.* Interest in naval reform continued to grow. It appeared that by December a commission would be appointed to consider the matter. "Hope on hope Ever!" Luce wrote Sims, "We'll get there some time."[36] They did. On 27 January 1909 President Roosevelt appointed a board headed by former Secretary Moody. It included former Secretary Paul Morton, Congressman Alston G. Dayton, and retired Rear Admirals Luce, A.T. Mahan, Robley D. Evans, William M. Folger, and William S. Cowles. Through Luce's urging, the board completed its work and submitted its recommendations to the President less than a week before he was to leave office. Roosevelt immediately forwarded the report to the Senate, but no action was taken.

When the new administration of President William Howard Taft took office on 4 March, the new Secretary of the Navy, George von Lengerke Meyer, immediately began to study the matter. Detailed plans were drawn up by a board headed by Rear Adm. William Swift, and in November 1909 Meyer ordered, without congressional authority, the establishment of a system of "aids" who would act as professional assistants to the Secretary and serve as an advisory council and general staff. The system was an improvement, although it did not represent the complete reformation that Luce and others had sought. It was a beginning, but it would take more than 5 years for Congress to finally authorize a reorganization of the Navy Department and provide for a Chief of

---

[35] Commodore Albert Lenoir Key (1860-1950).

[36] Luce to Sims, 29 December 1908, Sims Papers, LC.

Naval Operations "charged with the operations of the fleet, and with the preparation and readiness of plans for its use in war."[37] Other men were responsible for bringing this task to fruition, primarily Rear Adm. Bradley Fiske[38] and Congressman R.P. Hobson[39] of Alabama.

The effort to obtain strong military direction for the U.S. Navy was Luce's last great project. Shortly after he published his last article in December 1911, Luce became quite ill. He never again wrote another article; his efforts to influence the administration of the Navy subsided. The 84-year-old gentleman retired to his home at 15 Francis Street in Newport. There he died on 28 July 1917 shortly after his 90th birthday. His funeral was conducted in the simple, but impressive, Episcopalian liturgy amidst the colonial dignity of Trinity Church. Apprentices from the Naval Training Station lined the route to St. Mary's Churchyard, on the eastern side of the island, where Luce was buried beneath a simply inscribed black stone slab.

II

The contributions of Stephen B. Luce to his profession are difficult to measure. He was a teacher, a writer, an organizer, and an administrator, but more importantly he was the leader and the inspiration for several generations of American naval officers. In his own time his impact was large, but Luce's major contributions were for the most part intangible, a legacy for the future. The opinions of his contemporaries perhaps best intimate the nature of his impact. John S. Barnes, an able Civil War officer who served with Luce in two ships and at the Naval Academy and who later resigned to pursue a successful legal and business career, wrote of him:

> Stephen B. Luce, all through his distinguished career was one of the most capable officers in our or any navy. Besides his professional accomplishments, which were great, his

---

[37] The Act of 3 March 1915.

[38] Rear Adm. Bradley Allen Fiske (1854-1942) held more than 60 patents, including the stadimeter, gunfire control systems, and torpedo bomber. He served as Aid for Operations (1913-15) and wrote *The Navy as a Fighting Machine* (New York: Scribner, 1916).

[39] Capt. Richmond Pearson Hobson (1870-1937) graduated at the head of his Naval Academy class in 1889. He was awarded the Medal of Honor for exploits at Santiago during the Spanish-American War. He resigned from the Navy in 1903 and served in Congress from 1907 to 1915.

scientific and literary knowledge, increased by constant studying and reading, made him an ideal naval officer, fitted to fill any office with dignity and power within the scope of government action. My intercourse with him, then and later, I regard as one of the most fortunate intimacies of my life.[40]

A.T. Mahan in the introduction to one of his books credited Luce entirely for providing him with the direction for his career, something that he had not been able to find by himself.[41]

Adm. David D. Porter wrote of him to Assistant Secretary Fox: "He is a straightforward fellow and nature has not given him soft manners possessed by people who are all smiles to your face and abuse you behind your back."[42]

Bradley A. Fiske wrote in an obituary in the *Proceedings* of the U.S. Naval Institute in 1917:

Luce taught the Navy to think, to think about the Navy as a whole. . . . More clearly than any other man in American history he saw the relations that ought to exist between the central government and its military and naval officers . . . Luce saw strategy as clearly as most of us see a material object. To him, more than any other officer who ever lived are naval officers of every nation indebted for the understanding they have of their profession.[43]

Robley D. Evans described him as "that master of his trade,"[44] and Dudley W. Knox: "I never knew an officer to speak ill of him."[45] Luce's biographer, Albert Gleaves, wrote: "To such as he, there is no successor."[46]

To understand why influential men of his time were so deeply affected by Luce, the modern day historian must turn to the letters and published writings which he left behind. Much of his

---

[40] J.S. Barnes, "My Egotisography," pp. 112-133, Barnes Papers, Naval Historical Society Collection, New-York Historical Society.

[41] A.T. Mahan, *The Influence of Sea Power upon the French Revolution and Empire 1793-1812* (Boston: Little, Brown, 1893), p. vi.

[42] D.D. Porter to Gustavus Fox, 21 April 1866, Fox Papers, Naval Historical Society Collection, New-York Historical Society.

[43] B.A. Fiske, "Stephen B. Luce, An Appreciation," *United States Naval Institute Proceedings*, vol. XLIII, No. 9, September 1917, pp. 1935-40. In his autobiography *From Midshipman to Rear Admiral* (New York: Century, 1919), Fiske dedicated the volume to the memory of Luce, "who saw the light before others saw it and led the Navies toward it."

[44] R.D. Evans, *A Sailor's Log* (New York: Appleton, 1902), p. 44.

[45] D.W. Knox in a conversation with John D. Hayes, August 1954.

[46] Albert Gleaves, *Life and Letters of Rear Admiral Stephen B. Luce* (New York: Putnam, 1925), p. 256.

personal correspondence was deliberately destroyed by Luce, himself, and by his wife after his death. What remains, in the most part, is what he wanted to be remembered: his professional life.

Luce's thoughts and words on paper over the years fall roughly into eight categories: (1) practical sea training, (2) youth and the Navy, (3) officer education, (4) naval history, (5) naval administration and organization, (6) naval warfare, (7) military ethics, and (8) a few general subjects. Unlike some other writers, the body of Luce's writing does not demonstrate a readily discernible progression from beginning to end. An analysis of each category, however, shows the development of his thought on that particular subject. Because he sometimes thought about these categories simultaneously and wrote of them at about the same time, a complex interrelationship developed. This interrelationship can best be appreciated by briefly examining each category in turn and then viewing the broad aspect of his writing.

In the area of practical sea training, Luce's major contribution was his textbook on *Seamanship*. As each edition appeared, Luce ensured that the new aspects of shiphandling in steamships were considered, along with guidelines for the newly popular fore-and-aft sailing rig. His attention to these matters demonstrated his continuing interest in the practical aspects of the art, and as such his text provided up-to-date information for the Academy midshipmen.

At the same time, of course, Luce was an advocate of training under sail as the most appropriate method of teaching practical maritime skills. Not one to be reactionary or anachronistic, Luce strongly believed that practical experience under sail would teach a young man more about the basic nature of ships than experience in any other type of vessel. This opinion is still shared by significant portions of the maritime world today.

Luce's other textbooks, his small gunnery book, *The Young Seaman's Manual,* and contributions to the naval signal book are fragments of his larger contribution to practical training. However, all of them are devoted to his effort in obtaining a standard routine for all drills, maneuvers, and evolutions at sea.

Textbooks were only part of Luce's literary contribution to training. Within a decade after his first text appeared, he had expanded the scope of his work to the broad problems of a training system.

Closely connected with Luce's interest in training were his extensive writings for *Youth's Companion*. These articles, written for American youth and designed to arouse an interest in naval careers and sea life, emphasized the romance of the sailing era and the stalwart character of seamen. Written after his retirement, these articles carry with them a great feeling of nostalgia for the "Old Navy" of Luce's youth, yet at the same time, they express a hope that by thorough training, the future of the new steel navy will be equally satisfying. The articles underscore his faith in individual seamen as the greatest strength of the Navy.

The field of education was Luce's strong point. In every sense of the word, he was a teacher, and he devoted his entire career to the presentation of his concepts to the naval profession and to the Nation. In his thinking he drew a sharp distinction between practical training for specific tasks and the education of the mind for creative functions. Representative of much that was popular among the educational circles of his day, Luce's article "On the Study of Naval Warfare as a Science"[47] best reveals the substance of his educational concepts. With Herbert Spencer, he believed that education was an individual process whereby each person had to discover for himself the nature of the world around him. Largely for this reason, he established the methodology of the Naval War College around individual reading and research. Teachers were not to be sources of information, but rather to be guides in a cooperative search for knowledge. For Luce and many others, truth was something to be found in basic immutable laws of nature which were fully ascertainable by individual men. At that time the use of comparative study and analogy was popular in the arts, as it was among scientists. The scientists had demonstrated that there were basic laws of the physical universe, and it seemed logical that similar laws could be found in human nature. These were ideas which Luce brought together and applied in his own self-education and which he adapted to the Naval War College. They were not unusual ideas at this time, and they were not original with Luce. However, the depth of thought and the successful application of these ideas were unusual in a navy. Therein lies Luce's contribution.

By natural inclination, Luce endeavored to use history to explain and solve problems. He accepted Lord Macaulay's dictum that "no past event has any intrinsic importance; the knowledge of it is valuable only as it leads to form just calculations for the future." But he widened Macaulay's conception with his equally firm belief that "History is philosophy teaching by example."

Luce, however, made no pretense of being a professional

---

[47] Reprinted with commentary in chapter III.

historian. First and foremost he was a seaman and a naval officer: an activist, not a cloistered scholar. The study of history, in his mind, was merely the best means to an end. Remarkably broadminded in his approach, Luce was able to select from a plethora of historical data the evidence which he employed in his arguments. Every item he used was designed to underscore his argument and to relate to a current problem. There was no place in his thinking for historical problems which were unique or which were circumscribed by the conditions of their own time.

Luce devoted a large part of his writing to the subject of naval organization and administration. He did so not because he liked management problems as such, but because he saw this as the sphere in which there was the greatest need for reform. Having derived his interest in this subject from reflections on his own experience during the naval campaign along the South Atlantic coast in the Civil War, Luce felt that the Union Navy had failed simply because the Navy Department was not suitably organized to provide sound naval policy or feasible strategic plans. Appropriately, one of his first periodical articles, written in 1864, and his last, written in 1911, were both on this subject. His writing at every stage over this 47-year interval reflects the progress made within the Navy for improved administration. Throughout, Luce was highly influenced by the example of British naval administration. Time and time again he returned to the history of the Royal Navy to search for examples which illustrated the proper relationship between administration and the application of strategy.

In considering the subject of naval warfare, Luce recognized a great similarity between land and naval tactics. Although this perception was not unusual in contemporary European military thought, it was new in American professional thinking. Such a prominent writer as Emory Upton acknowledged Luce's insight in this regard as early as 1877.[48] Luce used the close relationship he saw between naval and military affairs as the foundation for some of the educational policies which he established at the Naval War College and promoted for the Navy as a whole. His reading of such writers as Gen. Sir Howard Douglas and Gen. Sir Edward Hamley reinforced his thoughts along these lines and encouraged him to create analogies between the two forms of warfare. In later life he would draw on the historical work of G.F.R. Henderson, John

---

[48] Upton to Luce, 16 October 1877, Luce Papers, LC; and Upton to Luce, 26 August 1878, U.S. Naval Academy Museum.

Fiske, and Brooks Adams to illustrate the correlations he found. Luce's perception started with an analogy between military and naval tactics, but as time went on it brought him to a broader understanding of warfare in general. By midcareer he was able to see beyond the purely naval point of view and to deal with the interrelationship between naval and military tactics, strategy, diplomacy, and national power. It was this area which he asked Mahan to consider in writing his lectures for the Naval War College.

A devout Episcopalian, he found himself faced, as had been his mentor, Rear Adm. S.F. Du Pont before him, with the apparent contradiction between the violence of war and the peaceful nature of the Christian tradition. He resolved this problem by perceiving the preparation for war as a means of its prevention, while giving benefit through strength.

He concluded one of his two essays on this subject:

The flaming sword that guards the way to sinless Eden will continue to prevail until man enters once more into that peace which passeth all understanding, when the lust of the eye and the pride of life shall no more be known. But mortal man cannot yet discern the coming of that day.

Meanwhile let practical Americans recognize the truth that war is a calamity that may overtake the most peaceful Nation, and that insurance against war by preparation for it is, of all methods, the most business-like, the most humane and the most in accordance with the teachings of the Christian religion.[49]

In considering this very difficult subject, Luce was able to maintain a professional outlook while at the same time giving a sympathetic hearing to the viewpoint of those who opposed military force, an opinion he found to be impractical.

One small group of writings stands in marked contrast to his other work. They were the only pieces he ever wrote that did not concern the Navy or the sea. These were three articles on what might be called general subjects,[50] one a tribute to an Italian "bone setter" who treated his son's dislocated hip, another on extrasensory perception, and a third essay on dreams. He became interested in these subjects in the mid-1870's when spiritualism was in vogue. Luce's interest in these matters is not mentioned in

---

[49] "The Benefits of War," p. 683. See items 94 and 124.

[50] See items 23 and 42.

the biography by Gleaves.[51] Perhaps Luce wished to remove these pieces from the record, as he eventually destroyed the vast portion of his personal, nonprofessional correspondence. The reason may never be known, but the articles that remain reveal a great deal about the author. Each deals with a phenomenon that, on the surface, seemed inexplicable; however, after careful analysis, Luce was able to develop an understanding of the basic principles involved and an appreciation for the problem presented. Here, as in his other writings, Luce examined and stripped away the nonessential information and reduced the issue to its basic elements. Dissecting these essentials, he then reached a conclusion concerning what he saw as the basic nature of the problem. The same procedure was characteristic of his approach to professional issues.

Luce's approach to the mysteries of spiritualism was a "scientific" one. Under the influence of an era in American history when the concept of scientific objectivity had reached a zenith in its prestige, he believed, like many others, that human events could be perceived in the same objective and analytical style used in physics and chemistry. An accumulation of accurately perceived historical facts could reveal, he thought, generalizations about the basic nature of man and his activities. A study of naval history, therefore, could reveal the basic laws which govern naval affairs. Luce may have fallen victim to a false understanding of the "scientific method," but neither scientists nor historians are entirely free of the egocentric problem, and in dealing with the broadest generalizations, they may both tend to interpret their observations in terms distorted by their own viewpoints. While the physical scientist may make fundamental assumptions which are essentially neutral, those who deal in human affairs cannot. The basic premises with which Luce and his followers built upon were subjective, not objective, ones. The very choice of topics, for example, "The Influence of Sea Power upon Nations" and the development of "Modern Naval Science" revealed a personal and professional predilection in an era of national expansion and naval development. While the modern reader can appropriately criticize this problem in Luce, it is essential at the same time to understand sympathetically the nature of "scientific enquiry" as Luce and his colleagues understood it. The scientific approach is an essential approach to the naval profession. It is an elementary factor in the intellectual forces which lead to the growth of professionalization

---

[51] Gleaves, *Life and Letters of Rear Admiral Stephen B. Luce.*

in the Navy. Despite its basic flaw, this approach allowed men such as Luce to see the Navy as an interacting system with a variety of relationships. Through it Luce perceived the Navy as an entity made up of many complementary elements, and thus he could define in broad terms the scope of naval science or, in modern terms, the naval profession. His interest in the comparative study of military history and in the naval history of all periods led him to see the relationships among tactics, strategy, seamanship, technology, education, training, organization, and administration. A reading of all Luce's writings documents for us the very direct interrelationship which he found among all the elements of his profession. Each individual subject is interlocking and complementary with the others. The binding element is his concept of a navy and the functions implicit in its being. Luce never wrote down this general concept in its entirety, but it can be pieced together from each of the parts.

Luce regarded the Navy as a flexible tool for applying force from the sea in wartime. For a maritime nation, this application must be closely allied with diplomacy and political purpose. He saw that a navy, to fulfill its functions successfully, must be efficiently controlled by men who are not only technically proficient, but who understand the limitations and the implications in the use of force. With this basic thesis, Luce conceived an administrative organization by which responsive control could be maintained. To staff this system effectively, he promoted standardized procedures throughout the service, established a training program for seamen and an advanced school of higher education for officers who would establish naval policy, develop strategy, and manage its functions. In short, Luce was a man with a basic concept about the nature of a navy, and his lifetime goal was to provide the structure for the U.S. Navy by which it could operate under the principles he conceived.

As with many constructive thinkers and activists, the ideas he built on rarely originated with him. Those on the study of history came from Macaulay and Buckle, J.K. Laughton, and later, Mahan. In tactics, his mentors were John Clerk, Paul l'Hoste, Jurien de la Graviere, Sir Howard Douglas and Foxhall Parker. Ideas about education came from Herbert Spencer, Henry Barnard, and Emory Upton. In strategy he was influenced by the expansionists of his own time, Henry Cabot Lodge and Theodore Roosevelt, as well as writers such as E.B. Hamley and Jomini.

He appreciated the technological revolution of his age and adapted to it. He saw changes, accepted them, and rose above them in order to preserve what he considered durable and essential. The technology of the day caused many others to become fascinated with its details, but Luce saw the innovations of ship design and ordnance only as additional reasons for improvement in education and administrative organization. This new technology would be a detriment, he believed, unless it was properly used and controlled. Education and organization were the key areas from which to achieve these ends.

Luce was a man with an idea and a purpose. He sought to implant his idea in the Navy and to form the Navy around it. By writing for periodicals, specifically those journals through which he could reach a particular audience, he was able to influence the interest groups essential to his cause. Professional military and naval officers were reached through the *United States Naval Institute Proceedings* and the *Army and Navy Journal,* as well as the short-lived *United Service.* Scholars and professional literary men were addressed in *The Critic,* and the leaders of the civilian community were his audience in *The North American Review. Youth's Companion* was widely read by youngsters and by their parents. He chose the columns of the local Newport, R.I., newspapers as the best means to influence popular support at home for his idea of a great naval base in Narragansett Bay. His contributions to *Johnson's Cyclopedia, Funk and Wagnall's Dictionary,* and Hamersly's *Naval Encyclopedia* gave him the position of an authority and allowed some of his basic ideas to become entrenched as standard concepts.

He also extensively used another literary means, personal letters, to achieve his ends. He had a reputation for being the most articulate and public relations-conscious flag officer of his day. He had command of the North Atlantic Station when the public was becoming conscious of its new seagoing arm. In response to this he made himself readily available to provide comment and information to members of the press. As President of the Naval Institute for more than a decade, he was the acknowledged leader of the intellectuals in the service. He influenced a number of rising young officers who considered him more of an associate than a senior: Tasker Bliss, Henry C. Taylor, Robley D. Evans, French E. Chadwick, Richard Wainwright, Bradley Fiske, William S. Sims, William McCarty Little, and Alfred T. Mahan.

Through his own position and prestige, Luce obtained direct access to several Secretaries of the Navy. While his ideas were not always readily accepted, men such as Hilary Herbert, W.C. Whitney, B.F. Tracy, and W.H. Moody, in particular, listened carefully to what Luce said and read his letters with interest. The relative degree of acceptance by these men was the measure of success in Luce's endeavors. Little could be accomplished without the support of the Secretary and as such the Secretary's office was always the prime target in Luce's efforts. At times he needed to employ the pressure of professional opinion, the public, the Congress, and even the President, but in the end, the ability to accomplish most of Luce's reforms lay within the power of the Secretary and needed his approval and support.

Luce's personal contacts outside the Navy were particularly important to the success of his endeavors. For example, while serving as senior member of a board inspecting the New York City reform schoolship *Mercury,* he came to know the elder Theodore Roosevelt, then a charities commissioner for the State of New York. Through this connection Luce met the commissioner's son, a Harvard student and future President. Later, Luce arranged for young Roosevelt to meet Mahan and to lecture at the Naval War College a few years after Roosevelt's *The Naval War of 1812* had been published.[52] Other useful connections were formed through the marriages of Henry Cabot Lodge, Brooks Adams, and Luce's son John, each to one of the three daughters of Rear Adm. Charles Henry Davis. These personal connections encouraged Luce to become an avid reader of Brooks Adams' writings, and their influence may be found in Luce's own articles. Henry Cabot Lodge, one of the Nation's leading expansionists, became a receptive correspondent.

His literary works, of course, generated significant contacts in themselves. Publisher Daniel Van Nostrand helped him get some early articles into print. William C. Church, founder-editor of the *Army and Navy Journal* and *The Galaxy,* had been with Luce at Port Royal during the Civil War. A future editor of *The North American Review* and *Youth's Companion,* William H. Rideing, was launched on a literary career by Luce when he arranged for the aspiring journalist to write an article for *Harper's Monthly*[53] about the schoolship *St. Marys.* Others in his literary circle were Jeannette and Joseph Gilder, founders and editors of *The Critic;* Lloyd Bryce, editor of *The North American Review;* and John Austin Stevens, author and founder-editor of the *Magazine of American History,* as well as a neighbor in Newport, R.I.

---

[52] S.B. Luce to T. Roosevelt, 13 February 1888, Theodore Roosevelt Papers, LC.

[53] "Nautical School Ship 'St. Marys,'" *Harper's New Monthly Magazine,* vol. LIX, No. 351, August 1879, pp. 340-49.

Through his position, his acquaintances, his letters, and his articles, Luce made his ideas known and took the measures necessary to implement them.

In evaluating the writings of Luce, one must remember that he was a subjective thinker, the leader of a reform faction in the U.S. Navy. He was strongly opposed in many of his plans, particularly by those Navy Department Bureau Chiefs with vested interests who saw his proposals as threats to their own power and position. He was also opposed by officers who saw no need for advanced education or for the type of theoretical work done by Mahan. Many of the technicists in the service saw little point in considering the broad aspects of warfare and preferred, instead, that all professionals would immerse themselves in the new technical developments of the era. Others were suspicious of Luce's interest in the history of the British Navy at a time when relations with England were strained. Those with opposing viewpoints often tried his patience and were targets for his barbs. As a result, Luce's writing often displays a pugnacious quality.

Stephen B. Luce was no theorist such as Clausewitz or Jomini. Neither was he a Mahan nor a Corbett. Although he never wrote a detailed philosophical statement encompassing his beliefs, Luce's major contribution to the U.S. Navy lies essentially in his unwritten concept of a navy. As a leader, it was this vision which he gave to his professional followers in the Navy. His writings were a means by which he contributed to the development of a practical, working framework on which the U.S. Navy could operate as a coherent entity. In this regard his books and articles illuminate only portions of his total vision. In each instance, however, they show only what was necessary to a specific reform or current problem. Although he took his ideas from a wide variety of sources, perhaps his most signficant contribution must be recognized in the transmission of many *avant-garde* ideas from contemporary European military thought to the American Navy. In one sense, Luce's work may be seen as an American naval extension of the general trend in European military thought, particularly evident after the Franco-Prussian War, to seek more effective methods for military control.

Luce's ideas made their greatest impact in the early years of American expansion. As the Nation moved outward from its continental base, many could see that the Navy might play an important role. Among those who were interested in further naval development, any new idea had an audience. Luce himself brought additional attention to his ideas by his own political efforts among powerful and influential men, his stubborn insistence on the veracity of his own opinion, and his effective leadership among many promising young officers. In his own time, he served as a catalyst for new ideas, ideas that in the future would be employed and elaborated upon as fundamental perceptions in the development of American naval education, organization, administration, tactics, and strategic theory. Taken with an understanding of the ideological sources, along with an appreciation for the practical results, the writings of Stephen B. Luce reflect a large part of the intellectual foundation of the United States Navy in the 20th century.

The Naval War College, *ca.* 1892

Begun in September, 1891, the new building was designed to house the staff as well as the class rooms and library for the College. Four sets of quarters were located in each of the four corners. The "Flemish" style building was completed in May, 1892. It was named in honor of Admiral Luce in 1934.

Photo: Naval Historical Collection, Naval War College

CHAPTER II

AN ADDRESS DELIVERED AT THE UNITED STATES NAVAL WAR COLLEGE NARRAGANSETT BAY, R.I., JUNE 2, 1903

By Rear-Admiral S.B. Luce, U.S. Navy.

Editors' Introduction

Stephen Luce's most enduring contribution to the U.S. Navy was the Naval War College. In this address delivered at the opening of the course in 1903, 18 years after he had founded the college, Luce made his most succinct statement on the contribution which he envisaged the college would make in developing more capable naval officers.

Luce firmly believed that intensive study and intellectual effort were necessary preparations for conducting successful operations at sea. In Luce's mind those in command at sea needed to comprehend more than the technicalities of their profession. They needed a broad outlook through which their own actions could be seen in the perspective of national and international affairs.

More than just a broad viewpoint for officers in general, Luce's address reflects his own opinions on the place of the Navy in the events of his day. One finds in this address a view of America's new role in the world and a direct recognition of the shift from European to global orientation in foreign policies. In this sense the address is an important example of the understanding which an influential officer had concerning the Navy's role at the turn of the century.

This address was published in the *United States Naval Institute Proceedings*, vol. XXIX, No. 3, 1903, pp. 1-8.

Mr. President[1] and Gentlemen:—

It is a great compliment to have been asked to welcome to the College the class of officers who are to attend the course which opens today, and one I highly appreciate.

---

[1] At the time this address was given, French Ensor Chadwick (1844-1919) was completing his term as President of the Naval War College. Chadwick was a strong supporter of the ideas on historical criticism and the historical lessons of seapower which were being promoted by Luce and Mahan. Chadwick later published *The Relations of the United States with Spain: the Spanish American War; The Graves Papers and Other Documents Relating to the Yorktown Campaign, July to October, 1781*; and *Causes of the Civil War*, vol. XIX in Albert Bushnell Hart's *The American Nation: a History*. Chadwick's contributions to the study of naval history are among the most important made by a naval officer in this period.

I perform this duty with pleasure and in behalf of the President and the faculty extend to you a hearty greeting.

As some members of the class are here for the first time, it will not be out of place to say something of the aims and objects of the College.

Although called a College, this institution differs from other seats of learning in having no teachers. A moment's consideration will show why this must be so. As its name implies the principal object of the College is the study of the Science and Art of War.

Now, war is a very large and comprehensive subject, and there are no professors competent to teach it. It would be the height of presumption on the part of the College to undertake to teach officers of mature years—such as generally make up the classes in attendance—any branch, whatever, of their profession, even the most elementary. All that the College can do; all that it professes to do, is to invite officers to come to it; and to offer them every facility for pursuing the study of the highest branches of their profession. All here, faculty and class alike, occupy the same plane, without distinction of age, rank, or assumption of superior attainments. All are pursuing one and the same end—the advancement of their profession. In the beginning I, myself, if you will pardon a personal allusion, announced myself as one of the class in attendance, and each succeeding year I have, when practicable, enrolled myself with the class, and still find I have much to learn.

We speak, habitually, of the Science and Art of War. As a science it recognizes certain general principles which are just as applicable today as they were in the time of the great Athenian admiral, Themistocles.[2] A strict adherence to those principles has not always insured victory, it is true; but a violation of them either through ignorance or neglect, has almost invariably led to defeat. Military writers have been careful to warn us that although war, in its most extended sense, may be called a science, yet it is not an exact science.

As an art, war is governed by rules which vary from age to age. Art, it has been well said, may be *learned* but it cannot be *taught*. This is particularly true of the Art of War. It cannot be taught, excepting in so far as one may teach oneself; and it is to offer to every officer the opportunity of teaching himself that the College doors are open.

Naval Tactics, for example, is an art, proficiency in which requires constant practice at sea, under conditions assimilating, as nearly as possible, to those of actual war. The rules of this art are laid down in the Signal Book. Having mastered these rules, the student finds there is an extension of the subject, on which the Signal Book is silent, viz.: the formations for battle. Military writers have called the former Minor, or Elementary, Tactics, the latter Grand Tactics, or the Tactics of Battle.

---

[2]Themistocles (ca. 514-450 B.C.) was an Athenian statesman, admiral, and general. Realizing the danger from Persia, as well as the inability of Athens to match Persian strength on land, Themistocles encouraged the development of an Athenian fleet and persuaded the Assembly to use the wealth from a rich new seam of Laurium silver for the construction of a modern navy. As the dominant leader in Athens at the time of Xerxes invasion, Themistocles was the main architect of victory at the battle of Salamis in 480 B.C. As Thucydides wrote, "it may be said that through force of genius and by rapidity of action this man was supreme at doing the right thing at the right moment."

A knowledge of the rules of minor tactics may be acquired in a comparatively short time. But grand tactics, or what may be designated as the tactics of admirals, present such a variety of conditions as to defy all rules. The successful conduct of a fleet, in battle, must depend very largely today, as it ever has done, upon the genius of the commander-in-chief. An admiral may rely, for guidance in battle, upon the inspiration of the moment, only when that inspiration is due to long and conscientious self-culture in the line of his profession, not otherwise.

It is to enable officers to prepare themselves for the hour of conflict that the College has been opened.

Strategy is based on immutable principles—principles just as applicable today as when illustrated by the campaigns of the great captains of an ancient civilization. As to naval strategy, in particular, your attention is called to the fact that some of its most valuable work is that which is accomplished in time of peace. This subject also can be mastered only by close study and reflection.

To the foregoing subjects must be added the laws of war, as treated under the head of Marine International Law.

One of the first steps in the establishment of an institution somewhat novel in its character, was to furnish the facilities for carrying on these studies and to suggest certain lines that might be followed to advantage.

The foundation once laid, it was assumed that those who were to conduct the course, *conjointly* with those in attendance, would rear the superstructure. To this end a few officers came together each one of whom took up a particular branch of study. The results of those studies were given out in the form of lectures, and the freest discussion invited. Contributions by members of the class in attendance were cordially invited and gratefully received. Such is the case today. In short the College is, to borrow a term from political economy, a sort of cooperative or joint-stock affair, where all work in unison for the common good.

The next step in the process of development was to get at the philosophy of navies, to show the reason of their being, their influence on the destiny of the state, and their true functions in peace as well as in war. The necessity of a navy to a maritime state having been shown, then its relative proportions were to be determined, as well as its character due to the position held by the state in the great family of nations, and the foreign policy sought to be carried out—whether the attitude of the state was to be purely defensive, or whether it was to be the offensive-defensive, that is to defend by assuming the offensive. If the latter then to show the necessity at all times for an advanced state of preparation. Thus was emphasized the fact that one of the most important factors of naval strategy belongs essentially to a time of profound peace.

These and kindred subjects are among the largest and most important that can engage the attention of the statesman and naval administrator.

That is the meaning of this College. It is a place of original research on all questions relating to war and to statesmanship connected with war, or the prevention of war.

That "war is the best school of war," is one of those dangerous and delusive sayings that contain just enough truth to secure currency: he who waits for war to learn his profession often acquired his knowledge at a frightful cost of human life.

We have often heard of the "Chess-board of European Politics." The game-board, now, is the great globe itself; and America, by her very geographical position, between two great oceans, is not the least important of the several contestants.

It is related that a gentleman living in one of the Eastern States, once remarked that the flow of the Mississippi was towards the north. His father's plantation, he said, was on the left bank of the river, and often, as a boy, he had noticed how the driftwood floated away to the right, which was to the north. No argument could convince him to the contrary. He had that evidence of his own senses and that was enough. Business matters required that he should revisit the home of his childhood. He sought the old steamboat landing, and there, just as he remembered it, the waters were carrying the driftwood to the north. He was right; right, that is, from the point of view of childhood. Watching still the driftwood he saw it whirled about in an eddy. Looking farther out he saw it carried by a counter-current beyond the bend of the shore where he stood, and into the great body of the mighty river which swept its resistless way to the gulf. This is not an inapt illustration of the so-called anti-imperialist who looks at the little eddies and counter-currents at his feet, and is blind to the great stream of human progress which has been setting in one undeviating way since the world began. "Westward the course of empire takes its way," can never become, to us, a hackneyed phrase. Its truth is receiving fresh proofs every day. From the day of the battle of Salamis, when a small, but highly disciplined Greek fleet beat back the tidal-wave of barbaric invasion, to the day our flag was planted on the Great Wall of China[3] is a far cry indeed. But the laws of motion are immutable, in the one case as in the other—in the flow of the great river, and the ever onward current of human events. The Mississippi can not give back its waters to their source; nor will the Star of Empire turn to the East.

Civilization is ever saying to the barbarian, and to the semi-civilized, "accept the bountiful gifts of nature, or make way for those who will." Thus there is a continual struggle for supremacy before which barbarism is constantly retreating. The stream of human progress is still sweeping on; and woe betide those who oppose its course. This means much for us, here, today.

Glance for a moment at the past and then contemplate the possibilities of the future. The invention of the Mariner's Compass,[4] the

---

[3] Luce is, no doubt, referring to the city walls at Peking where American forces fought during the Boxer Rebellion in August 1900, not the Great Wall along the northern border.

[4] Modern scholars place the first general, European use of the magnetic compass at sea in the 12th century. Chinese annals date the use of the compass from the period A.D. 1086-1093.

discovery of America, and the Reformation are three events which mark distinct eras in the world's history—grouped together, in their order of time, they illustrate in a remarkable manner the unity of purpose in working out the destiny of man.

The Mariner's Compass enabled the navigator to seek for the lost Atlantis amid the mysteries of an unknown sea; and led Columbus to a continent of vast proportions. Then came the Reformation when men fled from their homes across the waste of waters for opinion's sake. In the virgin soil of the new world new forms of political life germinated and bore fruit. Colonization followed. Oppression drove the colonies to rebellion and new states sprung into existence. These United States were still sparsely settled when the tempting bait of gold, in California, drew the tide of emigration across the mountains and peopled the Pacific slope. Then came the war with Spain, and Hawaii, Guam and the Philippines, those stepping stones across the Pacific, followed.

The world is growing impatient for an isthmian canal and will brook no frivolous excuses for delay.[5] Strategic points in the Caribbean, and in the Pacific, must be held and strengthened; and coaling stations and repair shops, under ample protection, must be provided.

The Monroe Doctrine alone demands a careful consideration of these questions.

Our Mercantile Marine.—An intelligent study of naval policy must necessarily include our shipping interests. The military marine and the mercantile marine are interdependent. The navy, while policing the sea, protects our foreign commerce, and in time of war, finds there its greatest reserves. It was once observed that we had "clipped the wings" of commerce and driven our carrying trade to foreign bottoms. The same is practically true today. Thus we are not only contributing indirectly to the support of foreign navies, which may some day be opposed to our own; but we are depriving ourselves of what would prove, in time of war, an auxiliary of incalculable value.

The remedy for this deplorable state of affairs must, necessarily be left to the wisdom of Congress. But the navy, with no other interest in the question save that dictated by the highest sense of patriotism, discharges an imperative duty, in urging as a military necessity, the re-habilitation of our mercantile marine.

These and kindred subjects belong to the strategy of peace, each topic finding its place in the College course.

The imprisonment of American Missionaries, and the massacre of Christians, by those under Turkish rule,[6] are a constant source of

---

[5] Serious American interest in building a canal began with explorations which were begun in 1870. Five months after this address was given, the United States obtained exclusive right to the Panama canal route in the wake of the Panamanian Revolution in November 1903. The canal was opened in 1914.

[6] Here Luce is referring to the Turkish massacre of Armenians in 1894-95. Until 1901 the major American difficulty with Turkey was the U.S. demand that an indemnity be paid for damages to missionary property during the Armenian troubles. After considerable diplomatic effort, highlighted by the appearance of the battleship U.S.S. Kentucky at Smyrna and the call of her captain, Colby Chester, on the Sultan in Constantinople, Turkey paid approximately $90,000 on the claim. In order to save face,

irritation to the people of this country; and may some day strain our foreign relations to the point of rupture. On the other hand the preservation in China, of what has come to be known as the "Open Door,"[7] a policy essential to our commercial interests, requires unremitting attention. With the map of the world constantly before us we must need be ever at the switch-board to keep in touch with whatever may be affecting our interests, hour by hour, in one quarter of the world or another.

Change, continual, unremitting change is the law of the universe. The solid earth itself is in a constant state of flux. Stagnation means atrophy and death. It is not enough for us to keep abreast of the times. This College must be in the very front rank of the advance guard of progress. To obtain some perception, however dim, of the future, we must study the past. This teaches us that the civilization we now enjoy was brought about by war. The proud position we, as a nation, now occupy, was rendered possible only by wars, and future problems in the destiny of man will be worked out through the instrumentality of the sword. There is no escaping it. Tears and tirades are here of no avail.

We are no apologists of war. Heaven forbid! We simply regard it, from a common-sense point of view, as one of the many evils flesh is heir to. War is a dreadful scourge we all admit. It is a relic of barbarism. We admit everything that can be said against war. But after all has been said, no student of history, however superficial, can deny that through that same dreadful scourge, ultimate good has been brought about. It has been so in the past, and, as far as human discernment can go, it must be so in the future.

War is not the only scourge man is heir to. Droughts, and resulting famines, by which thousands of innocent people have perished, as in India, through the slow torture of starvation, have proved more cruel than wars, and without their compensations.

The recent war with Spain cost but few lives, and comparatively little suffering, while Mt. Peleé, on the Island of Martinique,[8] swept out of existence an entire community of peaceful people. The war relieved

---

the Sultan disguised the indemnity payment as an installment on the cost for a new Turkish cruiser, *Medjidie,* to be constructed at the Cramp shipyard in Philadelphia. The ship was delivered to Turkey in early 1904.

In another incident during September 1901, an American missionary, Miss Ellen Stone, was kidnapped by Macedonian brigands and held for 5 months. Miss Stone's case became a *cause celebre* in American church circles. Nearly $70,000 was raised by public subscription in the United States. This sum was used to secure her release in February 1902.

[7]The U.S. "Open Door" policy was stated in a series of diplomatic notes issued by Secretary of State John Hay in 1899. Basically, the policy was a reflection of the U.S. concern that China might be parceled out into exclusive spheres of influences by other nations. The United States proposed that China remain territorially intact and independent but that nations which had special concessions in China should maintain the 5 percent Chinese tariff and, at the same time, allow all nations to trade in China without discrimination.

[8]Mount Peleé erupted on 8 May 1902 and destroyed the city of St. Pierre. Some 30,000 people died in the disaster.

Spain of colonies that had become burdensome, and in a manner that saved her honor. It was a war in the interest of civilization and human progress. But what end is served by pestilence and famine, and those convulsions of nature by which whole populations are swallowed up? The answer is locked up in the mysteries of an inscrutable Providence. All the Christian can reverently say is: "Thy will be done."

As between the various scourges inherited by man there is one marked difference. No human foresight can provide against earthquakes or volcanic eruptions or pestilence or famine. War, on the other hand, may in certain instances, be averted. But mark this well: It may be averted in one way only and that way is to be fully prepared for it. That is the meaning of this College: it is an instrumentality for the prevention of war by being prepared for it.

It is right here where the College joins hands with the Universal Peace Societies. To be prepared for war is the role of that naval strategy, which belongs to a period of peace. To be in the right place at the right time, and with adequate force, means success by checkmating your adversary in the first few moves. Campaigns have been won without firing a shot simply by skillful strategic movements. War has been defined as a question of positions and the most brilliant campaigns have been worked out on the map. It is the business of this College to study all the various problems of war as they may affect this country. The possibilities, indeed the probabilities, of future wars, and our duties in amply preparing for them, have been dwelt upon for the reason that contrary doctrines have been publicly proclaimed.

Every right-minded person must unite with the Church in praying to be delivered "from battle and murder and from sudden death." We all sincerely hope that arbitration may ultimately prove the sovereign panacea for the great curse of war; and that the doors of the temple of Janus may be forever closed. But Janus, though represented as a god, is also represented as "two-faced," and not always to be trusted; and arbitration fails, unhappily, when most sorely needed.

Do we not recall how it was said of old that the Lord sent a lying spirit to Ahab, King of Israel, that he might go up and fall at Ramoth Gilead?[9] And how the god of the Greeks sent a spirit in the form of a "deluding dream" to Agamemnon on the plains of Troy?[10]

"And thus the flattering Dream deceives the King!"

Beware of false prophets! The race is not extinct.

It is quite unnecessary to explain to such an audience as I have the honor of addresssing, that the College, itself, has no power, whatever, to act; nor authority to formulate a naval policy. Its aim, as stated in the beginning, is simply to invite officers to meet together to discuss questions pertaining to the higher branches of their profession, and enable each one, according to his own inclinations, to prepare himself

---

[9] I Kings 22.

[10] Homer, *The Iliad,* book II. The quotation is from the translation by Alexander Pope, book II, line 24.

for the highest and most responsible duties that can devolve upon a naval officer.

One thing must be borne in mind. At the firing of the first gun proclaiming war, the so-called "inspiration of genius" may be trusted only when it is the result of long and careful study and reflection.

Art is a jealous mistress; most of all so is the art of war.

If attendance here will serve, in any degree, to broaden an officer's views; extend his mental horizon on national and international questions, and give him a just appreciation of the great variety and extent of the requirements of his profession, the College will not have existed in vain.

CHAPTER III

THE INTELLECTUAL FOCUS:
ON THE STUDY OF NAVAL WARFARE AS A SCIENCE

"Science is applied knowledge."

By Rear-Admiral S.B. Luce, U.S.N.

Editors' Introduction

This article was presented as a lecture during the first session of the Naval War College in 1885. It was revised by Luce for the opening address at the second session on 6 September 1886. Subsequently, it was published in the *United States Naval Institute Proceedings*.*

Although the first session of the Naval War College had lasted less than a month and was presented to only nine students, it had been a definite success. For the moment, the fledgling school had friends in Washington who supported Luce's plans for an expanded course during the second year. With the conclusion of the first session on 30 September 1885, Luce and his small staff began to prepare for the following year. The second course would last nearly 3 months and have 21 students. Before the opening of the second session, however, Admiral Luce was reassigned as Commander in Chief, North Atlantic Station.

Departing on 22 June 1886 to take up a command which he hoped would develop into a squadron of evolution closely connected to the War College, Luce left the new school without a president. Although Luce had attempted to have Capt. Alfred T. Mahan assigned to the college staff as early as July 1884, Mahan did not arrive in Newport until August 1886 to take up his duties as professor, and now President.

After having arranged to have his flagship U.S.S. *Tennessee* in Newport during the new course, Luce delivered the opening address, "On the Study of Naval Warfare as a Science." In this speech he elaborated on the ideas that he had set down in his report to the Secretary of the Navy dated 13 June 1884 (bibliography item 75), and further refined the ideas in his article "The United States Naval War College" (bibliography item 73), published in January 1885, even before the first course had opened.

---

*"On the Study of Naval Warfare As a Science," *United States Naval Institute Proceedings*, vol. XII, No. 4, 1886, pp. 527-46.

This address is Luce's most complete expression of the intellectual concept behind the establishment of the Naval War College. The ideas which he expressed earlier had neither been tempered by the experience of the first course nor expanded by further reading and reflection. For Luce, the simultaneous study of the principles of military science and the opportunity to make comparisons between armies and navies at different points in history allowed students to classify and to generalize about human experience in warfare. Through an inductive method of reasoning by which a person proceeded from thinking about specific events to making broad generalizations and, at the same time, comparing and modifying these generalizations with tested principles, Luce believed that a theoretical structure could be developed for naval science. In the midst of a technological revolution in the world's navies, Luce was proposing an intellectual method by which professionals could develop the means to control more adequately the new capabilities of a steampowered, steel navy. Luce clearly understood that one first had to develop an understanding, a strategy, of what a navy was to do and why it existed, before one could properly select the means, the tactics, and the weapons by which it was to be done.

The article, in particular, emphasizes the complex intellectual heritage behind Luce's concept. In an era when Great Britain and France were the leading naval powers, one can clearly understand the impact which professional developments in those countries had on smaller navies. Certainly, Luce closely followed the latest naval thinking in the most prominent professional journals of both France and England. Luce's horizon was not limited only to the professional sphere, however. He was a voracious reader of history and literature as well. With Britain the dominant cultural center in the English speaking world, much of his reading and writing reflected a debt to British authors. Like many others in the 19th century, he followed closely the latest developments in science and technology. Perhaps something of a dilettante outside his own profession, Luce did find in his own thinking a close interaction between literature, science, technology, and education. His broad reading in the popular literature of the day had a profound impact on his professional contribution. In developing the theories behind this article, Luce was profoundly influenced by his reading of men such as the historian Thomas Buckle, the philologist Friedrich Max Muller, and the naval writings of Gen. Sir Howard Douglas and P.H. Colomb.

While this article draws its greatest importance from its elaboration on the basis for a new direction in naval education, it is important, too, for its relationship to the men who helped Luce implement his ideas. Among the staff who found their general guidance here were Army Lt. Tasker Bliss, a future President of the Army War College and Army Chief of Staff; Professor James R. Soley, international lawyer and future Assistant Secretary of the Navy; Lt. William McCarty Little, an innovator of tactics and the inventor of the naval war game; and the college's new President, Captain Mahan. In the course of their own careers, the contributions of each reflected something of the intellectual focus that Luce expressed in this address. The first to reach fame was Mahan. In 1886 he began the series of lectures that would be published 4 years later under the title *The Influence of Sea Power upon History, 1660-1783*.

Looking back on the address that had been an introduction for Mahan's work at the Naval War College, Luce remembered his final words, " . . . let us confidently look for the master mind who will lay the foundations of that science and do for it what Jomini had done for military science." Thirteen years later Luce would add, "He appeared in the person of Captain A.T. Mahan."

> Under date of May 3, 1884, the Secretary of the Navy appointed a board of three officers[1] to "report upon the subject of a post-graduate course for officers of the Navy."
>
> The board so appointed met, and, after careful deliberation, reported, under date of June 13, that there was "not only a reason, but an *absolute necessity*," for the establishment of such a school as contemplated by the order, the report dwelling most particularly on the importance of the study of war and international law. Much stress was laid upon the subject of war as the leading study of the proposed school. The board expressed the opinion that "a cogent reason for such a school was that there might be a place where our officers would not only be encouraged, but *required* to study their profession proper—war—in a far more thorough manner than had ever heretofore been attempted, and to bring to the investigation of the various problems of modern naval warfare the scientific methods adopted in other professions." And this idea of the study of war according to a certain prescribed method pervades the whole report. It is the central idea of the plan of operations, the very cornerstone, as it were, of the War College.
>
> The report of the board was adopted, and in October the Navy Department issued the following order:

---

[1] The board appointed by Secretary of the Navy William E. Chandler consisted of Commodore Luce, President of the Board, and two members: Comdr. W.T. Sampson and Lt. Comdr. Caspar F. Goodrich.

Commander Caspar Goodrich, (ca. 1886), had only recently returned from the European Station when he served on the Board which in 1884 recommended the establishment of the Naval War College. Goodrich had served as a naval observer on the staff of Lieutenant General Sir Garnet Wolsley during the Tel-el-Kebir campaign in 1882. He served as President of the Naval War College in 1889-92 and 1897-98.

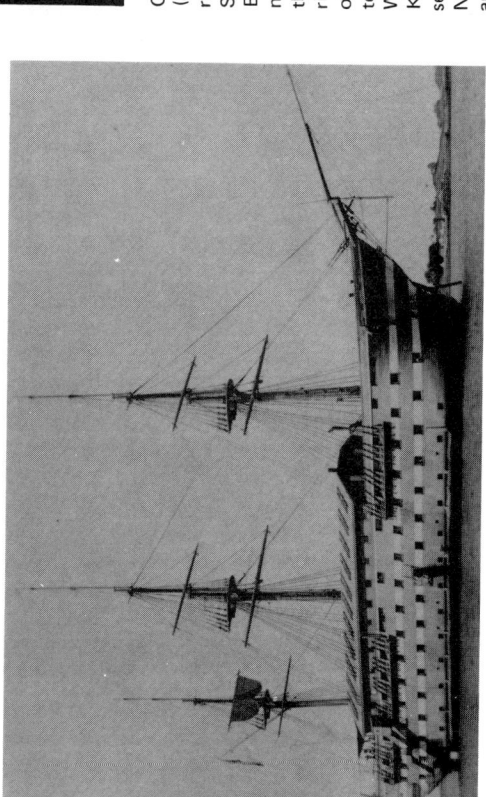

Below. The ship of the line U.S.S. *New Hampshire*, shown anchored off Coasters Harbor, (ca. 1882), was brought to Newport in 1881 to serve as the flagship of the Apprentice Training Squadron under Luce. In June 1884, Luce, Sampson, and Goodrich met as a board in the *New Hampshire* anchored where Luce placed her in 1881. He purposely anchored her away from the pier where she would swing to the wind and tide. Finding himself afloat and cut off from the rest of the world, the young apprentice could become accustomed to shipboard life and learn how to manage small boats as he travelled from his new home to shore. During Luce's absence on a training cruise to Europe in 1882, she was brought in and moored at the pier on Coasters Harbor Island by the advocates of battalion drill and close order marching. *New Hampshire* remained at Newport until 1891 when she was moved to New York. She was later named *Granite State*.

Photo: Naval History Division

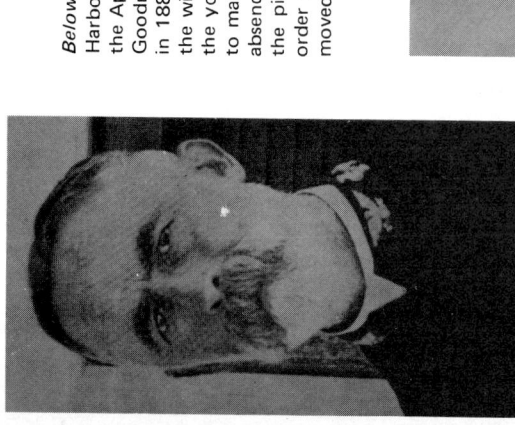

Captain William T. Sampson, (ca. 1898), in 1884 served as a member of the Luce Board which recommended the establishment of the Naval War College. Later, he became Chief of the Bureau of Ordnance, 1893-97, and Commander-in-Chief of the North Atlantic Squadron during the Spanish-American War.

"General Order No. 325.

"NAVY DEPARTMENT,
WASHINGTON, *October* 6, 1884.

"A college is hereby established for an *advanced course*[2] of professional study for naval officers, to be known as the Naval War College. It will be under the general supervision of the Bureau of Navigation. The principal building on Coasters' Harbor Island, Newport, R.I., will be assigned to its use, and is hereby transferred, with the surrounding structures and the grounds immediately adjacent, to the custody and control of the Bureau of Navigation for that purpose," etc., etc.[3]

"WILLIAM E CHANDLER,
Secretary of the Navy."

No immediate steps, however, were taken to carry out the order.

During the Second Session of the Forty-Eighth Congress the Senate adopted a resolution (Feb. 4th) calling upon the Secretary of the Navy for information in regard to an advanced course of instruction for naval officers. In answer the Secretary wrote, under date of February 11, 1885, as follows: "The reasons which have controlled the action of the Department are to be found in the recognized necessity for *an advanced course of military and naval education* in the United States. There are now existing three schools for the purpose in the Army and one in the Navy.[4] The latter is at the Torpedo Station at Newport, where a class of officers is assembled for a few months in each year for instruction in the art of manufacturing and using torpedoes and torpedo explosives. The constant changes in the methods of conducting naval warfare imposed by the introduction of armored ships, swift cruisers, rams, seagoing torpedo-boats and high-power guns, together with the more rigid methods of treating the various subjects belonging to naval science, render imperative the establishment of a school where our officers may be enabled to keep abreast of the improvements going on in every navy in the world. The Torpedo School only partially fufils the imperative requirements. The College is intended to complete the curriculum by adding to an extent never heretofore undertaken the study of naval warfare and international law and their cognate branches." (See Senate

---

[2] The italics used throughout the text of the address are Luce's.

[3] The remainder of the general order outlines the internal organization of the college, specifies that the course of instruction will be open to all officers above the grade of naval cadet, and states that Luce has been appointed "president of the college."

[4] The two Army schools were the Artillery School at Fort Monroe, Va., and the Infantry and Cavalry School at Fort Leavenworth, Kans. Luce published an extensive com.,entary on the Artil'"ry School in his article "War School:." (See bibliography item 68.) The Torpedo Station was located on Goat Island less than a mile south of Coasters Harbor Island and the Naval War College. The Torpedo Station was established in 1869 for the development of torpedoes, torpedo equipment, explosives, and electrical equipment. Until World War II nearly all torpedoes used by the U.S. Navy were manufactured there. A practical course of instruction existed from the beginning, but in 1873 an organized, 10-month-long course was begun.

Ex. Doc., No. 68, Forty-Eighth Congress, Second Session)[5] From this it would appear that the War College is not, in the estimation of the Department, for a post-graduate course merely, as that term is generally understood, but for the higher and much more comprehensive purpose of a greatly advanced course of professional instruction.

Now, it must strike any one who thinks about it as extraordinary that we, members of a profession of arms, should never have undertaken the study of our real business—war. For members of the naval and military profession it should be not only the principal study, but it should be an attractive study. War has been called a game, and as a game it possesses great interest to a majority of men, while to a certain order of minds it has a positive fascination.

We find in civil life men who love to study the campaigns of the great captains of history; who read the life of Alexander the Great, made up wholly of his campaigns, with the eagerness others peruse the pages of romance, and who follow Caesar through Gaul, and Hannibal across the Alps, with the keenest interest. No one can read the series of manoeuvres, the play and counter-play of Turenne and his great opponent, Montecuccoli; resulting in the untimely death of the former, without a thrill of admiration for the skill displayed by these two well-matched adversaries.[6] And, although confined entirely to the land forces, such campaigns are replete with valuable lessons to the naval officer. Marlborough, Frederick the Great, Napoleon, Wellington, and many of the great military leaders of our own country, have left us a rich legacy of many a skillfully played game which furnishes practical illustrations of great principles. It is for us, here and now, to familiarize ourselves with those principles, that we too may be ready to apply them when called upon to take a hand in the game.

Now, science is contributing so liberally to every department of knowledge, and has already done so much towards developing a truer understanding of the various arts, including that of the mariner, that it seems only natural and reasonable that we should call science to our aid to lead us to a clearer comprehension of naval warfare, as naval warfare is to be practised in the future. Steam tactics and naval warfare under steam are comparatively new studies, and readily admit of modern and scientific methods of treatment. The formation of the line-of-battle, composed of large ironclads, carrying heavy guns and auto-mobile torpedoes, the use of the ram as an independent arm, and the seagoing torpedo-boat and its place in the order of battle, are subjects which require the most careful consideration, and may well excite on the part of the naval officer, indeed *should* excite, an intelligent curiosity or inquisitiveness. Indeed, we may go further, and say that the naval officer who does not seek to inform himself on these points is

---

[5] *Letter from the Secretary of the Navy Reporting ... the Steps Taken by Him to Establish an Advanced Course of Instruction of Naval Officers at Coasters Harbor, Rhode Island, 1885.* See bibliography item 75.

[6] Henri de la Tour d'Auvergne Turenne (1611-1675) was *Marshal General of France,* and fought in the Thirty Years War. He was killed at the Battle of Sasbach on 27 July 1675. Raimondo, Count Montecuccoli (1608-1681) Turenne's opponent at the Battle of Sasbach, was an Italian-born general who fought in the service of Austria.

indifferent to the most important branch of his profession. That the whole subject is new and fresh and worthy of our most careful study is to be learned from the fact that the great naval powers of Europe still regard steam tactics as an unsolved problem. Thus we have the charm of novelty in our researches and a stimulant of a happy solution of a great problem.

What we need is, first, a clear conception of the problem itself, and then a solution of it so grounded in immutable principles as to admit of no doubt of its correctness. But it may be asked, "What is science?" and "How are we to regard as a science naval warfare, with all its various and complicated conditions?" and "How are we to treat such a subject in a scientific manner?"

In order to answer this very natural question, let us first understand what is meant by the word "science." Webster defines science to be "knowledge duly arranged, and referred to general truths and principles, on which it is founded, and from which it is derived." "In point of form," says Sir William Hamilton,[7] "it has the character of logical perfection, and in point of matter the character of real truth."

"A science," says Dr. Francis Lieber,[8] "is a branch of knowledge or collection of ideas systematically developed according to principles peculiar to the subject-matter itself. A science is independent within its own sphere. Everything is worthy of being scientifically investigated; that is, worthy of being investigated as to its essentials, separately and for itself, with a view of arriving at principles and laws. Every principle and law thus arrived at extends the sphere of knowledge, expands the human mind, increases the stock of civilization, and is emphatically useful."

Buckle[9] defines science as "a body of generalizations so irrefragably true that, though they may be subsequently covered by higher generalizations, they cannot be overthrown by them; in other words, generalizations which may be absorbed, but not refuted."

Both of the two last definitions may be illustrated by the history of the development of the physical sciences. By a series of experiments in chemistry many interesting and useful facts were discovered; but it was

---

[7] Sir William Hamilton (1788-1856) was a Scottish metaphysician who was influential in introducing the works of the German philosopher Immanuel Kant to the British public.

[8] Francis Lieber (1800-1872) was a German-born political philosopher and a veteran of the Napoleonic Wars. He came to the United States in 1827 and joined what would become the University of South Carolina. His code of military regulations for the conduct of the Civil War influenced similar codes in other countries and became the basis for the Hague Conventions of 1899 and 1907. Lieber was the first editor of the *Encyclopedia Americana*.

[9] Henry Thomas Buckle (1821-1862) was an English historian and the author of *History of Civilization in England* (New York: Appleton, 1922). Buckle believed that human progress was regulated by immutable principles similar to scientific laws. He attempted to determine the nature of these laws by the inductive study of history. For a study of the impact in America of Buckle's ideas and other historians with similar ideas, see W.S. Holt, "The Idea of Scientific History in America," *Journal of the History of Ideas*, vol. I, No. 3, June 1940, pp. 352-362.

not till the generalizations of Lavoisier[10] linked those facts together that the laws which govern the properties of matter were brought out. It was by this inductive method that chemistry was raised to a science.

In its earlier history geology was a crude mass of independent facts. But Cuvier[11] applied to the study the generalizations of comparative anatomy, and co-ordinated the study of the strata of the earth with the study of the fossil animals found in them. Thus he was the founder of the science of geology.

Astronomy furnishes a still more forcible illustration. Hipparchus,[12] Ptolemy,[13] Copernicus,[14] and Galileo,[15] each in his own time, made certain discoveries and demonstrated certain truths in relation to the movements of the heavenly bodies, and of the earth itself. And Tycho Brahe,[16] the Dane, far exceeded them all in the vast accumulation of observations of the stars. He undertook, in short, to catalogue the fixed stars, a labor originally essayed, though in a much ruder manner, by Hipparchus. But while Tycho Brahe himself knew not the real value of his own work, Kepler,[17] generalizing from the great mass of observations, was led to the discovery of those three great laws relating to the planetary system which won for him the proud title of "Legislator of the Heavens" and opened the way for the final generalizations of Newton.[18]

Taking its rise in the fanciful dreams of astrologers, astronomy has now become the most exact of all sciences. "By employing the deductive weapon of mathematics we can compute the motions and perturbations of the heavenly bodies; and by employing the inductive weapon by observation the telescope reveals to us the accuracy of our previous and, as it were, foregone inferences. The fact agrees with the

---

[10]Antoine Laurent Lavoisier (1743-1794), French chemist. He is considered the "father of modern chemistry."

[11]Georges Leopold Chretian Frederic Dagobert Cuvier (1769-1832), one of the great French naturalists and founder of the studies of comparative anatomy and paleontology.

[12]Hipparchus (fl. 146-127 B.C.), the greatest astronomical observer of antiquity. He is best known for his discovery of the precession of equinoxes.

[13]Ptolemy or Claudius Ptolemaeus (ca. A.D. 90-168). Modern historians believe that Ptolemy was more of a commentator on the works of his predecessors than an independent observer.

[14]Nicolas Copernicus (1473-1543) was the Polish astronomer who laid the foundation for modern developments in planetary astronomy. The Copernican theory rejected the Ptolemaic idea of an earth centered universe.

[15]Galileo Galilei (1564-1642) is credited with establishing the modern experimental method informally stating the principles later used by Newton in his first two laws and being the first to study the skies with the aid of a telescope.

[16]Tycho Brahe (1546-1601). He was the first to allow for the effect of atmospheric refraction and instrument error in his observations. His observatory at Uraniborg was the forerunner of the great modern observatories.

[17]Johann Kepler (1571-1630) was a German astronomer who worked closely with Tycho Brahe and inherited his collection of observations. Kepler's theories on planetary orbits were based on Brahe's observations and provided the starting point for Newton's investigations.

[18]Sir Isaac Newton (1642-1727), English scientist.

idea; the particular event confirms the general principle; the principle explains the event; and their unanimity authorizes us to believe that we must be right, since, proceed as we may, the conclusion is the same; and the inductive plan of striking averages harmonizes with the deductive plan of reasoning from ideas."[19]

Now, naval history abounds in materials whereon to erect a science, as science has been defined and illustrated, and it is our present purpose to build up with these materials the science of naval warfare. We are far from saying that the various problems of war may be treated as rigorously as those of one of the physical sciences; but there is no question that the naval battles of the past furnish a mass of facts amply sufficient for the formulation of laws or principles which, once established, would raise maritime war to the level of a science. Having established our principles by the inductive process, we may then resort to the deductive method of applying those principles to such a changed condition of the art of war as may be imposed by later inventions or the introduction of novel devices.

For a very simple and obvious illustration we may take the state of shipbuilding during the early and middle parts of last century. The French ships-of-war were of superior model and their bottoms were sheathed with metal. The English ships-of-war were of inferior model and were not sheathed.[20] The natural result was a constant gain of advantage in their sea fights of the former over the latter. The English ships were, on certain momentous occasions, so greatly retarded in their movements by the accumulation of marine growth, and their indifferent sailing qualities were of such great and manifest disadvantage to them in battle, and the fact is so often made a matter of historical record, that, by the method of generalization, we are enabled to lay down the broad principle *that speed is an essential element in naval warfare*—an axiom not needing an elaborate argument, but given as an illustration. This is the inductive system of proceeding from particulars to generals.

By reversing the operation and applying the deductive method of proceeding from generals to particulars, we deduce from the principle just stated the fact that the modern war ship must be modeled with special reference to speed, and must have her bottom protected from the fouling due to vegetable marine growth. Thus we arrive at a fundamental truth; and to disregard such teachings is not merely to commit a great blunder by shutting our eyes to the lessons of history, but it is to be unscientific in one's own profession, which, in these days, is to be culpably ignorant, if not criminal.

Nor are we obliged to go very far back for many important facts in regard to maritime war, on which we are to generalize. In our own very

---

[19] Buckle, *History of Civilization in England*, vol. II, pp. 337-38. This passage is part of Buckle's contrast between inductive and deductive reasoning.

[20] In 1761 the Royal Navy tested copper sheathing and by 1775, 12 ships had been coppered. By 1783 it had become standard practice to include it on all new British ships. In 1779-80, other European navies followed up on the early success of the English experiment. See R.J.B. Knight, "The Introduction of Copper Sheathing into the Royal Navy, 1779-1786," *The Mariner's Mirror*, vol. LIX, No. 3, August 1973, pp. 299-309.

limited experience in war the battle of Port Royal[21] furnishes a valuable illustration of the necessity of possessing a secure base of supplies within the theatre of war, and few naval conflicts have been so pregnant with results as that in which the monitor bore so conspicuous a part. As an illustration of that very important military element called the *moral effect* of a battle, it stands almost unrivaled.

The grouping together of a number of important facts gathered from the accounts of naval battles will enable the naval student who has acquired the habit of generalizing to lay down principles for his own guidance in war, and that is a work that each one can do for himself better than another can do for him. The passage from facts to principles in induction in its highest form is inspiration, says Tyndall.[22]

Again, it has been said that the philosophy of method bears the same relation to science that science does to art. "The progress of every science is affected more by the scheme according to which it is cultivated, than by the ability of the cultivators themselves." Some men, like Tycho Brahe, without a Kepler to follow, "have consumed their lives in fruitless industry, not because their labors were slack, but because their method was sterile."

Hence, to elevate naval warfare into a science, as we now propose doing, we must adopt the comparative method; and, as Cuvier co-ordinated the study of geology with that of comparative anatomy, so must we co-ordinate the study of naval warfare with military science and art. That is the theory on which we are now to proceed; and it is desirable that each one of us should comprehend this theory in its length and breadth, its height and depth, for it is on such perfect understanding alone that success in our present undertaking can be assured. It is by the comparative method that we have been led to a knowledge of the most important phenomena of the science of life. As it would be impracticable to study the living action of the various organs of the human body, the physiologist has recourse to other means whereby to carry on his investigation. All vertebrate animals, being constructed on the same general plan of organization, with corresponding organs of the same character common to all—their nervous and vascular systems, digestive apparatus, organs of locomotion, and the rest—can easily be recognized and compared with each other. From the study of the brain of a pigeon, for example, Dalton[23] was enabled to explain the functions of the human brain. From experiments on the

---

[21] Luce participated in the attack on Port Royal, S.C., on 7 November 1861. As a lieutenant he was in charge of a gun deck division in U.S.S. *Wabash*, the flagship of Samuel F. Du Pont, flag officer in command of the South Atlantic Blockading Squadron. The flotilla which sailed for Port Royal was made up of 75 ships, 25 of which carried coal and supplies. After the battle Port Royal became a major supply base for the Union blockade during the remainder of the war. Union control of Port Royal assured Gen. W.T. Sherman a secure supply base for his "March to the Sea" in 1864.

[22] John Tyndall (1820-1893), British physicist.

[23] John Call Dalton (1825-1889) was the first U.S. physician to devote himself to experimental physiology. He was a friend of Luce's who had served as an Army Brigade surgeon during the Port Royal expedition.

horse, Matteucci[24] demonstrated the rapidity of the circulation of the blood. Brown-Séquard[25] and Velpeau,[26] by experiments on animals, discovered the functions of the spinal cord. Bidder,[27] and Schmidt,[28] and Dalton illustrated the process of digestion by experiments on dogs; and the action of the heart and the circulation of the blood were, by the same process, illustrated by Harvey.[29] This gives us a hint pregnant with possibilities.

We have already referred, in passing, to the splendid results achieved by Cuvier through his adoption of the comparative method of investigation. Says Buckle: "By this union of geology and comparative anatomy, there was first introduced with the study of Nature a clear conception of the magnificent doctrine of universal change, while at the same time there grew up by its side a conception, equally steady, of the regularity with which the changes are accomplished, and of the undeviating law by which they are governed."[30]

. In his beautiful eulogy on Agassiz,[31] Professor Le Conte,[32] in explaining the comparative method of investigation (for the more general introduction of which he gives the great scientist high praise), says: "Anatomy only becomes scientific through *comparative* anatomy; physiology only becomes scientific through *comparative* physiology"; and we may add, without distorting the parallelism, that naval tactics, using that word in its more extended sense, becomes scientific only through *comparative* tactics. For, having no authoritative treatise on the art of naval warfare under steam, having no recognized tactical order of battle, being deficient even in the terminology of steam tactics, we must, perforce, resort to the well-known rules of the military art with a view to their application to the military movements of a fleet, and, from the well-recognized methods of disposing troops for battle, ascertain the principles which should govern fleet formations. Thus,

---

[24] Carlo Matteucci (1811-1868), Italian physicist.

[25] Charles Edouard Brown-Séquard (1817-1894), French physiologist.

[26] Alfred Armand Louis Marie Velpeau (1795-1867), French surgeon.

[27] Friederich Heinrich Bidder (1810-1894), Russian-born student of anatomy and physiology.

[28] Carl Schmidt (1822-1894) worked with Bidder in demonstrating the composition of gastric juices.

[29] William Harvey (1578-1657), English physician.

[30] Buckle, *History of Civilization in England*, vol. I, pp. 634-635.

[31] Jean Louis Randolphe Agassiz (1807-1873) was a Swiss-born geologist and naturalist who studied in Germany and later in Paris under Cuvier. As a professor at Harvard University after 1848, he exerted considerable influence in opposing the Darwinian concept of evolution.

[32] Joseph Le Conte (1823-1901), a geologist at the University of California, Berkeley, was one of the first students drawn to Harvard to study under Agassiz at the Lawrence Scientific School. Le Conte's eulogy, "Agassiz's Work and Method" was part of the Agassiz Memorial meeting at the California Academy of Sciences held in San Francisco, 22 December 1873. It was published in the Academy's *Proceedings* vol. V, 1873-74, pp. 220-243.

from the known, we may arrive at something like a clear understanding of what is now mere conjecture. *It is by this means alone that we can raise naval warfare from the empirical stage to the dignity of a science.*

It is important that this should be understood. We lay so much stress upon this method of treating our subject that, even at the risk of overburdening the argument, let us refer once more to the methods of investigation pursued by the most advanced thinkers of the age. We have drawn our illustrations so far from the physical sciences. Let us now go to other departments of learning, and we shall see what the comparative method has done for them.

"It was supposed at one time," says Max Müller,[33] "that a comparative analysis of the languages of mankind must transcend the powers of man; and yet, by the combined and well-directed efforts of many scholars, great results have been obtained, and the principles that must guide the students of the science of language are now firmly established.

"It will be the same with the science of religion. By a proper division of labor, the materials that are still wanting will be collected and published and translated; and when that is done, surely man will never rest till he has discovered the purpose that runs through the religions of mankind, and till he has reconstructed the true *Civites Dei* on foundations as wide as the ends of the world."

It has been by treating the subject of religion in a scientific manner that deep and hidden truths have been revealed, and passages of the Holy Scriptures otherwise obscure have been rendered clear and full of meaning. Thus, as the author says, "the science of religion will for the first time assign to Christianity its right place among the religions of the world; it will show for the first time what was meant by 'the fullness of time'; it will restore to the whole history of the world, in its unconscious progress towards Christianity, its true and sacred character."

Speaking in another place of the science of language, he says: "People ask, 'What is gained by comparison?' Why, all higher knowledge is gained by comparison, and rests on comparison. If it is said that the character of scientific research in our age is preeminently comparative, this really means that our researches are now based on the widest evidence that can be obtained, on the broadest inductions that can be grasped by the human mind." "What can be gained by comparison?" he asks again. "Why, look at the study of languages. If you go back but a hundred years and examine the folios of the most learned writers upon questions connected with language, and then open a book written by the merest tyro in comparative philology, you will see what can be gained, what *has been* gained, by the comparative

---

[33] Friedrich Max Müller (1823-1900), a German-born philologist and orientalist, was a leader in promoting the comparative study of both philology and religion in England. Luce's source for this quotation has not been located; however, the ideas in it are similar to those which Müller expressed in his *Lectures on the Science of Language* (New York: Scribner, 1862), and his *Lectures on the Science of Religion* (New York: Scribner, 1872). In the first portion of his *Lectures on the Science of Language,* Müller makes some of the same points which Luce uses here, with many of the same examples.

method." Reasoning thus, he advocates the comparative or scientific study of the religions of the world.

Lastly, we have the authority of Mr. Hutcheson Macaulay Posnett,[34] who, in his *Comparative Literature,* says: "The *comparative method* of acquiring knowledge is ... the peculiar glory of our nineteenth century."

Hence, we have not only comparative anatomy and comparative physiology, but comparative philology, comparative grammar, comparative religion, comparative literature, and why not, we ask again, comparative war, or a comparative study of the military operations of a sea army and a land army? Attention has been called repeatedly by various writers to the close analogy between military and naval operations. It has been successfully shown that among the ancients, or what has been termed the "oar period" of naval history, the military and naval tactics were as nearly identical as the nature of the elements would admit. The most distinguished soldiers of Carthage, Greece, and Rome commanded afloat, as occasion required.

Macaulay,[35] in speaking of the English Navy of the time of Charles II., says: "No State, ancient or modern, had before that time made a complete separation between the naval and military services. In the great civilized nations of the old world, Cimon and Lysander, Pompey and Agrippa, had fought battles by sea as well as by land. Nor had the impulse which nautical science received at the close of the fifteenth century produced any material improvement in the division of labor. At Flodden the right wing of the victorious army was led by the Admiral of England.[36] At Jarnac and Mon-Contour the Huguenot ranks were marshaled by the Admiral of France.[37] Neither Don John of Austria,

---

[34] Hutcheson Macaulay Posnett was a lawyer and professor of classics and English literature in University College, Auckland, New Zealand. The full quotation here is "The comparative method of acquiring or communicating knowledge is in one sense as old as thought itself, in another the peculiar glory of our nineteenth century," *Comparative Literature* (New York: Appleton, 1886), p. 73.

[35] Thomas Babington Macaulay (1800-1879). The quotation here may be found in *The Works of Lord Macaulay: History of England* (London: Longmans, Green, 1914), vol. I, pp. 314-315.

[36] The Battle of Flodden was an English victory over the Scots fought near Braxton, Northumberland, 9 September 1513. The Admiral of England, Thomas Howard, second Duke of Norfolk, first Earl of Surrey, (1443-1524) commanded 1,000 soldiers and sailors in the battle.

[37] The Battle of Jarnac was fought 12 March 1569 and the Battle of Moncontour was fought 3 October 1569. The French Huguenot forces were commanded by Gaspard de Châtillon, Comte de Coligny (1519-1572), the leader of the French Protestant cause in the first half of the Wars of Religion. Although he never commanded at sea, Coligny was made Admiral of France in 1552. With the death of the Prince de Condé in the Battle of Jarnac, Coligny was left as the sole experienced leader of the Huguenots. By 1570 he obtained for them the advantageous peace of St. Germain.

the conqueror of Lepanto,[38] nor Lord Howard of Effingham,[39] to whose direction the marine of England was entrusted when the Spanish invaders were approaching its shores, had received the education of a sailor. Raleigh,[40] highly celebrated as a naval commander, had served during many years as a soldier in France, the Netherlands, and Ireland.

"Blake[41] had distinguished himself by his skillful and valiant defense of an inland town before he humbled the pride of Holland and of Castile on the ocean.

"Since the Restoration the same system had been followed. Great fleets had been entrusted to the direction of Rupert[42] and Monk[43] — Rupert, who was renowned chiefly as a hot and daring cavalry officer, and Monk, who, when he wished his ship to change her course, moved the mirth of his crew by calling out, 'Wheel to the left!' Coligny was a colonel of infantry when, in 1552, he was made Admiral of France, and distinguished himself at the battles of Dreux[44] and Jarnac, and James II., served in the French army under Turenne, and received a thorough training as a soldier, before he was called upon to command the Channel fleet during one of the great Dutch wars."

About 1672 the French began to educate young men of good family especially for the sea, and England soon followed the example. In the process of time the two professions, the naval and military, became so distinct that everything of a military character began to be looked upon with contempt by those bred to the sea. The very name of "soldier" became among sailors a term of reproach, and when troops of the line were first placed on board ship they were made the subjects of endless ridicule among the rollicking sailors. Even to this day the older class of

---

[38] The Battle of Lepanto was a naval victory of Spain, the Pope, and Venice over the Turks. Fought on 7 October 1571, the battle was an important moral victory for the Christian forces. As the last battle fought between oared galleys, it marks an important turning point in the history of naval tactics and technology. Don John of Austria (1574-1578) was the son of Emperor Charles V.

[39] Charles, Lord Howard of Effingham, Earl of Nottingham (1536-1624) was made Lord High Admiral of England in 1584.

[40] Sir Walter Raleigh (1552-1618).

[41] Robert Blake (1599-1657) was the leading sea officer of the Parliamentary forces under Cromwell. During the first Dutch War he dramatically defeated the Dutch.

[42] Prince Rupert of the Rhine (1619-1682) was the third son of the Elector Palatinate, Frederick V, and grandson of King James I of England. The "Mad Cavalier" was a key military figure in the royalist cause during the English Civil War. After serving as generalissimo of King Charles I's army, he commanded the portion of the English fleet that remained loyal to the crown. He fled to France but returned after the Restoration to command the fleet with Monk against the Dutch in 1666. A general-at-sea and Admiral of the Fleet, he served as First Lord of the Admiralty, 1673-79.

[43] George Monk, Duke of Albemarle (1608-1670), was persuaded to join the Parliamentary forces of Cromwell after serving in the Royalist Army during the English Civil War. After the death of the Lord Protector, Monk was instrumental in bringing about the restoration of Charles II to the throne. He was a general-at-sea, joint commander of the navy, and served at sea in both the First and Second Dutch Wars. Monk was First Lord of the Treasury in 1667.

[44] The Battle of Dreux was a defeat by the Huguenot forces under Coligny and the Prince de Condé. The battle was fought 19 December 1562.

seamen despise "sojering," and look with contempt upon a "musket." This feeling was not confined to the seamen. It was shared by the officers, who prided themselves on their practical seamanship, and held military matters as beneath their notice. We have now reached a stage of progress which enables us to take such a broad and comprehensive view of nautical science as to avoid either of these extremes. While educating officers especially for sea service, they are yet taught the military character of their profession; and the close analogy between the operations of a fleet and an army has long been insisted upon, and is now generally acknowledged.

Even under sail tactics Paul Hoste,[45] and, later, John Clerk,[46] the author of the "Essay on Naval Tactics," noticed the military character of fleet evolutions. It is not surprising, therefore, that early in the history of steam tactics there should have been a number of writers who called attention to the same fact. Admiral Bowles,[47] R.N., remarked that we had "arrived at a new era, in which steam would enable naval commanders to conduct their operations on military and scientific principles,"[48] and Admiral Dahlgren[49] observed that the principles of military tactics would hereafter enter largely into the manoeuvres of a fleet. Sir Howard Douglas,[50] referring to these several authorities, adds that "the celerity and precision with which steam fleets may execute any evolution whatever will hereafter allow the

---

[45] Father Paul Hoste (1652-1700) was a Jesuit priest and professor of mathematics at the French Naval School in Toulon. In 1697 he published his *L'art des armées naveles*, the first recorded work on naval tactics. Hoste developed a system of tactics casend on the single line ahead and the independent action of squadrons. His influence can be seen in the tactical instructions of many English admirals as well as in later French tacticians. A second edition of Hoste's work was published at Lyon in 1727. Christopher O'Bryen published extracts in English from Hoste at London in 1762, but a complete translation did not appear until Capt. J.D. Boswall published his effort in Edinburgh in 1834.

[46] John Clerk (1728-1812) was a Scottish merchant who retired from a prosperous Edinburgh business in 1773 to devote himself to the study of naval tactics. The first portion of *Essay on Naval Tactics* was printed in a private edition of 50 copies in 1782. An expanded public edition appeared in 1790. Clerk claimed credit for Adm. Sir George Rodney's successful tactics in the Battle of the Saints, April 1782; however, in spite of similarities, Clerk's work did not influence Rodney in this battle. Later, his work did become extremely important to the English and the American navies. Throughout the 19th century the essay was a standard text for officers in the U.S. Navy.

[47] Admiral of the Fleet Sir William Bowles (1780-1869) was the author of the pamphlet *An Essay on Naval Operations* (London: Ridgway, 1849).

[48] Luce may have taken this quotation of Bowles' from Sir Howard Douglas, *On Naval Warfare with Steam* (London: Murray, 1858), p. 69.

[49] Rear Adm. John Adolphus Bernard Dahlgren, USN (1809-1870), was the inventor of the smoothbore naval gun that bears his name. Dahlgren was responsible for developing the U.S. Navy's ordnance factory at the Washington Navy Yard in the 1860's and 1870's. Luce's reference to Dahlgren's comment appears also to have come from Sir Howard Douglas, *ibid.*, p. 90.

[50] Sir Howard Douglas (1776-1861) was a British general, the son of Rear Admiral of the Blue Sir Charles Douglas. Sir Howard served in Canada and the Peninsula. He was Governor of New Brunswick, 1823-29, where he founded Fredericton University; Lord High Commissioner of the Ionian Islands, 1835-40; and Member of Parliament for Liverpool, 1842-46.

principles of tactics on land to be applied to the movements of ships on the ocean, with this advantage on the side of naval operations, that the inequalities of ground which so seriously embarrass the manoeuvres of troops do not exist at sea." This is quite true. The movements of an army may be, and very often are, obstructed by the physical conditions of a country; mountains, rivers, and forests must often be taken into account in planning a campaign, and the lines of communication with the bases of supplies, the lines of retreat, and the topography of the country within the field of operations must necessarily control the question of the proper distribution of troops for battle. None of these elements enter into the discussion of the operations of a fleet.

But beginning with the terminology of elementary tactics, and passing thence through the school of the battalion to grand tactics, and, finally, to strategy, it will be found that there is so much that is common to both the land and the sea forces, that we may by the comparative method, readily and intelligently, not only formulate correct theories in regard to naval warfare under steam, but confidently lay down unerring principles for our guidance in the conduct of battle. Commodore Parker's[51] "Fleet Tactics under Steam" is, as he himself tells us, "simply an adaptation of military to naval tactics."[52] Woods Pasha,[53] in a recent article on the naval tactics of the future, says: "It is hardly possible to glance at the development of the modern fighting ship without being struck by the analogy between military action afloat and ashore."[54] Indeed, it would help very materially in our investigations if we kept prominently in view that word *milites*, signifying fighting men, and thus have constantly before us the military character of our profession. We might then consider a fleet as a sea army, as the Latin races do, and adopt without reserve, as far as applicable, the tactical movements of the land forces for the management of an assemblage of ships-of-war. Such a step would have the advantage of clearing away or disposing of a great deal of useless material left over from the sail period, and enable us to bring to the consideration of our subject minds unembarrassed by obsolete formularies.

It would far exceed the limits of this paper, which is intended to be merely introductory, to point out in detail the close analogy between

---

[51] Commodore Foxhall Alexander Parker, USN (1821-1879) was a leader in the professional development of the U.S. Navy following the Civil War. During the Civil War he developed systems of naval tactics for steamships, served as Chief Signal Officer of the U.S. Navy, 1873-76, and drew up a code of signals for steam tactics. Parker was one of the founders and the first President of the United States Naval Institute. He died while serving as Superintendent of the Naval Academy.

[52] Commodore Foxhall A. Parker, *Fleet Tactics Under Steam* (New York: Van Nostrand, 1879), introduction.

[53] Sir Henry Felix Woods (1843-1919) was a British-born admiral in the Imperial Ottoman Navy. Commonly known as Woods Pasha, he served as naval adviser to the Sultan. He joined the Royal Navy in 1858 but was allowed to join the Turkish service in 1870. Woods was responsible for buoying the Dardanelles and its approaches. With Hobart Pasha (Adm. Augustus Charles Hobart-Hampden, 1822-1886), he reorganized the Turkish Fleet.

[54] Woods Pasha, "The Naval Tactics of the Future," *North American Review*, vol. CXLI, September 1885, p. 267.

the operations of land and sea forces. Many illustrations will doubtless suggest themselves to the naval student who reads military history, and it is especially recommended that the members of the class under instruction should, each one for himself, as we pass through the course of lectures on military science, note the points of analogy as they come up and make careful memoranda of those principles of military movements which are applicable to a floating force.

By way of illustrating our meaning more clearly, we may give a few examples of the more obvious principles common to both services. Guibert,[55] an eminent French writer on military science, has said that the art of fortification and that of field tactics are intimately connected with each other, and that the latter derives many of its principles from the art of constructing permanent fortresses. In both the important object is to dispose the parts, whether works or bodies of troops, so that they may afford mutual protection. He infers, therefore, that to be a good tactician a knowledge of military engineering is necessary. Now, these remarks apply with equal force to the naval tactician, for he too should so dispose the ships of his fleet that they may mutually support one another. Ships may be regarded as movable forts, and reasoned upon accordingly. "The inartifical practice," says Sir Howard Douglas, "of forming a fleet for battle in one long line, in which the ships are devoid of the power of protecting each other by reciprocal defense, and without a second line as a reserve, ought to be abandoned, as a corresponding practice with armies in the field has been renounced in warfare on land."[56] The advantages of the *echelon* formation for an army and its application to a fleet have been so fully and ably set forth by Sir Howard Douglas as to leave nothing to be added. The most striking illustration, however, is to be found in that peculiar method of attack to which Napoleon owed many of his victories on land and Nelson on the sea. It is expressed in that maxim which teaches the importance of so conducting a battle as to bring upon the point of attack a great superiority of force in such a manner that the enemy, even if numerically superior upon the whole, may be unable to succor the part so overpowered. The late Captain James H. Ward, U.S. Navy,[57] in commenting upon this point, says that this same maxim, so fully recognized by military writers, was in the contemplation of Byng in 1756; of Hood at Basseterre Roads (St. Kitts), 1782, and was carried

---

[55] Jacques Antoine Hippolyte, Comte de Guibert (1743-1790), was a French general and military writer. His *Essai general de tactique* (1770) has been considered one of the best essays by a soldier in the 18th century. Guibert predicted the establishment of national armies and presaged many of the innovations which occurred during the Napoleonic era. Napoleon himself was a careful student of Guibert's work.

[56] Douglas, *On Naval Warfare With Steam*, p. 103.

[57] Comdr. James Harmon Ward, USN (1806-1861), was killed in action while in command of the Potomac Flotilla, 27 June 1861. Ward was considered one of the most scholarly officers in the Navy at the outbreak of the Civil War. Long an advocate of a naval academy, he became the first Commandant of Midshipmen when the U.S. Naval Academy was opened in 1845. He published *An Elementary Course of Instruction on Ordnance and Gunnery* in 1845 and *Steam for the Million* in 1860. The reference here is to his *A Manual of Naval Tactics* (New York: Appleton, 1859), sec. II-III, pp. 49-127.

out by Rodney in his chase of the French in 1782; by Nelson at the Nile and at Trafalgar, and in a most remarkable manner by Perry at Lake Erie.

We have already laid down as a principle in naval warfare, clearly established by the method we have adopted for our investigations, that "speed is essential to success in war." This is true also in military science. Marshal Saxe[58] declared that "success in war is due to the legs of the soldiers." The rapid marches which preceded the battles of Gunzburg and Elchingen,[59] we are told, were the causes of the successes of Napoleon much more than those combats, brilliant as they were. To the bold and rapid movements which characterized the campaigns of Alexander the Great, Caesar, Hannibal, Frederick the Great, and Napoleon are to be attributed their uniform successes.

But there was a certain mobility, as distinct from speed, peculiar to the troops of Napoleon, which rendered them easily handled by a master of the art of war. This too is an important quality in ships. It was the speed and activity of the Greek triremes that led to their victory at Salamis. It was to the light, swift, and quick-turning Liburnian galleys that Octavius owed his victory at Actium. The Spaniards of the Invincible Armada were astonished by the speed and handiness of the English ships they encountered in the Channel. The Duke of Medina-Sidonia said they seemed to leave the Spanish ships and approach them at pleasure. In one of his plaintive letters to Parma he wrote: "We cannot bring the English to battle, for they are swift and we are slow."[60] The wretched sailing qualities of the Spaniards and their unwieldiness put them at a disadvantage for which skill and courage could not compensate.

Now, speed is a comparative quality. The English ships of that day, though fast when compared to the Spanish ships of the Armada, were slow when confronted later on with the superior models of France. It was during the greater part of the eighteenth century that the speed and handiness of the French ships-of-war enabled the French admirals to practise those tactics which so long rendered the high fighting qualities of the English of no avail. To the quality of speed, then, we must add,

---

[58] Maurice, Comte de Saxe (1696-1750), Marshal of France.

[59] The Battle of Gunzburg was fought 9 October 1805, and the Battle of Elchingen was fought 14 October 1805. Both were part of the Campaign of Austerlitz.

[60] Luce's source for this quotation has not been located; however, it is similar to the English translation of a letter from the Duke of Medina-Sidonia to the Duke of Parma, dated 4 August 1588:
> The enemy's ships have continued to bombard us, and we were obliged to turn and face them, so that the firing continued on most days from dawn to dark; but the enemy has resolutely avoided coming to close quarters with our ships, although I have tried my hardest to make him do so. I have given him so many opportunities that sometimes some of our vessels have been in the very midst of the enemy's fleet, to induce one of his ships to grapple and begin in the fight; but all to no purpose, as his ships are very light, and mine very heavy, and he has plenty of men and stores.

Gr. Br., Public Records Office, *Calendar of Letters and State Papers Relating to English Affairs Preserved Principally in the Archives of Simancas*, vol. IV, *Elizabeth, 1558-1603*) (London: H.M. Stationery Office, 1900), p. 360.

as another deduction, the quality of mobility, handiness, or the property of quick turning. The ocean racers of the great Transatlantic lines, with lengths ten, and often eleven, times their beam, have great speed, but very limited powers for quick turning.

There is still another quality of speed, or, more properly speaking, celerity of movement (if we may make the distinction), which is common to both land and sea forces, but which belongs more to the personal character of the commander-in-chief than to the troops or ships under his command. "It was not the Roman army which conquered Gaul, but Caesar," said Napoleon. "It was not the Carthaginian army which made Rome tremble at her gates, but Hannibal. It was not the Macedonian army which marched to the Indus, but Alexander. It was not the Prussian army which defended Prussia for seven years against the three most powerful states of Europe, but Frederick." The wonderful success of these great captains was due in a very large measure to the continuous celerity of their movements, to their great energy governed by an intelligent directive force.

In 1781 the English fitted out an expedition to capture the Dutch Colony at the Cape of Good Hope. DeSuffren sailed shortly afterwards from Brest (March, 1781), fell upon the English squadron under Commodore Johnson, at Porto Praya (Cape de Verde Islands), and after a drawn battle hurried on to the Cape of Good Hope, where he arrived one month in advance of the English, thus fully securing the object of his mission, which was to thwart the designs of colonization by the English in that quarter. History is replete with such examples of celerity of movements both in the land and in the naval service.

Nelson's chase of the French squadron under Villeneuve forms a chapter in itself. In connection with mobility of the units of organization must be considered still another element of success common to both services, the potency of drill. The talents of the naval architect and the skill of the marine engineer and the labors of the ordnance officer will have been put forth in vain, if the squadron of fighting ships be not in efficient discipline and thorough drill. History teaches no more important lesson than this, and here again the two armies stand on common ground. The Romans called an army *exercitus*, which also meant exercise. What a history in that one word! Frederick the Great paid more attention to mere parade drill than any modern general, to which fact he owed many of his victories, as well as his escapes from serious disasters.

"Unquestionably," says one military authority, "of two armies equal in all other respects, and equally handled by their commanders, that one must win which can manoeuvre with the greatest rapidity and precision." And one of the most distinguished writers of the day on naval matters says, in speaking of the necessity of a school of practice in naval tactics, "The fleet most thoroughly drilled in naval tactics will have the greatest advantage in war."

To say that "speed," "handiness" and "drill" are elements essential to success in war, seems to be stating such self-evident truths as to need no demonstration. That may be true, but it is equally true that the examples of history which inculcate these lessons are being disregarded every day by nearly all maritime powers, and by none more than our own. They are of that class of truths which everybody admits, but nobody heeds. A certain English essayist says that "the best way of introducing any subject is by a string of platitudes delivered after an oracular fashion." We have taken the hint.

Captain Maguire,[61] U.S. Army, following Guibert, shows the analogy between land and sea forces from the point of view of a military engineer. In speaking of the attack of forts by ships he says: "This attack by sea may be compared to a land siege. The fleet will first bombard the sea forts at long range, in order to silence their fire; thereupon it will approach nearer to the coast forts and batteries, in order to carry on with favorable chances the decisive fight intended for the complete subjection of the latter. Finally, it will turn its attention to those works more retired which bear upon the harbor entrance and its obstruction. This last act may be considered as entirely identical with the heavy and rapid fire of the siege batteries, which precedes the advance of the storming party. In case the obstructions consist of submarine mines, and the fleet must destroy them by torpedoes, this operation is identical with the counter-mining operations of a siege. Finally, as the storming of the breach is the crowning act of the siege, so must, or should, at least, the forcing of the harbor entrance be regarded as the last stage of the attack.

"This comparison leads us to the conclusion that the general principles of sieges may be applied to attack by sea. In place of the ground in front of the works to be attacked lies the sea, which, with its depths and shoals, rocks, islands, wide and narrow channels, represents the more or less favorable field of operations of the attacking party; while the powerful ships, in consequence of their armor, are very strong batteries, which, after being once completely equipped, need no subsequent aid, and, in consequence of their engines, can constantly and rapidly change their positions.

"The ammunition supply of the ships will limit their action against a sea fort to the duration of a few days; and this, in connection with their great mobility, will give to the attack the characteristics of a short, rapid engagement."[62]

But enough has been said to show the close analogy between the land army and the sea army to render further illustration unnecessary.

Having shown the system by which it is proposed to conduct the course of study in naval warfare, it is but just and proper to state, at the outset, that we are without instructors or even text-books. This should be distinctly understood. But we have an instructor in naval history to tell us some of the great lessons of the past; and we have an instructor in military science to teach those of us who are willing to learn what he knows of the general principles of that science. It is our part to learn what we can of them, to draw our own conclusions and to make our

---

[61] Edward Maguire (1847-1892) was a captain in the U.S. Army Corps of Engineers. A graduate of the Military Academy at West Point in 1867, Maguire served with the engineers on the Great Lakes and the western rivers as well as Secretary of the Fortification Board. He published nine articles and books on harbor improvement and technical subjects and one book on coastal defense.

[62] Edward Maguire, *The Attack and Defence of Coast-Fortifications* (New York: Van Nostrand, 1884), pp. 24-25.

own deductions, and to apply the principles which they illustrate by the operations of past wars, both at sea and on land, that we may formulate our own ideas on the subject of naval warfare. By doing this we adopt the *comparative method.*

It is obvious from what has just been said that, while learning naval history and the military art and science from professors of those branches, we must be our own instructors in the naval art and science. Says President Bartlett,[63] of Dartmouth College, in the *Forum* for September: "All higher education is essentially self-education. Teachers do not make the scholar. The impulse comes chiefly from within, and the student becomes the scholar when he ceases to confine himself to prescribed tasks or previous limits, and spontaneously reaches out beyond."[64] If we are to learn this highest, noblest branch of our profession at all, we must be our own teachers, for as yet the science has no professors. We are the pioneers. Not only is it true that we have neither instructors nor text-books on naval warfare under steam, but there are no foreign navies to which we can turn with confidence for instruction. In many of the essentials of an efficient navy, nearly every other maritime country has left us all but hopelessly in the rear. But in the theoretical knowledge of naval tactics under steam, it may be said that we all stand on common ground, with this advantage in our favor—that we are untrammeled with the traditions and formularies of an extinct period of tactics, and are, so far, free to prepare ourselves for a new study.

Let us glance for one moment at the state of "naval warfare under steam" as it was understood in England up to a very recent period. In an article on "Naval Tactics" which recently appeared in one of the most influential of the English reviews[65] occurs the following: "There appears to be a pretty unanimous agreement, on the part of all those who have made naval tactics a subject of study, that the art has, in its revived form, scarcely advanced beyond the merest rudimentary conditions of existence. It is impossible not to be struck by the strange singularity of such a fact, if fact it be." We may here interject the remark that it *is* a fact.

"In an age in which the greatest scientific skill and mechanical ingenuity have been unreservedly exerted in perfecting the warlike efficiency of the military marine, the one art needed to develop to its fullest extent that truly wonderful efficiency has been strangely neglected and overlooked.

"The great tactical revolution caused by the introduction of steam propulsion has been either quietly ignored, or its extreme significance has been left to be pointed out by a small company of prophets, who have not, as yet, succeeded in gaining more than a partial hearing for

---

[63] Samuel Colcord Bartlett (1817-1898) was a Congregational minister and the eighth President of Dartmouth College. He was a strong advocate of liberal education.

[64] S.C. Bartlett, "How I Was Educated," *Forum,* vol. III, September 1886, pp. 18-26.

[65] The following quotations are taken from an unsigned review article on the works of Hoste, Morogues, Mazarredo-Salazar, Clerk, Ramatuelle, Lullier, Boutakov, Campbell, Colomb, and Douglas, "The Past and Future of Naval Tactics," *Edinburgh Review,* vol. CXXXVI, October, 1872, pp. 288-303.

the statement of their views." And further on the author remarks: "It is somewhat humiliating to reflect that, as yet, in spite of the immense progress made in every other branch of the naval art, the very stones wherewith to raise our tactical structure are, as has been well said, still unhewn. Some malignant fairy appears to have been slighted at the birthtime of that mighty fleet (the English Channel Squadron and steam reserve combined in 1872) which has won the admiration and has become the model of all the navies of the world. It possesses all the elements of perfection, but lacks one gift—the power to use it with effect." And the writer concludes: "We have as yet found out no proper system of tactics, *not because the invention of one is impossible, but because we have neglected to follow the roads which lead to it.*"

This is certainly very plain language, but we believe it to have been absolutely true at the time it was written, some fourteen years ago—1872.

We may now come down to 1880. The Naval Prize Essay of 1880, by Captain the Honorable Edmund R. Fremantle, R.N.[66] is still fresh in our memory. "If," says that able essayist, "we attempt to derive inspiration from the numerous naval writers who have studied the subject of a naval engagement between ironclads of the present day, we are startled at the wide difference of opinion expressed, not only as to the strength of various formations, but as to the manner of fighting which will be adopted. As a rule, strong assertions have been made and decided opinions given, based on necessarily weak arguments and weaker facts.

"A very general belief, shared apparently by foreign writers, has been that fleets will clash together in 'line abreast,' and that they will subsequently pair off to decide the action, forming a series of independent duels." Some of the best of the English naval essayists represent the "line abreast," as they term the line, as a very weak tactical formation. "On the other hand," he continues, "we have foreign authorities advocating the 'line abreast' as the only effectual tactical formation, and objecting to the inherent weakness of the 'line ahead' (column); while the English naval writer who has given most attention to the subject (Captain Colomb)[67] prefers the 'line ahead' to

---

[66] Adm. Sir Edmund Robert Fremantle (1836-1929) was Rear Admiral of the United Kingdom, 1901-1927. He served as Commander in Chief in the East Indies, in China, and at Plymouth. A writer on naval subjects in a variety of magazines, he won the Naval Prize Essay for 1880 with his "Naval Tactics on the Open Sea with the Existing Types of Vessels and Weapons," *The Journal of the Royal United Service Institution*, vol. XXIV, No. 104, 1880, pp. 1-60.

[67] Vice Adm. Philip Howard Colomb (1831-1899) with his brother, Capt. Sir John C.R. Colomb, laid the groundwork for the reform of the Admiralty at the turn of the century. He invented a code of flashing light signals for use at sea. The essays on tactics which Luce refers to here, "The Attack and Defense of Fleets," *Journal of the Royal United Service Institution*, vol. XV, No. 64, 1871, pp. 405-437 and vol. XVI, No. 66, 1872, pp. 1-24, are not his best works. Although overshadowed by Mahan's *Influence of Sea Power upon History*, Colomb's *Naval Warfare* (London: Allen, 1891) has been recognized as the first soundly based British interpretation of naval history. Colomb was one of the prominent leaders in the movement to promote the professional study of naval history.

any other combination." The group system of Bouet-Willaumez,[68] the essayist treats with scant favor, though so strongly advocated by others. "The disagreement," he adds, "is not so much in the end sought for as in the means of attaining that end, Captain Colomb relying mainly on the GUN; the French writers mainly on the RAM." Now, as Captain Freemantle's essay received the prize, and as he exhibits the utmost familiarity with the Signal Book and the Manual of Drill, for neither of which he seems to entertain much respect, we may assume that he fairly represents the state of naval tactics in the English Navy of to-day, and that, to use his own language, they are still "groping in the dark."

It is plain there is little to be hoped for there. The French Navy is pretty much in the same category. Where, then, shall we look for light but to ourselves?

The position of our Military Instructor, it is hardly necessary to explain, is one of extreme delicacy. Entering upon an entirely novel undertaking, and thrown, I will not say among strangers, but among officers of another profession, it were singular, indeed, did he find himself wholly free from embarrassment.

Lieutenant Tasker H. Bliss,[69] 1st Artillery, U.S. Army, an officer who stands deservedly high in his own profession, has kindly consented to give us his time and his best endeavors to render his department of this Institution worthy of the profession he represents. He fully understands the theory on which our studies are to be conducted. He is not here to teach us *our* profession, as has been vainly imagined. Knowing little of our profession, he is here to teach us what he knows of *his own* profession. Let us co-operate with him, then, and by our attention and application attain such good results as to prove that comparative tactics is the true scientific method of studying naval warfare under steam.

We cannot close this paper without one or two allusions to the lessons of history which seem most pertinent to our subject. It has often been observed that the ancient Greeks are our masters in the art of war. The Greeks were so convinced of the necessity of the study of theory, and of the insufficiency of practice alone, that they instituted public schools where they taught upon fixed principles and rules the science of war. The Spartans, we are told, were the first who formed their tactics into a regular system, to be taught as a part of education. Other nations imitated the Greeks. Princes and states maintained, at their own expense, either military academies or skillful professors of tactics for instructing in the theory those young men who devoted themselves to the profession of arms.

The Greeks reduced the whole of the science to calculation and rule. This precision carried the military art among them at once to a high

---

[68] Vice Adm. Louis Edouard Comte Bouet-Willaumez (1808-1871) commanded the French Training Squadron, 1864-1866. While in that position, he developed tactics for steam warships which were published under the title *Tactique supplementaire a l'usage d'une flotte cuirassée* (Paris: Bertrand, 1868).

[69] Gen. Tasker Howard Bliss (1853-1930) was Professor of Military Science at the Naval War College from its opening in 1885 until 1888. Later, he became President of the Army War College, 1903-05, member of the Supreme War Council at Versailles during World War I, and Chief of Staff of the Army, 1917-18.

degree of perfection. "The Greeks," observes one military writer, "although they made their tactics the basis of the science of war according to examples given by their masters in the schools, nevertheless considered this as composing but a small proportion of the acquirements necessary to a general. The art of commanding an army was justly considered as a most important part of knowledge, and was taught accordingly. This embraced all the grand objects connected with war."

The story has often been repeated of Hannibal having ridiculed one of those professors of tactics who, with pencil and tablet in hand, had the assurance to debate with him upon the operations of war.[70] But the wisdom of the Greeks in establishing a regular system of military instruction rests upon too solid a foundation to be shaken by any such anecdote. Besides, Hannibal himself had enjoyed unusual advantages in respect to military education. He was early trained in arms under the eye of his father, Hamilcar, and probably accompanied him in most of his campaigns in Spain. He was certainly with him in the battle against the Vettones, in which Hamilcar perished, Hannibal being at that time but 18 years of age.

We do not find in history any mention made of naval schools among the ancients, but there is every reason for believing that the large fleets of galleys common to ancient Greece and Rome were fought by military men according to the military tactics of the times. The rules of the art of war, as then understood, comprehended both the land and the sea forces.

Here, then, is the philosophy of history teaching us by great examples. Inspired by the example of the warlike Greeks, and knowing ourselves to be on the road that leads to the establishment of the science of naval warfare under steam, let us confidently look for that master mind who will lay the foundations of that science, and do for it what Jomini has done for the military science.[71]

---

[70] Luce's source for this story is an anonymous book by a British author, *The Military Mentor: Being a Series of Letters Recently Written by a General Officer to His Son, on His Entering the Army: Comprising a Course of Elegant Instruction, Calculated to Unite the Characters and Accomplishments of the Gentleman and Soldier* (Salem, Mass.: Cushing and Appleton, 1808), vol. II, pp. 69-70.

[71] Writing to A.T. Mahan on 15 July 1907, Luce referred to this lecture and remarked, "Lastly, I say [in the article] we must look for one who will do for naval science what Jomini did for Military Science. After your lectures on naval strategy, I added to the above 'He is here; his name is Mahan.'"
In the Luce file, Naval Historical Collection, Naval War College, there is a photocopy of this article from an unknown source, which has this last sentence annotated in Luce's handwriting: "He appeared in the person of Captain A.T. Mahan, U.S.N." It is signed "S.B. Luce, Newport, R.I., July 26th 1899."

CHAPTER IV

TACTICS AND HISTORY:
ON THE STUDY OF NAVAL HISTORY
(GRAND TACTICS)

By Rear Admiral S.B. Luce, U.S.N.

Editors' Introduction

Like the last chapter, "On the Study of Naval Warfare as a Science," this essay was initially given as a lecture during the first session of the Naval War College in 1885, then revised, and presented again in September of the following year. It was subsequently published in the *United States Naval Institute Proceedings.**

Luce's title for this lecture, "On the Study of Naval History (Grand Tactics)" is somewhat misleading to the modern reader, but, in its older form, naval history was a study of tactics, not strategy, policy, and ideas. Here, Luce is not interested in presenting the philosophical basis for a study of naval history, as he did in his first lecture, but rather in making a direct and practical connection between the abstract study of warfare and the technical, professional knowledge of the day.

As the author of *Seamanship,* he had been recognized for years as one of America's great experts in the field of practical seamanship, but unlike the many naval officers who had become preoccupied with the new technical developments in the Navy, Luce saw beyond the engineering problems of steampower, steel ships, and big guns. In spite of the fact that he was a leading expert in one area of the naval profession, he was fully aware that deep, specialized knowledge alone was not sufficient for true professionalism in the officer corps. He recognized the need for a middle ground between the abstract theoreticians and the technicists who dealt only with the details of equipment. This was the area of grand tactics. In this sphere the traditional study of naval historians such as Hoste, Clerk, and Ekins could be used side by side with the most advanced tactical thinking of the day. The leading innovators of the day in this tactical thought were Englishmen such as P.H. Colomb, Fremantle, Noel, and Randolph

---

*"On the Study of Naval History (Grand Tactics)," *United States Naval Institute Proceedings,* vol. XIII, No. 2, 1887, pp. 175-201.

Naval War College, ca. 1885

Built in the 1820's as a Poor House, this was the home of the Naval War College from its founding in 1885 until 1889, when it was transferred to Goat Island and consolidated with the Torpedo Station. Luce had favored the original Coasters Harbor Island site for the College since the time he had first surveyed it in 1863 as a possible location for the Naval Academy. Through Luce's efforts, the War College's new building was constructed on Coasters Harbor Island in 1891-92.

and Frenchmen such as Penhoat, Aube, Bouet-Williamez, and Jurien de la Graviere. It is significant that in approaching this area of professional study, Luce was highly influenced by the pioneer naval historian Sir John Knox Laughton. In the 1870's Laughton had published two highly influential articles, "The Scientific Study of Naval History"[1] and "An Essay on Naval Tactics."[2] Luce had read both articles, and his writing in this period reflects the impact of Laughton's work. Luce's footnote in this article acknowledging Laughton, "to whom we are indebted for many valuable lessons," is substantive recognition of the impact which Laughton had on the U.S. Navy. Later, Laughton would be instrumental in bringing Mahan before the British public and serving as both inspiration and critic for his work. In 1890, shortly after the publication of Mahan's *The Influence of Sea Power upon History 1660-1783*, Laughton wrote to Luce that he would shortly publish a review of Mahan's book in the *Edinburgh Review*, and he added, "I shall take the liberty of reproducing some of the sentences in your letter, as to the origin and purpose of the work—I agree with you... that the *title* is not the best possible."[3]

In this article Luce betrays a serious shortcoming in his own scholarship. Unlike Laughton, who carefully verified his statements with original documents, Luce's quotations are not always accurate, and occasionally his information is simply incorrect. Luce's contribution is not derived from the quality and accuracy of the historical information he presents but from his application of historical scholarship to the development of naval education and to his conception of the different intellectual levels within the naval profession. In addition, this article documents the sources of many of the important intellectual influences which Luce transmitted to the U.S. Navy, not the least of which was that of Sir John Knox Laughton.

> The term "Naval Tactics" has been used in such a general way as to lead to some confusion of ideas regarding its true meaning. Some writers restrict it to the evolutionary movements of a fleet, and such as

---

[1] *Journal of the Royal United Service Institution*, vol. XVIII, 1875, pp. 508-527.

[2] In G.H.U. Noel, *The Gun, Ram, and Torpedo* (Portsmouth: J. Griffin, 1874), Essay II.

[3] Laughton to Luce, 3 August 1890, Luce Mss., Naval Historical Collection, Naval War College, Newport, R.I. Luce's letter to Laughton has not yet been located. Sir John Knox Laughton (1830-1915) was one of the pioneers in the field of naval history. For an excellent commentary on Laughton's contribution to British naval thought, see D.M. Schurman, *The Education of a Navy: The Development of British Naval Strategic Thought 1867-1914* (Chicago: University of Chicago Press, 1965), pp. 83-115.

are to be found in the Tactical Signal Book; others limit it to the manner of conducting a fleet in battle; while others again use the term in both senses, and often in such a careless way as to lead themselves and their readers into no little confusion. It is just as well that we should, in the very beginning, fully understand an expression which promises to be of frequent use.

Tactics has been well defined as the art of military movements. Naval Tactics is the art of conducting *the military movements of a fleet.* Battle being the chief object and end of a fleet, the order of battle constitutes the principal formation; and to bring the vessels composing a fleet, from any given order, to the order of battle, or any other order, is to perform an evolutionary or tactical movement. There are, besides the order of battle, various other orders and movements—such as chasing an enemy's fleet; escaping from a superior force; protecting a convoy; navigating the high seas; anchoring; going in or out of port, etc., etc.

These several orders, or formations, formerly called the "orders of sailing," etc., etc., were laid down in the Signal Book; and the methods of changing from one order to another were fully prescribed, a diagram accompanying each evolutionary signal number, showing the positions and movements of each individual ship. Thus, when, in 1790, Admiral Lord Howe[4] rearranged the Signal Book of the English Navy, he introduced "instructions for the conduct of the fleet in the execution of the principal evolutions which were illustrated by figures."[5] These evolutions may be termed Elementary or Minor Tactics. In thus revising the Signal Book, Lord Howe rendered a great service to the English Navy, and the value of his work was generously acknowledged by Nelson. In his letter to Earl Howe of January 8, 1799, giving some account of the battle of the Nile,[6] Nelson[7] writes: "This plan" [of battle] "my friends" [the captains of the several ships composing the fleet] "readily conceived by the signals, for which we are principally, if not entirely, indebted to Your Lordship...." Later on in the same letter he speaks of Earl Howe as "our great master in naval tactics and bravery."[8] The term "naval tactics," as here used by Nelson, is

---

[4] Admiral of the Fleet Richard, Earl Howe (1726-1799).

[5] Howe's 1790 tactical instructions were the last in a series of attempts during his career to reform British naval tactics. Throughout his reforms Howe attempted to develop methods by which captains could do as much injury as possible to the enemy at the least risk to themselves. Howe's work was the first blow against the old system of naval tactics. As it appeared in its final form in 1790, his work combined the best in current British theory with the best of the French influence that Rear Admiral of the Blue Richard Kempenfelt (1718-1782) had introduced in his signal book reforms of 1780.

[6] The Battle of the Nile was fought between the French and British in Aboukir Bay, 1 August 1798.

[7] Vice Admiral of the White Horatio Viscount Nelson (1758-1805).

[8] Sir Nicholas Harris Nicolas, *The Despatches and Letters of Vice Admiral Lord Viscount Nelson* (London: Colburn, 1845), vol. III, p. 230. This was not purely flattery on Nelson's part. He expressed a similar, although more tempered, sentiment in a letter to the Reverend Dixon Hoste, 22 June 1795, Nicolas, *ibid.,* vol. II, p. 45-46.

undoubtedly to be taken in connection with the revised Code of Signals, and refers to the Manual of Fleet Evolutions, which had been rearranged by Howe. Howe not only revised and greatly improved the Signal Book of the English Navy, including the Code of Tactical Signals, but he enjoyed the reputation of being indefatigable in the exercising of the fleet under his command in tactical evolutions, and the transmitting of orders by signals. He was, moreover, very exacting, requiring great precision in the execution of all manoeuvres. But this seems to be the limit of Howe's claim to be considered a tactician. He was skillful in Minor Tactics.

While Nelson was giving credit to Howe for a code of Minor Tactics, he, himself, was developing a system of Fighting Tactics (as it was formerly termed) till then little known in the English Navy. It was a system based upon sound military principles: that of beating the enemy in detail. In the letter just quoted, Nelson gives the gist of his plan of attack at the Nile. He says: "By attacking the enemy's van and centre, the wind blowing along their line, I was enabled to throw what force I pleased on a few ships." And it is this idea of placing two ships on one of the enemy, of doubling on him, that constitutes the merit of Nelson's fighting tactics.

Here, then, we have two celebrated tacticians. First, Howe, constantly exercising the fleet in Minor or Elementary Tactics, and preparing a school of officers who were subsequently to second Nelson in the development of the higher school of Grand Tactics; and, secondly, Nelson, who may be said to have founded a school of Grand Tactics. For it should be remembered that in Howe's great battle of the first of June (1794),[9] he exhibited no such fighting tactics as was afterwards practised by Nelson. With his accustomed exactness he formed his line with great precision, and stood down for the French fleet, each ship steering for her opposite, with the intention that all should pass through and haul to the wind, to leeward of the French line. There is no hint of crushing any one part of the enemy's force by overwhelming numbers; no indication of an intention of doubling on the van, or centre, or of placing the enemy between two fires. It was simply the old custom of placing ship against ship, and allowing a great fleet fight to resolve itself into a series of single engagements. The result was the customary indecisive battle, and consequent popular dissatisfaction. Howe, then, was not a tactician in the sense that Nelson was.

These two distinguished officers therefore represent the two different branches: the first Minor, Elementary, or Evolutionary Tactics; the second Fighting or Grand Tactics, or the Tactics of Battle.[10] These two branches, so inseparably connected, and which together with Strategy form one science, should, for the purpose of our present

---

[9] In the Battle of the Glorious First of June, Howe's fleet fought against the French Fleet of Admiral Louis Villaret de Joyeuse (1747-1812) in the Atlantic, some 350 miles west of Ushant, France.

[10] Other historians treat this division as two points in the continuing evolution of a single branch of study. See Julian S. Corbett, *Signals and Instructions 1776-1794* (London: Navy Records Society, 1909), and John Creswell, *British Admirals of the Eighteenth Century* (London: Allen and Unwin, 1972).

studies, be held separate and distinct. Nelson was also a great strategist; but this again is a distinct branch, which will be considered further on. At present we have to do with Grand Tactics alone—that is to say, with Fleet Fighting and its history.

The Signal Book furnishes, as already observed, the necessary instruction in the evolutions of a fleet. But there is no recognized code of Grand Tactics. In the early days of sailing tactics the navies of England and France had their Fighting Instructions, the latter contained in the Ordonnance du Roi. But it is quite safe to say that no navy of the present day can claim what may be called a satisfactory system of Fighting Instructions; or, we might go so far as to say, a satisfactory fleet organization. It is in the hope of obtaining clear ideas of the latter, so as to enable us to organize a fleet on sound principles, that one part of our studies is to be directed. Another essential part is to study the great sea fights of history, that we may form clear conceptions of how to fight the fleet we have organized. This is our present business.

The plan of attack drawn up by Nelson during his pursuit of the French fleet to the West Indies[11] contains the general principles which guided him in all his battles; principles which are in perfect harmony with the Science of War, and just as applicable now as they were then. In his memoranda he begins by enunciating the broad principle that it is the business of a commander-in-chief "to bring an enemy's fleet to battle on the most advantageous terms." One of these advantages he states to be "close action"; in other words, that the enemy is to be brought within effective range of his guns. He next assumes that the admirals and captains of the fleet will thoroughly understand his plan of battle; and, therefore, that few signals will be necessary.

This last expression has been, we may here remark parenthetically, misapplied and misunderstood.

Nelson closed the Signal Book because, having made his dispositions with great care beforehand, and fully instructed his captains as to his plan of battle, signals were no longer necessary. Battle once joined, every one was trusted to carry out his allotted part of the general plan.

Howe closed the Signal Book because he had no plan of battle beyond the simple method of the barbarian, to pit ship against ship.

It is easy to understand, therefore, how, when the opponents were fairly matched in military force, the results could be decisive in the former case and indecisive in the latter.

Having defined and illustrated the two branches of Naval Tactics, let us now take a cursory view of its history.

In the ardor of pursuit of a new study, such as we have declared "Naval Warfare under Steam" to be, we must not be unmindful of the lessons of the past. "History," it has been well said, "is Philosophy teaching by example."[12] We may add that history admonishes by its

[11] Nicolas, *Despatches and Letters*, vol. VI, pp. 443-45.

[12] Henry St. John, Viscount Bolingbroke (1678-1751), *On the Study and Use of History*, letter 2. The full quotation is "I have read somewhere or other, in Dionysius of Halicarnassus, I think, that history is philosophy teaching by examples."

warnings. It is by the knowledge derived from the history of naval battles that we will be enabled to establish a number of facts on which to generalize and formulate those principles which are to constitute the groundwork of our new science.

"History, as a means of instruction in the art of war, is obviously of the highest value," observes one military writer.[13] "But," he adds, "to make the study of history profitable, the mind ought, in the first instance, to be prepared so as rightly to distinguish between military events which may be analyzed and reasoned upon with advantage, and those which may be regarded merely as events in the world's history destitute of any important bearing on the art of war." It is only by a philosophical study of military and naval history that we can discover those truths upon which we are to generalize. "Thus," as the writer just quoted states, "the victory at Wagram[14] has been traced to the same primary cause by which the battles of Cannae[15] and Pharsalia[16] were gained, and the existence of fundamental principles, by which all the operations of war should be conducted, has been placed beyond doubt by the researches of Jomini[17] and other military writers." What has been done for military science is yet to be done for naval science. In the pride of an advanced civilization, we are too apt to look with contempt upon the old sailing tactics, and the battles fought under them. But even in these days of steam and electricity we may study with advantage the works not only of John Clerk and Paul Hoste, but of Thucydides and Herodotus.

Minor Tactics change with the change of arms or improvements in naval architecture.

Not so with Grand Tactics. But whether it was Phormio[18] or Agrippa[19] or Russell,[20] a Nelson or a Perry,[21] the victory has generally been with that leader who had the skill to throw two or more

---

[13] Luce's source for this quotation has not been identified.

[14] Napoleon's victory at the Battle of Wagram, 5-6 July 1809, ended the active phase of the Campaign of 1809 and resulted eventually in the Treaty of Pressburg and the capitulation of Austria.

[15] The Battle of Cannae was one of Hannibal's victories over the Romans during the Punic Wars in 216 B.C. It is considered the classic example of double envelopment.

[16] The Battle of Pharsalia or Pharsalus was Julius Caesar's decisive victory over Pompey in 48 B.C.

[17] Henri, Baron Jomini (1779-1869) was a Swiss soldier and military theorist. His best known work is *Precis de l'art de la guerre*.

[18] Phormio or Phormion (? - ca. 428 B.C.) was an Athenian admiral who fought in the Peloponnesian War.

[19] Marcus Vipsanius Agrippa (63-12 B.C.) was a Roman statesman and general who commanded the victorious naval forces of Octavian at the Battle of Actium in 31 B.C.

[20] Admiral of the Fleet Edward Russell, Earl of Orford (1653-1727) commanded the combined fleet of the English and Dutch in the battle against the French at La Hogue in 1692.

[21] Capt. Oliver Hazard Perry, USN (1785-1819), commanded the American Fleet against the British in the Battle of Lake Erie in 1813.

of his own ships upon one of the enemy. That is one of the most valuable lessons of all naval history, and that, it may be stated here, is one of the fundamental principles of our science. It is the capacity to carry out that principle that gives evidence of the skillful tactician. It is the ignoring of that principle that serves as one of the most impressive warnings of naval history.

Strategy is still less affected by the mutations of time and the advance of learning. Alexander the Great found it impracticable to reduce Tyre[22] without the aid of a fleet. On the appearance of the Cyprian and Phoenician war galleys, the Tyrians called in their own vessels and sunk triremes in the channel ways to block the entrance to their harbors. Twenty-two centuries later the combined fleets of England and France, co-operating with the armies on shore, compelled the Russians to resort to the same expedient; that is, to close the harbor of Sebastopol[23] by sinking vessels of war in the entrance. The Persian invasion of Greece taught the Athenians the necessity of having a navy. A navy was built, and at Salamis proved the salvation of the State.

England taught the United States the same lesson. Great strategic combinations it was found could not be formed without a navy; a navy was created—a navy small in numbers, but great in spirit—and the victories on Lake Erie and Lake Champlain[24] proved its inestimable value. History is full of such parallels. The invasion of Britain was once rendered possible by reason of the strength of the Roman fleet. But from the time of the Invincible Armada to the day of Trafalgar it has been impossible through the constancy and devotion of the English Channel Fleet. And although there have been such radical changes in the means of carrying on naval warfare, yet the same strategy which enticed Nelson to the West Indies in the vain pursuit of the French Fleet might be practised again to-day.

There are certain general principles which are just as applicable to the management of a sea army of the nineteenth century as they were in the days of Salamis or Actium, of Trafalgar or Lake Erie. Hence, it may be stated in general terms that, while the principles of the Science of War remain unchanged, the rules of the Art of War vary with the implements of war.

The introduction of the rules of the military art into the conduct of a fleet, and the revival of the spur, the rostrum of the galley period, has not only brought us back to the same general system of tactics in use during the ancient civilization, but has rendered a quasi-military education indispensable to the naval officer.

The great captains who achieved success at the head of the armies of Greece and of Rome, carried with them their fighting tactics to the

---

[22] The siege of Tyre was undertaken by Alexander in 332 B.C.

[23] During the Crimean War, Sevastopol was besieged by allied forces for 11 months from September 1854 to August 1855.

[24] The Battle of Lake Erie was fought on 10 September 1813. In the Battle of Lake Champlain, Capt. Thomas Macdonough, USN (1783-1825), led a small American Fleet to victory over the British. The two battles prevented the British Army from invading the United States from Canada during the War of 1812. The victory of Lake Erie also opened up the route to the West.

fleet, and on the decks of their galleys won the *corona navalis* for victories due to their military skill.[25]

It was so in the Middle Ages, King Edward III, who was distinguished for his military abilities, defeated the French in the great battle of Sluys[26] —a battle which, for the skillful manner in which it was fought, was thought worthy to be compared to the masterpieces of the ancient Athenian navy.

It was so at the dawn of modern civilization. Don John of Austria, who was essentially a soldier, gained at Lepanto one of the greatest naval battles of history.[27]

It was so during the earlier period of English naval history. Blake, Monk, Popham,[28] Deane,[29] Prince Rupert and the Duke of York,[30] all of whom held the highest commands during those terrible contests with the Dutch for the mastery of the narrow seas, were all men of military training. It was absolutely necessary, indeed, that men of military capacity should control the military movements of those large fleets on which the very existence of England depended, for the naval officer of that day knew little beyond the mere rudiments of his calling as a seaman.

As the navy of England developed into a distinct profession, the officers were sent to sea at a very early age and kept actively engaged, that they might become inured to the hardships and privations of ship life. With many undoubted advantages, the custom was open to certain objections. While it made them good, practical seamen, it gave them the sailor's proverbial distaste for acquiring knowledge through the medium of books. Thus they came to excel in all the practical details of their profession, but they knew little of the theory, or general principles, on which the science of that profession was based. To handle a ship in a seamanlike manner, and to preserve one's station in the fleet, seems to have been the highest point to which the practical education of that day aspired. True, that was much—indeed, it was a great deal; the value of that instruction was scarcely to be overestimated. When we consider the size of the fleets; their protracted cruises; their long and tedious blockades through all the changes of seasons; the vicissitudes of

---

[25] In vol. III, No. 1 (April 20, 1876), of the *Record* of the U.S. Naval Institute, an attempt was made to show more in detail than is now necessary the formation common to the fleets and armies of the Oar Period. [This is Luce's footnote. He is referring to his own article, "Fleets of the World." See bibliography item 41.]

[26] The Battle of Sluis or Sluys was fought in what is now the Netherlands on 24 June 1340. The battle secured for England control of the English Channel.

[27] For the latest interpretation of Lepanto, see Andrew C. Hess, "The Battle of Lepanto and its Place in Mediterranean History," *Past and Present,* No. 57, 1972, pp. 53-73.

[28] Edward Popham (1610-1651), General-at-Sea.

[29] Richard Deane (1610-1653), General-at-Sea.

[30] H.R.H. James, Duke of York (1633-1701), served as Lord High Admiral of England before his accession to the throne as King James II on 6 February 1685. He commanded the navy in the opening campaigns of the First and Second Dutch Wars. Through such men as Samuel Pepys, he did much to give the navy vitality.

weather, and the very poor sailing qualities of many or most of the ships before copper sheathing came into use, we cannot withhold our wonder and admiration for the skill, the devotion and courage of the English naval officers during those long naval wars which fill so large a space in the English history. But that severe school of practice, thorough as it undoubtedly was, proved wholly insufficient. The constant employment of the officers at sea, and the absence of a higher school, were an effectual bar to their acquiring even the rudiments of the military art. Generation after generation of English naval officers passed without the slightest attempt at methodical instruction in naval tactics. Such knowledge of the art as was acquired must have been by the process of absorption through observing the evolutions of the fleet and the manoeuvres of one's own ship. The Signal Book was the only manual of evolutions; and that was sedulously guarded from the eyes of the profane. For fear it might fall into the hands of the enemy, as it did on one or two notable occasions, or be surreptitiously copied by traitorous hands, it was heavily weighted with lead; and, when not in actual use, kept within the sacred precincts of the captain's cabin, whence none but the elect might take it. In the event of defeat it was to be cast into the sea. Furthermore, the flag officers of the English Navy were, for over a century, heavily handicapped by the Fighting Instructions of 1665,[31] which prescribed certain rules for the conduct of a fleet in battle—rules which proved to be not of general application, and not always in harmony with the principles of war. Unfortunately, these rules, insufficient as they were, received full confirmation by the mature judgment of two courts-martial which may be numbered among the *causes célébres* of the English Navy. The first was that of Admiral Thomas Mathews[32] for his failure in the engagement with the Franco-Spanish fleet off Toulon in the spring of 1744. The second was the trial of Admiral John Byng[33] for his failure in the battle with the French fleet off Minorca in May, 1756.

The Instructions,[34] on which, in a great measure, the judgment of the court in each case turned, were drawn up by the Duke of York in 1665.[35]

This was during those severe contests with the Dutch for the mastery of the narrow seas in which the conflicts took place. The line of battle, which was then for the first time observed according to Paul Hoste, though certain authors maintain that it was known previously by the Dutch, consisted of the close-hauled line ahead, in practice seven points from the wind. Owing to the limited sea room and the dangerous

---

[31] For a detailed discussion of the 1665 fighting instructions, see Julian S. Corbett, *Fighting Instructions 1530-1816* (London: Navy Record Society, 1905), pt. v.

[32] Admiral of the White Thomas Mathews (1676-1751).

[33] Admiral of the Blue the Honorable John Byng (1704-1757).

[34] The basis for this was the "Act for the establishing articles and orders for the regulating, and better government of his majesties navies, ships of war, and forces by sea." 13 Charles II, chapter 9 [1661].

[35] See "Fleets of the World," No. 1, vol. III of the *Record* of the U.S. Naval Institute, before alluded to. [Luce's footnote.]

coasts, the weather gauge was of the very first importance, and as a consequence it was necessary to preserve the order of battle with some degree of precision. When the field of operations was transferred to the broad ocean these conditions became greatly modified; yet, notwithstanding this, the Instructions continued to be binding, and were blindly observed to the frequent discomfiture of the English Navy. Thus, in Mathews' fight off Toulon, his vice-admiral, Lestock,[36] accused him of "rashness and precipitation in engaging the enemy before the line of battle was formed, contrary to the rules of war and the *practice of our best admirals;* therefore the sole miscarriage was chargeable on the admiral, who, by his imprudence in fighting, at first, at such a disadvantage, had endangered the whole fleet; and after, by a quite contrary conduct, suffered the enemy to escape."

Mathews, though he had exhibited the highest gallantry, was found guilty and declared to be "incapable of holding any further employ-[ment] in His Majesty's service."

Byng, on the other hand, failed from a too strict observance of the line of battle. Warned by the result of the former court-martial, he declared at the commencement of the battle that he "would not fall into that error with which Mr. Mathews was charged, and which proved his ruin," that of engaging the enemy before his line of battle was formed.[37] He was found guilty of the charges brought against him and condemned to death. He was said to have been "too great an observer of forms, of ancient rules of discipline and naval etiquette."[38]

During the Dutch wars the opposing fleets were no sooner out of port than they sighted each other; nor was it likely that the men who destroyed the shipping in the Thames, and whose guns were heard in London, would waste much time in manoeuvring. Battle was joined with eagerness on both sides, and the fighting was of the most stubborn character. But on the broad Atlantic, or even in the Mediterranean, fleets might cruise week after week without falling in with each other. When they did the English instinctively manoeuvred, as they had done in the Channel, for a windward position, which the French, committed to a different policy, and hampered by no such traditions, readily yielded. If the two fleets were on the same tack, and on parallel lines, the French would reduce sail, and under easy canvas await the enemy. If he came up astern, the van division of the English would first engage the rear of the French. The English could not use the lower-deck batteries in a fresh breeze, while the French, using their weather guns, could get all the elevation they needed. Firing high, they cut away the spars, rigging and sail of the English, which reduced their speed and

---

[36] Admiral of the Blue Richard Lestock (1697-1748). Mathews, who had engaged the French but who had broken the line of battle to do it, was blamed for failing to adhere to regulations. Lestock had not broken the written rules in the action, but he did disobey his commander in chief and unnecessarily endangered the fleet.

[37] Byng was well acquainted with the case. He had been the second senior member of the court-martial board which tried Mathews.

[38] Shortly after Byng's execution, Voltaire remarked in his satirical masterpiece *Candide,* "In this country it is thought well to kill an admiral from time to time to encourage the others."

threw the head of the line into confusion. Or, if the distance between the two lines was beyond the range of their guns, the English would stand on till the leading ships were abreast of each other, when they would run down to engage, each ship selecting her antagonist. But while they were standing down for the French, the latter would keep up a constant fire, raking their enemies as they approached; the English, meanwhile, unable to bring but a few bow guns to bear. When the English "brought by the wind," so as to use their broadsides, the French would bear up, make sail, and, running to leeward, reform their line and await another attack; this, the English, by being cut up by the French fire, were seldom able to make. Or, the two fleets might cross on opposite tacks, firing distant broadsides in passing. Again, the French Government had early submitted the various problems which enter into shipbuilding to rigid mathematical discussion at the hands of their most eminent mathematicians. The French ships, therefore, were superior to the English in the essential quality of speed, and the French naval authorities had recognized at the very first the necessity of sheathing their ships with metal. For these reasons the French admirals found no difficulty in avoiding a battle when it did not suit their purpose to fight; and, as the resources of their country did not enable them to build and fit out ships with the rapidity with which it could be done in England, it was their policy to avoid decisive actions unless the chances were greatly in their favor; hence, it frequently occurred that they declined to bring on a general engagement.

The many indecisive battles which resulted from these several causes gave great dissatisfaction in England, and finally culminated in the court-martial of Admiral Keppel[39] for his failure in the battle off Ushant in 1778.

As in the case of Mathews the charges were brought by his vice-admiral (Sir Hugh Palliser),[40] the second in command, and mainly for the same reason. The first charge declared in effect "that on the morning of the 27th of July, 1778, having a fleet of thirty ships of the line under his command, and being in the presence of a French fleet of a like number of ships of the line, the said admiral (Keppel) did not put his fleet in the line of battle, or into any order proper for receiving or attacking an enemy; but, on the contrary, by making signal for several ships to chase, increased the disorder of his fleet, and whilst in the disorder he advanced to the enemy and made signal for battle, the enemy's fleet being formed in a regular line of battle on that tack which approached the British fleet. By this unofficer-like conduct a general engagement was not brought about," etc., etc.

A brief abstract from Admiral Keppel's defense will show the line of his argument: "On my first discovering the French fleet at 1 P.M., July 23d, I made signal to form the order of battle, which being effected towards evening, the fleet was 'brought to' till morning, when, perceiving the French had gained the wind during the night, and carried a pressed sail to preserve it, I discontinued the signal for the time and

---

[39] Admiral of the White the Honorable Augustus, Viscount Keppel (1725-1786).

[40] Admiral of the White Sir Hugh Palliser (1723-1791).

made signal to chase to windward. If, by obstinately adhering to the line of battle, I had suffered the French to have separated from me; if the expected convoys had been cut off, or the coast of England had been insulted, what would have been my situation? Supported by the examples of Admiral Russell and other great naval commanders, who in similar situations had ever made strict order give way to reasonable enterprise, and particularly of Lord Hawke,[41] who, rejecting all rules and forms, grasped at victory by an irregular attack,[42] I determined not to lose sight of the French fleet by being outsailed, from preserving the line of battle," etc., etc. The court found the charges malicious and ill-founded.

In his official report of the battle the admiral had said: "The object of the French seemed to be the disabling of the King's ships in their masts and sails, in which they so far suceeded as to prevent many of the ships of my fleet being able to follow me, when I wore to stand after the French fleet. They took advantage of the night and made off. The wind and weather being such that they could reach their own shores before there was any chance of the King's fleet getting up with them, the state the ships were in—in their masts, yards and sails—left me no choice of what was proper and advisable to do." That was to return to Plymouth. The opinion of D'Orvilliers,[43] the French admiral who had been opposed to Keppel, is valuable: "During the fight," said he, "the English had the advantage, but after the firing ceased I out-manoeuvred Mr. Keppel."

The insignificant result of the battle and the court-martial which followed created great interest in England. But of the flood of literature that was poured upon the subject, the only publication that concerns us now is the pamphlet printed for private circulation by the Scotch country gentleman named John Clerk.[44] Up to his time there had been so many great battles the results of which were wholly out of proportion to the numbers engaged, that Clerk was led to believe the French "had discovered some new system of tactics; and that the English practice, since it was always unsuccessful, must have been radically wrong."[45]

In his more elaborate treatise, which appeared in 1790, he states that "after an examination of the late engagements it will be found that the French have never shown a willingness to risk making an attack, but

---

[41] Admiral of the Fleet Edward Lord Hawke (1705-1781).

[42] Alluding, no doubt, to the battle of Quiberon in 1759. [Luce's footnote.]

[43] Lieutenant Général des Armées Navales Louis Guillot, Comte d'Orvilliers (1708-1792).

[44] See "Life of John Clerk" by the eminent Scotch professor, Playfair. Clerk seems to have had a natural capacity for military affairs. Disappointed in his early hopes of entering the Navy, he gave much time to the study of Naval Tactics. [This is Luce's footnote. He is referring to John Playfair (1748-1819), "Memoir relating to the naval tactics of the late John Clerk, esq. of Eldin; being a fragment of an intended account of his life," *Transactions of the Royal Society of Edinburgh*, vol. IX, 1823, pp. 113-137.]

[45] John Clerk, *An Essay on Naval Tactics* (London: Cadell, 1790), p. 19. Luce is paraphrasing Clerk here.

have invariably made a choice of the leeward position; and when extended in line of battle they have disabled the English fleets in coming down to the attack. Upon seeing the English fleet disabled, they have made sail and demolished the van in passing, and upon feeling the effect of the English fire they have withdrawn, at pleasure, either a part or the whole of their fleet, and formed a new line of battle to leeward. The French have repeatedly done this. It will be found, on the other hand, that the English, from an irresistible desire of making the attack, have as constantly courted the windward position, and have repeatedly had their ships so disabled, by making the attack, that they have not once been able to bring them to close with, to follow up, or even to detain, one ship of the enemy. Therefore there was every reason to believe that the French had adopted and put in execution some system which the English either had not discovered, or had not yet profited by the discovery."

To illustrate his position he cites a number of cases, such as Byng's unfortunate action, already referred to; Pocock's[46] battles with M. D'Ache[47] in the East Indies in 1757; Admiral Byron's[48] engagement off Granada in 1779; Arbuthnot's[49] off the Capes of Virginia in 1781, and that of Graves[50] about the same time and place. The last instance in the series is Lord Rodney's[51] engagement off Martinique, April 17, 1780: "Notwithstanding the personal gallantry of Lord Rodney the French fleet bore alternately away and escaped, while the English, from the damage sustained in hulls and rigging, were unable to continue the pursuit."

Clerk further undertakes to show that whenever the French kept to windward, they were careful never to take the initiative and seek a battle, unless the odds were clearly in their favor.

This is illustrated by Rodney's two engagements on the 15th and 19th of May, 1780, near Martinique; Sir Saml. Hood's[52] engagement of the 17th of April, 1781, near the same place, and by Admiral Keppel's in 1778 off Ushant, already referred to. In each of these fights the fleets crossed on opposite tacks, exchanging their fire in passing. In the last case the French fleet, having the wind, ran down and reformed to leeward. Subsequently, in Arbuthnot's fight off the Chesapeake, the French admiral put in practice the same tactics. "It is by such investigations only," he says, "that it can be explained how two adverse fleets, amounting to thirty ships of the line each, carrying above 36,000 men, after having been brought in opposition of battle, and sustaining a

---

[46] Admiral of the Blue Sir George Pocock (1706-1792).

[47] Vice Admiral Comte d'Aché (ca. 1700-1775).

[48] Vice Admiral of the White John Byron (1723-1786).

[49] Admiral of the Blue Mariot Arbuthnot (1711-1794). Arbuthnot engaged the French Fleet off the Chesapeake Capes on 16 March 1781.

[50] Vice Adm. Thomas Graves (ca. 1725-1802).

[51] Admiral of the White George Brydges, Lord Rodney (1719-1792).

[52] Admiral of the Red Samuel, Viscount Hood (1725-1816).

furious cannonade from 4000 guns, besides musketry, have been brought to be separated again without effect, without the smallest apparent decision—that is, without the loss of a ship on either side, and sometimes without the loss of a man, although the rencounter has often been said to have been within pistol-shot."

On board the Ramilies,[53] Admiral Byng's flagship, in the fight with the French off Toulon, no one was even wounded.

Such, says an able English authority, in commenting upon Clerk's essay, was the state of Naval Tactics at the beginning of 1782. "During the whole war our fleets had invariably been baffled, disabled, worsted. Our admirals adhered, invariably, to the established mode of attack, and endeavored to obtain a windward position before they began to engage. The French, relying upon our want of penetration to discover, or of skill to counteract, this new system of defense, never failed to accomplish the object of their expedition, and to disable our ships, while they preserved their own. Dispirited by the failure of our arms in the American war, we beheld ourselves uniformly baffled on our own element, and we began to apprehend a decay of spirit in our officers and seamen."[54] When we consider that this language was used by McArthur,[55] the author of the well-known treatise on Naval Courts-Martial, and at one time Secretary to Admiral Lord Hood, it will add not a little to its significance.

Rear-Admiral Sir Charles Ekins remarks of Clerk: "In all his reasoning he shows with truth and success that our defeats were never owing to a want of spirit, but to *a deficiency of tactical knowledge.*"[56]

"No lessons in tactics," says one of the ablest naval essayists of the present day, "can be so valuable as those taught by the experience of the past . . . . In no case has a victory been won over a fairly equal force where the ignorance of the one commander-in-chief, or the skill of the others, has caused the strength of the fleet to be dispersed and has spread the attack over the whole, instead of concentrating it against a part. All the painfully notorious battles of the last century, notorious by reason of the bitter feeling and angry, tragical courts-martial which followed their want of success, come distinctly under this category. From the time of Mathews to the time of Rodney we were trammeled

---

[53] Read the account of the loss of the Ramilies in 1782 with Admiral Graves on board. She was hove to under the mainsail on the larboard tack. The admiral was saved and all the crew. [This is Luce's footnote. He probably read the account of the loss in Robert Beatson, *Naval and Military Memoirs of Great Britain from 1723 to 1783* (London: Longman, Hurst, Rees & Orme, 1804), vol. V, pp. 496-504.]

[54] Luce's source for this quotation from McArthur has not been located. It does not appear in McArthur's review of Clerk's *Naval Tactics* which appeared in the *Naval Chronicle,* vol. I, No. I, January 1799, pp. 32-42, and vol. I, No. 2, February 1799, pp. 137-140. The quotation is a paraphrase of Clerk, *Naval Tactics,* pp. 17-19.

[55] John McArthur (1755-1840) wrote *A Treatise on the Principles and Practice of Naval Courts Martial* (London: Whieldon and Butterworth, 1792). With the Reverend James Stanier Clarke (1765-1834), he edited the *Naval Chronicle.* In 1809 the two men jointly authored *The Life and Services of Horatio, Viscount Nelson.*

[56] Adm. Sir Charles Ekins (1768-1855) *Naval Battles from Life to the Peace in 1814* (London: Baldwin, Cradock and Joy, 1824), p. xiv.

and bound to a false system which, when skilfully opposed, could not, and did not, lead to any results other than disappointment and loss. The attack was made in line against line, if possible, ship against ship; and in no one instance was it attended with success. That the individual ships were, for the most part, skilfully handled and gallantly fought, may be conceded; that they were, singly, superior to the ships of the enemy, may be fairly maintained, but *collectively and as a fleet they were unable to accomplish anything.*"[57]

These are certainly very candid admissions; but they are fully justified by history.

Coming to us, as they do, from authors of high standing and of intimate knowledge of the subject, these statements are of the utmost value to the naval student; and we cannot feel too grateful to those gentlemen who have had the enlightened spirit, the sense of justice, and the love of truth, to give the plain facts, though it should not always redound to the credit of the profession they so worthily represent.

We now come to the true cause of the difficulty under which the English labored, and to the secret of the so-called "new system" devised by the French. McArthur goes on to say, "Our officers were eminently distinguished by their gallantry and seamanship, *but they had hitherto bestowed no adequate degree of attention upon Naval Tactics.*" And yet, for the fifty years preceding the treaty of Paris of 1783, the English naval officers had been constantly engaged in war.[58]

French officers, on the other hand, seem to have paid great attention to Naval Tactics. Tourville,[59] so highly eulogized by Macaulay, originated the best work on Naval Tactics (that of Paul Hoste) ever published.

D'Orvilliers,[60] who fought the drawn battle with Keppel, was the

---

[57] Prof. John Knox Laughton, R.N., Royal Naval College, Greenwich, to whom we are indebted for many valuable lessons.-S.B.L. [The quotation is from Laughton, "The Scientific Study of Naval History," pp. 521-522.]

[58] However fully we may share the incredulity of Lieutenant Hatchway, there is that about the utterances of Commodore Trunnion which plainly indicates the drift of popular opinion in his day (1751) in regard to the average sea-fight. In speaking of one of his exploits the Commodore says: "Finding the Frenchman—the Flower de Louse—took a great deal of drubbing, and that he had shot away all our rigging, and killed and wounded a great number of our men, I resolved to run him on board; but Monsieur, perceiving what we were about, filled his topsails and sheered off, leaving us like a log upon the water." (Dr. Smollett was a loblolly boy on board the Suffolk, Commodore, afterwards Admiral Sir Charles Knowles, and was present at the attack on La Guira in 1743. "Peregrine Pickle" first appeared in 1751.) [This is Luce's footnote. He is referring to the British novelist Tobias George Smollett (1721-1771). Smollett served as a surgeon's mate on board the ship of the line *Cumberland*, 80 guns, commanded by a Captain Stuart.] Smollett was present at the attack on Cartagena in 1741 and recorded his experiences in his novel, *Roderick Random*. Smollett was prosecuted for libel in 1759 by Adm. Sir Charles Knowles for remarks made in the journal *Critical Review* in May 1758. It is unlikely that Smollett met Knowles in the Caribbean. See Lewis Melville, *The Life and Letters of Tobias Smollett* (London: Faber and Gwyer, 1926), ch. 9.

[59] Marshall Anne Hilarion de Contentin, Comte de Tourville (1642-1701). Hoste was Tourville's chaplain.

[60] Lieutenant-General des Armées Navales Louis Guillouet, Comte d'Orvilliers (1708-1792), was Keppel's opponent in July 1779.

author of a work on Tactics; and the Viscount de Grenier[61] proposed a formation for battle and a system of tactics which was certainly a work of merit. The Viscount Morogues[62] and others of more or less note had written on the same subject. Ramatuelle[63] is worthy of careful study to-day.

Ramatuelle observes: "The French Navy has always preferred the glory of securing, or retaining a strategic advantage, or a conquest, to the more brilliant, perhaps, but really less substantial feat of making prizes; and in that they approach nearer to the true ends of war. For what would the loss of a few ships be to the English? The principal aim is to attack them in their possessions, the source of their vast commerce and their powerful marine."[64]

The superiority of the French as tacticians is well illustrated by the battles fought by Sir George Pocock and Monsieur D'Aché in the East Indies; and, better yet, by the series of battles between the Bailli de Suffren[65] and Sir Edward Hughes[66] on the same station in 1782 and 1783.

Both commanders-in-chief, being remote from their respective Governments, and beyond the reach of instructions, were thrown upon their own resources, and obliged to rely solely upon their own judgment in the conduct of affairs.

De Suffren recovered the Dutch ports of Trincomalee, which the English admiral had captured a short time before, and after a series of actions raised the blockade of Cudalore and relieved the garrison. The conflicts were terminated by tidings of peace, leaving the French, on the whole, masters of the situation.

In all the higher attributes of a naval officer, save hard and persistent fighting, De Suffren proved himself to be superior to his adversary.

Still another and more familiar illustration is to be found in our own early history, when, at one of the most momentous periods of the Revolutionary War, an English admiral was fairly outgeneraled by his more skillful adversary. It was when De Grasse[67] lured the English squadron away from the relief of Cornwallis.[68] The late Centennial

---

[61] Jacques-Raymond Grenier, Vicomte de Giron (1736-1803), hydrographer and author of *L'Art de la Guerre sur Mer* (1787).

[62] Lieutenant Général des Armées Navales Sebastien Francois Bigot, Vicomte de Morogues (1705-1781), founder of the French Naval Academy.

[63] Audibert Ramatuelle was termed an "ancien capitainne de vaisseau" when his book appeared in 1802.

[64] Audibert Ramatuelle, *Cours Élémentaire de Tactique Navale* (Paris: Baudouin, 1802), note 2, p. 363.

[65] Vice Adm. Pierre André de Suffren de Saint-Tropez (1726-1788), Marshal of France and Bailli of the Order of Malta.

[66] Admiral of the Blue Sir Edward Hughes (ca. 1720-1794).

[67] Lieutenant-Général des Armées Navales Francois Joseph Paul Marquis de Grasse, Comte de Tilly (1722-1788).

[68] Gen. Charles Cornwallis, first Marquis and second Earl Cornwallis (1738-1805).

celebration at Yorktown has revived the memory of the historical incidents of that period.[69]

At no time has the French Navy received full credit for its share in bringing a long and trying campaign to a successful termination.

While extensive preparations were being made by Washington in May, 1781, to capture New York, then occupied by the English, word was sent to De Grasse, in the West Indies, soliciting his cooperation. About the middle of May a message from De Grasse reached Newport,[70] where a portion of the French forces and a French squadron then lay, saying that he had sailed, not for New York, but for the Chesapeake. This completely changed the whole plan of operations and made the army of Cornwallis the objective point. Continuing the demonstration against New York, with a view to misleading the English commander-in-chief, the combined armies took up their march for Virginia, distant about four hundred miles, and in about one month's time came within sight of the English at Yorktown. On the 14th of September, Washington held a consultation with De Grasse on board the Ville de Paris, when arrangements were made to prosecute the siege of Yorktown.

Clinton[71] meanwhile, learning that the French squadron under Count de Barras[72] had sailed from Newport for the Chesapeake, dispatched Admiral Graves with his squadron to intercept him.

On reaching the Capes of Virginia, Graves was surprised to find the French squadron at anchor in the Bay. De Grasse, on his part, expecting to see the squadron of De Barras, was surprised to see the English ships. It was now that the skill of De Grasse displayed itself in the exercise of the highest order of strategy. He immediately proceeded to sea, and, practising the policy so often resorted to by the French, of allowing the English to gain the much-coveted weather gauge, he commenced a series of those indecisive actions which, as we have seen, so often characterized the naval battles of that day.

After each partial engagement the French would edge away to leeward, and, reforming the line of battle in a new position, await the attack. This manoeuvring was kept up for five days; the English eager for a general and decisive battle, the French luring them away from the one objective point in the whole theatre of the war, the key of the entire plan of operations so laboriously prepared by Washington and his allies. At the end of about five days, judging the squadron under De Barras to be safe, De Grasse returned to the Chesapeake.

When Graves reached the Capes, he had the mortification of finding both French squadrons at anchor in the Bay, their united forces being much superior to his own. Completely outgeneraled, he returned to New York. The last avenue of escape left open to Cornwallis being thus

---

[69] See *Report of the Commission in Charge of the Yorktown Centennial Celebration*, 20 February 1883, Senate Report No. 1003, 47th Congress, 2d session.

[70] Newport, R.I., was a French base between July 1778 until August 1781.

[71] Gen. Sir Henry Clinton (ca. 1738-1795).

[72] Lieutenant-Général des Armées Navales Louis, Comte de Barras (ca. 1700-1788).

closed by the French fleet, the destruction of the English army became inevitable.

To estimate the value of the service rendered by the French, and the full significance of the tactics of De Grasse, we have only to suppose that Admiral Graves, instead of following the French outside the Cape, had stood up the Bay for York River and effected a junction with Cornwallis. Notwithstanding the disparity of forces, the French having twenty-four ships of the line to nineteen of the English, he could have rendered his position so strong that the French, exercising their extreme caution, would not have ventured to attack, even when joined by De Barras with ten ships of the line. Moreover, Admiral Digby,[73] with a squadron, shortly after arrived at New York, so that when thus reinforced the fleet of Admiral Graves consisted of twenty-seven ships. Had the English commander-in-chief succored the besieged army, as a French admiral would have done, had their relative positions been changed, it would have given an entirely different complexion to the whole campaign of Washington, if it had not completely frustrated it.

The position of Admiral Graves may be likened to that of an army interposed between the parts of an enemy's extended lines in such a way as to be able to concentrate on either one of those lines before the other could be brought to its assistance.

Napoleon practised that species of tactics, which enabled him to beat his adversary in detail with brilliant success.

In this case before us, the objective point, Yorktown, was left open, so that the English admiral, without fighting, had only to sail in between the two French squadrons, establish himself in an impregnable position on the York River and render the relief so earnestly looked for by the English army. That De Grasse, with a numerically superior force, should have avoided a conflict with the English squadron, leads to the belief that the French must have been sensible of some inherent weakness, which is not fully explained by their known inability to refit their ships or replenish stores with the thoroughness and expedition of their adversaries. No doubt De Grasse was right in saying, on the occasion of his subsequent surrender to Rodney, that the English were, in naval matters, a hundred years ahead of them. We may except, as the English have so candidly done, the practical knowledge of Naval Tactics. Their superior skill in handling their fleets was forced upon them as necessary to their existence: it was the instinct of self-preservation.

The object of Clerk, to refer once more to the "Treatise on Naval Tactics," was to point out the grave defects of the English Fighting Instructions and to suggest the remedy. There seems to be no doubt that the English naval officers profited by the lesson, and, the ice once broken, there was no longer any hesitation in putting in practice the principal suggestion thrown out by the author, and one which is conformable to one of the oldest and best-known rules of the art of war—viz: to inflict upon the enemy a decisive blow by concentrating an overwhelming force upon a given point of his line, thus beating him in

---

[73] Admiral of the Red Robert Digby (1732-1814).

detail. It was to just such a manoeuvre that Rodney owed his success on the 12th of April, 1782. How far Rodney was indebted to Clerk for the tactics which gave him the battle, it is unnecessary to discuss. Suffice here to say that in the memoirs of that officer the claim of Clerk is wholly denied; and that Sir Howard Douglas, in an able pamphlet, claims the honor in behalf of his father, who was Rodney's flag captain. Moreover, it has been pointed out by Clerk himself that the same manoeuvre was performed by De Suffren, though not with equal success, in the battle with Sir Edward Hughes off Ceylon, in the East Indies, the very same day of Rodney's victory in the West Indies (April 12, 1782). The same tactics were referred to by Paul Hoste long before. They had been practised by Count d'Estrees[74] when, in 1673, he cut through Prince Rupert's line.

It is quite certain, however, that the essay became an accepted authority, and led to a change in the Fighting Tactics of the English Navy. Thus it came that the naval battles of the French Revolution opened a fresher and brighter chapter in the history of English Naval Tactics.

Lord Howe, upon whom devolved the labor of reorganizing the English fleet and the Signal Book, after ten years of peace, led off in 1794 with the victory of the 1st of June. This was followed by the defeat of the Spanish squadron off Cape St. Vincent in 1797, where Nelson played so conspicuous a part; and in the same year Duncan, in two irregular columns, smashed through the centre and rear of the Dutch line at Camperdown, winning a brilliant victory.

The period culminated in Nelson and Trafalgar.

It is but fair to say here that it is claimed for Hawke, and with justice, that he founded the school of which Nelson became the most brilliant exponent.[75]

The English naval officers had, at last, begun to study Naval Tactics, leaving no longer to the French the monopoly of that secret of success. It is interesting to know that Nelson not only studied Clerk's Naval Tactics, but that it was his custom to give out to his captains problems in tactics for their solution. This had the tendency of leading their thoughts into those channels best calculated to prepare them for any emergency of battle that might arise, thereby laying down in advance the foundations for victory.

As the history of naval warfare may be divided into the three great periods of *Oars, Sails,* and *Steam,* so it is convenient for our present purpose to divide the history of Naval Tactics under Sail into three periods. The first begins shortly after the peace of Westphalia, 1648, which terminated the Thirty Years War, and includes the three Dutch wars, when the English and Dutch contended for the sovereignty of the seas. It was during this time that James, Duke of York, originated the Naval Tactics of the English Navy and first established a regular order

---

[74] Jean, Comte d'Estrées (1624-1707), Marshal of France, Vice Admiral of Ponant, and Viceroy of America. In 1673 d'Estrées commanded a fleet in conjunction with Rupert against the Dutch in the Channel.

[75] Montagu Burrows, *The Life of Edward, Lord Hawke* (London: Allen, 1883), pp. 497-98.

of battle.[76] It ended in 1673 with the defeat of De Ruyter[77] by Prince Rupert. During this period the principal commands in the English fleet were held by officers who had enjoyed the advantages of a military training, and the battles were of the most decisive character.

The second period includes the times referred to by Clerk: the War of Succession, beginning in 1712; the war with Spain in 1718; the Spanish War in 1739; the war with France in 1744; the Seven Years War, from 1756 to 1763; and the American War, ending with the treaty of Paris in 1783. During this period the fleets of England were commanded by seamen pure and simple, who, ignoring the science of their profession, permitted themselves to be hampered by a set of arbitrary and insufficient rules. The battles fought during this period were, with few exceptions, indecisive.

The third and last period is characterized by a close attention to Naval Tactics and decisive battles.

It may be said to begin with Rodney's victory in 1782, and end with Nelson and Trafalgar in 1805.

The conclusion, which is not at all strained, is that the landsman with a military training was more capable of conducting the military movements of a fleet than the mere sailor who knew nothing of the science of war.

Charnock, in speaking of the Earl of Sandwich (Admiral Montague),[78] says that "at the age of 30 (1655), bred to the Army, he was appointed joint commander of the fleet with Blake, a man undoubtedly possessed of the highest gallantry, but, like himself, totally unacquainted with every principle of Naval Tactics; yet under these very men, even at their first outset in their new profession, the British flag spread everywhere a terror and commanded a respect which, without intending to depreciate in the smallest degree the merits of their successors, we may truly say the greatest professional skill has never yet enhanced."[79] It is evident that their ignorance of "every principle of Naval Tactics" was amply supplied by their knowledge of Military Tactics, which enabled them to direct those more extended movements of a fleet comprehended in the term Grand Tactics, or the Tactics of Battle.

Prince Rupert and the Duke of Albemarle (Admiral George Monk) were styled "His Majesty's Generals at Sea." Monk may have excited the mirth of his sailors by calling out, "Wheel to the right," or "left," when he wished to tack ship; but he defeated the celebrated Dutch admirals, Van Tromp[80] and De Ruyter, and was one of the best naval administrators England has ever had. Monk, it should be said, had enjoyed, during the earlier years of his life, a short experience at sea.

---

[76] Luce, "Fleets of the World," p. 18.

[77] Adm. Michiel Adriaanszoon De Ruyter (1607-1676).

[78] Admiral of the Fleet Edward Montague, first Earl of Sandwich (1625-1672).

[79] John Charnock (1756-1807), *Biographia Navalis* (London: R. Faulder, 1794), vol. I, p. 30.

[80] Adm. Maarten Harpertszoon Tromp (1598-1653).

On the other hand, it was said of Sir Edward Hughes, a typical officer of the middle part of the eighteenth century, that he could handle his ship to admiration, but knew little about managing a fleet. Much the same may be said of Admiral Byng. A part of the evidence given on his trial conveys a valuable lesson. Captain Gardiner,[81] of the Ramilies, 90, the flagship of Admiral Byng, testified that "he advised Mr. Byng repeatedly to bear down, but without effect; *for that on the day of the action the admiral took entire command of the ship upon himself*"; which means that he had no conception of the duties of his high office of commander-in-chief of a fleet. So of Mathews: he understood the practical part of his profession better than the theory, and "knew better how to fight, himself, than to command others to fight."

We cannot refrain from giving here a couple of pen-and-ink portraits of two distinguished officers whose services have been referred to. Of ·De Suffren the writer says: "He was cool and daring in action, crafty in policy, of ready wit, and of singular genius as a tactician, with much practical skill, added to a vast fund of theoretical skill: the most illustrious officer, without exception, that had ever held command in the French Navy." Opposed to him was Sir Edward Hughes: "Brave, skilled in his profession, of the old school, not fitted to receive new ideas, opinionated, perverse, with but little idea of tactics and less of policy, he was still, at all times, ready for battle. *He did not know much about manoeuvring a fleet,* but he could handle his own ship to admiration; he had not much judgment as to the proper time to fight, but when he did fight, he did so with a courage that was proof against all odds."[82]

Sir Charles Ekins, in commenting upon the want of success of Admiral Graves, remarks that, "unfortunately, the fate of Mathews and Byng was still fresh in the recollection of our naval commanders; and as in those cases disgrace or punishment alike awaited both the daring and the cautious, the conducting of a fleet in the presence of an enemy became a duty at once perilous and perplexing."[83]

It is curious to note, as we may here, how the traditions of the English Navy seem to have completely usurped the place of original investigation. Keppel justified his conduct as having been formed on that of Russell, Hawke, and other great commanders, and the sentences inflicted upon Mathews and Byng affected generations of their successors.

The great lesson to be drawn from this cursory review of the history of Naval Tactics under Sail is, that the highest achievements of a navy are to be secured when, to the practical training from boyhood in all

---

[81] Capt. Arthur Gardiner (? - 1758).

[82] J.K. Laughton, "Le Bailli de Suffren," *The United Service Magazine,* May and June 1867, reprinted in Laughton, *Studies in Naval History* (London: Longmans, Green, 1887), ch. IV, pp. 125 and 147.

[83] Ekins, p. 123.

the details of the naval profession, there is added proper instruction in the science and art of war.[84]

We must pause here for a moment to disclaim any intention of undervaluing the character of those many great seamen whose deeds embellish and adorn the pages of English naval history.

Drake,[85] Hawkins[86] and Frobisher[87] (Lord Howard was not a seaman in the sense that Drake was), aided by the elements, scattered the Invincible Armada; but they lived before any regular system of tactics had been devised. And Anson,[88] Hawke and Boscawen[89] won their victories for the most part by superior numbers, wherein skill and tactics had little part. The battle of Quiberon, fought in bad weather, on a dangerous and unknown coast, must, however, stand out as a brilliant and exceptional victory.

If history be that "vast Mississippi of falsehood" Arnold[90] has called it, the earnest student in his search for truth must carefully weigh the evidence, for and against, before concluding on the respective merits of the Fighting Tactics of the English and the French Navies of the last period of Tactics under Sail. Much praise is undoubtedly due to Nelson and his school; but what was the condition of the French Navy during the Revolution and the Consulate? Says an English naval essayist on this point: "The French, by their careful study of, and attention to, the details of naval architecture, of strategy and tactics, held their own against us for nearly one hundred years—not brilliantly, perhaps, but at any rate sufficiently—and it was not till the close of the century, when the study of tactics had been, in a measure, *forced upon us,* that we recovered our old superiority. As we improved, the French, victims of anarchy and internal confusion, deteriorated, and thus, by the happy combination on our part of tactical study, practical skill, and constant experience; on the part of the enemy of ignorance and presumption, we won those great victories which mark the annals of the end of the last century and the beginning of this."[91]

These "great victories," then, were not due wholly to the prowess and skill of the English, but in a measure to the deterioration of the French; how great a measure that was, English writers themselves tell us.

But let us continue our study of English Naval Tactics.

In 1827 was fought, at Navarino, the last great fleet fight under sail; and the year after appeared the second edition of "Naval Battles," by Rear-Admiral Ekins, from which we make the following extract. He

---

[84] This sentence summarizes Luce's view of naval education.

[85] Sir Francis Drake (ca. 1540-1596).

[86] Sir John Hawkins (1532-1595).

[87] Sir Martin Frobisher (ca. 1535-1594).

[88] Admiral of the Fleet George, Lord Anson (1697-1762).

[89] Admiral of the Blue Edward Boscawen (1711-1761).

[90] Matthew Arnold (1822-1888), English poet and literary critic.

[91] Laughton, "The Scientific Study of Naval History," p. 524.

quotes another English admiral of distinction who uses this language: "If I commanded an English fleet opposed to a French one, I should not have the least objection to their cutting my line. I should probably myself break all order of battle, in order to prevent their cutting off any particular ships, and then, behold! the old story: I have them in action, ship to ship. This is the great secret of *our* tactics; that of the French to prevent it.

"I fairly own," he continues, "that I hope close action, ship to ship, will ever be the first object of a British naval commander-in-chief." And Admiral Ekins adds, with a burst of fine enthusiasm: "This is bravely said by the gallant son of a noble chief, and let the British Navy say, *Amen!*"[92] This may be admirable as a specimen of rhetoric, but, certainly, very poor tactics. The passage is not without value, however, as corroborative of one of two theories: Either the English had been betrayed into over-confidence by the demoralized condition of the French Navy, and the consequent ease with which victories over it were gained, rendering skillful tactics unnecessary—and there is much to support this view—or, that after Trafalgar the English Navy relapsed into what has been well called the "Dark Age" of Naval Tactics. As late as 1828 two distinguished British admirals coolly tell us that the secret of their tactics is "close action, ship to ship"—a principle directly opposite to what their own Nelson and his school taught. His teaching, and the teachings of all great captains, both on shore and afloat, is to put *two* against *one*. To understand this fundamental principle is to understand the very root and groundwork of Grand Tactics; and to be able to carry out this principle in battle, is to exhibit the highest skill as a tactician. What, then, must we say of the Ekins school? Sir Samuel Hood, with twenty-two ships, when standing in to engage the French fleet of thirty-three sail of the line under De Grasse (anchored at Basseterre, St. Christopher, in 1772), designed to throw the whole weight of the attack on the head of the French column and crush that before the rear, which would have been thrown out, could possibly come to its succor. The French, notwithstanding their superiority, as a whole, no doubt escaped an overwhelming defeat by getting under way and standing out to sea. The same plan of battle was carried out at the Nile. The head of the French column was doubled upon and crushed, while the rear was completely thrown out of action. What Nelson meant by writing to Duncan, after Camperdown, that he [Nelson] had profited by his [Duncan's] example, is not precisely clear.[93] In the battle of Camperdown, October 12, 1797, Duncan made signal to form line; but, not waiting for all the ships to come up, he and his

---

[92] Sir Charles Ekins, *The Naval Battles of Great Britain* (London: Baldwin and Cradock, 1828), pp. 19-20. This quotation also appears in the first edition, pp. 8-9.

[93] Admiral of the White Adam, Viscount Duncan (1731-1804). This letter is not included in Nicolas, *Despatches and Letters*, and it is not referred to in modern studies of Nelson. By a letter from Duncan to the First Lord of the Admiralty, Julian Corbett shows that Duncan was not purposefully innovating any new tactical ideas. See J.S. Corbett, ed., *Private Papers of George, second Earl Spencer, First Lord of the Admiralty, 1794-1801* (London: Navy Record Society, 1914), vol. 2, p. 197, Duncan to Spencer 15 October 1797.

vice-admiral, Onslow,[94] led down on the enemy in two irregular columns, not unlike the manner in which Nelson and Collingwood[95] led the attack on the allied fleets off Trafalgar. In both cases the entire English fleet did not cut through the enemy's line, but some "brought to" to windward, thus placing the enemy between two fires.

Nelson, in his general order, dated on board the Victory off Cadiz, Oct. 18, 1805,[96] divided the fleet into two lines, sixteen ships in each line, with an advanced squadron of eight of the fastest-sailing two-decked ships, which eight ships, added, if wanted, to either of the two lines (as the commander-in-chief might direct), would swell that line to twenty-four ships. Those eight ships constituted the reserve. Having made his general disposition, he adds—and here lies the gist of the whole matter[97]—"The impression of the *whole British fleet* must be made (with the intention of overpowering it) on that *portion* of the enemy's line rearward from the third or fourth ship ahead of its commander-in-chief presumed to be in the centre. I will suppose the twenty enemy's ships ahead untouched."[98] That is to say that, by doubling on the enemy's centre and rear, he threw the entire van out of action.[99] And yet, nearly a quarter of a century after Nelson's splendid

---

[94] Admiral of the Red Sir Richard Onslow (1747-1817).

[95] Vice Admiral of the Red Cuthbert, Lord Collingwood (1740-1810).

[96] This is the secret memorandum of 9 October 1805, Nicolas, *Despatches and Letters*, vol. VII, pp. 89-92.

[97] The full quotation is as follows:
  The Whole impression of the British Fleet must be to overpower from two or three Ships ahead of their Commander-in-Chief, supposed to be in the Centre, to the Rear of their Fleet. I will suppose twenty Sail of the Enemy's Line to be untouched, it must be some time before they could perform a manoevre to bring their force compact to attack any part of the British Fleet engaged, or to succor their own Ships, which indeed would be impossible without mixing with the ships engaged.
Nicolas, *Despatches and Letters*, vol. VII, p. 90.

[98] On taking command of the fleet that was destined to operate against the combined forces of the enemy, Nelson summoned the admirals and captains of the fleet into the cabin of the *Victory*."When I came to explain to them the 'Nelson touch,'" he wrote to an intimate friend, "it was like an electric shock. Some shed tears; all approved—'It was new—it was singular—it was simple!' and from Admirals downwards, it was repeated 'It must succeed, if ever they will allow us to get at them.'" Collingwood said the plan of attack was irresistible. [This is Luce's footnote. Nelson's intimate friend was Emma Hamilton to whom he wrote on 1 October 1805, Nicolas, *Despatches and Letters*, vol. VII, p. 60.

[99] It may not be out of place to call attention just here to the expression "breaking the enemy's line," so often met with in naval history. In Capt. Montagu Burrows' "Life of Lord Hawke," the author says that "Lord Rodney was not the first to whom credit is due for 'breaking the enemy's line,' an operation he put in practice with distinguished results in his famous battle of Dominica, and which after 1782 became the tactics of the British Navy."
  Now, simply breaking the enemy's line amounts to very little in a tactical point of view and may, if the opponents are fairly matched, be attended with evil results. But the author goes on, in tracing the development of fighting tactics, to explain that "the next step was to cut through the enemy's line and *double the force* on each ship so cut off. After the time of Nelson any other method seemed inconceivable." [This is Luce's footnote. The quotations are from Burrows, pp. 69-71.]

illustration of a well-known principle of the science of war, we find two distinguished admirals of the British Navy telling us that the secret of their tactics is to "place ship against ship."

Leaving the sail period, let us now consider the state of Naval Tactics at the present day.

In an exhaustive article on the subject, which appeared a few years ago, the very able writer declared that, in the British Navy, Naval Tactics *"had not been so much neglected as despised."* Just think of that! *"Not so much neglected as despised."* He says: "In that service no tactical maxim has ever been held in so much honor as the simple phrase which asked only for a fair field and no favor."

"Plenty of sea room and a willing enemy," he continued, "was a formula which adequately expressed the aspirations of a body of men strong in their confidence of their superior seamanship and of their undoubted valor and endurance." Evidently, for such men, if such indeed there be in the English Navy, the lessons of Hawke and Nelson have been given in vain.

As late as 1872 there were a number of English writers who agreed in thinking that, notwithstanding their magnificent fleet of ironclads, they were still "no more than groping after something definite which it was hoped might arise at a future time." They had not yet a perfectly settled drill to guide them in their fleet evolutions.

Another author, writing about the same time, says: "The naval student is brought face to face with the great difficulty of modern Naval Tactics—the choice of weapons. What would be the English choice, should war come upon us now? It is somewhat painful to note that we have no choice. We vaguely hope that a wise choice will in some way be disclosed to us, and we do not take a great deal of trouble to see how things point. The position we hold is dangerous and improper." He continues: "While each of the four modern naval weapons, the gun, the ram, the Harvey torpedo, and the Whitehead torpedo, has its advocates, the great mass of naval men simply look on."

In the English Naval Prize Essay of 1879[100] the author says: "Evolutions are not tactics. Evolutions are simply fleet drill: the Signal Book is a drill book."[101] He then proceeds to criticise the Signal Book, winding up with the remark: "Are there no broad principles which might be shadowed forth in the Signal Book? At present, it must be admitted, we are groping in the dark. Our evolutions and manoeuvres have no direct bearing on battle formations.[102] ... Modern naval warfare has so changed," he says, "and is in such a state of transition, that, failing a direct order from higher authority to deal with tactics, modern Signal Book committees *have agreed to ignore them*, except so far as an occasional verbal change in an old signal might be adapted to

---

[100] Luce is referring here to the Naval Prize Essay of 1880, not 1879: Captain, the Honorable E.R. Fremantle, "Naval Tactics on the Open Sea with the Existing Types of Vessels and Weapons," *Journal of the Royal United Service Institution*, vol. XXIV, No. 104, 1880.

[101] *Ibid.*, p. 33.

[102] *Ibid.*, p. 45.

modern warfare." Here, then, lies the whole trouble: the English have made no serious effort to get up a modern Code of Fighting Instructions. The essayist is not without words of praise, however, for the Signal Book, deficient as it is. "If," says he, "we turn to the definitions, we see a great improvement has taken place in recent editions, the terms 'guide of a fleet,' 'guide of a column,' and others, being comparatively new. The term 'column' is also new, and is now used to mean *any number of ships in a distinct body, whether in line ahead, line abreast, or otherwise.*' The word," he adds, "has been objected to, with justice, as having a forced meaning, but at least it *describes clearly* a body of ships in any formation, and this was previously much required."[103]

Further on he says: "Alluding to the old Signal Book" (and the new one, he tells us, is a mere transcript with a few extra notes and observations), "we ask if we are right in supposing that *all these signals, evolutions and manoeuvres are intended as a groundwork for tactics? And, if so, where are the tactics?*"[104]

Another writer[105] asks the same question: "But are even the evolutions prescribed for the squadrons sufficient? *If battle is their object, where are their formations or plans of attack which they recommend?*" The former essayist answers the question himself by saying: "We have been living in peaceable times, and battle *and action signals have been dropping out of the Signal Book. What remains?* Just ten articles of instructions for action which are mostly obsolete."[106]

It must be admitted that these remarks of English Prize Essayists hold out small encouragement to hope for much instruction in tactics from the English Navy. And there is reason to believe that other navies are pretty much in the same unsettled state as to the best system of Steam Tactics, both Minor and Grand. Commander Hoff,[107] who has taken great pains to gather together under one cover all that is latest and best of the published opinions on the subject, quoting from English, French, German, Italian, and Russian and Belgian writers, comes to the deliberate conclusion that "all of them are more or less unsatisfactory."

The conclusion forced upon us is inevitable—that we must begin *de novo* and build up this science for ourselves.

We might very well conclude here, but for one or two remarks of the distinguished officers just quoted which require a passing notice.

---

[103] *Ibid.*, p. 43.

[104] *Ibid.*, p. 45.

[105] Adm. Sir George Cranville Randolph (1818-1907), *Problems in Naval Tactics* (Portsmouth: Griffin, 1879), p. iv.

[106] Fremantle, *ibid.*, p. 45.

[107] William Bainbridge-Hoff, *Examples, Conclusions and Maxims of Modern Naval Tactics*, Office of Naval Intelligence, Bureau of Navigation, Navy Department, General Information Series No. III, Information from Abroad (Washington, D.C.: U.S. Govt. Print. Off., 1884). The statement in quotations appears to be Luce's deduction from Bainbridge-Hoff's concluding remark that he hoped the presentation of this material would "develop research in a direction at once very interesting and very important."

One writer says: "Evolutions are not tactics, though they may form the basis on which tactics are founded." And again, speaking of the Signal Book as a manual of drill in fleet evolutions, he asks, "Where are the tactics?" And again, another officer asks, in speaking of fleet evolutions in the Signal Book, "If battle be their object, where are their plans of attack?"

To these several remarks we may repeat that "Tactics is the Art of Military Movements." This applies to the movements of a fleet, or its evolutions. Hence, the evolutions laid down in the Signal Book do constitute, in themselves, what is known as Minor Tactics. Further, that the writers quoted have confounded two distinct branches, viz.: Minor or Elementary Tactics, which is limited to evolutions (see Introduction), and Grand Tactics, or the Tactics of Battle. This distinction is made by military writers, and it would be well for us to adopt it, here and now, for our Naval Terminology. We will thus avoid any confusion of ideas. In the English Navy they had for generations of flag officers the Fighting Instructions, and in France the Ordonnance du Roi, to both of which reference has been made. These comprised the Grand Tactics of the Sail Period. The great want now felt in both those navies are modern Fighting Instructions. That is what they are striving for. But, as we have said, and say again, nobody, to our knowledge, has arisen, so far, who has shown himself competent to draw them up.

Now, Elementary Tactics, or the system of fleet evolutions laid down in the Signal Book; Grand Tactics, or the manner of forming a fleet for battle, and for conducting it in battle, and Strategy, together constitute the science of naval warfare; and that is what we are now to study.

In starting out with a new study, it is not desirable to retain the terminology of an obsolete system. The English and French have both fallen into this error. The English still cling to the terms *line ahead, line abreast,* and *line of bearing;* while the French retain the terms used by Paul Hoste; *La Ligne de File, La Ligne de Front,* and *La Ligne de Relevement.* Now, strictly speaking, the term *line of bearing,* having reference to the wind, is inapplicable to steam tactics. It was a line six points from the direction of the wind, and a fleet was on the starboard, or larboard, line of bearing according as the ships composing it could fetch, by a simultaneous movement, into the line of battle on the starboard or larboard tack. The term is a convenient and expressive one, however, and having been adopted by writers on steam tactics, it should have a modified and precise definition given it.

Unhampered by traditions as we are, let us at once adopt the shorter, simpler, and equally expressive terms of *Line, Column* and *Echelon,* and their derivatives, to express the various formations of a fleet. We shall then avoid such clumsy expressions as *line ahead in single column,* and many similar ones common to writers of the day.

Our terminology should be precise, our definitions clear. Where old terms will answer, it is certainly well to retain them, even if the sense must be modified. But when we are actually wanting in terms, we may be safe in taking such as have passed into the currency of military literature.

Our attention, then, will be first directed to Elementary Tactics; next, to the Tactics of Battle, and lastly, to Strategy.[108]

---

[108] Luce is referring to the course of study at the Naval War College.

Captain Alfred T. Mahan, *ca.* 1896

Luce selected Mahan to give lectures at the Naval War College on the subject of the influence of navies on nations. Mahan arrived in 1886 to take up his position as a history professor, and took on additional duties as Luce's successor in the Presidency. He served as President of the Naval War College, 1886-89 and 1892-93. He was formally connected with the College again in 1910-12 while preparing some of his lectures for publication.

Photo: Naval Historical Collection
Naval War College

CHAPTER V

LITERARY CRITIC: THREE BOOK REVIEWS

Editors' Introduction

In these three book reviews, one may catch a glimpse of Luce in the role of a literary critic. All three of the selections for this chapter were published anonymously during the decade of the 1890's in Joseph B. Gilder's journal, *The Critic*.

The initial selection is Luce's commentary on Mahan's first major work, *The Influence of Sea Power upon History 1660-1783*. It was the first review of this book to appear in a major American literary journal. Indeed, *The New York Times*[1] took no notice of the work until 9 months later when it published an excellent two-column review. Shortly after *The Critic*'s review appeared in print, Luce sent a copy of it to John Knox Laughton in England. Apparently without knowing that Luce was the author of the clipping, Laughton replied,

> I have to thank you for the cutting from the *Critic* which you have been good enough to send me. I hope I shall be able to do Capt. Mahan justice on this side of the water. His chapters on strategy & policy are excellent: the details of his history he has, I think, taken too exclusively from French sources, and many of them are certainly inaccurate. I see the *Critic* refers with disapproval to Clark Russell's Life of Nelson. It is no doubt a scandalous performance, I took the opportunity of saying as much in the *Atheneum* of 31 May . . ..[2]

For Luce the writings of Mahan were another way of publicizing the work of the Naval War College to the community of naval scholars. His review and his correspondence with influential students of naval affairs such as Laughton[3] stressed the connection between Mahan's work and the college. In a letter to the editors[4] of *The Critic* several years later, Luce noted that it "was about the only periodical in the United States to review [the book] . . . and to call attention to its surpassing merits." He noted, too, that Mahan's work had received far more attention abroad than it had at home.

---

[1] *The New York Times*, 19 April 1891, p. 19:1. Theodore Roosevelt's unsigned review appeared in the *Atlantic Monthly*, vol. LXVI, No. 396, October 1890, pp. 563-567.

[2] Laughton to Luce, 12 August 1890, Luce Papers, Naval Historical Collection, Naval War College.

[3] See Editors' Introduction to chapter IV.

[4] *The Critic*, vol. XXIII, No. 597, 29 July 1893, p. 77.

In his review of Mahan's second seapower book *The Influence of Sea Power upon the French Revolution and Empire, 1793-1812*, Luce once again lauded his friend's work. Many historians found this a much more profound work than Mahan's first but continued to criticize him for his dependence on secondary sources. In response, Luce points out in his review that the author had not only consolidated the essence from a mass of books but had been able to seize the substance from the works and use it "to fatten his own theme." At the same time that he appreciated Mahan's skill as a historian, he recognized the continuing opposition by a significant group within the naval profession who saw little practical value in the theoretical abstractions of history. Offering a word of encouragement in the face of criticism, Luce remarked, "to be sneered at and twitted is sometimes a spur to a man of mettle." As shown in these reviews, the public support which Luce gave to Mahan and to his writings through his many connections emphasized the relationship of Luce as Mahan's mentor and champion in his early writing career.

In the third selection Luce offered enthusiastic praise to the work of Col. G.F.R. Henderson. The Englishman's work *Stonewall Jackson* represented the best then being written by any military theorist and was designed to illustrate the problems of strategy, military policy, leadership, and the science of war. Such books were rarely read in the quarters that needed them the most. Shortly after the publication of *Stonewall Jackson*, Henderson complained to an acquaintance, " . . . so far from its [*Jackson*] having attracted any notice I find that very few of the senior officers even know of its existence. We are certainly not a literary army, and the unfortunate soldier with a turn for writing history does not get much encouragement from the service."[5] The situation was no different on the western side of the Atlantic, with a similar attitude in the Navy. Luce was one of the very few men in the service who saw that the book held many lessons for Americans in his day. It showed the need for the study of history, a deeper study of strategy, and the establishment of a general staff. When Luce viewed Henderson's work in 1899, he saw that it touched on many of the nascent developments in the American military, some which had been only recently illustrated in the Spanish-American War.

---

[5] Sir Henry Brakenbury, *Some Memories of My Spare Time* (Edinburgh, 1909), p. 86, quoted in Jay Luvaas, *The Education of an Army: British Military Thought, 1815-1940* (Chicago: University of Chicago Press, 1964), p. 244.

The Influence of Sea Power upon History
By Captain A.T. Mahan, U.S. Navy. $4. Boston: Little, Brown & Co.[6]

This is an altogether exceptional work: there is nothing like it in the whole range of naval literature. Prepared originally as part of an extensive course of lectures on the art and science of naval warfare, to be delivered at the U.S. Naval War College, before classes of officers of varied experience, the author took the broadest and most comprehensive view of his subject, looking into the primary causes which have brought navies into existence, the conditions under which they have grown in power, and their influence—as the suggestive title of the book states—on national development. No other author with whom we are acquainted, has ever undertaken to treat the subject in such a liberal, not to say philosophical spirit, or to weave the story of the navy and its achievements into the affairs of state so as to bring out its value as a factor of national life. The work is entirely original in conception, masterful in construction, and scholarly in execution.

Military science, like certain other sciences, has been built upon precedent. Military writers have recorded, not only the campaigns, but the *dicta*, of the great captains of every age of which history gives us any account. Napoleon's maxims might almost be called a compendium of the art of war; while the general principles illustrated by the campaigns of Alexander the Great, of Hannibal and Caesar, in ancient times, and of Napoleon, Wellington, Marlborough, Frederick and Prince Eugene, in modern times, constitute in themselves the science of war. Thus we have military history the base of military science. Naval history has never been conceived in this spirit. It is now undertaken, for the first time, to write such a naval history as may be justly regarded as the foundation of naval science. It is a work that was demanded by the progressive spirit of our Navy. Called to the Chair of Naval History at the War College, the author, finding no work which adequately treated of naval warfare, was obliged to bring forward its leading features and to discuss them from his own standpoint. Such was the genesis of this admirable treatise.

Dealing largely with general principles of universal application, the naval student is led to deduce from the story of past wars lessons for his guidance in those of the future. In treating of the old French wars, as well as those of a later date, the author is at once just and discriminating. He views the momentous struggle between the two great sea-powers for supremacy in the West Indies with the calm eye of professional criticism, bestowing the need of praise, or bringing under the rod of reprobation, the great sea-captains of the age; whether they fought for the Lilies of France or under the red Cross of St. George. Each is judged with an inflexible regard for a high standard of professional ability. Bravery of a personal order is conceded, as well as excellence in practical seamanship; but the admirals of the English and French fleets stand or fall according as they prove themselves skilled in the art of war upon the ocean.

---

[6]This review appeared in *The Critic*, vol. XVII, No. 343, 26 July 1890, pp. 41-42.

These are "The Lessons of War as Taught by the Great Masters;" they are just the lessons to set before professional men. They bring into prominence the great value of naval history when properly studied; and they discover a higher and, we might almost say, unsuspected field of investigation: the problems of modern naval warfare, examined by the light of history—studies which might well engage the brightest minds of the profession. They are lessons in naval history which, for obvious reasons, could not have been so well drawn by writers of either country immediately concerned: the element of impartiality would have been wanting. The work itself is just such a one as could have been produced only by an American free from bias; by an American naval officer who had made naval and general history the subjects of profound and exhaustive study; by an American scholar who to elegance of diction and wealth of illustration could add the charm of narrative style to render his book instructive to the professional and pleasing to the general reader. Indeed, it places the former class of readers under a deep debt of gratitude by dispelling the harmful delusion that everything that is old in naval warfare is obsolete; that there is nothing profitable in the story of the battles of the past, to assist in forecasting those of the future. Even so clever a writer as W. Clark Russell[7] has fallen into this error—an error which, uncorrected, would sap the very foundations of the science of war. In his Life of Nelson,[8] he questions, when summing up the character of his hero, that "his genius can 'longer be serviceable in suggestion to a posterity whose hopes are lodged in steel plates.'" Now the gist of the entire work under consideration is a standing protest against such a fallacy. The principles so ably illustrated by Nelson are just as applicable in this day of steam, steel plates and heavy guns as they were in the days of "tacks and sheets." Nor does the author fail to dissipate the popular delusion that Nelson's tactics consisted, as Mr. Clark Russell, puts it, in 'dashing at the enemy'. There certainly was 'dash' in the manner in which Nelson carried his ships into action; but his plans of battle, carefully matured in advance, were the result of a deliberate application of well-established military principles. Such are the lessons as taught by the great masters; and such are the lessons that, for the three or four years last past, the author has been laying before successive classes of officers who, in the near future, are to command our ships and squadrons—some of whom, indeed, are even now in command afloat.

But the work takes a still higher range, and furnishes lessons for the administrator and legislator alike. An English writer thus sketches the

---

[7] William Clark Russell (1844-1911), novelist. After engaging in journalism, he produced some 60 nautical tales of adventure; his writings led to improved conditions in the merchant marine. He wrote on the lives of William Damper in 1889, Lord Collingwood in 1891, and with W.H. Jaques, *Nelson*.

[8] W. Clark Russell and William H. Jaques, *Horatio Nelson and the Naval Supremacy of England* (New York: Putnam's, 1890). What Luce did here was to write a book review within a book review. He does not mention the coauthor, a fellow naval officer, William Henry Jaques (1848-1916). Jaques published short books on torpedoes and on modern armor; he resigned from the Navy in 1887 to become an adviser to the Bethlehem Iron Works in the manufacture of heavy armor.

province of a great administrator in time of war. Speaking of the leading incidents of English history during the period included in the Seven Years' War, he says:

> In Westphalia the English infantry won a great battle which arrested the armies of Louis XV, in the midst of a career of conquest; Boscawen defeated one French fleet on the coast of Portugal; Hawke put to flight another in the Bay of Biscay; Johnson took Niagara; Amherst took Ticonderoga; Wolfe died by the most enviable of deaths under the walls of Quebec; Clive destroyed the Dutch armament in the Hooghly and established English supremacy in the Carnatic. The nation, while loudly applauding the successful warriors, considered them all, on sea and on land, in Europe, in America, and in Asia, merely as instruments which received their direction from one superior mind. It was the great William Pitt,[9] the great commoner, who had vanquished French marshals in Germany and French admirals on the Atlantic, who had conquered for his country one great empire on the frozen shores of Ontario, and another under the tropical sun near the mouths of the Ganges.

The mental horizon of this great man took in vast continents and boundless seas, while to his genius as a statesman he added the strategy of an accomplished soldier.

Compare to such an extended field of operations our naval and military establishments, organized with a single eye to perennial peace, dwindle into utter insignificance. Small as our navy is, however, we have yet to learn its true functions, and its value as an exponent of national power—to learn, in short, the inadequacy of moral influence, such as this peace-loving country should exert, unsupported by material force. The work before us is eminently calculated to educate the public mind as to what that force should be and the limits it should attain. We have said enough to make clear its *raison d'etre,* and to show why it must take a high place—the highest of its kind, if it be not absolutely *sui generis*—in naval and military literature. Let us hope the author may be induced to continue his labors so as to include the War of 1812.

We have been unstinting in our praise simply because the work deserves it. It has its defects, undoubtedly, but they are so far overshadowed by what is deserving of commendation, as hardly to be noticed. The book, as already stated, consists of lectures which formed part of a course on the art and science of naval warfare. That this fact should be wholly ignored by the author is immaterial to the general reader. But the student of naval and military history would undertake its perusal in a far different spirit, were he informed, at the outset, that the author aimed at something more than the mere showing of how national life is affected by the sovereignty [sic] of the seas.

---

[9] William Pitt, Earl of Chatham (1708-1788).

England and France on the Sea[10]

The Influence of Sea Power upon the French Revolution and Empire: 1793-1812. By Captain A.T. Mahan, 2 vols. $6. Little, Brown & Co.

To be sneered at and twitted is sometimes a spur to a man of mettle. In the changed condition of modern naval warfare, and with the vastly different nature of its materials as compared with earlier days, there was some ground for the rather discouraging comment of a senior officer in the United States Navy to Capt. Mahan. When asked to lecture upon naval history and naval tactics in the United States Naval War College, the comment was made, "You won't have much to say about history." Nevertheless, by his two books, Capt. A.T. Mahan has not only given us a fine exhibition of his powers, but has shown how out of the nettle of history he has plucked the flower of science. To him the naval records of the past are not merely masses of archaeology, but they have a distinct lesson for to-day, notwithstanding that the ships and powers of offence and defence are something undreamt of a half-century ago.

In the work now before us, a proper continuation of his "Influence of Sea Power upon History: 1660-1783," he begins with a survey of events in Europe 1783-1793, and then goes on to show what were the elements in the coming struggle between France and England, and also to analyze the causes leading to the overthrow of Napoleon. France and England, like two gladiators, were pitted against each other, and it was a question which could longest submit to blood-letting and treasure-losing. Sooner or later, one of the combatants must yield through sheer exhaustion. Had England been Germany or Spain, the long battle would probably have been fought out on land, and would have been much more quickly decisive. Great Britain, being insular in situation, soon found out that the real struggle was to be settled on the waves, and the great statesman who ruled the destinies of Great Britain was able to make accurate forecast of the struggle and the results. Capt. Mahan gives us, even to minute touches of line and color, most interesting pictures of the ships, men and guns at the opening of the year 1793. He declares that Great Britain was in a genuine state of naval unpreparedness. He shows what strenuous efforts were put forth, which culminated in the finest navy of Europe, and how the spirit of the nation became incarnated in such heroes as Nelson and Collingwood. He penetrates to the real meaning of the mass of books, diplomatic, political, naval and historical, which have been written to describe the state of things in Europe during the last decade of the eighteenth century, and his power of seizing the point in each author in order to fatten his own theme is very striking. For example, he quotes from Fyffe's "History of Modern Europe,"[11] to show that after Trafalgar,

---

[10] This review appeared in *The Critic*, vol. XXII, No. 569, 14 January 1893, p. 17.

[11] C.A. Fyffe, *A History of Modern Europe* (New York: Holt and London: Cassell, 1880), vol. I, p. 282. Charles Alan Fyffe (1845-1892), barrister-at-law, historian, fellow of University College, Oxford.

the campaign of which he describes so brilliantly, Napoleon was forced "to impose his yoke upon all Europe or to abandon the hope of conquering Great Britain. Nelson's last triumph left England in such a position that no means remained to injure her but those which must result in the ultimate deliverance of the continent." He also demonstrates, by a masterly familiarity with both the detail and principles of naval equipment and morale, that Nelson, so far from being a mere bulldog fighter or dashing commander, was thoroughly and unpoetically scientific. Not only was he the chief to lock yardarms in battle and to sweep decks with grape and cannister, but he was also the man of foresight who refused to sail from port until the four inches of flannel had been furnished to the tails of the shirts of his sailors, while for their stomachs, and what went into them, he was as careful as for the food of their minds. With the eye of a strategist as well as a tactician, and in every chapter a critic and appraiser, the author follows the fortunes of Napoleon, which, seemingly rising to zenith, were all the more hastening to their inglorious setting; while the naval power of Great Britain was increasing upon the sea and becoming a permanent force. England having achieved the mastery of the ocean and the annihilation of the fleets of the only naval powers having any claim to be considered as such—the Netherlands, France and Spain,—an opportunity arose for the neutral carriers, among them the United States.

Most worthily does Capt. Mahan give credit to Pitt, who was a great master, not only in finance, but of war. He gave a general direction to the naval effort, and by his unprecedented naval development he secured also commercial prosperity. In this he was enabled to make the question depend upon the ultimate exhaustion of either of the great contestants, and having control of the sea and of the great pathway to the British colonies, and being able thus to command the resources of many parts of the world, the ultimate issue was not long in doubt. Indeed, in a certain sense, the conflict between 1783 and 1812 in Europe was in many striking respects like that decided in America a few years before, in the same eighteenth century. France, though holding Canada and controlling all the inland of America by line of forts to Louisiana, was yet unable to hold her own against England, which had full command of the ocean and constant access to her colonies.

It will be good news to those who admire the author's power to know that he proposes to devote an entire work to the war between Great Britain and the United States in 1812-1815.

Stonewall Jackson and the American Civil War[12]
By Lt. Col. G.F.R. Henderson. 2 vols. Longmans, Green & Co.

These volumes fall easily within the category of "books that are books." They are admirable—admirable both as to matter and the treatment thereof.

Stonewall Jackson was a born soldier, and, as far as mortal man may be permitted to judge, a true Christian. Indeed, in certain aspects of his

---

[12]This review appeared in *The Critic*, vol. XXXIV, No. 859, January 1899, pp. 65-67.

character he reminds one of the Cromwellian soldier who "fought so well because he prayed so well." It is, however, in depicting Jackson as a strategist and tactician, and in describing the campaigns in which he bore so conspicuous a part, that the author has laid all Americans, north, south, east, and west, under a deep debt of gratitude.

Colonel Henderson, the author, is singularly well equipped for the task he has so happily accomplished. An educated soldier himself, and Professor of Military Art and History at the Staff College, Sandhurst (England), he has brought to his work a familiarity with the campaigns of the great captains of every age. This knowledge has enabled him to form an intelligent estimate of the leaders of our Civil War, both North and South, and to institute a just comparison between them as masters of the art of war, and the most noted names of military history. Amid this galaxy the author places Jackson's resplendent star. Colonel Henderson's treatment of military questions, whether dealing with the broad principles of war regarded as a science or with the accepted rules of the art, brings forcibly to mind the writings of the lamented Colonel Cornwallis Chesney, whose "Campaigns in Virginia and Maryland" and "Essays in Military Biography" are well known in this country. Colonel Chesney was one of the best military critics of his day, and enjoyed a reputation for absolute impartiality. Colonel Henderson, while equally able as a military writer, is yet possessed of a certain charm of style which lightens up the dryest details, and makes clear the most complicated movements on the field of battle. It is this clear and luminous style that will render the book most attractive to the non-professional reader.

The similarity pointed out by the author between the various phases of the campaigns in Virginia and those of the historic battle-fields of Europe give a very substantial value to the work. So, too, the parallels drawn between the principal leaders in the American conflict and those who have become famous in other lands.

> "If Jackson's military characteristics are compared with those of so great a soldier as Wellington," observes the author, "it will be seen that in many respects they run on parallel lines. 'I can do,' said Jackson, 'whatever I will to do"; while the Duke, when a young general in India, congratulated himself that he had learned not to be deterred by apparent impossibilities. Both were patient, fighting on their own terms or fighting not at all. Both were prudent, and yet when audacity was justified by the character of their opponent and the condition of his troops, they took no counsel of their fears . . . Both were masters of ruse and stratagem, and the Virginian was as industrious as the Englishman.
>
> Although naturally impetuous, glorying in war, they had no belief in a lucky star; their imagination was always controlled by common-sense, and, unlike Napoleon, their ambition to succeed was always subordinate to their judgment. Yet both, when circumstances were imperative, were greatly daring. The attacks at Groveton and at Chancellorsville were enterprises instinct with the same intensity of resolution as the storm of Badajos and Ciudad Rodrigo, the passage of the Douro, the great counterstroke of Salamanca . . . It has already been pointed out that Jackson's dispositions for defence differed in no degree from those of the great Duke. And much more to the same effect. (Vol. II., p. 603.)

Woven in with the texture are threads of discourses on strategy and tactics, both minor and grand, such as are not to be found even in such a standard work as "The Operations of War" of General Edward Bruce Hamley. Speaking of the mighty host put in the field by the North and the thoroughness of its organization as a fighting machine, one factor was overlooked—"intelligent control." This was during the earlier days of the war. "Men," he observes, "who, aware of their own ignorance, would probably have shrunk from assuming charge of a squad of infantry in action, had no hesitation in attempting to direct a mighty army, a task which, Napoleon has assured us, requires profound study, incessant application, and wide experience."

Many statesmen and even soldiers are ignorant of the fact that strategy is an art in itself, to attain success in which one must serve a long apprenticeship. "The rules of strategy," he continues, "are few and simple. They may be learned in a week. . . . But such knowledge will no more teach a man to lead an army like Napoleon, than a knowledge of grammar will teach him to write like Gibbon." He then draws the pathetic picture of the great and good Lincoln "poring, night after night, when his capital was asleep, over the pages of Jomini and Clausewitz," trying to master the art of war, with the result that, when Grant was appointed to supreme command in 1864, he said: "'I neither ask nor desire to know anything of your plans. Take the responsibility and act, and call on me for assistance.' He had learned at last that no man is a born strategist."

It is a significant fact, remarks the author, that, during the three years the control of the armies of the North remained in the hands of the Cabinet, the balance of success lay with the Confederates. But "when Lincoln abdicated his military functions in favor of Grant, the Secretary of War had nothing more to do than to comply with his (Grant's) requisitions. Then, for the first time, the enormous armies of the Union were manoeuvred in harmonious combination, and the superior force was exerted to its full extent." (Vol. I., page 255.) Farther on (page 503, Vol. I.), he justly observes that "it by no means follows that because a man has lived his life in camp and barracks, had long experience in command, and even long experience of war, he can apply the rules of strategy before the enemy." He may lack the mental and moral qualities. Again, there are few schools where strategy may be learned—"the light of common-sense alone is insufficient: nor will a few months' reading give more than a smattering of knowledge. 'Read and re-read,' said Napoleon, 'the eighty-eight campaigns of Alexander, Hannibal, Caesar, Gustavus, Turenne, Eugène, and Frederick.'"

It has not yet been recognized in this country that if armies are to be handled with success they must be directed by trained strategists. "No *Kriegsakademie*, or its equivalent, existed in the United States, and the officers whom common-sense induced to follow the advice of Napoleon had to pursue their studies by themselves." Jackson was one of these. As a strategist, Napoleon was undoubtedly his model. "If Napoleon himself, more highly endowed by nature with every military attribute than any other general of the Christian era, thought it essential to teach himself his business by incessant study, how much more is such study necessary for ordinary men?"

As one result of his studies the author draws the conclusion that "the campaigns of the Civil War show how much may be achieved, even with relatively feeble means, by men who have studied strategy, and have the character necessary for its successful practice; and what awful sacrifices may be exacted from a nation ignorant that such a science exists." "Fabius and Scipio, Wellington, Nelson, and St. Vincent, Grant, Sherman, and Farragut [and he might have added Porter] have replaced the mere tacticians; and the superior resources, wielded with strategical skill, exert their inevitable effect." (Preface, xii.)

As a sequence of his earnest advocacy of a close study of the higher branches of the military profession such as marked Jackson's ten years as Professor of Artillery Tactics at the Virginia Military Institute, Lexington, follows, naturally, the equally earnest plea for a carefully trained staff. Referring to the deplorable results flowing from the interference of the civil authorities with the military—both North and South—one of those results being Jackson's letter of resignation,—the author states that the organization of the armies was very largely the work of civilians, and the advice of the higher officers was very generally disregarded. In the North "cavalry was considered an encumbrance and a staff a mere ornamental appendage." (Note on the Evils of Civilian Control, page 264.)

He freely admits the blunders made by the staffs of the three armies—English, French, and Prussian—in the Waterloo campaign; but adds, very truly, that the art of war has made great strides since then, and even since 1870. "Under Moltke's system,"—the careful training of officers and men to fit them for service in the general staff,—"which has been applied in a greater or less degree to nearly all professional armies, the chance of mistakes has been much reduced. The staff is no longer casually educated and selected haphazard; the peace training of both officers and men is far more thorough; and those essential details on which the most brilliant conceptions, tactical and strategical, depend for success, stand much less chance of being overlooked than in 1815. It is by the standard of a modern army, and not of those whose only school in peace was the parade-ground, that American armies must be judged." (Vol. I., page 530.)

The "Moltke system" is still unknown to our army. We have no general staff; no system of education of officers for staff duties. The story of the recent campaign on the southern coast of Cuba, when compared with the exposition made in these pages of the radical defects of our military organization in 1862, furnishes abundant proof that we have failed utterly to profit by the lessons of the Civil War.

Colonel Henderson, we repeat, has accomplished in these volumes a great work, and one for which every American ought to feel thankful. They should be read by the statesman, the soldier, and the scholar, in short, by every one who has at heart the good of his country and the efficiency of the army.

CHAPTER VI

ADMINISTRATIVE REFORM: THE FLEET

By Rear Admiral S.B. Luce, U.S.N. (Retired)

Editors' Introduction

This essay was originally published in the *North American Review** in October 1908. The subject is the establishment of an effective form of naval administration capable of efficiently directing the fleet in wartime. Unlike the other selections in this volume, it was read and discussed in influential places long before it was published.

The first draft of the article was written in May 1907, about the same time that Luce was preparing his "Memoranda" to the Secretary on naval efficiency. It was designed to follow up the memoranda, to point out general problems in the Bureau system, and to underline the inherent difficulties in this system for the proper direction of the fleet. Luce sent the first draft of the article to the Secretary of the Navy asking permission to publish it. The Secretary, however, was vehemently opposed to publication on the grounds that it "might stir up strife." Luce, at that time, felt dutybound not to publish it without approval.

In October he delivered it as an address on the closing day of the Naval War College's Summer Conference, but it was still not heard by the audience that Luce sought. A year later, in April 1908, Luce sent a rough copy of it to Comdr. William S. Sims, the President's Naval Aide, in hope that he could induce President Roosevelt to read it and become directly involved in the effort to reform the naval bureaucracy. In mid-June, Roosevelt gave his permission to publish the article in any "technical journal" that Luce desired, but he declined to read it on the grounds that he might "be held accountable for every little phrase in it." On 17 June, Luce wrote to Sims,

> Now the President himself is the audience I desire to reach. If he does not take enough interest in naval affairs to read a paper in defense of his own policy in regard to naval

---

*"The Fleet," *North American Review*, vol. CLXXXVIII, No. 635, October 1908, pp. 564-576.

questions of the highest import there is no use in going any further—I do not care to fire in the air. It's the appointment of a Commission in the Navy Department I am after.[1]

At this point Luce nearly gave up his hopes for a commission to reorganize the Navy, but with encouragement from Sims, Luce decided to publish his article. With some changes and deletions, Luce went ahead to "fire off my little guns."[2] He submitted the article to the *North American Review,* one of the most widely respected American journals of the day; it was quickly accepted for publication. As "The Fleet" was going to press, Roosevelt decided to take the lead. Sims let Luce know that Roosevelt was about to take action. Luce replied, "I am delighted to know that M. RACINE [as Luce called the President] will take hold and be our Standard bearer—that in itself will ensure Victory—One blast upon his bugle-horn is worth a thousand men."[3] Typically, Luce went on to suggest that Sims have the Navy Library sent up copies of his previous articles on naval administration. "M. Racine may perhaps get one or two pointers from them. They, the articles, date back nearly twenty years."

By January 1909 a board, headed by former Secretary Moody, was appointed to review the problem of reorganization. Luce received notification from Secretary Truman Newberry that he would be ordered to Washington for duty on the Moody Board. Shortly after he received the news, Luce wrote, "The rift in the cloud grows wider,"[4] His article "The Fleet" had doubtlessly played a part in the effort to get the President to take the lead in reforming the Navy. While the article laid out the argument for Luce's case, in another sense it was a way of prodding the bureaucracy into action. As he wrote in the postscript of a letter to Capt. William J. Barnette, the Secretary to the General Board, "Why do not you Washington chaps get on a hustle? Hey?"[5]

> That the United States has taken a fresh departure from the erstwhile even tenor of her way is now acknowledged and acquiesced in. It is only by looking back a few short years that one can realize the great changes that have brought this country prominently before the notice of the world. The year 1898 has been called the year of Europe's

---

[1] Luce to Sims, 17 June 1908, Sims Papers, LC. This was a comment about Theodore Roosevelt's letter to Luce, 16 June 1908, Luce Papers, LC.

[2] Luce to Sims, 22 June 1908, *ibid.*

[3] Luce to Sims, 2 November 1908, *ibid.*

[4] Luce to Sims, 7 January 1909, *ibid.*

[5] Luce to Barnette, 13 March 1908, *ibid.*

Commander William S. Sims

Sims served as naval aide to President Theodore Roosevelt between 1907 and 1909. In this key position, he was able to transmit many of Luce's ideas to Theodore Roosevelt, as well as to promote his own. He earned his fame as "the man who taught the Navy how to shoot." Later, he commanded U.S. Naval Forces in Europe during World War I, and was President of the Naval War College.

discovery of America.⁶ The accession of colonies and of battleships was synchronous. Beginning in a quiet and unobtrusive way, this wide departure from a traditional policy that had come to be regarded by many as sacred, attracted little attention. It requires no great discernment, now, to understand that both our colonial interests and our fighting ships will continue to increase until there will be an American colonial system⁷ and a fully organized fleet⁸ commensurate with our territorial expansion and the development of our resources.⁹

The colonies will need for their intelligent government a Colonial Secretary, who will be a member of the Cabinet; and the fleet will need intelligent government, not only to insure its efficiency, but to keep within reasonable bounds the great expense its maintenance entails: over one hundred million dollars a year. The question is—and it is a very grave one for the country—How is the efficiency of the fleet to be kept up, and an economical disposition of its funds insured? For the days of prodigal expenditures must soon end.¹⁰

The wisdom of the framers of the Federal Constitution is not to be questioned; but, with all its advantages, the wide separation between the legislative and executive branches of the government has, in practice, certain disadvantages. This separation is not conducive to harmony. Indeed, it has led at various times to what has savored of hostility on questions vitally affecting the interests of the country. Mutual understanding on naval matters is wanting. It is undoubtedly true that Congress has been extremely liberal in its appropriations for the navy; but, as far as one can learn, this liberality has not been in accordance with any well-digested plan of naval development.

To the lay mind it would appear that herein lies one fruitful source of trouble; there seems to be no settled plan of naval development upon which the Executive and Congress can agree. Were such a plan to be matured, and accepted, both branches of the government could act in

---

⁶The published version has been compared with a typed manuscript in the Lecture Collection, Naval Historical Collection, Naval War College. This version is annotated and signed by Luce. Dated "Newport, R.I., May 16th, 1907," Luce has added in his own hand. "Read before the Conference of Officers at the Naval War College, Oct. 1st, 1907. S.B.L." This sentence does not appear in the manuscript.

⁷In the 1907 version the remainder of the sentence is, " . . . and, for its protection, a fully organized fleet."

⁸The word "Fleet" is used here in its general sense to signify the total number of vessels of war available for active service. In England, "Fleet" and "Navy" are synonyms. [This is Luce's footnote.]

⁹The 1907 version adds
This accretion will come about, not because "we, the people," wish it; nor will it be retarded because "we, the people," do not wish it. It will come neither by accident, nor by design, but through the operation of the law of "manifest destiny;" a destiny manifest to the student of the philosophy of history and to the political seer. The unity and continuity of purpose apparent in the conduct of human affairs, bears ample evidence that the Great Lawgiver of the universe, He who marks the sparrow's fall,—will shape the country's ends,"rough-hew them how we will."

¹⁰This sentence was added to the published version.

harmony on most matters concerning the navy. There is such a thing as a naval policy. The building up of a navy without a definite plan is like the directing of a number of artisans to build some houses without stating how many houses were required, of what material they were to be constructed, or for what purpose they were to be used. The naval policy of England, for example, is very simple. It is known as the "two-Power standard"—that is to say, the strength of the English navy must at all times be maintained at a strength equal to that of any two naval Powers that may be combined against it. In the House of Commons not long since, the Prime Minister[11] was asked if it was the policy of the Government to make equality with the two next strongest fleets the standard of England's naval strength. The Prime Minister's answer was: "The present strength of the British navy is in excess of the two-Power standard." That is the naval policy, in a nutshell, of the greatest naval Power of the world.

In more specific terms, we find the First Lord of the Admiralty saying,[12] "The test the Admiralty applied to naval efficiency and the standard they had set up for years past, as that which must be maintained, was that we must be strong enough in *battleships* alone to defeat any combination of any two Powers, and that we should have a margin over and above this, for contingencies, of some ten per cent. This was the minimum which they had considered safe. With respect to our cruiser power," he added, "we need, and must maintain, far more."

The word "efficiency" as used here refers to the strength of the line of battle.[13]

---

[11] Sir Henry Campbell Bannerman (1836-1908), Liberal Party Prime Minister from December 1905 to his death in April 1908. He made this statement in Parliament on 12 November 1906. See Great Britain, *Parliamentary Debates,* 4th series (London: H.M. Stationery Office), vol. CLXIV, p. 1067.

[12] Edward Marjoribanks, second Baron Tweedmouth (1849-1909), First Lord of the Admiralty from December 1905 to April 1908. He made this statement on 3 November 1906, according to Luce's notation in the typescript; Luce's source for this quotation has not been located.

[13] The 1907 manuscript continues here with the following:

It has been the naval policy of France since Trafalgar, as we gather from the foreign press, to keep two objects steadily in view. One, that it shall not be so far inferior to that of England as to put her diplomacy completely at the mercy of the British Government; the other that it shall be equal in strength to the navies of any two other naval powers in Europe, next in importance to those of England and her own. It has been found by experience that a proportion of battleships of the first class (which constitutes the real strength of navies) of two-thirds of those of England, satisfies, in the main, those conditions.

It is obvious that while France maintains its navy in about this proportion it can, by alliance with one or more of the other naval powers, be in a position not far short of that of England; and the British Government would, consequently, be compelled to think seriously before attempting to force the hands of France at any time when the relations between the two countries might become strained.

In this connection a distinguished statesman of England frankly admitted that, whatever confidence Englishmen may have in the sense of justice and moderation of their own Government they must admit that in any difficulty with France, their language, and attitude, on many international questions would be different, and less conciliatory, if the navy of France were reduced to a point where it would give them no concern whatever. It cannot be denied, then, that looked at

Naval Policy.—The expressions "Naval Policy" and "Naval Efficiency," it may be observed, have been used by certain writers as convertible terms. This has led to no little confusion of thought on naval matters. England's naval policy, as we have seen, is to maintain the two-Power standard; while the naval policy of France is to keep the main body of her fleet in the Mediterranean, for France applies the principles of the Monroe Doctrine to certain sections of the north of Africa. In the one case it is a question of the number of battleships of the first category; in the other the disposition made of those ships.

"Naval Efficiency" is construed by some authorities as meaning the number of battleships available for war, as in the case just quoted from the speech of the First Lord of the Admiralty; by others again as the normal state of discipline of the fleet, and the judicious use made of it. There have been fleets powerful in numbers of ships and guns, manned by a personnel of good fighting material, and yet wholly inefficient for purposes of war. Mere numbers do not constitute efficiency. To the unskilled, excess of numbers means discomfiture.

From the English we get the very expressive term "fighting efficiency." Thus, in "A Statement of Admiralty Policy,"[14] we gather from the Navy Estimates Committee that the following considerations obtained: "first, the whole object of the Navy Estimates is to secure the fighting efficiency of the Fleet and its instant readiness for War; secondly, the least amount [of money] compatible with that end."

The Hon. Joseph G. Cannon,[15] Speaker of the House of Representatives, is represented in an alleged interview as saying: "Our navy will be of no benefit to us unless the men know how to handle the ships, and how to work the guns. Efficiency is more important than any other consideration, and it can be gained only through practice. I feel there is a strong sentiment throughout the country in favor of maintaining an efficient navy, and, as I said before, *efficiency is more important than size.*" These words are the words of wisdom.

Efficiency is the power to accomplish a desired end: the possessing of adequate skill for the performance of a duty. "The swordfish can kill the whale," said an American gentleman[16] when asked, in 1894, of the probable outcome of the War then imminent between China and Japan.

Naval policy, in its broadest sense, comprehends Statesmanship. It is the relative rank, as a naval Power, which the State aims to assume and

---

by the light of experience in such matters the policy of France in this respect is wise, and gives to its diplomacy a force, which, otherwise would be wanting. Nelson said, a line-of-battleship was a great aid to diplomacy.

[14] Dated 30 November 1905.

[15] Joseph Gurney Cannon (1836-1926) served in the U.S. Congress as a Representative from Illinois between 1875-91, 1893-1913, and 1915-1923. "Uncle Joe" served as Speaker of the House from 1901 through 1911.

[16] William Alexander Parsons Martin (1827-1916) was a Presbyterian missionary, educator, and author. He served as President of Imperial University in Peking, China, and wrote a number of books on international law, natural science, Christianity, and Chinese affairs. This quotation is from his book, *The Awakening of China* (New York: Doubleday, Page & Co., 1907), p. 171.

maintain in the family of nations. It includes: first, the creation of a floating force adequate to make good its pretensions; and, secondly, the ability to use that force effectively—in brief, the weapon and the skill to wield it.

Despite its alleged structural defects, no American can have looked upon the fleet of battleships now circumnavigating the globe without a feeling of pride.[17] The Navy Department is certainly entitled to credit for this imposing display of sea power. But the credit must be shared by others—it must be shared with the iron and steel industries of the country and by the great ship-building plants now in operation.

To the Navy Department alone belongs the credit of initiating the movement which has led to this result—a movement which has given the country for the first time in its history a fleet in the true technical sense.

The genesis of what is called the "new navy" was in 1881. In that year the first Advisory Board convened by the Secretary of the Navy, the Hon. W.H. Hunt,[18] recommended the building of steel ships on the ground "that such a step would give an impetus to the steel industries of the country."[19] That end has been accomplished far beyond what the most fervid imagination could have pictured; and it is largely to those same steel and shipbuilding industries that we are indebted for the formidable line of battle we now have.[20] Taken together they have trained up a body of skilled artisans which it would be difficult to duplicate in any part of the world. Congress is wise and far-seeing in providing them with work.

By what means soever the fleet has been brought into being, its existence is an established fact, and its continued growth is assured. The weapon has been forged. Where is the hand to wield it? Where is the power to insure efficiency? These are very present questions, and call for intelligent answers.

As to Naval Efficiency.—In a speech delivered on June 22nd, 1905, President Roosevelt is reported to have declared that he would give up the Monroe Doctrine and the Panama Canal, rather than refuse the means which can alone render our attitude as a nation worthy the respect of mankind. "Therefore," he added, "keep on building

---

[17]The manuscript version of this sentence reads: "No American could have looked upon the fleet of battleships assembled in Hampton Roads, to assist at the Jamestown celebration, without a feeling of pride." Luce is referring here to the naval review which was part of the Jamestown Ter-Centennial Exposition. See U.S. Congress, Senate, *Final Report . . . of the Jamestown Exposition,* Senate Doc. 735, 60th Congress, 2d sess., 1909.

[18]William Henry Hunt (1823-1884). Born in South Carolina, he served as an Associate Judge of the U.S. Court of Claims and then Secretary of the Navy in 1881-82. After a brief administration in the Navy Department, he became Ambassador to Russia, 1882-84.

[19]See *Annual Report of the Secretary of the Navy, 28 November 1881,* Appendix I: "The Advisory Board-Proceedings" (Washington: U.S. Govt. Print. Off., 1881), pp. 27 ff.

[20]Here the manuscript adds: "The South Bethlehem Steel Works, the Midvale Steel Works, the Fore River Ship Building Co., the Cramps, and the Newport News Ship Building Co., and others on the Pacific Coast, all representing millions of dollars of capital, must not be suffered to languish for want of work."

[battleships] and maintaining at the highest point of efficiency the United States Navy, or quit trying to be a big nation."[21] That, in brief, is the President's Naval Policy. It includes the power, coupled with the ability to wield that power effectively.

The building programme of Congress has supplied the power. It only remains to consider the question of efficiency—the consummate ability to wield that power.[22] The duty of devising measures for securing naval efficiency rests, under wise laws, exclusively with the Executive. This all-important factor of Naval Policy the President must, perforce, leave to his Secretary of the Navy. The latter, a civilian, well versed in public affairs, but unfamiliar with naval or military arts, must in turn defer to his advisers in the Navy Department. The Secretary on assuming office finds himself associated with a civilian Assistant Secretary and eight "admirals," so called,[23] each one of the latter presiding over one of the eight Bureaus of which the Navy Department is composed.[24] Five of these admirals belong, singular to say, to the non-combatant class, and three of them to the combatant class.[25] The five non-combatant admirals naturally regard questions of naval efficiency from the non-military point of view: the admirals of the combatant class from the military point of view. Moreover, each of the offices over which these admirals preside—combatant and non-combatant alike—belongs to the civil branch of the Department, and have to do with material and finance. It does not take long for the Secretary of the Navy on assuming office to discover that naval efficiency is a very broad and comprehensive subject, and one which belongs exclusively to the military side of his office. With this discovery is revealed the fact that the military side of his office does not exist. There is no such thing. This fact, taken in conjunction with the fact just stated, that there is a radical and irreconcilable difference of opinion on the part of his advisers on vital questions affecting naval efficiency, would, in time of

---

[21] Theodore Roosevelt speech at commencement, Williams College, Williamstown, Mass. See report "Big Navy or No Canal," *The New York Times*, 23 June 1905, p. 1:5.

[22] The manuscript adds here: "Naval efficiency rests under wise laws solely, and exclusively with the executive."

[23] The phrase "so called" has been added to the published version. In another draft copy of this article in the Luce Papers, Library of Congress, Luce has made a footnote here in his own hand: "Swiss admirals all." The reference is from Jacques Offenbach's *La Vie Parisienne*.

[24] Section 7 of the Personnel Act of March 3, 1899 prohibits the changing of titles of officers. [Luce's footnote.]

[25] The Act of July 5th, 1862 provided that the Chiefs of four of the Bureaus should be appointed from the list of officers of the Navy not below the rank of commander. This gave the advisers of the Secretary of Chiefs of four line Bureaus and the Chiefs of four staff Bureaus. As this equal division did not accord with the views of the civics, a clause was introduced in the naval appropriation bill of June 29th, 1906, providing "that the Chief of the Bureau of Yards and Docks (which, by the Act of '62, had been assigned to the line officer) shall be selected from the members of the corps of Civil Engineers of the Navy, having not less than seven years' active service." This gave the non-combatants a majority. [Luce's footnote.]

war, leave the Secretary of the Navy in an unenviable position. Divided counsels are fatal to military operations.

A navy that requires time for preparation after war has been declared is far from being in an efficient condition. On February 5th, 1904, Japan severed diplomatic relations with Russia, and at midnight of the 8th Port Arthur was startled from its slumbers by the guns of the Japanese fleet. It was a complete surprise.[26] Three days after the diplomatic rupture Japan struck the first blow at Port Arthur and Chemulpo. There was no such trifling as is said to have occurred at Fontenoy: "Fire first, gentlemen," about the military movements of the Japanese. They knew the great moral and military advantages of taking the offensive, and they assumed it at once and effectually.[27] But they were enabled to do so only by a long and thorough course of preparation during peace. So much for the readiness to strike. The point where the first blow is to fall can be determined best by those who have made such questions the subject of careful study, undisturbed by administrative duties. There must be no mistake as to the true objective. To be master of the situation at the outset may prevent a war. Some of the most important strategic moves are those made during peace.

It may be stated right here once for all, without circumlocution, that naval efficiency, in its true sense, is unattainable under our present form of naval administration. It is far better that the people should know this in order that the responsibility may be placed where it belongs. The truth of this statement we now purpose showing.

How the American method of governing the fleet, a purely military organization, works in practice may be illustrated by examples taken from official documents of recent date, documents which are easily accessible to all the world.

The President, recognizing the inherent defects in the constitution of the Navy Department, knowing that the efficiency he has so much at heart is not attainable under existing conditions, urged Congress to amend the law under which the Navy Department is organized with a special view to increasing the efficiency of the navy. In his message to Congress of December, 1903, Mr. Roosevelt said: "We need the establishment, by law, of a body of trained officers who shall exercise a systematic control of the military affairs of the navy, and be the authorized advisers of the Secretary concerning it."[28] In order to carry out the views of the President, the Secretary of the Navy prepared and presented to the Naval Committee of the House *"a bill to increase the*

---

[26] This sentence has been added to the published version.

[27] Compare the prompt action of the Japanese with ours when we left it to a British Colonial Governor to "request" Commodore Dewey to leave Hongkong, April 24th, 1898. See Luce, "Naval Administration II," *United States Naval Institute Proceedings*, vol. XXVIII, No. 4, December 1902, pp. 848-49. [This is Luce's footnote. See item 117.]

[28] Theodore Roosevelt, "Third Annual Message to Congress, 7 December 1903," *The Works of Theodore Roosevelt, State Papers as Governor and President, 1899-1909* (New York: Scribner, 1925), p. 234.

efficiency of the Navy," the object of which was to legalize the General Board. In presenting the bill to the Naval Committee of the House, its adoption, by Congress, was ably advocated in person by the Secretary of the Navy, the Hon. William H. Moody.[29] He was followed by the Admiral of the Navy (Admiral Dewey)[30] and by the Chiefs of three Bureaus representing the combatant class of the Department. Secretary Moody's presentation of the case, on the part of the administration, was lucid, logical and learned, leaving absolutely nothing to be said in advocacy of the President's plea for naval efficiency. But the majority of the Secretary's advisers—the non-combatant admirals—would not have it. The bill was vehemently opposed by the non-combatants, represented by the Assistant Secretary of the Navy of that day, and the Chiefs of what are known in the navy as the five Staff Bureaus.[31] As the bill has never been heard of since it was presented to the Naval

---

[29] William Henry Moody (1853-1917) was a Massachusetts-born Harvard graduate who had studied in the law offices of Richard Henry Dana, Jr., author of *Two Years Before the Mast*. Later, while serving as District Attorney for eastern Massachusetts, Moody gained wide recognition for his prosecution in the famous "Lizzie Borden Case" at Fall River, Mass. A popular chant of the day proclaimed,

> "Lizzie Borden took an axe
> And gave her mother forty whacks;
> When she saw what she had done
> She gave her father forty-one!"

Although legally acquitted, she was convicted in the popular mind, and the case became the subject of plays, novels, a ballet, an opera, and a musical revue. Elected to Congress, Moody served in the House of Representatives from 1895 until 1902. A pugnacious master of fact and detail on the floor of the House, he attracted the attention of President Theodore Roosevelt who appointed him Secretary of the Navy in 1902. He served in the Navy Department until Roosevelt selected him as Attorney General in 1904. During his 2-year tenure in the Department of Justice, he attracted attention again by personally arguing the Government's successful position in the Beef Trust Case (*Swift & Co. v. U.S.* 196 US 375). In 1906 he was appointed to the Supreme Court where he served until forced to retire by failing health in 1910.

[30] Admiral of the Navy George Dewey (1837-1917), the victor of the Battle of Manila Bay in 1898, was given the rank of Admiral of the Navy by a grateful Congress. As the senior officer in the Navy, he served as President of the General Board from its inception until his death in 1917. His personal prestige did a great deal to increase the effectiveness of the Board.

[31] The Chief of Bureau of Supplies and Accounts [Rear Admiral H.T.B. Harris] publicly criticised the President's plea for naval efficiency. (See "Admiral Harris on General Staff" *Army and Navy Journal*, 30 January 1904, vol. XLI, no. 22, p. 574.) This flagrant violation of Navy Regulations seems to have elicited no comment.

[This is Luce's footnote. In Harris' statement he criticizes Luce's and Mahan's proposal for a British style staff. In April 1904 the following men were the Navy's Bureau Chiefs: Rear Adm. M.T. Endicott, Bureau of Yards and Docks; Rear Adm. H.T. Mannly, Bureau of Equipment; Rear Adm. H.C. Taylor, Bureau of Navigation; Rear Adm. G.A. Converse, Bureau of Ordnance; Rear Adm. W.L. Capps, Bureau of Construction and Repair; Rear Adm. C.W. Rae, Bureau of Steam Engineering; Rear Adm. H.T.B. Harris, Bureau of Supplies and Accounts; Rear Adm. P.M. Rixey, Bureau of Medicine; Capt. S.C. Lemly, Judge Advocate General. The Assistant Secretary of the Navy was Charles Hial Darling.]

Committee on April 11th, 1904, it is natural to suppose that it received its quietus then and there.[32]

The motives of the Committee in thus turning down the General Board are not open to question. But, as the record stands, it would appear, to the world at large, that the Chiefs of the five Staff Bureaus had influence enough to defeat an urgent measure of the administration to increase the efficiency of the navy.

In plain terms, the President was defeated by Bureaucracy. This was the literal fulfilment of a prophecy. During the "Investigation of the Navy Department" in 1875-6, Commodore D. McN. Fairfax, U.S.N.,[33] stated, in his testimony before the House Naval Committee, that "the Bureau system was gradually undermining the discipline of the Navy Department and must sooner or later be changed." The time for the change has arrived. "If a house be divided against itself that house cannot stand."[34]

True, the General Board continues a potentiality, but this is due to the President and not to Congress. The General Board was established by the Navy Department, General Order No. 544, March 13th, 1900, which order was embodied in the Navy Regulations of 1905, thus giving it for the time being the force of law (Sec. 1547 R.S.). But as it is competent for some administration of the future to rescind this order and delete it from the Navy Regulations, it is obvious that the character of the General Board lacks the quality of permanence which statute law alone can give. To insure this permanency of character was the request preferred by the President, as we have seen; a request to which the House Naval Committee declined to accede.

Some Functions of the General Board.[35] —The General Board represents the military element of naval administration—hitherto wanting—as distinct from the civil branch represented by the eight Bureaus. It is the legitimate Council of War of the civilian Secretary of

---

[32] Those interested in this subject should read U.S. Congress, House, *Hearing before the Committee on Naval Affairs, House of Representatives, April 11th, 1904, on "A Bill (H.R. 15403) to Increase the Efficiency of the Navy."* 58th Congress, 2d sess., pp. 909-989.

[33] Rear Adm. Donald McNeill Fairfax (1821-1894) was Commandant of the Naval Station at New London, Conn., when this testimony was given. In 1861 he had been executive officer in U.S.S. *San Jacinto* under Capt. Charles Wilkes when that ship captured the Confederate agents James M. Mason and John Slidell from the English ship *Trent*. Taking charge of the Confederates, Fairfax is credited with such tact that he was able to take the men into U.S. custody without allowing the English captain to surrender his ship as a prize. Fairfax served as Commandant at New London from 1873 to 1878. He then served as Governor of the Naval Asylum before retiring in 1881. See Fairfax's testimony in 44th Congress, 1st sess., House Miscellaneous Doc. No. 170, serial 1703-05.

[34] This quotation from Abraham Lincoln's speech of 16 June 1858 was added for the published version at this point. In the manuscript it appears several pages beyond. See footnote 39.

[35] The following four paragraphs were added for the published version. For a detailed study of the General Board in this period, see Daniel J. Costello, "Planning for War, A History of the General Board of the Navy 1900-14," Unpublished Ph.D. Thesis, The Fletcher School of Law and Diplomacy, Medford, Mass., 1968.

the Navy on all matters pertaining to war and to the preparation for war.

When the Spanish War broke out, it was seen at once that, to meet a foreign naval Power on the ocean, further trifling with our radically defective system of naval administration must cease at once. One of the first steps, therefore, in this direction was the convening of a Naval War Board, a body separate and distinct from the Bureaus, but in close touch with the office of the Secretary of the Navy. To this Board was intrusted the very responsible duty of a careful study of the whole theatre of the war, and of watching closely the movements of the enemy's fleet, squadrons or single cruisers, as far as could be done by means of the reports which were constantly reaching the Department, day and night, by wire or mail. These reports, sometimes of a conflicting nature, had to be carefully sifted, differences reconciled, and the real designs of the enemy penetrated as far as possible. The questions arose: "What was the objective of Cervera's[36] fleet?" and, after the battle of Manila Bay, May 1st, 1898, and the destruction of the Spanish squadron, "What would be Spain's next move in that direction?" These were questions the members of the War Board were obliged to study carefully and to answer out of their knowledge of naval strategy. As a result of these studies, the Naval War Board was enabled to keep the Secretary of the Navy fully informed, at all times, of the movements of the enemy, and to place before him recommendations for such counter movements of our own forces as the conditions, varying from day to day and even from hour to hour, required. Incredible as it may appear, these highly important military duties had not been provided for in our scheme of naval organization. It will be seen from this that the Naval War Board was not of the nature of an advisory board, as that term is understood in the Navy. It had higher, and vastly more responsible, functions: The transactions of the War Board cover 860 typewritten pages of copies of communications sent and received. This was departmental duty performed mainly by officers having no part in the organization of the Department; hence its extra-legal character. The nature of the War Board and the necessity for its existence are so clearly set forth by Secretary Moody in his testimony before the House Naval Committee, on April 11th, 1904, as to leave little to be said.

On the conclusion of the war with Spain, the Naval War Board, through some singular misconception, was dissolved. But it had proved itself so indispensable as a part of the organization of the Navy Department that the Secretary of the Navy issued General Order No. 544 with a view to its permanent establishment under the title of the "General Board."

Once more the President essayed to induce Congress to increase the efficiency of the Navy. In his special message to Congress of December

---

[36] Adm. Pascual Cervera y Topete (1839-1909) commanded the Spanish squadron in the Caribbean during the Spanish-American War. He had served as the Spanish Minister of Marine when Luce represented the United States at the Columbian Exposition in Madrid in 1892. Cervera was captured by the U.S. Navy when his squadron was destroyed at Santiago de Cuba in July 1898.

17th, 1906,[37] on the Personnel of the Navy, Mr. Roosevelt made certain specific recommendations, failure to adopt which, "by judicious legislation, the future of our Navy will be gravely compromised." "In my last three annual messages I have invited the attention of Congress to the urgent necessity of such legislation . . ." but the Commander-in-Chief of the Navy did not take into the account the deep-seated defection in the ranks of his own immediate command, in his own official family, as it were. The Personnel Bill, so earnestly advocated by the administration, was strangled in its birth. Congress has thus, through its House Naval Committee, put itself on record as opposing measures which have for their object the increasing of the efficiency of the Navy. It is clear that the views of the administration on naval affairs carry little weight with the Naval Committees of the two houses of Congress. There is a good reason for this. The Navy Department is divided against itself, and the majority of the Secretary's Colleagues[38] are opposed to any change in the present method of administering the affairs of the Navy. Congress has endowed them with great powers, and it is only natural that they should exert those powers to protect their vested rights—rights which must be safeguarded though the heavens fall.[39]

As political power goes with the control and expenditure of the revenues of the State, so power, patronage and influence go with the expenditure, with limited accountability, of considerably over one hundred million dollars a year by the Chiefs of the eight Naval Bureaus. This explains why a Chief of Bureau has in certain directions, far more influence than the responsible head of the Department—the Secretary of the Navy himself. It is scarcely necessary to say that in this discussion of the business methods of the Department, not the slightest reflection is intended to be cast, either directly or by implication, upon the high character and strict integrity of the Chiefs of the several Bureaus. We sincerely trust that goes without saying. One may be permitted to criticise a system without impugning the high character of the components of that system—the Bureaus.

It will be seen from the foregoing that the navy, a distinctively military body, is governed, practically, by an oligarchy of non-military men. To govern, in its original sense, means to pilot or to steer. Hence we are led to conclude that our fleet is piloted or steered by "admirals," who belong neither to the military nor to the seaman class. This method of governing a navy is saved from being preposterous only because of the fiction that it is in accordance with the will of the people, as expressed through their representatives in Congress. Mr.

---

[37] Roosevelt's message was reprinted in the *Army and Navy Journal*, vol. XLIV, No. 17, 22 December 1906, p. 450.

[38] The Secretary's Colleagues.—This is the only Executive Department where the law places the Secretary and his associates in office on an equal footing. [This is Luce's footnote.]

[39] The "House divided" quote from Lincoln originally appeared here. The following paragraph was added to the published version.

Secretary Bonaparte[40] acted wisely in recommending, as he did in effect, the total abolition of this archaic and demoralizing form of naval government by Bureaus. Put none but militant seamen at the helm.

Bureaucracy.—"My experience during the past year," declared Secretary Bonaparte, in his annual report of November 28th, 1906, "has greatly strengthened my belief, as expressed in the last annual report of the Department, that the system of autonomous Bureaus is open to very grave theoretical objections; and that only the very high character of the personnel employed in these Bureaus . . . prevents these theoretical objections from seriously affecting the *efficiency* and *economy* of the Department's work. It seems to me, therefore, desirable *that a very radical and thoroughgoing change should be made in the organization of the Department.*"[41] He then outlines a plan (the appointment of a commission on the Navy Department) which, he says, appears to afford a reasonable promise of satisfactory results and which in effect would, as already observed, abolish the present archaic system of trying to govern the navy by Bureaus.

Secretary Bonaparte's diagnosis of the case was perfectly correct. His prescription—a commission to examine into, and report upon, the whole subject of naval administration, pointing out the defects of the present system, and suggesting the remedy therefor, would result in immediate relief at the hands of Congress. There can be little doubt of that. To insure intelligent legislation Congress must have bed-rock facts to go upon; and those facts can be ascertained and formulated best by a board of experts appointed for the purpose. Such is the disease which afflicts the Navy to-day and its remedy.

Bureaucracy aims exclusively at augmenting its own official powers at the expense of more extended interests. It is characterized, asserts one authority, "by the inefficient and obstructive performance of duty through minute subdivisions of functions, by inflexible formality and pride of place." A Bureaucrat is defined as "an official who endeavors to concentrate administrative powers in his own bureau."

All the privations and suffering of the English Army in the Crimean War, through lack of provisions and clothing, resulting in the loss of thousands of lives, was due directly to army bureaucracy; and English army bureaucracy repeated its mismanagement fifty years later in the Boer War. Bureaucracy greatly damaged our own military prestige during the war with Spain, and might have been fatal to the navy but for the timely advent of the Naval War Board. It was Russian

---

[40] Charles Joseph Bonaparte (1851-1921) served as Secretary of the Navy from 1905 to 1906. He was a Harvard educated lawyer from Baltimore, Md., and had attracted the attention of Theodore Roosevelt by his activity in the area of civil service reform. In 1906 he succeeded W.H. Moody as Attorney General; he left office in 1909 with Roosevelt. Bonaparte was a grandson of Jerome, King of Westphalia, one of Napoleon Bonaparte's brothers.

[41] U.S. Navy Dept., *Annual Report of the Navy Department for the Year 1906,* (Washington: U.S. Govt. Print. Off., 1907), p. 5.

bureaucracy, not Togo,[42] that defeated Rodjestvensky[43] in the Sea of Japan. Togo simply gave the *coup de grace*. Villeneuve,[44] Du Pont,[45] Cervera and Rodjestvensky, each in turn, was the victim of inefficient naval administration. Is there a demand for another American victim? Said Premier Stolypin:[46] "My hope and purpose are, with the aid of the Duma, to get rid of the bureaucratic system. Such is the Emperor's firm and unshakable will." Bureaucracy defeated President Roosevelt in his efforts to promote naval efficiency in 1904; and Bureaucracy dominates the Navy of the United States to-day. Let this truth be pondered by that portion of an irresponsible press that so airily fans the flame of enmity between this country and our good friend, Japan.

A decision of the United States Supreme Court defining the administrative authority of the Secretary of the Navy sanctioned the exercise by the Secretary, of the military functions of the President, as Commander-in-Chief of the Navy. The principle enunciated in that decision has been applied to the relations sustained by the Chiefs of the several Bureaus to the Secretary and through him to the President. Thus the Chiefs of the several Bureaus have become the representatives of the Commander-in-Chief of the Navy, and clothed with all his authority touching the affairs of their respective Bureaus. Their orders must be respected and obeyed as the orders of the Commander-in-Chief. The Act of August 31st, 1842, makes this very clear. It declares explicitly that "the orders of a Chief of Bureau shall be considered as emanating from the Secretary himself, and shall have full force and effect as such." But, as the orders of the Secretary are to be regarded as the orders of the President, it is plain that the orders of a Chief of Bureau must also be regarded as the orders of the President. This makes practically nine Secretaries of the Navy, with power in their respective spheres, equal to those of the constitutional Commander-in-Chief. All the evils of bureaucracy are thus aggravated by the law which put it in operation. Sixty-five years' experience and the testimony of numerous Secretaries of the Navy show conclusively that this unbusiness-like

---

[42] Count Heihachiro Togo (1847-1934) was a Japanese admiral trained at Greenwich, England. He was Commander in Chief of the Japanese Navy in the Russo-Japanese War in 1904-05. He bombarded Port Arthur and defeated the Russian Fleet at the Strait of Tsushima on 29 May 1905.

[43] Adm. Zinovi Petrovich Rozhdestvenski (1848-1909) was Commander of the Baltic Fleet that was sent to the Pacific in the Russo-Japanese War. He was defeated by Togo at the Battle of Tsushima in 1905.

[44] Vice Adm. Pierre Charles Jean Baptiste Sylvestre Villeneuve (1763-1806) opposed Nelson at Trafalgar.

[45] Rear Adm. Samuel Francis Du Pont, USN (1803-1865), led the South Atlantic Blockading Squadron in the victory at Port Royal, S.C., in 1861 and in the defeat at Charleston in 1863. Luce served under him during the time he was at sea in the Civil War. He dedicated his *Seamanship* to him. See John D. Hayes, ed., *Samuel Francis Du Pont: a Selection From His Civil War Letters* (Ithaca, N.Y.: Cornell University Press, 1969), 3 vols.

[46] Petr Arkadievich Stolypin (1862-1911) was Premier of Russia from May 1906 until his assassination in September 1911. He was the sponsor of the last major government reform attempt before the Revolution.

system is conducive neither to efficiency nor to economy, but the very reverse. It insures the greatest amount of extravagance with the least amount of accountability, and is fatal to efficiency.

While we are vainly struggling to increase the efficiency of the navy, Germany continues building big ships according to a carefully matured plan.[47] She remembers that the Hague Peace Conference of 1899 was the precursor of a great war.[48] In her next conflict she does not purpose being found wanting either in ships or in naval efficiency. Japan indulges in no idle dreams of universal peace, or Utopian restrictions of sea power. In the late war she demonstrated to all the world the absolute necessity of an efficient naval administration, without which naval efficiency is absolutely impossible. This she devised and perfected long in advance of the collision she saw to be inevitable. Russia, also, taught us the equally valuable lesson that naval efficiency does not consist in the number of ships alone. The battle is not always to the strong. Strength, to be effective, needs intelligent direction.

Fortunately, Congress has authorized the building of two more 20,000-ton battleships,[49] coupled with the assurance of a continuous building programme. But on the vital question of naval government—the power to handle the forged weapon, the means of insuring naval efficiency—it is the purpose of the oligarchy which shapes the conduct of our naval affairs to maintain the *status quo.*

It is now the naval oligarchy *versus* the people. The question of the hour is: Which shall prevail?[50]

S.B. Luce

---

[47]The typescript version reads: "... Germany, regarding with ill concealed contempt the solemn mockery of a Hague Conference for the limitation of armaments, continues building big ships according to a carefully matured plan." For two excellent studies of the origins of German seapower in the 1890's see Jonathan Steinberg, *Yesterday's Deterrent: Tirpitz and the Birth of the German Fleet* (London: MacDonald, 1965), and Holder H. Herwig, *The German Naval Officer Corps: a Social and Political History 1890-1918* (Oxford: Clarendon Press, 1973).

[48]Luce is referring here to the International Peace Conference held at the Hague, May-July 1899, and the Russo-Japanese War of 1905. A.T. Mahan was a delegate to the Conference at the Hague.

[49]Luce is probably referring to the Act of 2 March 1907 which authorized the 20,000 ton battleship U.S.S. *North Dakota* (BB-29) and to the Act of 29 June 1906 which authorized the 20,380 ton *Delaware* (BB-28).

[50]The last paragraph was added for the published version.

125

CHAPTER VII

FLEET CONTROL: NAVAL STRATEGY

By Rear Admiral Stephen B. Luce, U.S. Navy

Editors' Introduction

The work of the Moody Board was completed on 26 February 1909 when its final report was sent to the President. The statement which serves as the philosophical basis for its recommendations, the section entitled "General Principles Governing Naval Organization" was actually written by Mahan, but the document clearly shows the influence of Luce.[1] Most importantly, the board's proposals incorporated Luce's concept of an office for "Naval Operations," but there were still difficulties to be surmounted. While the general public seemed confused over the subtlety of the issue, a large number of professional officers did not understand or appreciate the rationale behind the proposal. In addition, Roosevelt's term as President had only a few days to run when the final report was submitted to Congress. Luce feared that the reform effort might easily fail without a nationally known standard bearer. It was essential, therefore, that professional opinion support and sustain the President's initiative. An article in the spring of 1909 would help to keep the issue alive, and at the same time it could help to clarify the nature of naval strategy and to delineate the area of responsibility for the proposed office. To accomplish this Luce resurrected a lecture that he had delivered on 17 July 1902, during the summer course of the Naval War College. He revised it and nearly doubled its length in order to focus on the most current issues. Then he submitted it for publication to the *United States Naval Institute Proceedings*, where it appeared in April 1909.[2]

In contrast to his article on "The Fleet," which concentrated on the inadequacy of the Bureaus in dealing with the fleet, this essay focuses directly on the problem of fleet control. The conclusion, however, is the same; the Navy needed a group of officers who

---

[1] U.S. Congress, Senate, *Certain Needs of the Navy: Message from the President of the United States Transmitting Two Preliminary Reports of the Commission Appointed to Consider Certain Needs of the Navy*, 25 February 1909, Senate Doc. 740, 60th Congress, 2d sess., pp. 2-3.

[2] "Naval Strategy," *U.S.N.I. Proceedings*, vol. XXXV, No. 1, 1909, pp. 93-112.

were trained to deal with the broad problems of naval operations and educated in the principles of strategy.

Published toward the end of his writing career, this article is significant in that it illustrates the balance which Luce maintained, at the end of his life, between his exhaustive reading and his practical knowledge of the Navy.

His reliance on Mahan for historical data is, of course, a change from his earlier work. Taken as a historical document, it provides an interesting contrast between the naval writing in the pre-Mahan era, as illustrated in chapters III and IV. Like many others, Luce, too, had come to rely on his prodigy. He did not, however, become totally absorbed in the maritime view. He retained his old interest in all aspects of warfare. He continued to read the latest military studies, as well as to keep up with the new developments in naval thought. Luce went so far as to emphasize the importance of military history for the naval student. " . . . Military movements on land," he wrote, "suggests the continuity of similar rules in military movements at sea." Luce's insistence on this relationship between military and naval thought seems to have had an impact upon his friends and colleagues at the Naval War College. For it was at about this time that the War College staff began to become interested in the ideas developed by the German General Staff.[3] The "applicatory system" and "the philosophy of the order form" would develop into the American military planning process used during World War II. In the years between 1909 and 1912, the seeds were being planted for the adoption of these ideas. Luce's writing was undoubtedly one of the influences that contributed to the acceptability of these concepts in the U.S. Navy.

In March 1909, while this essay was in the press, Luce received a letter from the editor of *Navy Magazine,* who asked "As to the present status and outlook of our reform movement." Luce replied confidentially,

> The "present status" is the *old* status of chronic friction between line and staff; and the "outlook for reform" is not encouraging. The campaign of reform is scarcely yet begun, and while I am not without hope of ultimate success, I realize that the struggle for reform will be long and arduous.[4]

---

[3] See Charles W. Cullen, "From Kriegsacademie to the Naval War College: The Military Planning Process," *Naval War College Review,* January 1970, pp. 10-15; and J.B. Hattendorf, "Technology and Strategy: A Study in the Professional Thought of the U.S. Navy, 1900-1916," *Naval War College Review,* November 1971, p. 31.

[4] Luce to W.D. Walker, 29 March 1909, Luce Papers, LC.

Luce in his later years.
Photo: Newport, R.I. Historical Society

The first results of the reform movement appeared before even Luce may have hoped for them. Within a month after the "Aid system" was established by Navy Secretary George Meyer, W.S. Sims wrote to Luce:

> I congratulate you with all my heart upon the final success of the long fight you have made for a military organization of the navy. Too many forget that you began this fight before we youngsters understood much about its object and its importance. You planted the seed, and you may repose for years in the shade of the sturdy tree that sprang from it. We kids have the satisfaction of knowing that we got in a good lick now and then, but your work prepared the service to brave the pain of a (to us) new idea and finally to see the light.[5]

Sims was certain that the Congress would fully support Meyer's action. His optimism was premature, but his analysis of Luce's contribution was accurate.

> War is *not* a game of chance, as so often asserted. The saying is true only when the game is undertaken by those unprepared for it by previous study. There are games in which there is a large element of chance; but we see proofs every day of that element being discounted, or neutralized, by the superior skill of one or the other of the players. Ordinary participants in the game, guided by a few fixed rules, are often surprised to find that, although favored by fortune at the outset, they yet lose the game. The skill of their opponent had offset the advantages which in the beginning had been all their own. The truth is forced upon them that a superficial knowledge of a few elementary rules of the art is no match for an opponent's familiarity with the principles on which the rules are founded, and an automatic readiness to apply them.
>
> The same may be predicated of the great game of war. A knowledge of the principles of the science, combined with skill in the application of the rules deduced from them, will reduce to a minimum the chances of defeat, and enable an adept in the art to convert the errors of a more powerful adversary into a means of success.
>
> War in its more extended sense may be regarded as a science. The growth of a science is simple. The science of law, for example, founded upon human rights and the principles of truth, equity and justice, could not have been built up save by the enunciation of those principles by eminent jurists. The precedents established by the recorded opinions of great lawyers, and the rulings of the bench, have been handed down through long lines of judges, carrying with them all the weight and force of law; indeed the findings of the courts have not infrequently been formulated into statute law. The principles of the science would lie dormant did not man breathe into them the breath of life by giving

---

[5] W.S. Sims to Luce, U.S.S. *Minnesota*, 13 December 1909, Luce Papers, LC.

expression to them in due form. Thus has it been with the science of war. Its principles have found expression in the deeds and maxims of eminent seamen and soldiers. Great captains, gifted by nature with a genius for war, have illustrated its principles in their campaigns and have put them down in writing, or have had them recorded by competent writers. We owe the graphic account of the "Retreat of the Ten Thousand," so famous in military annals, to Xenophon[6] himself, and Thucydides, an admiral of the Athenian Navy,[7] was the best naval historian of antiquity. His works should be read by every naval student to-day. In reading Arrian,[8] observes Sir Edward Creasy,[9] we read General Aristobulus[10] and General Ptolemy[11] —two of the generals of Alexander the Great—on the campaigns of the Macedonians, and it is like reading General Jomini or General Foy[12] on the campaigns of the French. Achilles,[13] who according to an ancient belief was of divine origin, his mother being Thetis, a sea-nymph, served as the model warrior on whom Alexander aspired to form himself. This belief no doubt suggested to Napoleon the idea that war should be represented by the head of Achilles, to indicate its divine origin. Hannibal and

---

[6] Xenophon (ca. 430 B.C. - after 355 B.C.), Greek historian, was one of the "Ten Thousand Greeks" who went to Asia to seek their fortunes. In his *Anabasis* he recorded his experiences as a leader in the Army of Cyrus during the rebellion against Artaxerxes II of Persia. His description of the retreat northward along the Tigris toward the Black Sea prompted the historian J.B. Bury to remark that Xenophon could have made his fortune as a war correspondent.

[7] Thucydides (ca. 460 B.C. - ca. 404 B.C.) is best known for his history of the Peloponnesian War. However, in 424 B.C. he was elected 1 of the 10 strategoi for the year in Athens and given command of the fleet based at Thasos. Unable to prevent the capture of the city of Amphipolis, he was recalled, tried, and exiled. His *Peloponnesian War* was written during his 20 years of exile.

[8] Flavius Arrianus Arrian (ca. A.D. 96 - ca. A.D. 180) was a Greek historian and philosopher whose *Anabasis of Alexander* is the most reliable source for the military career of Alexander the Great. Arrian served as Governor of Cappadocia under the Emperor Hadrian and Archon of Athens.

[9] Sir Edward Shepherd Creasy (1812-1878) was an English historian. The reference here is to his most popular work, *Fifteen Decisive Battles of the World from Marathon to Waterloo* (New York: Alden, 1885), p. 88.

[10] Aristobulus of Cassandreia (fl. fourth century B.C.) was one of the Greek technicians who accompanied Alexander the Great's army. He wrote an account of Alexander's campaigns which, while best for its geographical and ethnological information, was used as a source by Arrian, Strabo, Plutarch and others.

[11] Ptolemy I Soter (367-283 B.C.) was the founder of the Ptolemaic dynasty in Egypt. He was one of Alexander's most trusted generals. Upon Alexander's death he was appointed Satrap of Egypt.

[12] General Maximilien Sebastien Foy (1775-1825) was a French general during the Napoleonic Wars. His *Histoire de la guerre de la Peninsula sous Napoleon* was published from his notes in 1827.

[13] Achilles was the great warrior and hero of the Trojan Wars.

Scipio[14] studied the character and achievement of Alexander and emulated his example; while Caesar studied all three and wrote his own incomparable works, which form the basis of the science of war. Each successive school of war was founded upon the campaigns of the successful leaders who had gone before, till Napoleon came to reconstruct the art and adapt it to modern conditions. He, too, studied the campaigns of the great captains who had preceded him, and bore witness to the truth that the principles of the science never change: that what was true in the time of Alexander and of Hannibal and of Caesar was true in his own day.

Thus step by step has the science of war been built up. The principles form the basis of the rules; and, other things being equal, he is most successful in war who has the greatest aptitude for applying those principles and putting those rules in practice. When it is found, observes one writer, that a general always attacks the key of an enemy's position with superior forces, well supported; or, in receiving an attack, opposes the enemy with greater numbers or with men securely intrenched, we need only enough instances to know that he is superior to chance. He may, in one or two cases, be called lucky; but when he is found always to do the same thing, and is always on the right spot, at the right time, with his men rested and his trenches dry, we then understand that he knows his business—that he is a past master in the art of war. Thus has it been going on for ages. The maxims of Napoleon alone form a compendium of the art of war, and their interest to the naval student is that they apply in many cases to the operations of a fleet just as well as they do to the operations of an army.

It is well understood that rules cannot be given to suit in every instance, and when they do cover a given case, blind aherence to them does not always ensure victory. During the War of the Spanish Succession, Lord Galway,[15] an experienced soldier, thought it more honorable to fail according to rule than to succeed by innovation. This great commander, we are told, conducted the campaign of 1707 in the most scientific manner. On the plains of Almanza[16] he encountered the army of the Bourbons. He drew up his troops according to the methods prescribed by the best writers and in a few hours lost eighteen thousand men, one hundred and twenty standards, all his baggage and all his artillery.[17]

---

[14] Publius Cornelius Scipio Africanus, the elder (236 - 184 B.C.), was the Roman general who fought Hannibal and the Carthaginians in the Second Punic War.

[15] Henri de Massue de Ruvigny, second Marquis de Ruvigny, Earl of Galway (1648-1720), was the son of a French general who became a naturalized Englishman following the revocation of the Edict of Nantes. In 1707 he was appointed Commander in Chief of all English forces in Spain.

[16] The Battle of Almanza was fought in June 1707.

[17] The War of the Spanish Succession gave to England Gibraltar and Minorca, separating the southern parts of France from the western, neutralizing Toulon, which Louis XIV had designed as a great naval depot. Gibraltar and Port Mahon in the hands of England enabled her to control the trade of the Levant. The war was terminated by the treaty of Utrecht in 1713. [This is Luce's footnote. His source for this information was T.B. Macaulay, "War of the Succession in Spain," *The Miscellaneous Works of Lord*

A knowledge of military and naval history shows us what errors in war have been committed, and instructs us how they may be avoided. A knowledge of principles enables us to form our own rules to meet special needs, and a knowledge of the rules will often enable one to avoid committing blunders which have become historic. The most that can be claimed for a knowledge of the science of war is that it so prepares the student that he may *make the least number of mistakes.*

The greatest captains known to history have made mistakes in war. Caesar, it is said, accomplished his self-training in war by dint of many errors. His knowledge of the art was acquired by the mistakes he had made and intelligently profited by. Turenne, on being asked how he had lost the battle of Muriendahl,[18] replied, "by my own fault; but," he added, "when a man has committed no faults in war he can only have been engaged in it but a short time." The great Frederick[19] candidly acknowledged that no general had ever committed greater faults than he had. But to the reverses of the campaign of 1744 he always ascribed his subsequent successes. It was in the midst of difficulty and disgrace that he caught the first clear glimpse of the principles of military science. Napoleon, himself, confessed that he had been so often mistaken that he no longer blushed for it. "Don't be discourgaged! It was my fault this time!" cried out General Lee[20] to the retreating Confederates on the third day's fighting at Gettysburg; a frank admission that disarms all criticism.

Military and naval histories, observes one authority, while warning the student against such mistakes, are yet the depositories of maxims which genius has suggested and experience confirmed. They both lighten the way and shorten the road of the traveler and render the labor and genius of past ages tributary to our own. These teach us most emphatically that the secret of successful war is not to be found in mere legs and arms, *but in the head that shall direct them.* If this be either ungifted by nature or uninstructed by study and reflection, the best plans of campaigns are of no avail. This is true of naval operations. Ships and guns may be all that the most advanced science and the highest state of art can produce; but if the genius to combine the various units to the greatest advantage, to direct their movements with skill, and supply their needs, be wanting, they can contribute but little to success in war.

What the great soldiers of past ages have done for the military art, the great seamen have in a measure failed to do for the naval art. The

---

Macaulay (New York: Knickerbocker Press, n.d.), vol. III, p. 200, and Burrows, *Life of Lord Hawke*, p. 16.]

[18] In the Battle of Marienthal (Mergentheim), half of Turenne's army was lost to the Bavarians in 1645.

[19] Frederick II the Great (1712-1786), King of Prussia. Luce is referring to Frederick's disastrous campaign in Silesia against Austria. It was followed in 1745 by a series of victories for his army.

[20] Gen. Robert Edward Lee (1807-1870), Confederate general. See Douglas Southall Freeman, *R.E. Lee: a Biography* (New York: Scribner, 1935), vol. III, p. 130, for a different version of this incident and quotation.

latter were not men of letters. The orders of battle of many of the celebrated admirals known to history, the maxims by which they have been guided, the opinions on naval operations they have given utterance to have seldom been recorded, or when they have been, the records are not always easy of access. Up to a very recent date no one had appeared to gather together the mass of valuable material that lay scattered about in all but forgotten volumes, classify and arrange in order all that was of value, and sift out and reject the volume of fable interwoven with serious history and from the residuum deduce the science of naval warfare.

The naval student has not as a rule appreciated the full value of military history as a guide and helper in his studies. And yet the constant recurrence of the application of certain rules of the art of war observable in military movements on land suggests the continuity of similar rules in military movements at sea.

"I am struck," writes General Lord Wolseley,[21] in his articles on our Civil War, "I am struck throughout the whole story of the minor operations of this period by the illustrations they afford of the regularity with which the old rules and principles of war assert their supremacy." He then instances two battles (Wilson's Creek, May 10, 1861, and Pea Ridge, March 7, 1862) "curiously alike in the military lessons they furnish." "Both failed," he adds, "as might have been predicted."[22] That is to say, failed through ignorance of first principles.

Colonel Henderson, R.A.,[23] observes that, of the mighty host put in the field of the Civil War, by the North, and the thoroughness of its organization as a fighting machine, one factor was overlooked— *intelligent control*. This was during the earlier days of the war. "Men who, aware of their own ignorance, would probably have shrunk from assuming charge of a squad of infantry in action, had no hesitation in attempting to direct a mighty army, a task which Napoleon has assured us requires profound study, incessant application, and wide experience." Strategy is an art in itself, to attain success in which one must serve a long apprenticeship. The rules of strategy are few and simple and may be mastered in a week. But such knowledge will no more enable a man to lead an army as Napoleon did, or conduct a naval campaign as Nelson did, than a knowledge of English grammar will teach a man to write as Gibbon did.[24] A truly pathetic picture is drawn of the great and good Lincoln poring night after night, while all

---

[21] Field Marshal Garnet Joseph Wolseley, first Viscount Wolseley (1833-1913), visited America during the Civil War. He met Gen. T.J. "Stonewall" Jackson and Robert E. Lee. Wolseley published his observations of the war in *Blackwood's Magazine* in 1863. This has been edited by James A. Rawley, *The American Civil War: An English View* (Charlottesville: University of Virginia Press, 1964).

[22] Rawley, *ibid.*, pp. 129-30.

[23] Col. George Francis Robert Henderson (1854-1903) was a military writer, historian, and lecturer at Sandhurst.

[24] Edward Gibbon (1737-1794), English historian, author of *Decline and Fall of the Roman Empire*.

Washington was asleep, over the pages of Jomini and Clausewitz,[25] trying to master the art of war and only too glad to shift the load onto Grant. "I do not ask for your plans," he said; "go ahead, and when you need assistance call on me." He had learned that a man cannot become a strategist by cramming!

"It is a significant fact that during the three years the control of the armies of the North remained in the hands of the Cabinet the balance of success lay with the Confederates. But when Mr. Lincoln abdicated his military functions in favor of Grant, the Secretary of War had nothing more to do than comply with his (Grant's) requisitions."[26] This practice—the Cabinet directing the operations of war—was repeated at the outset of the Spanish War, and with equal want of success. We failed to profit by our own experience in war and are still in the same condemnation.

General Sherman,[27] in a very interesting and instructive article, points out that in our Civil War it was the "educated soldiers" who made the fewest mistakes; and that, when mistakes were made, the movement was *in violation of the "lessons taught by the great masters of the art."*[28] Hence the necessity of studying the great masters, a necessity imposed upon the seaman as well as upon the soldier.

"Out of the experience of great soldiers," says General Sherman, himself a great soldier, "arose certain rules which made the art of war. These rules are as true as the multiplication table or the law of gravitation; their operation is as certain as that of any of the physical laws. The art of war has grown into a science demanding as much, if not more, study than most of the sciences in which the human mind is interested." "Grant's[29] attack on Grand Gulf, and subsequent landing at Bruinsburg; the movement on and battle at Port Gibson; the rapid march to Jackson, whereby he drove Pemberton[30] to his trenches and then invested him till his surrender, July 4, 1863, all these operations illustrated the highest principles of war, one of its maxims being to

---

[25] Gen. Karl von Clausewitz (1780-1831), Prussian military theorist. Luce appears to be mistaken here. Jomini's works were known in the United States before the Civil War, chiefly through the efforts of Dennis Hart Mahan, A.T. Mahan's father. Clausewitz' works were not translated into English until 1873 or French until 1886. By the late 1880's, Clausewitz' thought had penetrated the most important military circles in those two countries. His work was not well known in the United States until after 1900.

[26] G.F.R. Henderson, *Stonewall Jackson and the American Civil War* (London: Longmans, Green, 1898), vol. I, p. 255. Luce also quotes this in his review of this book in *The Critic*, See chapter VI.

[27] Gen. William Tecumseh Sherman (1820-1891), Union general. During the Civil War, Luce's encounter with Sherman at the siege of Savannah, Ga., in January 1865, was the beginning of Luce's interest in strategy. Luce describes this in his article, "Naval Administration III." See bibliography item 122.

[28] W.T. Sherman, "Grand Strategy of the War," *Century Magazine*, vol. XXXV, February 1888, pp. 582-598.

[29] Gen. Ulysses Simpson Grant (1822-1885).

[30] Lt. Gen. John Clifford Pemberton (1814-1881) was the Confederate general who held Vicksburg against Grant.

divide your enemy and beat each moiety in detail." The same principles precisely apply to naval operations. It was through ignoring this sound maxim that the English Admiral Graves, in 1781, permitted the junction off the Cape of Virginia, of the French fleets under de Grasse and de Barras, respectively, and missed his great objective, the beleaguered army of Cornwallis at Yorktown; and during the Trafalgar campaign the English Admiral Cornwallis[31] made a similar mistake.

Another well established rule applicable alike to an army operating on land and an army operating on the high seas is that an army having assumed the offensive must maintain the offensive. This General Sherman illustrates by the series of movements of the Union Army under Grant in 1862 and 1863, having Chattanooga for its objective. "All these movements were made strictly according to the lessons of war as taught by the great masters."

The object of General Sherman's admirable article is to show that the Civil War brought forth, on both sides, the knowledge, talents, and qualities necessary to the occasion; that success resulted from the same qualities, the same knowledge of, and adherence to, the rules of war, which have achieved success in other ages and in other lands, and that military knowledge acquired beforehand was most valuable, though not always conclusive. The same knowledge might have been and was acquired in actual war, though often at a terrible expense of human life and misery.

General Sherman's conclusion is that "there may be such men as born generals; but I have never encountered them, and doubt the wisdom of trusting to their turning up in an emergency." The whole tenor of this instructive article is to emphasize the value in war of the educated seaman and soldier and is the strongest possible appeal for the higher education of officers of the military and naval services. "Of all the professions of life," observes Prof. John Fiske,[32] in writing of our Civil War, "there is none in which the imperative need of professional training is so forcibly demonstrated as in warfare, where errors of judgment are visited with such prompt and terrible penalties."[33] Says that profound thinker, the "father of modern political economy,"[34] "the art of war is the noblest of all arts and has become the most complicated. In order to carry it to any degree of perfection it is

---

[31] Luce is referring to the division of Adm. Sir William Cornwallis' squadron in August 1805. Cornwallis retained 18 ships of the line to guard the entrance to the channel and sent 18 of the line under Rear Adm. Sir Robert Calder to blockade Villeneuve at Ferrol. Mahan severely censured Cornwallis for this in his *The Influence of Sea Power upon the French Revolution and Empire*. Other historians have not agreed with Mahan. See Julian S. Corbett, *The Campaign of Trafalgar* (London: Longmans, Green, 1910), pp. 250-51.

[32] John Fiske (1842-1900), historian and philosopher, was an important exponent of the ideas of Darwin, Spencer, and Huxley in America. He was professor of American history at Washington University, St. Louis, Mo., from 1884.

[33] John Fiske, *The Mississippi Valley in the Civil War* (New York and Boston: Houghton Mifflin, 1900), p. 207, in a section entitled "The Evils of Amateur Generalship."

[34] Adam Smith (1723-1790).

necessary that it should become the sole or principal occupation of a particular class of citizens."[35]

Naval Strategy.—If we now consider the subject of naval strategy, it will be found that in this branch of the art of war the analogy between military operations and naval operations loses itself in identity. In the definitions of strategy given by military writers one has only to substitute the word fleet for army. The field of battle, observes Hamley,[36] is the province of tactics. The whole theatre of war is the province of strategy. It is the object of strategy so to direct the movements of a fleet that when the decisive collision occurs, it shall encounter the enemy with increased relative advantage. When the movements of one of two fleets have been so directed as to increase the chances in its favor, by forcing the enemy either to engage at a disadvantage, or to abandon a strategic point, or position of advantage, under penalty of worse disaster, there is proof of a power (brain power) which differs from the mere ability to fight. The Trafalgar campaign, which deserves careful study, furnishes illustrations of the soundness of these views.

Of two fleets, each having equal chances of victory, the defeat of one may be simply a reverse, with a large residuum of recuperative power; while, to the other, defeat would be absolute ruin. The defeat of the American squadron at Manila, May 1, 1898, would have been a disaster, the effect of which it would be difficult to compute. Failure to gain a decisive victory, even, would have been almost as fatal as actual defeat, for Admiral Dewey had no base to fall back upon, no *point d'appui*. The risks taken were enormous, but fully justified by the event.

The triumph of strategy is complete when the commander of one of two originally equal forces succeeds by the combinations of the campaign in bringing his adversary's fleet into a position where the chances of victory are greatly against it, and where defeat will entail disasters beyond the mere loss of the battle. Had the Spanish squadron under Cervera, on first reaching the West Indies, fallen in with a small portion of the American forces in those waters, the defeat of the latter would have been of comparatively minor importance, whereas the defeat of the Spaniards would have resulted, as it actually did, in ruin so complete and results so far-reaching as to practically end the war.

It may, and sometimes does, happen that the results of a campaign depend more upon strategy than upon tactics, more upon movements than upon victories gained in battle. From the French army of the Danube the left wing of General Kray[37] marched rapidly through

---

[35] Adam Smith, *An Inquiry into the Nature and Causes of the Wealth of Nations.* Book V, chap. I, pt. I.

[36] Gen. Sir Edward Bruce Hamley (1824-1893). See his *The Operations of War Explained and Illustrated* (London: William Blackwood, 1878), pp. 59-62.

[37] Field Marshal Freiherr Paul Kray von Krajova (1735-1804) commanded Austrian troops in Italy, and later on the Rhine, in the Napoleonic Wars. In 1800 he was defeated at Biberach and Misserkirch and then driven to Ulm. By a skillful march around the flank of the French Army, Kray's army escaped into Bohemia.

Switzerland to the right extremity of the Austrian line and by that movement alone conquered all the country between the Rhine and the Danube without pulling a trigger. In 1805 the army of Mack[38] was completely paralysed and the main body forced to surrender at Ulm without a single important battle. In 1898 Spain ordered Admiral Camara[39] with a squadron to proceed to the Philippines to retrieve the loss of Montojo's[40] command and regain Manila. He got as far as the Suez Canal, when the squadron under Rear-Admiral Watson[41] threatened, through the press of the country, the coasts of Spain. The news of this projected movement caused the immediate recall of Camara. (It was a well-known practice of Napoleon to contrive to have his emissaries, carrying important dispatches, captured by the enemy. These dispatches were so artfully worded as to completely deceive the enemy. This led to the suggestion that there should be in our Navy Department a Bureau of Misinformation.)

It is one of the oft-quoted sayings of Napoleon that to acquire the secret of the art of war one must read, again and again, the campaigns of the great captains. "Model yourself upon them," he said. But of strategy he has assured us that there is only one means of mastering it, and that is by incessant study and exhaustive thought. And Nelson's legacy to us, observes a recent English writer, is that "strategy and tactical study is that which above all things a naval officer should occupy himself with."[42]

Of all the great games of war of modern times, the one possessed of most interest to the naval student is that in which the British Admiralty was pitted against one of the greatest masters of the art of war of all times—Napoleon. The stake played for was nothing less than an empire. Great Britain, including her entire colonial system, was the prize. It was a struggle against sea-power by the first captain of the age, and sea-power prevailed. The theatre of the war embraced practically the four quarters of the globe.

The story of Trafalgar has been so admirably well told in a course of lectures delivered at the Naval War College, and now to be found, under

---

[38] Lieutenant Field Marshal Freiherr Karl Mack von Leibrich (1752-1828) was Quartermaster General of the Austrian Army. He was the responsible commander of the army which opposed Napoleon in Bavaria.

[39] Rear Adm. Manuel de la Camara commanded the Spanish reserve squadron which was to have sailed from Spain through Suez and the Red Sea for the Pacific to relieve Montojo.

[40] Rear Adm. Don Patricio Montojo y Pasaron (1839-1917) commanded Spanish naval forces in the Philippines against Dewey.

[41] Rear Adm. John Crittenden Watson (1842-1923). As a commodore, Watson had command of the North Cuban Blockading Squadron in May and June 1898 under Rear Adm. W.T. Sampson. From June to September 1898 he commanded the "Eastern Squadron" which was organized and ready to be dispatched to the Spanish coast. Its purpose was to force the recall of Camara's reserve squadron and prevent the reinforcement of Montojo's fleet in the Philippines.

[42] The source of this quotation has not been identified; however, it is the thrust of J.K. Laughton's comments in his articles, "The Scientific Study of Naval Warfare" and the "Last Great Naval War."

the title of Sea Power,[43] in every library, as to leave little to be said save in the way of drawing from it lessons for our instruction.

"Let us be masters of the English Channel for six hours," said Napoleon, "and we shall be masters of the world!"[44] That was the war problem he undertook to solve. But the British Admiralty understood the game better than its opponent, and Napoleon lost. The first object of Napoleon was to lure away the English fleet in order to get control of the Channel. With that view the French fleet, under Villeneuve, was sent to the West Indies to threaten the English possessions in that quarter. Nelson followed in pursuit. On June 4, 1805, the hostile fleets were about 100 miles apart, Nelson with 12 ships of the line at Barbadoes, Villeneuve at Martinique with 20.

June 12, Nelson, then off Antigua, feeling convinced that the French fleet had sailed for Europe, hurried off the brig *Curieux*, Captain Bettesworth,[45] with dispatches to the Admiralty conveying the intelligence that Villeneuve had left the West Indies but that his destination could only be surmised. Captain Bettesworth was to deliver the dispatches in person. Carrying a heavy press of sail, the *Curieux* reached Plymouth July 7. Captain Bettesworth posted to London, where he arrived at 11 o'clock on the night of the 8th. The First Lord of the Admiralty, Admiral Lord Barham,[46] having gone to bed, Nelson's dispatches were not given him till early next morning. He exclaimed angrily, on receiving them, of the loss of so many precious hours. Without waiting to dress, he at once dictated orders, with which, by 9 a.m. of the 9th, Admiralty messengers were hurrying to Plymouth and to Portsmouth.

Cornwallis was directed to raise the blockade at Rochefort, sending 5 ships to Sir Robert Calder,[47] who was then watching off Ferrol with 10. The latter was ordered, with the 15 ships thus united under his command, to cruise 100 miles west of Cape Finisterre to intercept Villeneuve and prevent his junction with the Ferrol squadron. Cornwallis received his orders on the 11th, and on the 15th, eight days after the *Curieux* anchored in Plymouth Sound, the Rochefort ships joined Calder. The latter at once proceeded to the post assigned him. On the 22d the sudden lifting of a dense fog revealed to each other the hostile forces of Calder and Villeneuve, the British 15 sail of the line, the Allies 20. This was one of the most dramatic scenes of the whole campaign. Was it mere chance that brought these two opposing forces to confront

---

[43] A.T. Mahan, *The Influence of Sea Power upon the French Revolution and Empire* (Boston: Little, Brown, 1893), 2 vols.

[44] *Ibid.*, vol. II, p. 130.

[45] Capt. George Edmund Byron Bettesworth (1780-1808) was given a post captain's commission by the First Lord of the Admiralty for delivering the dispatches. Three years later, at age 28, he was killed while in command of the frigate H.M.S. *Tartar* during action with a schooner and five gunboats near Bergen.

[46] Admiral of the Red Charles Barham, first Baron Barham (1726-1813).

[47] Admiral of the White Sir Robert Calder (1745-1818).

each other at that particular time and place? Was it not rather a fine exhibition of skill of two accomplished strategists?

"It is difficult," observes the author, "to praise too highly the prompt and decisive step taken by Admiral Lord Barham when so suddenly confronted with the dilemma of either raising the blockade off Rochefort and Ferrol or permitting Villeneuve to proceed unmolested to his destination, whatever that might be. To act instantly and rightly in so distressing a perplexity, to be able unhesitatingly to make a sacrifice of advantages, long and justly cherished, in order to strike at once one of the two converging detachments of an enemy, shows generalship of a high order."[48]

Napoleon, himself, was entirely misled by Lord Barham's prompt measures, whose rapidity even he could not have surpassed. "The *Curieux*," he said, "only reached England on the 9th, and the Admiralty could not decide on the movement of its squadrons in 24 hours."

Charles Middleton, Admiral Lord Barham, was at this time 80 years old, too old, some English writers maintain, to be at the head of the Admiralty during a time of war or even in peace. He had been but two months in office. His prompt action on the morning of the 7th, they say, was simply the carrying out of plans already matured by the Board of Admiralty. However that may be, the plans were well conceived by somebody in the Admiralty, be the credit for them whose it may, and the strategic combinations were identical with those laid down by the best military authorities.

The rest of the story, omitting details, is soon told. Sir Robert Calder was unequal to the task imposed upon him. After an indecisive action the two fleets separated. Villeneuve was enabled to reach Vigo on the 28th of July; few days later, favored by the wind, he reached Coruña (August 1) and effected the junction with the allied forces in the harbor of Ferrol, which it had been the very object of the English Admiralty to prevent. On learning (August 13) that Villeneuve had reached Coruña, Napoleon wrote to his Minister of Marine. "If with thirty ships my admirals fear twenty-four British, we may as well give up all hope of a navy." No more forcible illustration could be given to show that *numbers* do not mean efficiency. It is not an uncommon cry with us to-day: "Give us more ships, for we *must* have an efficient navy." *Numbers do not constitute efficiency.* The fighting qualities of the Spaniards none can dispute. And yet Napoleon reckoned one French ship of the line as equal to two of the Spanish; it was simply a question of the relative efficiency of the two navies.

Calder now joined Cornwallis[49] off Brest, raising, with some of Nelson's ships, that force to 34 ships of the line, all admirably disciplined. The Allies had in Brest 21 ships, in Ferrol 29, neither of which was equal in number, still less in quality, to those under Cornwallis. The naval situation, continues the author, was now

---

[48] Mahan, *French Revolution*, vol. II, p. 169.

[49] Admiral Sir William Cornwallis, brother of Lord Cornwallis who surrendered at Yorktown in 1781. [Luce's footnote.]

comparatively simple. Cornwallis was superior to either of the enemy's detachments, and he held the interior position. In case Villeneuve approached, it was scarcely possible that the two hostile fleets, dependent upon the wind, which, if fair for one, would be foul for the other, could unite before he could crush one of them. It was equally improbable that, with all their lookout frigates, or, as we now call them, scouts, Villeneuve could elude the British fleet and gain so far the start of it as to cover the straits of Dover during the time required by Napoleon.

"In his concentrated force, therefore," continues the author, "and his interior position, Cornwallis controlled the issue."[50] But to borrow General Sherman's form of expression, he acted "in violation of the lessons of war as taught by the great masters." He threw away his great advantage. On learning that Villeneuve had put to sea with 27 or 28 ships of the line, he at once dispatched Sir Robert Calder towards Ferrol with 18 sail, keeping 16 for himself. This separation of the two parts of his fleet, says the author, is condemned by the simplest and most generally accepted principles of warfare. It transferred to Villeneuve all the advantage of central position and superior force and was stigmatized by Napoleon himself as a glaring blunder. So much for not knowing one's business!

"While the British squadrons were concentrating in the Bay of Biscay, and the diligence of Nelson was bringing the Mediterranean ships to the critical center of action, Napoleon, from the heights overlooking Boulogne, was eagerly awaiting news from Villeneuve, from whose skill, zeal and courage everything was to be hoped."[51] He leaned upon a broken reed. Villeneuve's heart failed him. Instead of making for the Straits of Dover he steered for Cadiz!—and the game was practically up.[52]

The sudden collapse of all of Napoleon's long and carefully thought-out plans of invasion calls to mind another occasion, when a thoroughly efficient but comparatively small fleet turned back what promised to be a tidal wave of subjugation of a free people:

> A king sate on the rocky brow
> Which looks o'er sea-born Salamis;
> And ships, by thousands, lay below,
> And men in nations;—all were his!
> He counted them at break of day—
> And when the sun set, where were they?[53]

Let us now go back and ask who it was that directed all these great movements of the English fleets? For even Nelson himself, with all his genius for war, was but a single factor in the hands of the supreme

---

[50] Mahan, *French Revolution*, vol. II, p. 176.

[51] Luce identifies his source here as simply "Mahan." The sentences in quotation marks are a paraphrase of Mahan, *French Revolution*, vol. II, p. 173.

[52] At this point the close similarity of the text to the 1902 lecture ends. Luce wrote the remainder of the article for the published version in 1909.

[53] George Gordon Noel Byron, sixth Baron Byron (1788-1824), *Don Juan*, LXXXVI, 4.

directorate of the various strategic movements. It matters not whether the master mind was Lord Barham's or that of his staff. For our purpose it was the British Admiralty. And therein lies the question for our navy to consider—the creation of a directive agency to project strategic movements covering the entire theatre of war, embracing, it may be, the four quarters of the globe. The study of naval battle tactics is eminently proper—say rather, indispensable; but it is, after all, providing for contingencies more or less remote; while the creation of an intelligent directive force that can, during peace, foresee and provide for the contingencies of war, and efficiently direct the operations of the fleet when war does come, is a practical question of the present.

To avoid the possibility of misapprehension it is proper to state, in this connection, that our form of government, and the genius of our people, demand that the Secretary of the United States Navy must, and always should be, a civilian, selected by the President with a special view to his fitness for the office. Our insistence is, that the civilian who occupies this high and responsible position shall have at his elbow, at all times, able and responsible advisers on all questions relating to war and to the preparation for war. He should be furnished, by law, with a Board of Directors, by what name soever it may be called.

Having defined strategy as it is applied to military and naval operations, and shown by ample illustrations what a prime factor it is in war, let us now proceed to inquire how the United States manages such matters. The head of our Admiralty[54] has put it on record that for the first *seven months* of the Civil War, "but for some redeeming naval successes at Hatteras and Port Royal, S.C., ... the whole belligerent operations would have been *pronounced weak and imbecile failures.*" *Per contra*, the Prussian campaign of 1866, during which the naval battle of Lissa[55] was fought, lasted *but seven weeks*, resulting in the consolidation of the German Empire!

In regard to one of the greatest strategic movements of the Civil War, the capture of New Orleans and the control of the Mississippi river, the head of our Admiralty wrote: "In general and desultory conversation with military and naval men and others, the passage of the forts and the capture of New Orleans was spoken of as desirable, but not a practicable undertaking." The views of the Department on the subject were "speculative and uncertain."[56] The movement which led to the

---

[54] Gideon Welles (1802-1878), Secretary of the Navy 1861-69. See John Niven, *Gideon Welles* (New York: Oxford University Press, 1973).

[55] Luce is referring to the second Battle of Lissa which was fought during the Austro-Prussian War between Italian and Austrian squadrons off the Dalmatian island of Lissa in the Adriatic on 20 July 1866. The Italians were defeated in this, the first battle fought at sea by fleets of modern ironclad warships. The first Battle of Lissa was fought between the British and a Franco-Venetian squadron, 13 March 1811.

[56] Gideon Welles, "Admiral Farragut and New Orleans, with an Account of the Origin and Command of the First Three Naval Expeditions of the War," *The Galaxy*, vol. XII, Nos. 11-12, November-December 1871. This article has been reprinted in Albert Mordell, comp., *Civil War and Reconstruction: Selected Essays by Gideon Welles* (New York: Twayne, 1959), pp. 129-30.

capture of New Orleans and the ultimate control of the Mississippi was the result of fortuitous circumstances, and the active part taken by parties not connected with the Navy Department. The latter heartily cooperated in the movement, it is true; it simply did not take the initiative, as it should have done, and would have done had the Secretary of the Navy enjoyed the advantages of presiding over a Board of Directors, and listening to the counsel of expert advisers. It is submitted to an intelligent, patriotic and practical people if that is the way to carry on naval operations in war—by "desultory conversations of a civilian with military and naval men"? An endeavor has been made to show that war is, in one sense, a science, to master which requires profound study. In another sense it is an art, to become an adept in which a man must devote all the faculties with which nature has endowed him. To assign to the control of the Admiralty, with all its vast responsibilities, a civilian, however eminent, without a staff of naval experts, is only to imperil the highest interests of the country, to sacrifice precious lives, to waste munitions of war, and place the civilian head of the navy in an utterly false position. That is what was done in the Civil War and repeated up to a certain point in the Spanish War. In respect to naval affairs Americans seem incapable of profiting by their own mistakes in war.

A generation after the Civil War came the war with Spain, only to find our Admiralty as incompetent as ever. The battleship *Maine* was destroyed in the harbor of Havana, February 15, 1898. Ten days later (February 25) the Assistant Secretary of the Navy telegraphed to Commodore Dewey at Honkong: [sic]

> Secret and confidential. Order Squadron, except *Monocacy*, to Hongkong. Keep full of coal. In the event of declaration of war [with] Spain, your duty will be to see that the Spanish Squadron does not leave the Asiatic Coast, and then [begin] offensive operations in Philippine Islands. Keep Olympia[57] until further orders.
>
> (Signed) ROOSEVELT.

From the date of the Assistant Secretary's dispatch, February 25, to the actual breaking out of the war, April 21—nearly two months—much precious time was lost in preparing for hostilities.[58] Three days later, April 24, came the dispatch from Commodore Dewey which ran as follows:

> Hongkong, April 25, 1898. Secretary of the Navy, Washington. In accordance with the request of the Governor of Hongkong, the Squadron leaves to-day for Mirs Bay, China, to await telegraphic instructions. Address, Hongkong. I will communicate by tug.
>
> (Signed) DEWEY.

---

[57] The cruiser *Olympia* had been ordered home. From this time on all the dispatches sent out from the Navy Department indicate that the Government fully anticipated a war with Spain. [Luce's footnote.]

[58] For additional information on the preparation for and details of the Battle of Manila see Nathan Sargent, *Admiral Dewey and the Manila Campaign* (Washington: Naval Historical Foundation, 1947), and U.S. Navy Dept., *Annual Reports of the Navy Department for the Year 1898* (Washington: U.S. Govt. Print. Off., 1898), vol. II,

142

One would have supposed that with all our experience during the four years of the Civil War prompt measures would have been taken to meet the crisis which everybody saw was at hand; and that Commodore Dewey would not have been left so long in suspense and finally placed in the humiliating position of being requested to leave Hongkong. Such, unfortunately, was not the case.

The dispatch to Commodore Dewey from the Assistant Secretary of the Navy, who seems to have been the only one of the administration to comprehend the necessity of action, was dated February 25, 1898. The dispatch from Commodore Dewey announcing the action of the Governor of Hongkong was dated April 25, an interval of sixty days. Now it required but 54 days for the powerful monitor, *Monterey*, and the collier, *Brutus*, to go from San Francisco to Manila. Had those vessels been ordered to join Commodore Dewey at the date of the dispatch of the Assistant Secretary of the Navy, they would have reached their destination in time, if not to take part in the action of May 1, they would have at least exercised a wholesome moral effect on natives and foreigners alike, and would have relieved Commodore Dewey of all cause of anxiety. As a matter of fact the *Monterey* did not leave San Francisco till *41 days after the battle of Manila!* The excuse is that the monitor was not ready for sea. Of course she was not: How could she be ready? The Commandant of the Mare Island Navy Yard, California, where she then was, could not fit her out for sea without orders from headquarters, and there was no one at headquarters upon whom that duty devolved. The civilian Secretary of the Navy knew absolutely nothing about such things, and his advisers, the several Chiefs of Bureaus, foreseeing that war was imminent, were fully taken up with matters pertaining to their respective bureaus which had to do with other matters. The Chief of the Bureau of Navigation, who has a quasi-military character, in default of a special office for the direction of military operations, was already overloaded with the details of his own bureau. The Naval War Board did not come into existence till May 2, the day after the battle of Manila.

The dispatch from Commodore Dewey of April 25 informing the Secretary of the Navy that he had been "requested" to leave Hongkong was received at the Navy Department on Sunday morning. The Department was practically deserted. But the Bureau of Navigation was never closed, during the war. The dispatch was received by Lieut. H.H. Whittlesey, U.S.N.,[59] then on duty in the Bureau. Lieut. Whittlesey took it at once to the house of Captain Crowninshield,[60] the Chief of the Bureau of Navigation. Captain, the late Rear-Admiral, Crowninshield,

---

Appendix to the *Report of the Bureau of Navigation*. [Documents relating to the operations of the war with Spain.]

[59] Lt. Comdr. Humes Houston Whittlesey (1861-1943) was a graduate of the U.S. Naval Academy in 1884. He retired from the Navy as a lieutenant commander in 1905.

[60] Rear Adm. Arent Schuyler Crowninshield (1843-1908) served as Chief of the Bureau of Navigation from 1897 to 1901.

under date of July 9, 1901,[61] gave out the following very interesting account of the dictating by President McKinley of the now "famous dispatch" to Admiral Dewey. This account, we may premise, is now of no little historic value as an incident of our naval annals:

> On Sunday, April 24, 1898, Lieutenant H.H. Whittlesey called at my home with a despatch from Admiral Dewey, stating that the Governor of Hongkong had notified him that he must leave that port with the force under his command within forty-eight hours.
>
> Deeming it of the greatest importance that a reply should be sent as soon as possible to Admiral Dewey, I took the despatch to the White House and laid it before the President. The President directed me to go and find Mr. Long,[62] the Secretary of the Navy, and Judge Day,[63] the Secretary of State, and bring them to the White House. Upon returning to the White House, I was shown to the western end of the upper corridor, where the President was sitting with the following persons: Secretary Day, Attorney-General Griggs,[64] Senator Hale[65] and one other, possibly Secretary Bliss,[66] though I am not sure. The late Senator Davis[67] joined the party later.
>
> A discussion of the despatch from Admiral Dewey and the reply which should be sent to him was taking place when I arrived, in which I took part for several minutes. The President then turned to Attorney-General Griggs and said: "Griggs, you write a despatch for Dewey to proceed to Manila and attack the Spanish naval force assembled there," whereupon Attorney-General Griggs turned to me and said: "Captain, you know how to write that better than I do; you go and write it. You will find some blanks in the Cabinet room."
>
> I at once proceeded to the Cabinet room and wrote the despatch. Returning to the Presidential party I handed the despatch I had prepared to Attorney-General Griggs, who said it was satisfactory and handed it to the President, who read it aloud.
>
> The only change that was made in the despatch as I wrote it was the addition of either the word "capture" or the word "destroy." The despatch as originally written by me contained but one of these words, but which one I do not recall.

---

[61] The Secretary of the Navy, John D. Long, addressed the Massachusetts Club at Nantasket, Mass., on 2 July 1901. His remarks were published in the local papers and read by A.S. Crowninshield at his home in Peabody, Mass. The following day, 3 July 1901, the admiral wrote Long correcting him and pointing out that he, Crowninshield, was the author of the telegram to Dewey. This letter from which Luce took the quotation and other correspondence relating to this incident was published in the *Papers of John Davis Long* (Boston: Massachusetts Historical Society Collections. 1939), vol. LXXVIII, pp. 379-82, 387.

[62] John Davis Long (1838-1915) was a Governor of Massachusetts, Congressman, and Secretary of the Navy, 1897-1902.

[63] William Rufus Day (1849-1923) was Assistant Secretary of State in 1898-99 and later an Associate Justice of the Supreme Court.

[64] John William Griggs (1849-1927), Attorney General, 1898-1901; member of the Permanent Court of Arbitration at the Hague, 1901-12; president of the Marconi Wireless Telegraph Company.

[65] Eugene Hale (1836-1918), U.S. Senator from Maine, 1881-1911. Hale was a prominent supporter of the Navy in the Senate.

[66] Cornelius Newton Bliss (1833-1911), Secretary of the Interior, 1896-98. Bliss was offered the Vice Presidency by McKinley in 1900, but he declined it in order to continue his career in textile manufacturing.

[67] Cushman Kellogg Davis (1838-1900), lawyer; Governor of Minnesota, 1873-75; U.S. Senator from Minnesota, 1887-1900. An outspoken expansionist, Davis served on the Senate Foreign Relations Committee from 1891 until his death.

I then went over to the Navy Department, handed the despatch to Lieutenant Whittlesey and directed him to go ahead and put it into cipher. Lieutenant Whittlesey reported to me the same evening that the Secretary had signed the despatch and that it had been sent.

The experiment that had failed lamentably in 1862 was tried again in 1898. During the first three years of the Civil War, as already related, the President had exercised his military functions as constitutional commander-in-chief, with what unfortunate results we have seen. The President was now to try it again in the war with Spain with no better success. As early as March 9, Congress voted $50,000,000 for national defense; and Admiral Dewey testified before the Senate Committee, June 26, 1902, that war with Spain was regarded out there (China) as certain as early as April 1, and that if he had had timely reenforcements the insurrection which cost so many precious lives would have been averted.[68]

It is a fatal mistake to adapt the amenities of peace to the prosecution of war. "If there be any truth established by the universal experience of nations, it is this, that to carry the spirit of peace into war is a weak and cruel policy. The time of negotiation is the time for deliberation and delay. But when an extreme case calls for that remedy which is, in its own nature, most violent and which, in such cases, is a remedy only because it is violent, it is idle to think of mitigating and diluting."[69]

The Naval War Board came into existence not a day too soon. It stood for a Naval Staff, and was successful in pulling the Department through the war. The Secretary of the Navy of that day pays it the following well merited compliment: "The Board [Naval War Board] possessed high intelligence and excellent judgment and its service was invaluable in connection with the successful conduct of the war."[70] And yet it was summarily dissolved at the close of the war! Its great value as a permanent office was not understood.

The Naval War Board had to do with the very questions of naval strategy, the subject of which we have been dealing. Some of the most important strategic measures are those adopted during peace—adopted perhaps many years in advance of even the prospect of hostilities. The British Admiralty has matured plans for the construction of a large dockyard, comprising about fifty-two acres, at Rosyth, on the north side of the Firth of Forth. It will become in no great while one of the most important naval stations in the kingdom. As a strategic point it will furnish a base for naval operations in the North Sea, should the tide of war ever tend in that direction.

It may readily be seen, from what has gone before, that by the timely occupation and security, during peace, of an important strategic

---

[68] See U.S. Congress, Senate Committee on the Philippines, *Affairs in the Philippine Islands,* Hearing before committee, 31 January-28 June 1902, Senate Doc. 331, 55th Congress, 1st sess., 1902.

[69] The source of this quotation has not been identified.

[70] John D. Long, *The New American Navy* (New York: Outlook, 1903), vol. I, p. 163.

point, a war may be averted. It is that consideration that makes a Naval Staff an indispensable part of an enlightened system of naval administration, not less in peace than in war. Pearl Harbor, Hawaii, is another illustration of the wisdom of securing during peace an important strategic point. The value from a military point of view of a naval base in those islands can scarcely be exaggerated. The navy is indebted for this great acquisition to the happy accident of a gentleman, in no way connected with the executive branch of the government, visiting Hawaii not long since.[71] Becoming convinced, from personal observation, of the manifold advantages of Pearl Harbor for naval and military purposes, he resolved that active measures for the establishment there of a naval base should no longer be delayed.

In 1893, while Captain A.T. Mahan, the President of the Naval War College, was still engaged in his studies and resultant lectures on naval strategy, there appeared in the *Forum* of March of that year an article from his pen entitled "Hawaii and our Future Sea Power."[72] This article attracted just enough attention, at the time, to cause the author to be summarily detached from the War College and sent to sea, the administration of that day not being in favor of the taking over of the Hawaiian group. But the cogent arguments advanced by the eminent author, showing the great advantages, from a strategic point of view, of the possession of those islands, served to crystallize current thought of the past sixty years on the subject, and matters finally began to take definite shape. On the 6th of April last, bill H.R. 20308 to establish a naval station at Pearl Harbor, Hawaii, being under discussion in the House, there were disclosed some interesting facts in connection with our methods of conducting the affairs of the navy.[73] For whereas the naval station at Rosyth was established by the English Admiralty, the naval station at Pearl Harbor was established by Congress on its own initiative.

In the hearing before the Naval Committee of the House, January 29, 1908, on the subject of Pearl Harbor, one of the delegates from Hawaii[74] said: "The importance of Pearl Harbor as a naval and military base has been repeatedly urged by men able and experienced in military and naval science, among them Captain A.T. Mahan, who pointed out with unanswerable arguments the commanding importance of Pearl

---

[71] Luce may be referring to the railroad promoter and sugar plantation promoter, Benjamin Franklin Dillingham (1844-?) whose firm eventually received the contract for dredging and drydock construction at Pearl Harbor.

[72] A.T. Mahan, "Hawaii and our Future Sea Power," *Forum*, vol. XV, March 1893, pp. 1-11. The article was included as chapter One in *The Interest of America in Sea Power, Present and Future* (Boston: Little, Brown, 1897).

[73] See *Congressional Record*, 6 April 1908, pp. 4562-63. [Luce's footnote.]

[74] Jonah Kuhio Kalanianaole (1871-1921) was a Prince of the Kingdom of Hawaii and a cousin of Queen Liliuokalani. He served as a Delegate to the U.S. Congress from 1903 to 1921. See A.L. Bates, "Report from the Committee on Naval Affairs Favoring H. 18120 to Establish a Naval Station at Pearl Harbor, Hawaii," 2 March 1908, House Report 1132, 60th Congress, 1st sess., serial 5225; and "Report ... Favoring H. 20308 ... " House Report 1385, 60th Congress, 1st sess., serial 5226.

146

Harbor as the key to the Pacific." The Hon. A.L. Bates,[75] having in charge the bill for the "establishment of a naval base at Pearl Harbor," in his report, March 2, 1908, quotes the opinions of Captain Mahan as to its great importance from a naval and military point of view. And Senator George C. Perkins,[76] member of the Naval Committee of the Senate, in a powerful plea for the establishment of a naval base at Hawaii, states that "in 1893 our greatest authority on sea power and naval strategy, Captain A.T. Mahan, wrote with reference to the proposed annexation of Hawaii," etc. The Senator then quotes from the *Forum* article of March, 1893, in which the strategic importance of the islands is fully set forth.

We put it fairly and squarely to the naval profession and to the public generally, if the operations of war, involving naval strategy, as we have endeavored to define and illustrate it, can be successfully conducted save by a directorate composed in part, at least, of those who have made the study of the Science and Art of War their chief occupation?[77]

---

[75] Arthur Laban Bates (1859-1934) was a member of the House Naval Affairs Committee who introduced the bill which made Pearl Harbor a naval base. He was Congressman from the 25th Pennsylvania District from 1901 to 1913.

[76] George Clement Perkins (1839-1923), shipowner, banker, Governor of California, 1880-83; U.S. Senator from California, 1893-1915; Chairman of the Senate Committee on Naval Affairs, 1909-13.

[77] Perhaps Luce meant to say here: "We put it fairly and squarely to the naval profession and to the public generally, that the operations of war, involving naval strategy, as we have endeavored to define and illustrate it, cannot be successfully conducted save by a directorate composed in part, at least, of those who have made the study of the Science and Art of War their chief occupation."

CHAPTER VIII

NAVAL BASES: THE NAVY AND ITS NEEDS

By Rear Admiral S.B. Luce, U.S.N.

Editors' Introduction

Even at the age of 83, Luce still had much to teach the Navy. The perspective which he had gained in six decades of naval service, along with his broad vision, allowed him to gage dispassionately the growth of the Navy into a properly functioning organization. He saw clearly that the ideas which he had advocated in the past had not been fully appreciated. There were many in the service and in Congress who failed to understand, in broad terms, the meaning of a navy. As the battleship building race in Germany and Britain caught the attention of his contemporaries, he could see that many still focused solely on the instruments of iron and steel, the details of battleships, and the size of guns. They seemed unable or unwilling to grasp the intricate interrelationship between administration and strategy, between ships and men, between fleets and bases.

In one of his last major lectures at the Naval War College, "A Short Study in Naval Strategy," Luce turned directly to the problem of naval bases. Speaking before the Naval and Military Conference on 27 August 1910, he pointed out that the U.S. Navy had made considerable improvement since 1881. It had a fleet, its administration had been bettered, but the subject of bases still had not become prominent. Little attention was being given to the new requirement for base development for the "new Navy." Few had bothered to consider bases in terms of their strategic as well as their technical significance. In order to bring this issue clearly to the forefront, Luce delivered his lecture at the Naval War College, and then submitted it for publication in the *North American Review*.[1]

As he had done so many times before, Luce extensively revised his work before it appeared in print. In his original lecture[2] he

---

[1] "The Navy and Its Needs," *North American Review*, vol. CXCIII, No. 665, April 1911, pp. 494-507.

[2] "A Short Study in Naval Strategy," Lecture Collection, 1910, Naval Historical Collection, Naval War College.

devoted several pages to the sudden rise of Germany as a naval power. He noted the influence of Mahan on Kaiser Wilhelm, and he went on to speculate.

> If it should so happen that Germany should seize the island of Jamaica what would be the course of the United States? We know that many Germans regretted that at the termination of hostilities of the Franco-German War they had not exacted in part payment the ceding of the island of Martinique, for Germany has long wanted a naval base in the West Indies. Does all this explain the reason for the Canadian Navy?[3] England could be starved into submission in a week were it not for her fleet.

As interesting as such comments are to us today, Luce took them out of the published version of his lecture. He wanted to focus directly on the issue of bases, so he removed most of the peripheral comments from his lecture. He retained, however, the part which promoted Narragansett Bay, R.I., as the best site for a naval base on the eastern seaboard. Luce had first become attracted to this area in 1862 while assigned to the Naval Academy which had been temporarily located in Newport during the Civil War. He strongly supported the effort to permanently locate the school there instead of returning it to Annapolis after the war. In the 1880's he located the Training Squadron in Narragansett Bay, and in 1884 his report to the Secretary of the Navy specifically placed the location of the proposed Naval War College on Coasters Harbor Island. Luce lived out the remainder of his life in Newport, on the shore of Narragansett Bay.

This essay appeared in the April issue of the *North American Review*, which also featured a biographical sketch of the author. A few days after its appearance, Capt. Bradley Fiske, then a member of the General Board, wrote Luce:

> I have read your article in the *North American* very carefully, and I think it is very, very good. Admiral Dewey spoke of it to me this morning, and asked if I had read it, adding "it is a splendid article."
>
> I don't know when we are going to get any money for bases. Congress has been educated up to a dim appreciation of a battleship—but no further; except that some of them appreciate submarines a little too much.[4]

---

[3] The Canadian Navy was established by the "Naval Service Act," 9-10 Edward VII, ch. 43. Assented to 4 May 1910.

[4] B.A. Fiske to Luce, 12 April 1911, Luce Papers, LC.

Naval War College and Narragansett Bay, *ca.* 1916. This photograph illustrates Luce's dream for Narragansett: A major fleet base crowned by the navy's highest educational institution.

Luce published this article precisely for the purpose of educating the general public and their representatives in Congress in the importance of the Navy's need for something more than ships alone.

History furnishes some notable examples of the degeneration of navies after a great war. It is the natural result of action and reaction. Such was the experience of the United States Navy following the Civil War. For twenty years after the close of that war the United States had dropped out of the list of naval powers.

In undertaking the building up of the "new navy,"[5] as it has been called with questionable propriety, there are certain well-established facts that must be taken into account. First of all, we are, as a people, averse to "entangling alliances." We abjure the use of force. We "seek peace and ensue it." The genius of our people lies in the direction of trade, commerce, the industries and the development of the vast resources of the country. We have no known enemies. Our only fear, and that a remote one, is in being drawn into the quarrels of others.

President Taft[6] well expressed the feeling of our people when he declared recently that all international disputes should be settled by arbitration. But while awaiting the establishment of the International Court of Arbitral Justice, so earnestly advocated by Mr. Root,[7] when Secretary of State, every American must subscribe to the sound views of Mr. Roosevelt as expressed in his address before the Nobel Prize Commission—to wit: *"Each nation must keep well prepared to defend itself until the establishment of some form of international police power competent and willing to prevent violence as between nations."*[8] That our development as a naval power is to proceed on those lines—the prevention of hostilities by preparation for them—has already been declared by Congress through its building programme of two first-class battleships a year and by its liberal appropriations for the maintenance of the naval establishment. Such being the naval policy of Congress, it is

---

[5] "The Forty-seventh Congress during its sessions of 1881-82 and 1882-83 authorized the construction of three steel cruisers and one steel despatchboat. These ships were the nucleus of the New American Navy, the development of which, in peace, has potently aided the upbuilding of numerous industries of the nation and the achievements of which in war rival in glory and results those for which the Old Navy is justly famous." John D. Long, *The New American Navy*, vol. 1, p. 1. [This is Luce's footnote.]

[6] William Howard Taft (1857-1930) succeeded Roosevelt as President and served from 1909 to 1913. After serving as Kent Professor of Constitutional Law in Yale University from 1913 to 1921, he was appointed Chief Justice of the Supreme Court.

[7] Elihu Root (1845-1937) was Secretary of War, 1899-1903; Secretary of State, 1905-1909; U.S. Senator from New York, 1909-15. He was awarded the Nobel Peace Prize in 1912.

[8] Roosevelt's mediation of the Russo-Japanese War of 1904 won him the Nobel Peace Prize. He addressed the prize committee at Christiana (now Oslo), Norway, on 5 May 1910. See Herman Hagedorn, ed., *The Works of Theodore Roosevelt* (New York: Scribner, 1925), vol. XVIII, pp. 410-15.

in order to examine into the constituents of a navy to the end that a healthy, all-round growth may be assured.

With the regeneration of the United States Navy in 1881 there arose the necessity for the adoption of three measures of the highest importance—namely:

1. The placing of the administration of the affairs of the navy on a war footing.
2. The creation of a fleet.
3. The establishment of naval bases.

The first measure is in a fair way of accomplishment. The second, a fleet, is an accomplished fact, leaving only the third measure to be considered.

In the building up of a navy the public mind seems to be centred on ships alone. Tables are published from time to time showing the comparative strength of navies as measured by the number of battleships of each country, together with their tonnage and gun power. Engrossed by the continued development of the battleship, we overlook the important fact that there should be maintained a fixed ratio between tonnage and personnel. With the increase of number and size of battleships, moreover, comes the increased demand for the means of taking proper care of them, which necessitates ample docking facilities and repair-shops. Keeping the under body of a battleship clean enables her to maintain her normal speed (her cruising radius) without an undue expenditure of coal (or oil), a very important factor during hostilities. A battleship should be docked for cleaning at least once every six months.

But the very important item in the process of naval development is the establishment of naval bases. A base, in a military sense, is simply a basis of operations or a point from which supplies may be drawn.[9] A naval base means that and much more.

The term "naval base," it may be observed, is new to our naval vocabulary. Naval students knew of such things only through reading of them. For, having no fleet, naval bases did not enter as a factor into our naval life. Our first ships after the termination of the Revolutionary War—those built during the latter part of the eighteenth century—were set up, some of them at least, in private shipyards which were conveniently located for the purpose. These were utilized by the Secretary of the Navy and their purchase was subsequently authorized by Congress. Such was the shipyard owned by John Jackson. It was situated on or near a mud flat on Wallabout Bay, Brooklyn, New York. It was here that the "Adams," a small twenty-eight-gun frigate, was

---

[9]"The first point in a plan of operations is to be assured of a good base; this name is applied to the extent of the frontiers of a state from whence an army will draw its resources and reinforcements; that from whence it will have to depart for an offensive expedition and where it will find a refuge in time of need." [This is Luce's footnote. The quotation is from Baron de Jomini, *Summary of the Art of War or a New Analytical Compend of the Principles of Strategy, Grand Tactics, and of Military Policy* (New York: Putnam, 1854), art. XVIII, pp. 88-89. This translation was by Maj. O.F. Winship and Lt. E.E. McLean of the U.S. Army.]

built for the Government by Jackson[10] in 1779. It seems to have been the policy of that day to utilize whatever happened to be at hand and to make the most of it. Those private shipyards, coming under Government control, gradually took on the character of, and came to be known as, navy-yards. They served their purpose in their day, but for some of them that day has long passed. The utilitarian policy no longer obtains. In looking to the further growth of the navy, we must adjust, and readjust, our focus to modern conditions, as they grow and expand, that all the various elements that go to make up a navy may be seen in their true proportions and their proper relations. The old navy-yards were naval bases only in such a very limited sense that they were never known as such. The selection of sites was dictated by utility, not by reason of their strategic position or their value in a military sense.

In fitting out a fleet and its auxiliaries during war, or in anticipation of war, a permanent naval base in a situation favorable for operations in the field of hostilities is of the first importance. After a battle a naval base is a necessity, whatever may be the result of an engagement. We know from recent naval history that even a victorious fleet will suffer serious losses and will be obliged, in parts at least, to fall back on its base for supplies and repairs. If worsted in the fight, then the whole fleet, or what is left of it, will have to seek the shelter of its base, and badly damaged ships—ships, perhaps, in a sinking condition—must be speedily docked, or beached, or go down in deep water. A naval base, moreover, is necessary for the assembling of the reserves of battleships of the second category—ships with all but perishable stores on board and ready at short notice to fill gaps in the line of battle. A glance at foreign Naval Powers will show the military value attached to naval bases and to the imperative necessity of organizing the reserves of the line of battle.

The great military ports of England, Germany, France, Russia, Italy and Japan serve as illustrations in point. After the unification of Italy in 1859[11] there was constructed at Spezia a dockyard that for capacity and completeness was equal to all of our navy-yards of that day combined. It was designed for nine building-slips and ten dry docks. At Kiel and at Wilhelmshaven the Germans boast of two of the finest dockyards in the world, the creation of recent years. The magnificent roadstead and dockyard of the former (Kiel) has been rendered impregnable by the defensive works planned by a commission presided

---

[10] *Adams* was launched 8 June 1799 by the firm of Jackson and Sheffield. In 1801 the land for the New York Navy Yard was purchased from Jackson. It was part of the decision by Congress to appropriate funds for the establishment of shipyards at Washington, Norfolk, Philadelphia, Boston, Portsmouth, and New York. Luce obtained much of this information while preparing the report of the Commission on Navy Yards (see item 70) and in writing "On Navy Yards and Their Defense" (see item 102).

[11] Italy was unified in March 1861 at the time Victor Emmanuel was declared King of Italy. La Spezia, a part of the Duchy of Genoa in the Kingdom of Sardinia, became a naval headquarters after the military fleet was transferred from Genoa in 1857.

over by von Moltke[12] himself. Wilhelmshaven, with its three dry docks, each one capable of taking in a battleship of 25,000 tons displacement, gives one an idea of what constitutes a primary or permanent naval base. In addition to these, there was begun in May, 1909, at Brunsbettel on the Elbe, just at the entrance of the Kiel Canal, two dry docks which surpass any yet constructed. They are in length 330 metres (1,072.50 feet) and 45 metres (146.25 feet) wide, to cost thirty million marks.[13]

England, fully alive to the possibilities of the near future, has established new naval bases at Malta, Gibraltar (new by reason of the new dry docks), Dover and Rosyth. It is the intention of the Admiralty, according to recent reports, to establish still another naval base. Harwich, on the North Sea, is the place designated. It is already strongly fortified. The old dockyards at Chatham, Sheerness, Portsmouth, Plymouth, Pembroke and others no longer suffice. The Government dry dock No. 1 at Gibraltar is 863 feet long and 95 feet wide. The harbor recently opened at Dover is said to be the largest artificial harbor in the world. It encloses an area sufficient for the accommodation of a fleet of twenty-five first-class battleships and auxiliaries. Dover harbor was begun in 1898 and is said to have cost $20,000,000.

"This harbor has taken eleven years to construct and has cost the Government $20,000,000. By its erection the ancient English port of Dover has been transformed into a powerful naval base. The reason for this transformation is not far to seek. It is the policy of the British Admiralty to have the strength and bulk of their ships lie nearest their strongest rival. That rival to-day is Germany, hence the desirability of equipping Dover with an efficiently protected harbor, where the ships can lie safely at anchor and yet be in a position to strike quickly at the North Sea."[14]

Rosyth, on the north side of the Firth of Forth, Scotland, is now nearing completion.[15] Japan has at Yokohama three dry docks and four at Yokosuka. The French have their principal military ports at Brest, Cherbourg, Toulon and Bizerta, near Tunis, where there are three dry docks. Then we have Port Arthur and Vladivostok as other examples of great military ports.

In the scheme for the rehabilitation of the Chinese navy, one of the very first steps has been the establishment of a primary naval base. This has been done, not at one of the commercial ports, but at Hai Fu Wan

---

[12] Field Marshal Helmuth Johannes Ludwig von Moltke (1848-1916), the younger, was Quartermaster General in 1903 and Chief of the General Staff in 1906. He was the nephew of Helmuth Karl Bernhard Graf von Moltke (1800-1891), the victorious leader of Prussian forces in 1866 and 1871.

[13] About $6½ million (U.S.) in 1911.

[14] The recent proposition to fortify the mouth of the Scheldt with a view to the establishment there of a naval base is fraught with danger. If carried into effect it would not only prove a serious menace to England, but would lead, undoubtedly, to international complications of the gravest character. [This is Luce's footnote.]

[15] Luce's source here was *Engineering*, vol. LXXXV, No. 2202, 13 March 1908 [London], p. 348. This untitled and unsigned article provides details and a chart of Admiralty plans for Rosyth.

in Nimrod Sound. This strategic point bears about the same relative position to the Sea of Japan that Dover (England) does to the North Sea.

There are *military* ports, it may be observed in passing, and there are *commercial* ports. Out of the experience of long and exhausting wars, as in the past between England and France, the importance of certain harbors on either side of the Channel and in the Mediterranean became manifest. They were those most conveniently situated for projecting naval campaigns against an enemy and as harbors of refuge in cases of disaster or defeat. They were the principal strategic points within the theatre of belligerent operations. As bases for such operations they gradually developed into military ports. In the absence of the stern school of war naval students, in anticipation of possible hostilities of the future, have determined the most important strategic points on their coasts for the establishment of naval bases, such as we have seen at Wilhelmshaven in Germany, and Dover, England, and Rosyth in Scotland, looking to coming events forcing the centre of disturbance in the North Sea. Commercial ports, on the other hand, grow out of the necessities of commercial enterprises without regard to military considerations.

The following in regard to German naval bases is taken from a recent English paper:[16]

"Wilhelmshaven and Emden, Borkum and Heligoland,[17] the greatest quadrilateral of naval fortresses the world has ever beheld, are nearing completion. Within two-thirds of a day's steaming of the British coasts, within half a day's reach to the entrance of the Baltic, they proclaim to the world that Germany is preparing for a great naval conflict."

The recent transfer of the principal German naval base from Kiel to Wilhelmshaven

"is the announcement that the fortified island of Borkum combines with Emden to accentuate the importance of the Ems estuary in the new scheme for the future, while Borkum connects with Heliogoland through the impassable chain of the East Frisian Islands; and Heligoland—the northern Gibraltar—closes to an enemy the estuaries of the Weser and the Elbe and completes, with the mighty fortress harbor of Wilhelmshaven, the vast quadrilateral, Emden, Borkum, Heligoland, Wilhelmshaven, which encloses in its enormous bastion configuration —one hundred miles long on each of its faces and sixty on each of its flanks—a score of islands bristling with forts, together with linking positions on the mainland of huge strength and extent. The great waterways of the Ems, the Weser and the Elbe bring the resources of populous provinces to the wharves and quays. A vast system of strategic railways can carry thousands of trained soldiers to the mighty embarkation docks of Emden. It is appalling to think of the situation if those unparalleled preparations and armaments represent enemies or rivals."[18]

The foregoing, while somewhat hysterical in style, presents some interesting features of Germany's naval projects and conveys a good idea of what constitutes a permanent naval base of the first order. From *our* point of view the great works the writer describes are all in the interests of peace. From an examination of these and other of the great

---

[16] F. Hugh O'Donnell in the *Pall Mall Gazette,* 8 April 1908. [Luce's footnote.]

[17] Heligoland is an islet only about one-fifth of a square mile in area. [Luce's footnote.]

[18] *Pall Mall Gazette,* 8 April 1908. [Luce's footnote.]

military ports of the world we are led to conclude that the constituents of a naval base of the first order are, roughly speaking, about as follows:

1. Its situation must be at the best strategic point within the area under consideration.

2. It must afford a safe harbor for a fleet of at least from twenty-five to thirty battleships with their auxiliaries, aggregating a total of about sixty heavy-draught ships and numerous small craft.

3. Such anchorage must be within the lines of defence.

4. It must afford ample docking facilities, at one and the same time, at least four ships of 45,000 tons displacement, each of, say, thirty-eight feet draught.

5. The interior lines of communication to the sources of supply should be such as may be fully secured in time of war.

6. It should be easy of access and egress and admit at mean low water, and without constant recourse to dredging, ships of the heaviest draught of water—say, thirty-eight feet.[19]

7. It should be in proximity to a community able to furnish skilled labor in the departments of iron shipbuilding and marine enginery.

8. The facilities of the neighborhood for furnishing the materials which enter into these industries should be ample.

9. The character of the soil of the littoral should be such that the dry docks and wet basins in numbers sufficient to meet all probable demands of the future can be constructed at moderate cost and its area sufficient for all the structures that may be needed for a repairing yard and a naval arsenal combined.

10. It should enjoy a salubrious climate.

11. It should be difficult to blockade.

With the exception of Wilhelmshaven and one or two other of the great military ports of Europe, it is not to be assumed that all these conditions can be found at any one place. But accepting the principal points, it is plain that the United States has no naval bases. All the components of naval bases exist save only the will to assemble them.

Twenty years ago America had no fleet. All the various parts that go to make up a battleship lay scattered about in every direction. By the exercise of the creative power the thousand and one units have been marshalled into order, and first a battleship and then a fleet have sprung into existence. So far so good. But our naval development has been one-sided. In the ardor of building a fleet naval bases have been overlooked. In this respect the constructive genius is still wanting. We have navy-yards, naval stations, naval rendezvous; but, in a technical sense, we have no naval bases. The elements have yet to be assembled. This one-sided growth is not progress. We may double the number of battleships and still make no naval progress unless the other constituents of sea power keep pace with the building programme.

---

[19] We have not yet reached the limit of size of ships. The White Star liners "Olympic" and "Titanic" are 860 feet long, 92 feet beam and at 37½ feet draught have a displacement of 60,000 tons. These ships could be docked at Gibraltar. [Luce's footnote. These were the largest ships of the day.]

With the development of the battleship goes, or should go, the development of all that makes her an efficient instrument of war; her motive power, armament, personnel, munitions, victualing, means of repairing, docking, and so forth. And as battleships increase in numbers and size so must all the heterogeneous elements that contribute to their efficiency increase, otherwise there is no real naval progress. The visible manifestations—the great ships and their war-like appearance—delude the public into thinking increase of tonnage is progress. Those of the profession know better. It is their duty to point out defects and instance cases of retarded development in the several parts.

On examining the map of our Atlantic seaboard, to which this discussion is confined, three principal strategic points[20] at once attract attention: Narragansett Bay, Chesapeake Bay and the Florida Keys. Chesapeake Bay has the making of a permanent or primary naval base. In the days of the old navy, Hampton Roads fulfilled all the requirements of our little floating force. Fort Monroe furnished the necessary defence, and the navy-yard at Norfolk, established in 1801, with its narrow approaches and limited facilities, was equal to the light demands made upon it. Those advantages no longer suffice. The army is already planning for an advanced line of defences. In 1906 the "Taft National Coast Defence Board," so called because the Hon. William H. Taft, then Secretary of War, was its president, in recommending the fortification of the entrance of Chesapeake Bay reported in part as follows:

"Commercially and strategically Chesapeake Bay is to-day, as it always has been, of the very first importance. With the entrance unfortified, as it is now, should a hostile fleet gain control of the sea, it could establish a base on its shores without coming under the fire of a single gun. It could pass in and out at pleasure, have access to large quantities of supplies of all kinds and paralyze the great trunk railway lines crossing the head of the bay."[21]

The proposition is to create an artificial island on the Middle Ground whereon to erect a fort mounting heavy guns. These, with heavy guns on Capes Charles and Henry, would effectually close the entrance of the bay to an enemy.

If, coincident with the construction of these defensive works by the army, the navy should build up-to-date dry docks at some carefully selected point in the bay for the docking of the 30,000-ton ships now provided for, Chesapeake Bay would become in time a naval base of the first order.

---

[20] "Every point in the theatre of war which should have a military importance, either from its situation at the centre of communication or from military establishments and fortified works of whatever description which would have an influence over the strategic field, will be, in reality, a territorial or geographical strategic point"—not a geometrical point. [This is Luce's footnote. The quotation is from Jomini, *ibid.*, art. XIX, p. 97.]

[21] U.S. Congress, Senate, *Report of the National Coast Defense Board*, 5 March 1906, Senate Doc. 248, 59th Congress, 1st sess., serial 4913.

Key West, Florida, is the most important strategic point on the southern coast. The prospect of the early completion of the Panama Canal emphasizes its value from a naval point of view. Its great natural advantages have been materially enhanced by the construction of the Florida East Coast Railway, which connects it with the mainland. An interesting report on Key West as a naval base will be found in the "Congressional Record" of April 5th, 1910, page 4436.

Guantanamo, Cuba, is valuable as an advanced post or rendezvous for the same reasons that apply to Key West. In the event of the Caribbean Sea becoming the theatre of naval operations, it would prove as a strategic point of very great importance. It cannot, however, come within the category of permanent naval bases, unless Congress should authorize the expenditure of money for defensive work, machine-shops and dry docks. Situated in an alien country and its lines of communication and sources of supply liable to be cut off by an enemy, its defences should be of the most formidable character. It would still be wanting in skilled labor.

Limon Bay, Panama, itself furnishes an advanced naval base. The entrance to the Canal must be strongly fortified and ample docking facilities will without doubt be provided: dry docks of at least 1,000 feet in length and wide in proportion.

At the Atlantic Deeper Waterways Convention, Norfolk, Virginia, November 17-20, 1909, President Taft[22] is quoted as speaking of Norfolk as the "most important navy-yard and navy base that we have in the United States . . . . and Chesapeake Bay as the greatest strategical point of naval rendezvous in the United States."

Accepting that authoritative statement, it may be confidently affirmed that next after Chesapeake Bay comes Narragansett Bay, which is the "greatest strategical point of naval rendezvous" north of the Capes of Virginia. Narragansett Bay seems to have been intended by nature for a permanent naval base of the first order.

English naval officers who had become familiar with our coasts and harbors were quick to recognize that fact at an early day. In 1773-74 British engineers made a careful study of Narragansett Bay with a view to the establishment of an extensive naval station with dry docks, shipyards, marine hospital and a system of fortifications. In a report to the Board of Admiralty, under whose instructions the work was undertaken, it is stated that:

"The whole bay is an excellent man-of-war harbor, affording good anchorage, sheltered in every direction and capacious enough for the whole of His Majesty's navy were it increased fourfold. There are no dangerous ledges or shoals within the bay or near its entrance, which is easy of access with all winds. Another advantage it possesses over any other harbor on the northern coast in the winter season is that it is very seldom obstructed by ice, and the tide is not sufficiently strong to render drift ice dangerous to ships lying at anchor. The harbor has not been frozen up so as to prevent ships coming in to safe anchorage since 1740, and the oldest inhabitants do not recollect to have heard that it was ever so frozen up before since the settlement of the colony. It has other advantages that cannot be found elsewhere in America. A whole fleet may go out under way and sail from three to five leagues on a tack, get the trim of the ships and exercise the men

---

[22] See report in "No Cash, Says Taft, for Foolish Plans," *The New York Times*, 20 November 1909, p. 5:3-5.

within the bay, secure from attack from an enemy. The vicinity of the ocean is such that in one hour a fleet may be from their anchorage to sea or from the sea to safe anchorage in one of the best natural harbors the world affords. Its central situation also in His Majesty's North-American colonies and its proximity to the West Indies are advantages worthy of consideration, as it regards the protection of every part of His Majesty's widely extended possession in this quarter. . . .

"Whether it is feasible of defence is a question which your lordship [the Earl of Sandwich] very justly considers of the highest importance and to which my particular attention is directed. . . . Of expense I say nothing. . . . Suffice it to say that it is completely feasible and that the importance of the position as a naval station is worth the expense, be what it may."[23]

Written one hundred and thirty-seven years ago, the natural advantages pointed out in this report which Narragansett Bay affords as a naval staton exists to-day, while the defensive works suggested in the report have been thoroughly carried out by our own military engineers. The breaking out of the Revolutionary War put a stop to all further proceedings in this direction on the part of the English Admiralty.

Mr. Joshua Humphreys,[24] Naval Constructor, who designed the "Constitution" class of forty-four-gun frigates, having been ordered by the Secretary of the Navy under date of January 29th, 1802, to examine sites for naval stations on the eastern coast, reported, in part, as follows:

"Having compared and considered the advantages and disadvantages of situation, with capacity of harbor, depth of water, rise of tide, expense in building docks, prices of land, facility of navigation and capability of defence previously stated at each port, I am decidedly of opinion that Newport, Rhode Island, is by far the most suitable port for the establishment of dry docks and a great naval port for our navy for the ease and safety of entry at all seasons of the year. Its eligibility, in preference to any other eastern port, is universally acknowledged. The principal and only objection is the great expense of fortification, which may amount to more than a million of dollars."[25]

Under date of April 25th, 1802, the Secretary of the Navy, Hon. Robert Smith,[26] transmitted to the President the report of Mr. Humphreys. In the letter of transmittal the Secretary wrote:

"Mr. Humphreys was also instructed to examine the different ports and harbors eastward of New York with a view to the selection of the situation for one of the docks for repairing ships directed by Congress. . . . His report on that subject corresponds with the opinion the Secretary of the Navy has long entertained from the best lights in his power that Newport, Rhode Island, affords advantages which give it a superiority over other places. . . . It is easy of access and can be gained under circumstances which would render it almost impossible

---

[23] "A British Navy Yard Contemplated in Newport, R.I., in 1764," *Rhode Island Historical Magazine*, vol. VI, No. 1, 1885, pp. 42-47. This article attributes the report to Robert Melville, Governor of Grenada, in 1764 or 1765. Internal evidence leads one to doubt this attribution; however, extensive search in the Public Record Office, National Maritime Museum, Ministry of Defence Hydrographic Office, and the British Museum, London, failed to locate the original report at the time this study went to press.

[24] Joshua Humphreys (1751-1838), shipbuilder, and naval architect, was considered the leading designer in America. His ships were famous for their speed and individual accomplishments.

[25] U.S. Congress, *American State Papers; Naval Affairs* (Washington: Gales and Seaton, 1834), vol. XXIII, p. 91.

[26] Robert Smith (1757-1842), Secretary of the Navy, 1801-09; Secretary of State, 1809-11.

for a ship in a crippled state to reach any other port to the eastward of Chesapeake Bay. It has a capacious and very safe harbor in all kinds of weather, and it is the very point of which a maritime enemy would endeavor to get possession for the purpose of annoying our own coast, our own trade and of cutting off one-half the maritime strength of our country from the other half.

"The objection to this place is the expense of fortifying it. . . . France or England could take possession of Rhode Island and make it a second Gibraltar."[27]

No one can read the exhaustive report of Mr. Humphreys, to which the Secretary gives such hearty approval, without feeling that he was thoroughly well qualified to deal with the subject under discussion.

Our own officers were not slow to recognize the importance of these waters from a naval as well as a military point of view. Agreeably to the terms of a Senate resolution of February 13th, 1817, a mixed commission of naval officers and officers of the United States Army Engineer Corps examined and reported upon a proper site "for a naval depot, rendezvous and dockyard" east of Delaware Bay. The commissioners were General Swift[28] and Colonel McRee[29] of the Corps of the United States Engineers and Commodore Bainbridge[30] and Captains Samuel Evans[31] and Oliver H. Perry of the Navy.

As between Boston and Newport Commodore Bainbridge preferred the former, as it was "favorably situated for obtaining timber for shipbuilding"—all the others favoring Narragansett Bay. The majority report, dated Navy-Yard, New York, October 30th, 1817, states that:

"The commissioners (except one), [Commodore Bainbridge] are of the opinion that Narragansett Bay presents the best site for a naval depot in the Union north of Chesapeake Bay. . . .

"An examination of this bay has satisfied the commissioners (with one exception) that the best site for a great *naval depot east of Chesapeake Bay* is to be found in this bay [Narragansett] and the various positions upon the waters of it. . . .

"The commissioners have in their survey and examination only determined where it will be best to locate a *great naval depot* and where sites for defence should be selected."[32]

The three lookout stations at Gay Head,[33] Block Island and

---

[27]*American State Papers, ibid.,* p. 87.

[28]Brig. Gen. Joseph Gardner Swift (1783-1865) saw his first tour of duty as a cadet at Fort Adams, Newport, R.I., in 1800-01, before joining the first class at West Point. He served as Chief Engineer of the Army, 1812-18. Swift is considered the first engineer of distinction to have received his training entirely within the United States.

[29]McRee did not serve on this commission, but on another similar one which considered, at the same time, possible navy yard sites in the South.

[30]Capt. William Bainbridge (1774-1833), hero of the Barbary Wars. He dissented from this report. See note 32.

[31]Capt. Samuel Evans (? - 1824) joined the U.S. Navy in 1798, served in the quasi-war with France.

[32]This admirable report may be read with profit to-day. [This is Luce's footnote. The report is printed in *American State Papers, ibid.,* pp. 490-92. Bainbridge's dissenting report is on pp. 487-88.]

[33]The western point on the island of Martha's Vineyard.

Montauk Point,[34] which in time of war would give notice of the approach of an enemy's fleet, gives an exceptional advantage to Narragansett Bay as a naval base. It is the natural outpost of New York City. As an industrial centre it ranks high. During the Civil War a firm in Providence,[35] Rhode Island, made a large quantity of shot and shell for the navy and more than 300 6.4-inch guns. Since 1891 the same firm has made for the United States Government seventy-three 12-inch breech-loading rifled mortars with cast-iron bodies hooped with steel and fifty with steel bodies similarly hooped. Altogether Narragansett Bay and its tributaries can furnish all the skilled labor a naval base could need during peace or in time of war. The fact that it has a channel forty feet deep which can be carried ten miles up from the entrance, and that, too, without dredging, furnishes another advantage enjoyed by no other harbor on our Atlantic seaboard.

On the northwest shore near Greenwich[36] will be found an excellent place for a fresh-water basin for destroyers, torpedo-boats and small craft generally, an advantage that can be claimed by no other harbor on the coast save Philadelphia, which is too far from the sea.[37]

The one and only objection to Narragansett Bay in 1773, 1802 and 1817 as "a great naval port" was the expense of fortifying it. That objection has been overcome. Narragansett Bay is now well fortified.[38] It has, therefore, all the constituents of a naval base of the first order save the docking facilities. It only awaits the time when its exceptional advantages shall have been passed upon officially by a duly appointed mixed commission of army and navy officers, as has been our practice in the past, and the question of its adoption taken up by Congress.

It was a very wise move to establish a naval base at Pearl Harbor, two thousand miles off the coast of California. It would be equally wise to establish one at home right at our door. The argument against the establishment of a naval base in Narragansett Bay is that we have too many naval stations already and that the administration would scarcely be justified in asking Congress for the large sum necessary to erect another and an entirely new one. That question is for Congress to decide, not for the navy. It is for Congress to decide whether the paramount necessities of the entire country are to be sacrificed to the political interests of localities having little or no military value.

We have seen from what has been said the importance, from a military point of view, attached to naval bases by the great naval

---

[34] The eastern point of Long Island.

[35] Builder's Iron Works.

[36] East Greenwich, R.I.

[37] In the manuscript of his 1910 lecture, Luce notes here, "One very great advantage of Narragansett Bay and one which must not be overlooked is that it is not a commercial port."

[38] "In 1900, Narragansett Bay was defended by a half dozen separate forts, all well within the bay, whose armament in 1900 comprised three dozen heavy pieces." E.R. Lewis, *Seacoast Fortifications of the United States: an Introductory History* (Washington, D.C.: Smithsonian Institution Press, 1970), p. 9.

Powers abroad. We have noticed that naval bases are not placed up narrow streams nor at commercial centres. It has been made plain that naval bases are at the most important strategic points near the sea and that, while easily accessible to friends, they are yet strongly fortified against foes.

To recapitulate: The question of naval bases has not been until recently seriously considered for reasons not far to seek. As long as America had no fleet the need of naval bases did not exist. With the regeneration of the navy and the creation of a fleet the establishment of naval bases became a prime necessity. Again: The great majority of Americans are prone to shut their eyes to the possibilities of war, hence they are averse to preparing for such a contingency. The Spanish War was an illustration of that fact. Is the next war to prove that we are incapable of profiting by the mistakes of the Civil War and of the war with Spain? But the principal reason why the question of naval bases received no consideration was the defective system of naval administration commonly known as the "Bureau System," now happily extinct.

Bureaus are indispensable to any form of naval administration, under what name so ever they may be designated. But they all had to do with *materiel* and belonged to the civil branch of naval administration. The military branch did not exist. The sole reason for the existence of the Navy Department and its several bureaus is the preparation for war. One of the first essentials in war is the mapping out of naval campaigns and one of the essentials in campaigns is naval bases. The subject of naval campaigns, in which naval strategy forms so large a part, can be dealt with only by specialists, and the "Bureau System" discouraged the training of specialists in the very branch to which the Navy Department owes its existence—the art of war.

The current work of the Navy Department was, and still is, ably carried on by specialists in the arts of *ordnance, navigation, naval architecture, steam engineering* and the rest, but, strange to say, there was no specialist in the art of war, the art to which the Navy Department owes its existence, as we have already stated. The art of war includes the subject of naval strategy and naval strategy deals with naval bases. One of the chief requisites of a naval base is that it shall be placed in the most advantageous strategic point in the field of possible operations. These points can be determined only by careful study of the question in all its bearings, and when the site has been settled much time and money is required for its development. Military history furnishes examples of fortifications erected at great cost of time and labor only to serve as monuments to the lack of foresight of those who designed them. The point selected was of no strategic importance. It is a curious fact that the navy, up to the present time, has failed to appreciate its own character as a strictly military organization. A one-sided development seems no longer possible. The "Bureau System," by which is meant the control of the navy by independent bureaus belonging to the civil branch of the Navy Department, has no part in the "new navy."

S.B. Luce

Lieutenant S.B. Luce, *ca.* 1861

As head of the Seamanship Department at the Naval Academy Luce wrote to the Commandant of Midshipmen on 26 February 1861: "Compared to the Army with their wealth of professional literature, we may be likened to the nomadic tribes of the East who are content with the vague traditions of the past. Does it seem creditable then, Sir, to this institution that it should possess no textbook on the most important branch taught within its hall?" Luce's *Seamanship* first appeared in 1862, and it remained the leading textbook in the field until 1901.

Photo: U.S. Naval Academy

CHAPTER IX

ANNOTATED BIBLIOGRAPHY OF LUCE'S WRITINGS
ACTIVE DUTY YEARS: 1862-1888

Editors' Introduction

The enduring quality of the writings of Stephen B. Luce becomes readily evident when one considers the large number of his articles that were either reprinted within his lifetime or were expanded by sequels. Indeed, the maritime world today could still gain a great deal from the inheritance left by this gifted officer, and it would be valuable to publish all of his writings in the manner of the first seven chapters.

However, the sheer volume of Luce's published words, over 148 separate pieces, makes such an effort clearly prohibitive so the balance of his writings will be presented in abstract form. This appears as the best practical substitute. A similar effort made almost 20 years ago was evidently beneficial to the scholars who sought it out and, to some degree, inspired this work.[1]

This and the following chapter include all the identified material that Luce published in the period from 1862 through 1911—essays, book reviews, letters to the editors, newspaper articles, interviews, encyclopedia pieces, instructions and reports in Government publications, introductions to articles and books by other authors, short pieces repeated in several publications and editions of his books.

There are 58 of his essays, including one translation from the French, which must be reckoned as the core of his writings. Added to these are 12 book reviews which, in many cases, equal the impact of his essays. The well-known text on *Seamanship* went into eight editions, five of them in 10 years, the last still in print. His second and lesser known book *Naval Songs* had two editions and three added printings, but even today this work remains relatively unknown despite a continuing interest in sea songs and the shanties of the sailing age.

Many of Luce's earlier writings appeared anonymously, thus following a practice customary in publishing well into the 19th

---

[1] John D. Hayes, "The Writings of Stephen B. Luce," *Military Affairs*, vol. XIX, Winter 1955, pp. 187-196. See also Samuel P. Huntington, *The Soldier and the State* (New York: Belknap Press, 1957), pp. 232-233, 236-237, 492, 493; John A.S. Greenville and George B. Young, *Politics, Strategy, and American Diplomacy, 1873-1917* (New Haven: Yale University Press, 1966), pp. 15-18.

century. Also, bearing in mind the restrictions of active duty, Luce was careful to what he signed his name, particularly near the end of his naval career when he held high public office and many of his articles dealt with the sensitive issues of Navy Department reform.

Identifying much of this anonymous material was as difficult as it was fascinating. Numerous tearsheets and newspaper clippings among Luce's papers appear to bear the stamp of his ideas and interests, and attributing to him material written by others was a constant temptation. This was particularly the case with service periodicals such as the *Army and Navy Journal,* where Luce was virtually naval editor for 15 years. However, only those pieces which we can be reasonably certain to have come from his pen are included here. The primary means of identification was Luce's own correspondence and initialed or signed copies of articles found in his papers and books. Nevertheless, numerous of his writings were found to which there are no references or even indications in his papers. He may have forgotten them or may have simply wished them to remain unknown.

Abstracts of most of the pieces herein are necessarily short, but the more significant articles are given comparatively extensive treatment with appropriate historical references. Each article, book, issue, and edition has been arranged chronologically and given a number for ready reference. Cross-references within these two chapters use the bibliographical item number to specific works, listed here with their full citations. The appendix to chapters IX and X provides interested readers with item numbers of articles that specifically treat subjects within the categories listed.

1. *Instruction for Naval Light Artillery, Afloat and Ashore.* New York: Van Nostrand, 1862. Prepared and arranged for the U.S. Naval Academy by William H. Parker, Lt., USN., 2d ed., revised by Lt. S.B. Luce, USN, Asst. Instructor of Gunnery and Tactics at the U.S. Naval Academy.

    This first literary work of Stephen B. Luce may be said to be Civil War induced. Lieutenant Parker, an intellectual like Luce, had originally written the work in 1859 while on duty at sea in the steam frigate *Merrimac,* after a 4-year tour as instructor at the Academy. It was published and adopted as a textbook in 1860 after he had returned to Annapolis for his second tour on the faculty. Parker resigned his commission when his native state, Virginia, seceded on 19 April 1861 and joined the Confederate Navy. In 1863 he became Superintendent of its Naval Academy on board CSS *Patrick Henry.* He served after the war as master of Pacific coast steamers and as president of Maryland Agricultural College, later the University of Maryland.

An inveterate raconteur, his *Recollections of a Naval Officer*[1] is a delightful sea classic.

Luce assumed Parker's duty as instructor in gunnery. Continuing to use at the U.S. Naval Academy a text by a "rebel" officer would have been unthinkable, so the Superintendent, Comdr. George S. Blake, had Luce revise it. It was dated Naval Academy, Newport, R.I., March 29th 1862. This revision contained an added section by the ordnance specialist, Capt. John A.B. Dahlgren, USN.

---

[1] See W.H. Parker, *Recollections of a Naval Officer* (New York: n.p., 1885).

2. *Seamanship: Compiled from Various Authorities for the Use of the United States Naval Academy, Newport, R.I.* Newport, R.I.: Atkinson, 1862.

    This first edition of the Seamanship text was compiled by Luce with the assistance of Lt. E.O. Matthews, a fellow instructor on the staff of the Naval Academy. In the preface to this anonymous volume, the compilers remark, "The materials composing this volume have been hastily drawn from Totten, Murphy, Boyd, and Nares, and given to the printer to publish in time for the use of the Midshipmen, during this summers cruise. It is too crude and imperfect to be considered as a text book." The preface is dated "Newport, R.I., May 12, 1862."

3. *Seamanship: Compiled from Various Authorities and Illustrated with Numerous and Selected Designs, for the Use of the United States Naval Academy.* 2d ed., Newport, R.I.: Atkinson, 1863.

    The second edition appeared with the name of Lt. Comdr. S.B. Luce on the title page. In the preface dated "Naval Academy, Newport, R.I., Feb. 1863," Luce points out

    > That for the present at least, the introduction of Steam and Iron-Clads into the Navy, in no degree lessens the necessity that officers should be skillful seamen, skillful in the management of ships under canvas, and fertile in all the resources known to seamen, as well as prompt in the application of them when meeting the accidents and disasters incident to men-of-war.

    He goes on to point out that the text will assist midshipmen in acquiring a knowledge of the duties of seamen, petty officers, and lieutenants, in learning how to take charge of a watch and a "division of great guns." Admitting that proficiency in seamanship can only come from practical experience on deck and in the tops of seagoing men of war, he believed that the text would be useful as a guide for observation and instruction. In support of his view that young seamen should continue to be trained in the way of a sailing ship, Luce faces his preface with an extensive quotation from Sir Howard Douglas' *Naval Warfare with Steam* which concludes, "It must not, therefore, be assumed, in preparing for steam-warfare, that the sail will be entirely supplanted by steam, or that steam fleets may dispense with crews of able seamen."

The volume is dedicated to Rear Adm. Samuel F. Du Pont under whom Luce had recently served as a watch and division officer in the flagship of the South Atlantic Blockading Squadron. Upon his detachment in January 1862, Du Pont had written a complimentary letter on Luce's behalf which allowed him to be returned to his proper position for promotion on the Navy List. Luce had been dropped 72 numbers in 1850 because of his participation in a demonstration against the decision of the Superintendent of the Naval Academy not to allow midshipmen to participate in the inauguration of President Zachary Taylor.

This edition includes a translation of "Le Manoeuvrier" by Bourdé de Villehuet. The translation in part two, "Theory of Working Ship," was not done by Luce, but he has made a number of corrections to it.

4. *Seamanship: Compiled from Various Authorities and Illustrated with Numerous Original and Selected Designs: for Use of the United States Naval Academy.* 2d ed. New York: Van Nostrand, 1863.

This edition is identical to item 3. Like the Newport issue, the title page also states that it is the second edition. Apparently, Van Nostrand used it without alteration when he published it for a larger audience.

5. "On Training-Ships, No. 1," *Army and Navy Journal*, vol. I, No. 9, 24 October 1863, p. 132.

This is the first of a series of articles which Luce submitted to the *Journal*. (See items 5-9.) They comprise his first publication in a periodical and were the fruits of his inspection of British and French naval training ships during the summer cruise to Europe by the Naval Academy practice ship *Macedonian*, his first command.[1]

Luce's reporter friend William C. Church, whom he met while the latter was covering the Battle of Port Royal, had founded the *Army and Navy Journal* the previous August. Luce submitted this material to him in two parts, the first two articles were sent shortly after his return from Europe, and the others from the monitor *Nantucket*, the command of which he assumed on 10 November 1863 at Wassaw Sound, Ga. These pieces were all unsigned, as were subsequent articles by him in this magazine.

Luce claimed that with the Naval Academy well established, something must be done for the seamen, "the bone and sinew of the Navy," who were basically artillerists. He asked for a system that would keep these men in the Navy and make them a part of it. He then describes how the French and British had succeeded in doing this, primarily by long-term enlistments of boys and training them in special schoolships. He indicated also that boys could be trained in cruising men-of-war if they were kept separate from the rest of the crew and their instruction closely supervised by the commanding officer. "It is the future we must look to—the future."

---

[1] The official report of this cruise is in Luce to G.S. Blake, Superintendent of the Naval Academy, 23 September 1863, Luce Papers, LC.

6. "Seamen and Training-Ships, No. II." *Army and Navy Journal*, vol. I, No. 10, 31 October 1863, p. 150.

   This installment is devoted to the French Navy.

7. "Training Ships. Educated Seamen and Warrant Officers." *Army and Navy Journal*, vol. I, No. 16, 12 December 1863, p. 250.

   This installment discusses the French training system in detail and quotes at length from British reports of 1858-59 on naval training. Beginning with this article, the remainder of this series was written in the cramped quarters on board the monitor *Nantucket*.

8. "Training Ships. Educating Boys for Seamen." *Army and Navy Journal*, vol. I, No. 17, 19 December 1863, pp. 260-261.

   Luce discusses in detail his visit to the English training ships. He goes on to explain,
   > But how is it that in our country, where education is so popular and where public schools are scattered broadcast over the land, the Navy should form an exception to the general rule? Where are all the philanthropists? What are they doing? They have succeeded in ejecting "cats" and the "grog-tub" from the Navy, and with them the old school of seamen: let them go on with their work and give us training ships and a "new school," that our ship's boys may be well instructed and thoroughly trained to their business, their moral tone elevated and their whole nature improved. . . . to improve the men, they must begin with the boys.

9. "Training Ships. Instruction of Ship's Boys." *Army and Navy Journal*, vol. I, No. 18, 26 December 1863, pp. 276-77.

   In this installment, Luce discusses the training of boys in general, as well as outlining a proper course for them to follow.

10. "What the Navy Wants." *Army and Navy Journal*, vol. I, No. 34, 16 April 1864, p. 564.

    Here Luce publicly stated for the first time that the U.S. Navy needed some form of a Board of Admiralty. Written in the form of a letter to the editor, this was the initial step in a half century of untiring effort to get line officer direction of the Navy Department.

To make his point, he uses some previous *Journal* material by other writers: a long article, two published letters to the editor, and an editorial by Church himself. These appeared in the issues of 16 January, 12 March, and 19 March. The first (vol. II, pp. 322-323) was a long unsigned piece with the title: "About Promotions in the Navy," which might have been written by Luce himself, but positive verification has not been made. This piece first discusses the value of competition in all endeavors and the need for more of it in the U.S. Navy. To this end the writer recommends selection for promotion, similar to the French Navy where up to the rank of lieutenant, one-third of the promotions were by selection; up to commander, one-half; and all in the grades of captain and flag ranks.[1]

The letter of 12 March 1864 (vol. II, p. 489) signed with the pen name, Sam Pennant, also recommended selection, but by boards of officers and not by political favoritism, as he charged was the case in the U.S. Navy. Church's editorial of the same date (vol. II, p. 489), on the need for systematic training of seamen, was based entirely on Luce's 1863 *Journal* articles (see items 5-9). The 19 March letter (vol. II, pp. 499-500) recommended measures to correct the deplorable officer promotion situation in the Marine Corps.

Luce used the four pieces to summarize convincingly the major personnel improvements required in the Navy at that time: selection of officers for promotion, education of marine officers, and the training of seamen.

He wanted to know, however, what was to become of such earnest expression of ideas. "*Who is to take it in charge and bring it before Congress in the proper form? or who even is to bring it to the notice of the Secretary?*" At this time he was engaged in a frank and fruitful exchange of correspondence with Assistant Secretary of the Navy Gustavus V. Fox[2] on training of seamen and boys.

Although signed with the initials "J.F.P." this item is identified as Luce's by his letter to W.C. Church enclosing "a few lines."[3]

---

[1] From *Reglement sur Service de Interior*, then available at Van Nostrand's. The letterwriter advised every officer desiring professional improvement to read it.

[2] See Luce to Fox, 27 January and 15 March 1864; Fox to Luce, 1 March 1864, Luce Papers, LC. See also John D. Hayes, "Captain Fox—He is the Navy Department," U.S.N.I., *Proceedings*, vol. XCI, September 1965, pp. 64-71.

[3] Luce to Church, 30 March 1864, Church Papers, LC.

11. *Seamanship: Compiled from Various Authorities, and Illustrated with Numerous Original and Select Designs, for the Use of the United States Naval Academy.* 3d ed., rev. and enlarged. New York: Van Nostrand, 1866.

Luce revised and enlarged his seamanship book shortly after

he returned to the Naval Academy as Commandant of Midshipmen. In this edition he removed the translation of the "Theory of working ship," since other departments at the Academy would teach the principles involved. In addition, the recent publication of new naval regulations allowed him to remove the sections on shipboard routine and the duties of officers. In the place of this information, additional chapters on seamanship were added.

With this edition, the textbook became one devoted entirely to the art of seamanship. The book earned its fame as the leading seamanship text in the United States essentially in the form of the 1866 revision. The preface to this edition is dated, "U.S. Naval Academy, May 1866."

12. "A Nautical College." *Army and Navy Journal,* vol. IV, No. 14, 24 November 1866, p. 217.

    This item is a short letter to the editor. In his letter, Luce mentions the incident which had moved him to action: the sinking of the coastal steamer *Evening Star* on 3 October 1866. En route from New York to New Orleans, with 278 people on board, the ship was struck by a hurricane. Only 34 survived. An inquiry showed that the disaster was caused by an incompetent master who had taken no precautions, an insufficiently trained crew, and defective lifeboats.

13. "Nautical Schools." *Army and Navy Journal,* vol. IV, No. 18, 22 December 1866, p. 281.

    This offering for Church's paper was part of his endeavors at this time to promote safety in American flag passenger ships through training of merchant marine officer candidates in state schoolships. He had been shocked by a series of serious accidents at sea with heavy loss of life, and he recalled the limitations of officers of the Volunteer Navy during the Civil War, most of whom came from the merchant service.

    Characteristically, Luce decided to do something about this. On 17 November 1866 he sent a circular letter to a large number of public officials, prominent businessmen, and leaders in education, including the Secretary of the Treasury Hugh McCulloch and his friends, Senator Charles Sumner and Mr. Robert B. Forbes, a prominent shipowner, China merchant, and writer on maritime affairs. He argued for "establishing a nautical school for the professional instruction of such as are now or may desire to become officers of the merchant marine." Response was encouraging. On 24 November there appeared a brief letter signed "L" on the same subject, in which he emphasized the reserve of trained seamen that would be available in event of a foreign war. (See item 12.)

14. "Nautical Schools." *Army and Navy Journal,* vol. IV, No. 19, 29 December 1866, p. 298.

    In a long letter of 29 December, also signed "L" (item 14),

he described the proposed school. The first third of the work is a long extract from the 1864 Report of the Board of Visitors to the Naval Academy. It had been written by one of the board members, Henry Barnard. Barnard was president of St. John's College, Annapolis, Md. (1866-67) while Luce was Commandant of Midshipmen at the Naval Academy. Founder of the *American Journal of Education,* Barnard was the first U.S. Commissioner of Education, 1867-70.

15. "Routine for Fleet Maneuvres under Sail." *The Naval Signal Book of the United States of America.* Prepared under the authority of Hon. George M. Robeson, Secretary of the Navy, Bureau of Navigation, Washington: U.S. Govt. Print. Off., 1869.

    This three-page section provides the standard commands, signals, and basic procedures for fleets to get underway, come to anchor, furl sails, loose sails, cross topgallant and royal yards, send down light yards, and reef topsails.

    This section remained unchanged when the *Signal Book* was amended in 1873.

16. "French Naval Tactics—No. I." *Army and Navy Journal,* vol. VIII, No. 49, 22 July 1871, p. 782.

    On 23 June 1871 Luce wrote W.C. Church from the U.S.S. *Juniata* at Gravesend, England, that he had personally obtained a copy of *Considerations Generales sur la Tacticque Navale Escadre d'Evolutions 1868-1870*[1] by Vice Adm. Jean Baptiste Edmond Jurien de la Graviere (1812-1892). He had made a free translation under the title "French Naval Tactics" and offered it to Church for publication in his *Journal.* He stated, however,

    > I should observe that the style of the original is far from elegant or classical. It will not for a moment compare with the writings of De Joinville for example, hence it is hard for an inexperienced scribbler to make a hasty translation of an inelegant style read smoothly in the vernacular. I do not wish to be known as the translator.[2]

    He did not have to be ashamed of his new type of literary effort. Examination indicates that it was superior to one done for the Royal Navy, shortly after the original publication. Luce had requested a copy of this translation from the Admiralty when he was in England, but he never received the copy promised by the First Lord of the Admiralty, George J. Goschen's private secretary. While visiting Villefranche, Luce went to Jurien himself, who obliged him with a lithograph copy of the original manuscript. This autographed copy is in the Luce Papers, Naval Historical Collection, Naval War College.

    Jurien had taken command of the French Mediterranean Fleet in 1868. Its ironclads were formed into a Squadron of Evolution for the purpose of developing a system of tactics as well as a signal book for this new type of warship. Church divided the translation into seven segments for publication in serial form (items 17-23). In the first three, Jurien outlined the history of tactics in the age of sail and the complete transformation in this art and science required by the introduction of the steam ironclad fitted with a ram. He told of efforts made with the new signal book of 1861 to adapt to the change. The success of ramming tactics of the Austrians against the Italians at the Battle of Lissa off the Dalmatian coast on 20 July 1866, however, forced the two leading maritime nations to hurriedly revise their ironclad tactics. (See item 104 for Luce's excellent account of this battle in "Naval Warfare Under Modern Conditions.") As usual, the French were first and did the more thorough job.

In the final four segments, Jurien recounts how this job was done and surprisingly gives details of the general instructions proposed for the new signal book such as, orders for steaming and of battle, formations, evolutions, getting underway, and coming to anchor, et cetera.

Jurien de la Graviere was the son of an admiral who served through the Revolutionary and Napoleonic Wars. The young Jurien entered the navy in 1828 and commanded the squadron that convoyed the French forces to Mexico in 1861. His literary accomplishments matched his professional ones. He was a prolific author of naval history and biography, although only one of his works, *Guerres Maritimes sous la Republique et l'Empire* (1845-1846) has been translated into English. It was published under the title *Sketches of the Last Naval War* (London, 1848). In 1866 he was elected to the Academie des Science and to Academie Francaise.

---

[1] See Vice Admiral Jurien de la Graviere, "Considérations Générales sur la Tactique Navale apropos de la révision du livre des signaux," *Revue Maritime et Coloniale*, vol. XXIX, June 1870, pp. 429-54.

[2] Luce to Church, 23 June 1871, Luce Papers, LC.

17. "French Naval Tactics—No. II." *Army and Navy Journal*, vol. VIII, No. 50, 29 July 1871, p. 798.

In this installment Graviere discusses the difference between a maneuver and an evolution.

18. "French Naval Tactics—No. III." *Army and Navy Journal*, vol. VIII, No. 51, 5 August 1871, p. 814.

In this installment Graviere discusses battle tactics in the age of the ironclad warship.

19. "French Naval Tactics—No. IV." *Army and Navy Journal*, vol. VIII, No. 52, 12 August 1871, p. 829.

Here, Graviere discusses "natural tactics" and the relationship between ships' captains and the admiral in the midst of battle.

20. "French Naval Tactics—No. V." *Army and Navy Journal*, vol. IX, No. 1, 19 August 1871, p. 10.

   In this section the topic is the organization of the fleet and orders for steaming, sailing, and battle.

21. "French Naval Tactics—No. VI." *Army and Navy Journal*, vol. IX, No. 2, 26 August 1871, p. 22.

   This installment discusses formations and evolutions.

22. "French Naval Tactics Conclusion." *Army and Navy Journal*, vol. IX, No. 3, 2 September 1871, p. 42.

   This installment discusses general instructions for getting underway and coming to anchor, the fleet underway, and the fleet in battle.

23. "Regina Dal Chin." *The Galaxy*, vol. XIII, No. 5, May 1872, pp. 685-92.

   Luce's first nonprofessional article and also the first with his own byline was a testimonial to the Italian woman who treated his son's dislocated hip. He begins it with:

   "This is the story, short, simple, and imperfect as it may be, of one of the most remarkable women of our day. It is the story of a female surgeon, and as I hope the reader will presently admit, the story of a veritable disciple of Hippocrates."[1]

   The essay appeared in the periodical that W.C. Church and his brother Frank[2] founded in 1866. Described on its title page as "A Magazine of Interesting Reading," it remained in publication until 1878 when it was absorbed by its competitor, *The Atlantic Monthly* of Boston.

   Luce had several articles in *The Galaxy* which put him in good literary company. (See items 42 and 44.) Among its contributors were Walt Whitman, Mark Twain, Henry James, John W. De Forest, Sidney Lanier, Bayard Taylor, Bret Harte, Anthony Trollope, and Gideon Welles.

   ---

   [1] Hippocrates (ca. 460 - ca. 377 B.C.) Greek physician, who is often called "The father of medicine."

   [2] Francis Pharcellus Church (1839-1906), after the demise of *The Galaxy*, served until his death as editorial writer for the New York *Sun* specializing in religious and theological subjects. One of his editorials, "Yes, Virginia, There Is a Santa Claus" is still frequently reprinted. See *New York Times*, 12 and 13 April 1906.

24. "Nautical Schools in the U.S., a Historical Sketch." *The Nautical Gazette*, vol. IV, No. 86, 15 February 1873, p. 266.

   In this letter to the editor, Luce refers to an article of 18 January 1873, which he may also have written, and gives the text of a bill providing for examination of merchant marine officers and the establishment of marine schools.

   In this piece he recalls that Mr. Thomas Goin of New York, a ship booker, started a naval school in 1835 that was received with much enthusiasm along the Atlantic coast. At that time only 9,000 of the 100,000 seamen sailing under the American flag were, in fact, Americans. Goin's enterprise did not succeed.

Two years later, in 1837, Congress enacted a law providing for the enlistment of boys. The Secretary of the Navy in his report of 1839 was very sanguine, and, at one time, there were 2,000 boys enlisted, but there had been no well-thought-out plan. Boys were herded into receiving ships and sent to cruising vessels where they learned the bad habits of the older crew members. Initially, many had expected to become midshipmen, but requests for discharges swamped the Navy Department. Enlistments were eventually stopped although the law remained on the books and provided the executive authority for apprentice training when it was tried in 1863 and again in 1875.

All of this history was introduced to support the bill which proposed that the Federal Government examine merchant marine officers and provide schools which look "directly to the elevation in tone and professional improvement of the *personnel* of the entire body of our great commercial navy."

Bradley S. Osbon (1828-1912), editor of *The Nautical Gazette*, was a merchant marine officer turned maritime reporter. He had met Luce while covering the Port Royal operation for the *New York Herald*. Flag Officer S.F. Du Pont considered his report the best newspaper account. Osbon was later Farragut's clerk and also reported the Battle of New Orleans in April 1862. He established *The Nautical Gazette* and remained its editor-owner until 1876. Luce sent him news items from time to time, one in October 1871 after his ship suffered heavy damage in a Bay of Biscay storm.

The popular biographer Alfred C. Paine wrote *A Sailor of Fortune: Personal Memoirs of Captain B.S. Osbon* (New York: n.p., 1906), a delightful yarn, but an unfortunate historical fabrication.

25. *Seamanship: Compiled from Various Authorities, and Illustrated with Numerous Original and Select Designs, for the Use of the United States Naval Academy.* 5th ed., rev. and enlarged. New York: Van Nostrand, 1873.

No copy of *Seamanship* has been located for the fourth edition. The publishers may have taken into account the two "second editions." See items 3 and 4. This is the fifth issue of Luce's book under this title. It appears to be identical with item 11 which was published in 1866. Although no new preface was written for this edition, this item includes the 1863 preface as well as that of 1866.

26. *Manning and Improvement of the Navy. Address Delivered at the United States Naval Academy,* by Capt. Stephen B. Luce of the U.S. Navy, n.p., n.d.

A copy of this item is in the Library of Congress. Research has shown that it is not a Government document and there is no record of its publication by the Naval Academy. It may possibly be an early imprint of the Naval Institute before its journal was being published, or it might have been printed by Van Nostrand. The early records of both organizations have been destroyed.

The text of this piece is nearly identical to item 27, including the introductory paragraph, the discussion after the address, and the synopsis of the bill on maritime schools that would amend the Act of 28 February 1871.

27. "The Manning of Our Navy and Mercantile Marine." *The Record of the United States Naval Institute Proceedings,* vol. I, No. 1, 1874, pp. 17-37.

"Our uneducated seamen will not stand a chance against the trained gunners of England and France." So wrote Luce early in this opening article in the initial issue of the *Proceedings*.[1] In it Luce outlines what he had advocated throughout his 1863 and 1866 pieces in the *Army and Navy Journal,* the need to improve the education of officers of the merchant service and the general character as well as the training and discipline of the Navy's enlisted men. He again discusses the excellent system for training boys in the British and French navies and the steps taken to provide capable officers for Great Britain's merchant marine. He explains at length his proposed bill to promote the efficiency of masters and mates and to encourage the establishment of public maritime academies.

Luce presented this as the second lecture at the Annapolis chapter of the newly formed United States Naval Institute. He had been invited by his friend Commodore Foxhall A. Parker, an intellectual like himself, who was the moving spirit in founding the Naval Institute. Parker had given the first lecture before the institute on the Battle of Lepanto, but he withdrew his paper from publication to incorporate it into his book *The Fleets of the World* (New York: Van Nostrand, 1876). Luce, therefore, had the good fortune to be harbinger of this long-lived professional journal.

---

[1] Early issues of this journal carried titles of both *The Record and The Papers and Proceedings.* Publishing was intermittent until 1880. From then the title *Proceedings* only was used. The magazine became a quarterly with the first issue of 1881. Further references in this bibliography will use "U.S.N.I. *Proceedings."*

28. "Chapter II." *History of the United States Marine Corps* by M. Almy Aldrich. From official reports and other documents compiled by Capt. Richard S. Collum. Boston: Shepard, 1875, pp. 21-30.

Luce wrote this chapter in 1874 while at the Boston Navy Yard. At that time Captain Collum was in command of the Marine Barracks at Boston. While serving there from 1872, Collum collected documents for this volume and wrote a rough draft which he submitted to Boston publisher Henry L. Shepard before being detached for duty in Washington and on the Asiatic Station. Apparently Shepard asked the journalist M. Almy Aldrich to edit Collum's work and put it into publishable form. The first edition appeared under Aldrich's name in the centennial year of the Marine Corps. Appearing at a time when the separate existence of the Marine Corps was being seriously questioned, this volume made a notable contribution defending the corps. This volume was rewritten by Collum in 1890, and his new work saw a second edition in 1903. Luce's chapter dated "Navy Yard Boston, December 20, 1874," was included without alteration. (See items 90 and 120.) Collum is remembered today as the first Marine Corps historian in uniform.

Luce presents in his chapter the general subject of marines in three sections: (1) their employment in antiquity, (2) the Royal Marines of Great Britain, and (3) a closing tribute to American Marines. He devotes these early pages to an account of marines in the navies of Greece and Rome. The Greek word, *Epibatae,* has been defined by various scholars as "marines," the heavy armed soldiers who served on board ships. The crews of swift triremes consisted of two classes: the *Epibatae* appointed to defend the vessel and the sailors. These marines were entirely distinct from the land soldiers. They belonged to the ship.

The *Epibatae* used arrows and darts at a distance, spears and swords in close combat, and, as ships increased in size, they added *ballistae* (large stone throwers) and *naves turritae* (turrets) and fought with these as though from castles on land.

In earlier periods of naval history, when issues of battle were decided by hand-to-hand ship combat, the number of marines was as large as could be accommodated on board. However, when naval tactics became more of an art, skillful maneuvers were then used to disable enemy craft. The number of marines in a trireme was reduced to 10 in a crew of 200.

The Corps of Marines was established in the Royal Navy in 1664. They were trained in sea fighting and in ship maneuvers in which many hands were needed. In 1774 three regiments were raised in the colonies. In 1760 the sea soldiers in the British Navy numbered over 18,000. Marines did not join in the general mutinies at Spithead and the Nore in 1797. Marine guards put down several mutinies on ships between that time and 1802. As a reward for this loyalty to the crown, the corps was designated Royal Marines in 1802, and in 1804 the Royal Marine Artillery was established. Luce includes one pertinent remark. "Happily for us, our seamen have never been driven to mutiny." But he always contended that marines should be retained on board ship for the contribution they made to the ship's military atmosphere.

The education of Royal Marine officers was thorough, and Luce wished that something similar could be made available to U.S. Marine officers. The U.S. Marine Corps Commandant had attempted to get graduates of West Point without success. Luce's final sentences support improved education for Marine officers and urge improved organization for the U.S. Marine Corps.

29. *The Young Seaman's Manual. Compiled from Various Authorities, and Illustrated with Numerous Original and Select Designs. For the Use of the U.S. Training Ships and the Marine Schools.* New York: Van Nostrand, 1875.

This manual was published anonymously by Luce as a textbook for the schools that he had helped to establish. The material in the volume was taken directly from his *Seamanship* text. Luce very carefully restricted the contents of this manual to the basic material which would be useful in the education and training of cadets. It includes chapters on the compass and lead, knotting and splicing, the log, rope, blocks, tackles, the mast and rudder, cutting and fitting rigging, masting, rigging ship, sails, and boats. There is some evidence which indicates that two issues of this manual may have been made in 1875.

30. "Modern Navies. No. I–Navy of the United States." *Army and Navy Journal,* vol. XIV, No. 1, 12 August 1876, p. 7.

This article is devoted to an outline history of the Continental Navy and the origins of the U.S. Navy between the years 1775 and 1781.

Four of this series of six articles analyze the U.S. Navy; the fifth, the navies of Great Britain and France; and the last, the other navies of Europe. (See items 31-35.) Those on the Navy of the United States offer its political and administrative history, stressing the superiority of American warship design before the Civil War. In the third article he reminds his readers of the Navy's peaceful achievements: the Naval Academy, Coast Survey, Hydrographic Office, Torpedo School, the scientific expeditions, suppression of the slave trade, and the opening of Japan.

The proper duty of the U.S. Navy, he claimed, was not coast or river defense, but that of the offensive on the high seas. Luce ended his series on the U.S. Navy with a statement by Lewis Cass:[1] "It is on our maritime frontier that we are most exposed . . . Our great battle upon the ocean is yet to be fought, and we shall gain nothing by shutting our eyes to the nature of the struggle, or to the exertions we shall find it necessary to make."

---

[1] Lewis Cass (1782-1866), brigadier general in the War of 1812, Governor of Michigan Territory, 1813-31; Secretary of War, 1831-36; Ambassador to France, 1836-42; U.S. Senator from Michigan, 1845-48, 1849-57; Secretary of State, 1857-60; Democratic candidate for President, 1848.

31. "Modern Navies. II–Navy of the United States." *Army and Navy Journal,* vol. XIV, No. 2, 19 August 1876, p. 26.

This installment continues the outline history of the U.S. Navy from 1783 to 1812.

32. "Modern Navies. No. III—Navy of the United States." *Army and Navy Journal,* vol. XIV, No. 5, 2 September 1876, p. 62.

   This installment outlines the U.S. Navy's contributions to naval science between 1842 and the Civil War.

33. "Modern Navies. No. IV—Navy of the United States." *Army and Navy Journal,* vol. XIV, No. 6, 9 September 1876, p. 71.

   In this installment Luce discusses privateering and the relationship of the Navy to deep sea commerce.

34. "Modern Navies.—V." *Army and Navy Journal,* vol. XIV, No. 8, 23 September 1876, p. 110.

   This installment is divided into two sections under the headings "Great Britain" and "France."

   In the section on the Navy of Great Britain, Luce refers to the British Admiralty, to the training of boys for which there were 22 school and drill ships, and to the ironclad fleet. He draws attention to the Royal Navy's steam reserve, consisting of vessels in reduced commission, some prepared to go to sea within 48 hours, others kept in thorough repair with all required armament and equipment on board.

   In describing the Navy of France, Luce first gives a brief description of the organization of that country's Navy Department and then compliments its ironclads, especially the squadrons of evolutions.

35. "Modern Navies.—V. The Navies of Europe." *Army and Navy Journal,* vol. XIV, No. 10, 7 October 1876, p. 135.

   This article devotes a brief descriptive paragraph and comment each to the navies of Austria, Denmark, Germany, Greece, Italy, Russia, Spain, Sweden and Norway, Turkey, and the navies of South America and Asia.

   Luce, in command of *Juniata* in 1870, had been sent, during the Franco-Prussian War, to observe the French blockade of German North Sea ports. He took advantage of this to gain considerable information on the new German Navy which was first organized in 1849. The Germans, he claimed, were carrying out a farsighted naval policy that would provide a balanced fleet with 23 ironclads by 1882. Their naval ports then were at Kiel, Danzig, and Williamshaven on the North Sea. The last had one of the finest dockyards in the world. He notes that Japan then had the former Confederate ship *Stonewall* and one other ironclad. The Imperial Naval College at Yeddo [Tokyo] had 150 cadets, with a schoolship.

36. "Sovereignty of the Sea." *Potter's American Monthly,* vol. VII, November 1876, pp. 345-63.

   During the winter of 1876-1877, Luce published three articles in *Potter's American Monthly*[1] (see items 37 and 43), his first attempt to reach directly the general public on professional subjects. Two of these pieces were signed, the third appeared under a thinly veiled pseudonym. To make his professional subjects appealing to the magazine's readers, he included a great deal of history.

Luce defined the term, "Sovereignty of the Sea," the title of the first, as "a certain predominance of maritime influence possessed by one particular state over all others." In ancient days it meant trade dominance as in the case of Phoenicia or naval power in the case of Athens. In the Middle Ages the concept of maritime strategy became one of domination of large water areas, in some cases including whole seas or segments of the ocean. Where such areas were virtually enclosed within a country's landform, this construction has survived in international law. Luce pointed to the case of the United States asserting the right of domain over Long Island Sound. The Kings of England, beginning in the 13th century, asserted a control over the English Channel and North Sea based on the then Norman possession of both bordering coasts that they did not relinquish until 1807. Luce then devotes about half the article to a history of Britain's claim to sovereignty of the sea. It is known that Luce had read English history since his days as a midshipman in 1845, when one of his shipmates on board U.S.S. *Congress* presented him with a history of the Royal Navy. Since Luce was acquainted with many English journals, he may have used an article by John Knox Laughton as the source for this piece. (J.K. Laughton, "The Sovereignty of the Sea," *Fortnightly Review*, vol. V, August 1866, pp. 718-33.) No connection with Laughton has been documented for this early date; however, 3 years later, Luce obtained a copy of Laughton's 1879 article from the *Journal of the Royal United Service Institution*, "The Heraldry of the Sea—Ensigns, Colours, and Flags." The item in the Luce Papers, Library of Congress, is inscribed, "Captain Luce with kind regards. J.K. Laughton, 21 March 1879."

While Laughton's work was devoted to England's claim to the "narrow seas" of the English Channel, Luce was interested in the analogy to the littoral problems of the United States. American writers[2] on international law in Luce's time agreed that the extent of our coasts and the shallowness of the waters off them, together with the natural boundary of the Gulf Stream, entitled the United States to freedom from belligerent warfare out to that limit. He was concerned most about the Florida Channel, then as now, a great highway of ocean commerce. Spain at the time held Cuba and also had seven ironclads, whereas the United States did not have an effective fighting ship.

---

[1]Named the *American Historical Record*, edited by Benson J. Lossing, until January 1875 when John E. Potter became its publisher and made it more general in character. See Mott, *A History of American Magazines*, vol. II (1865-1885).

[2]Theodore W. Woolsey, *Introduction to the Study of International Law* (New York: Scribner, Armstrong, 1874), p. 85; Henry Wheaton, *Elements of International Law* (Boston: Little, Brown, 1866), pp. 214ff; Henry W. Halleck, *Elements of International Law and the Law of the Sea* (Philadelphia: Lippincott, 1872), pp. 76-84.

37. "Reorganization of the Navy." *Potter's American Monthly*, vol. VII, December 1876, pp. 422-25.

Luce's previous article in Potter's "Sovereignty of the Seas" may have been a screen for this, a subject on which he wanted to address himself directly to the American people. It would have been improper for him to sign it without permission from the Navy Department, but the pen name he used, "Luke B. Stephens," was certainly sufficiently close that he could be recognized as the author. However, there was no marked official or service opposition to his efforts at this time, and Luce evidently enjoyed good relations with George M. Robeson, Secretary of the Navy in Grant's administration.

Luce liked all things French, and he was particularly partial to France's naval administration which he depicted clearly for his civilian readers. He pointed out, however, that in France and other continental countries the Navy Minister is selected from the active list of admirals. This practice would not be acceptable in Great Britain or in the United States where a supposedly eminent statesman is placed in charge of the sea arm. In the United States the Secretary, as a Cabinet member, is also an adviser to the President on naval policy. But at that time, there was no senior officer assigned to advise him on professional and technical matters. Here, Luce contended, was the fatal defect in the organization of the U.S. Navy Department.

He then discussed Lt. Matthew Fontaine Maury's part in creating the bureau system of organization. Maury wrote a series of articles in 1841-1842 entitled "Scraps from the Lucky Bag" which appeared under his pseudonym "Harry Bluff" in the *Southern Literary Messenger* of Richmond, Va. He proposed that the bureau type organization be adopted for the Navy Department to replace the Board of Commissioners. This was enacted into law in 1842. However, his additional proposal for an under secretary who would be a post captain was ignored by Congress.

Luce ends the article with a proposal that he was to reiterate for the next 30 years. "The proper way of proceeding to reorganize the Navy is to have a commission especially organized to make an exhaustive study of the subject and to report to Congress, in the form of a bill, exactly what is needed."

Luce was not the only author writing on this subject. Richard W. Meade anonymously wrote a remarkable series of 18 articles on a proposed naval organization for the United States which ran in the *Army and Navy Journal* from October 1875 to

May 1876. Its title was "Thoughts on Naval Administration—the Nation that Controls the Sea Controls the World."

38. "Naval Government." *Army and Navy Journal*, vol. XIV, No. 21, 30 December 1876, p. 329.

Although no documentary evidence has been found in the Luce or Church correspondence to attribute concretely this item and the following item to Luce, the style is so characteristically Luce and the subject matter so parallel to his correspondence at this time that this assumption may be made.[1]

The first paragraph outlines the American difficulties in endeavoring to achieve ideal naval government. The best possible would include a well-qualified naval administration and the limitations of the American methods.

Comments by Chancellor Kent and Justice Story were included which supported the concept of a naval adviser.[2]

---

[1] Luce to D.D. Porter, 17 November 1874, Porter Papers, LC; Luce to W.C. Church, 22 December 1875, Church Papers, LC; Luce to W.C. Whitthorne, 8 February 1876; Luce to Jurien de la Graviere, 1 May 1876, Luce Papers, LC.

[2] James Kent (1763-1847), jurist, legal writer, Chancellor of the New York Court of Chancery, 1814-21, author of *Commentaries*. Joseph Storey (1779-1845), Associate Justice of the U.S. Supreme Court, was noted for his masterful opinions, many of which concerned admiralty matters and the law of war at sea. He was an early supporter of a strong navy.

39. "The Mixed Commission." *Army and Navy Journal*, vol. XIV, No. 22, 6 January 1877, p. 344-45. See item 38.

The content of this article is the same as a letter Luce wrote to Washington C. Whitthorne,[1] Chairman of the House Naval Affairs Committee. In his article and letters, the naval officer mentions an editorial from the *Army and Navy Journal*, vol. XIII, No. 49, 15 July 1876, p. 787, which he may also have authored. Luce had drafted a bill for Whitthorne establishing a mixed commission to investigate the organization of the Navy and to propose the legislation needed to provide for a proper reorganization of the Navy. Luce wanted the commission to include two naval officers, an Army officer, and two distinguished civilians. The Army officer would enable the commission to define the military function of the Navy, while the civilians could judge the moral effect of the Navy on the Nation. In his letter to Whitthorne, which paralleled this article, Luce suggested that Charles F. Adams and George Bancroft be the "eminent civilians" appointed to the commission.[2]

Luce had obtained many of his ideas for a joint commission from his correspondence with French Vice Adm. Jurien de la Graviere. Jurien described for him the appointment of the French parliamentary inquiry appointed 31 October 1849. However, Jurien himself placed little faith in the work of such commissions. He personally preferred general inspections by competent officers.[3] That commission achieved for the French Navy what Luce wanted for the United States. In essence, this came about through the Moody Board in 1909.

---

[1] Luce to W.C. Whitthorne, 8 January 1876, Luce Papers, LC.

[2] Charles Francis Adams (1807-1886), diplomat, Minister to Great Britain during the Civil War, son of President John Quincy Adams. George Bancroft (1800-1891), historian, diplomat, Secretary of the Navy, 1845-46, founder of the Naval Academy, Ambassador to Great Britain, 1846-49, and to Germany, 1867-74.

[3] Luce to Jurien de la Graviere, 1 May 1876; Jurien de la Graviere to Luce, 30 May 1876, Luce Papers, LC.

40. *Seamanship: Compiled from Various Authorities, and Illustrated with Numerous Original and Select Designs, for the Use of the United States Naval Academy.* 6th ed., rev. and enlarged. New York: Van Nostrand, 1877.

This edition appears to be identical to item 25. The title page still carries the author's name, "S.B. Luce, Lieutenant-Commander, United States Navy," in spite of the fact that he had been promoted to captain. See items 11 and 25.

41. "Fleets of the World." U.S.N.I. *Proceedings*, vol. III, No. 1, 1877, pp. 5-24.

This second Luce article for the Naval Institute has the same name as a book published recently by his friend Foxhall A. Parker. In fact, the article was a commentary based on two books by Parker, *Fleet Tactics Under Steam*, New York: Van Nostrand, 1870, and *Fleets of the World: The Galley Period*, New York: Van Nostrand, 1876. This paper was read before the Naval Institute on 20 April 1876.

Luce was supposed to produce a book review, but the subject carried him away and he ended up with a 20-page naval history of the world, treating the subject in three maritime ages: Oar, Sail, and Steam. Parker had limited his volume to galley warfare by the Mediterranean powers and by the Norsemen, expecting eventually to compile a trilogy on the subject. However, he died suddenly in 1879, while Superintendent of the Naval Academy.

Luce begins his long "review" with definitions, the most significant being the word "tactics." The Greeks not only coined this word but became masters of the art of war at sea. The Romans adopted the Greek systems of maneuvers, applying it to their wide experience in land warfare.

The first seafight entirely under sail, according to Luce, was in 1217 at North Forelands in the English Channel; the last decisive battle under oars was Lepanto, 1571. Tactics for the age of sail, notably the line ahead, finally evolved after the Battle of Texel, 1665. Luce calls attention to the first scientific treatment of naval warfare under sail by Paul Hoste.

In this article Luce demonstrates the similarity between ancient tactics and Parker's tactics for steam warships. By footnoting the exact signal from the *U.S. Naval Signal Book*, Luce brings together a detailed knowledge of ancient naval warfare and current U.S. naval tactics. Parker's *Fleet Tactics Under Steam* and *Squadron Tactics Under Steam* were the basis for *U.S. Naval Signal Book, Naval Tactics, 1874*, an 85-page supplement to the general *U.S. Naval Signal Book*.

Luce notes:

in establishing the fact of similarity between two tactical systems widely separated by time . . . there is no intention of holding up the tactics of the ancients as worthy of imitation. Though we acknowledge the Greeks to be our masters in the art of war, yet tactics change with the change in weapons; what may have been admirable in their day might prove, therefore, utterly impracticable now. With strategy it is not so . . . ..

In summation, Luce remarks " . . . We are forced to the conclusion that the true way to study naval tactics is to do so in connection with the study of Military and Naval history and the science of war as taught at the best military schools." Looking back to the books under review, Luce sees them as "a brilliant illustration of the change from the 'rough and tough old Commodore' to the higher culture of the modern school." He also remarked with some compunction: "In the ardor of pursuing the theme we have been led somewhat beyond the range of the volumes under consideration." He closes with a tribute to Parker's scholarship and takes occasion to mention the great but now almost forgotten sailor-poet of English literature, William Falconer.[1] For another review of this book by Luce, see item 44.

---

[1] William Falconer (1732-1770), author of the epic poem *The Shipwreck*, based on his own experience in a disastrous stranding on a Greek island in the Aegean Sea. He was one of three saved. He lost his life in another shipwreck while en route to India. The first edition of *The Shipwreck*, London: n.p.. 1762, is superior to the revised 3d edition (1769). See his *Poetical Works* with a biography by J. Mitford in the Aldine Edition, London, 1836; Philadelphia, 1852. He is also author of the *Universal Marine Dictionary,* London: n.p., 1769, Luce probably read *Falconer's Works*, Boston: n.p., 1877.

42. "The Modern Pythia." *The Galaxy,* vol. XXIII, February 1877, pp. 209-16.

This unusual essay on extrasensory perception shows the range of Luce's interests and reveals his tendency toward dilettantism.[1]

In Greek mythology, Pythia was the high priestess of the oracle of Apollo at Delphi. Luce's "modern Pythia" was planchette, later called Ouija, a small, heart-shaped board supported by two casters and a pencil. This device, when touched by two persons mentally concentrating on a question, moved apparently by itself across a surface marked with letters and symbols. In doing this, it traced messages revealing evidence of extrasensory perception, telepathy, clairvoyance, and precognition.

The article details Luce's own experience with planchette while on board a Pacific Mail Steamer[2] in November 1868 en route from Panama to San Francisco to take command of the gunboat *Mohongo* at Mare Island. He actually conducted experiments with the assistance of a lady partner, evidently a Civil War widow en route to a new life in California. The essay lists over a page of test questions put to planchette, with all of its replies. When he received answers that he already knew, he first thought that he was being hoaxed, but he soon realized that this vehicle was only revealing information implicit in the inquiries that had been made.

Passengers crowded the room to ask questions and to hear predictions. One can easily picture the personable and alert Luce captivating these people. Answers to factual queries, such as the recent presidential election or the position of ships at sea, were found to be glaringly wrong when checked with the actual facts.

Luce decided that what needed to be investigated was not the degree of faith to be placed in planchette, but why it should be consulted at all. He immediately falls back on history and comes to the conclusion that the explanation lies in man's twofold nature: the outward side that we present to the world and the inner depth about which we know little. Xenophon indicated this twofold nature in his *Cyropaedia*[3] as had St. Paul.[4] Luce gives the several Greek words that distinguish differences in our inner nature but for which there are no English equivalents. The poet Byron alludes to the mystery "with no less truth than beauty."[5] Luce explained the phenomenon of telepathy by analogy to the popular scientific wonder, electricity. It was not difficult to understand how psychic stimuli on nerve fibers were transmitted to the muscles and, thus, to planchette and the letters and symbols on the board. Practitioners were in no way aware of the operation, except through its results.

The phenomenon was known to the ancients in the time of Nebuchadnezzar (ca. 605 - ca. 562 B.C.) the King of Babylon. The Chaldean priests, magicians, astrologers, and Magi, with their understanding of visions and dreams, possessed all the knowledge in this sphere which was transmitted to Egypt and then to Greece. The intellectual Greeks, however, were not to be imposed upon by a priesthood. Themistocles made a tool of them, and the great orator Demosthenes denounced them. Because of this, much of this ancient knowledge was lost.

Luce concludes that few observers of human nature would doubt that "we are bound by an 'electric chain,'" and that there are abnormally sensitive individuals, but professional mediums fail to show the slightest use, despite the antiquity of their profession. "It remains to be shown wherein the modern medium is entitled to a particle more of respect than the medium of Endor."⁶

---

[1] In the Luce Papers, LC, there is an additional undated piece by Luce on dreams. He had it published about this time in an unidentified Germantown, Pa., periodical.

[2] See J.H. Kemble, *The Panama Route 1848-1869*, New York: De Capo, 1972. Ships in which Luce might have taken passage were *Golden City, Golden Age*, and *Montana.* it is interesting to note that W.H. Parker was a master of Pacific Mail Line ships between 1865 and 1874. See item 1.

[3] Xenophon. *Cyropaedia*, Book VI, i, 41. Walter Miller, trans., Xenophon *Cyropaedia (London and New York: The Loeb Classical Library*, 1914), vol. II, pp. 141-142.

[4] Hebrews 4:12; 1 Corinthians 15:15-44.

[5] George Gordon Lord Byron, *Childe Harold's Pilgrimage*, canto IV, XXIII, 4 to IV, XXIV, 2.

[6] Samuel 28:7. In the King James versions, the medium is termed the "Witch of Endor."

43. "Signals and Signaling." *Potter's American Monthly*, vol. VIII, April 1877, pp. 297-302.

In this article Luce attempts to present a popular, entertaining history of naval signaling. This same material is better presented in his article, "Naval Signals," in *Johnson's Cyclopedia* (see item 45). In this piece Luce reveals his wide range of sources for his research in professional subjects. In addition to classical writers such as Homer, Polybius, Plutarch, Caesar, Thucydides, and the Bible, Luce has also consulted Sir Harris Nicolas' history of the Royal Navy, George Preble on the history of the flag, as well as the current International Code of Signals and information on the Army's signal system. Luce was particularly interested in the subject of signaling in this period. In early 1877, while in command of U.S.S. *Hartford*, he noticed that the United States Code list assigned signal letters to all vessels in the U.S. Navy and merchant marine, but the vessels of the Revenue Marine were omitted. In a letter to the Chief of the Bureau of Navigation on 22 January 1877, Luce formally recommended that the next code list include these vessels and that an order be issued to all naval ships requiring them to exchange numbers with Revenue vessels, as was common practice between naval ships. "The object of this," he wrote, "is to bring the Commercial Code of Signals into more frequent use and familiarize officers and men with them of both services."

44. "Literature." *The Galaxy*, vol. XXIII, May 1877, pp. 717-18.

This unsigned book review of Foxhall Parker's *Fleets of the World* appeared in a section of *The Galaxy* devoted to reviews of current literature. It has been identified by a letter to W.C. Church[1] in which Luce states:

> By note from Mr. Van Nostrand I learn that you are willing to accept a notice of "Fleets _____" for the "Galaxy". I have never before written a book notice, & am so much engaged now that I have no time to study up on methods. I have done my best, however, in this instance and hope it will suit, as I wish to do something in that line out of my friendship for the author.

In the review itself, Luce summarizes the volume and concludes that it is a valuable contribution to the profession. He felt that the book amply demonstrated that "naval archaeology is not a mere idle amusement, suited to the elegant leisure of the scholar." It had practical value in that it enabled an officer to understand his profession more thoroughly.

---

[1] Luce to W.C. Church, 12 February 1877, Church Papers, LC.

45. "Marines, U.S. Corps of." *Johnson's New Universal Cyclopedia: a Scientific and Popular Treasury of Useful Knowledge. Editors-in-chief Frederick A.P. Barnard and Arnold Guyot with Numerous Contributors from Writers of Distinguished Eminence in Every Department and Science in the United States and in Europe.* New York: Johnson, 1878, vol. IV, p. 734.

Luce contributed five articles to the first edition of this popular encyclopedia. (See items 46-49.) Foxhall A. Parker was the naval editor for this edition. Luce succeeded him in this position for later editions.

The first piece on the Marine Corps is a typical encyclopedia article, condensed and more informative than the one he did for Collum (see item 28).

46. "Naval Signals." *Johnson's Cyclopedia,* vol. IV, p. 734.

The article on naval *signals* treats this means of distance communication in ancient time, during the Eastern Roman Empire, and in British naval history. He discusses in considerable detail, day and night signals in the U.S. Navy and explains the U.S. Army Myer system which was used extensively by the Navy during the Civil War. The primary advantage of this system is that it does not require a code book. The international code of signals provided a universal language for the entire maritime world. One system of flags had been adopted by all maritime nations with a common signal book but each printed in the user's language. This system is still employed.

47. "Naval Tactics." *Johnson's Cyclopedia,* vol. IV, pp. 734-35.

In the article on "Naval Tactics," Luce separates the periods of naval history as he did in the review of Parker's work (item 41) into the Ages of Oars, Sails, and Steam and pointing out the resemblance of the tactics of the third with that of the first.

48. "Navy." *Johnson's Cyclopedia,* vol. IV, p. 744.

The article "Navy," 2,000 words long, includes a definition

of the term, a philosophical discussion of warfare at sea, and the unqualified requirement that a nation exposed to the sea or with large overseas trade must have a good navy. He uses the Persian-Greek War and the Battle of Salamis to aptly illustrate the function of a navy. He inserts his claim that powerful navies are not dangerous to civil liberties (see item 53).

A short history of the U.S. Navy describes its organizations, officer corps, ships, and navy yards. The President, he points out, is authorized to keep as many ships in commission during peace as he thinks proper, but Congress really determines the size of the active Navy by the amount annually appropriated for its maintenance.

49. "Rope-Making." *Johnson's Cyclopedia,* vol. IV, pp. 1718-19.

    Luce's piece on "Rope-Making" was derived from personal experience. The famous ropewalk at the Boston Navy Yard had been under his jurisdiction from 1872 to 1875.

50. "Naval Training Schools." *Brentano's Aquatic Monthly and Sporting Gazetteer,* new series vol. I, No. 1, April 1879, pp. 34-36.

    This piece is a long letter written to the editor of a yachting, rowing, and swimming magazine which was published under various names between 1872 and 1891. Luce informs his readers of the activities of the apprentices of his Training Squadron. He points out that in the sailing days, seamen were equally familiar with merchant ships and men of war, and that it was only necessary to train them to handle marine artillery and to use boarding pikes and cutlasses. But in 1879 guns were heavier and seamen were often called upon to land ashore under arms, therefore more extensive training was needed. At this time Luce was frequently landing the apprentice battalion for exercise, training, and parades. He then goes on to explain the training, pay, cruises, and other details of preparing his naval apprentices to become petty and warrant officers. The piece is signed and dated U.S. Frigate *Minnesota,* Brooklyn, March 1879.

    Articles on the Training Squadron and its apprentices appeared in the Providence *Commercial Journal,* Newport *Mercury,* Waterbury (Conn.) *American,* Norfolk *Landmark,* New York *Herald, Times,* and *Sunday Star,* papers in Poughkeepsie and Newburgh, N.Y., and in *Frank Leslie's Illustrated Newspaper.*

51. "United States Naval Training Ships." *The United Service,* vol. I, July 1879, pp. 423-43.

    Ici on parle Anglais.—This notice, frequently seen in the shop windows of Paris, was not very long ago placarded in the starboard gangway of one of the ships of our Mediterranean squadron: "English spoken here." The few American sailors who belonged to that ship had good reason to give such notice a conspicuous place . . . . The jest had at least the merit of a good point, and that point was a severe commentary on the character of the crews we have been for years employing to maintain the honor and integrity of the American flag upon the ocean.

So goes the first paragraph. The humorous reference was to Luce's own command, the steam sloop of war *Juniata*. Shortly after his return in her from the European station in 1872, he made an official detailed report to the Secretary of the Navy on the deplorable personnel situation, not only in his own ship, but in those of the entire squadron.[1]

About this time Capt. R.W. Shufeldt became head of the Bureau of Equipment and Recruiting. He soon established procedures to enlist and train American boys in order that the Navy could acquire a body of native-born petty officers and leading seamen. Moreover, changes in the methods of warfare were requiring a higher type of men-of-warsmen, able to perform an extended range of enlisted duties, many of which were mechanical.

In 1877 Luce was assigned command of the steam frigate *Minnesota*, stationed at New York with the mission of recruiting and training these boys. It is such training that Luce describes in this article. He stresses that the discipline and routine of ship's life is of far more consequence in training and character development than formal instruction. The schoolship, to succeed, must be a school of practice.

"On board a well-disciplined ship exercises are carried on and everything is kept in beautiful order, while the crew has plenty of spare time on their hands. It is this 'spare time' that, on board the school ship, is devoted to study."

In 1964, this article was reprinted in pamphlet form by the Naval Historical Foundation, Washington, D.C.

---

[1] Luce to Navy Department, 12 November 1872, Luce Papers, LC. The copy of this report in his papers was requested from the Navy Department by Luce while preparing this article.

52. *The Young Seaman's Manual, Compiled from Various Authorities, and Illustrated with Numerous Original and Select Designs. For the Use of the U.S. Training Ships and the Marine Schools.* 2d ed. New York: Van Nostrand, 1880. (This issue is identical to item 29.)

53. "A Powerful Navy Not Dangerous to Civil Liberty." *The United Service*, vol. II, No. 1, January 1880, pp. 109-13.

In this first of three articles on military ethics, Luce takes issue with the view, expressed by Theodore D. Woolsey, then President of Yale College, in his work, *An Introduction to the Study of International Law*, par. 122, p. 210. The article in *The United Service* was basically the same as a letter Luce had addressed to Woolsey shortly after the book appeared.[1]

Luce took issue with the view that powerful navies are detrimental to national prosperity and dangerous to civil liberty.

He showed from both ancient and modern history that navies are compatible with democratic institutions. He also established that an American Navy of respectable size could be maintained from one-sixth of the custom revenues provided by foreign commerce. This article was reprinted in 1906. (See item 128.)

---

[1] Luce to Woolsey, 13 April 1875, Luce Papers, LC.

54. "Administration, Naval." *A Naval Encyclopedia: Comprising a Dictionary of Nautical Words and Phrases; Biographical Notices, and Records of Naval Officers; Special Articles on Naval Art and Science, Written Expressly for This Work by Officers and Others of Recognized Authority in the Branches Treated by Them. Together with Descriptions of the Principal Naval Stations and Seaports of the World.* Philadelphia: Hamersly, 1881, pp. 19-21. [Hereafter referred to as Hamersly's *Encyclopedia*.]

This excellent volume is still a useful literary tool for maritime historians, writers, editors, yachtsmen, and naval students. Contributors to L.R. Hamersly's volume numbered 66, most of them naval officers. Major contributors were Lt. F.S. Bassett who wrote 26 articles; Medical Director Edward Shippen, a talented naval historian, contributed 23 articles; Lt. E.T. Strong, 13 articles; and Luce, who contributed 12. (See items 54-65.)

55. "Admiralty." Hamersly's *Encyclopedia*, p. 23.

This article discusses the office of Lord High Admiral of England and the commissioners for executing that office.

56. "Anchoring." Hamersly's *Encyclopedia*, pp. 35-36.

This article discusses anchoring by square-rigged vessels, schooners, and steamships, along with anchoring by the stern and with a spring.

57. "Commission." Hamersly's *Encyclopedia*, p. 154.

Here, Luce draws a contrast between an officer's commission, a commission of inquiry, and the commission of a vessel.

58. "Corvette." Hamersly's *Encyclopedia*, p. 174.

Luce discusses the use of this term in France and Britain.

59. "Emergencies at Sea." Hamersly's *Encyclopedia*, pp. 244-45.

This article discusses shipboard procedures during a fire at sea, collision, grounding, springing a leak, a squall, man overboard, and loss of the rudder.

60. "Government, Naval." Hamersly's *Encyclopedia*, pp. 316-17.

In this article Luce contrasts the British and American systems of government. His last paragraph reads: "The proof of the inefficiency of this [the U.S.] form of naval government is to be found in the fact that it utterly failed to stand the test of war. The foregoing will serve to illustrate the principle of naval administration."

61. "Mooring." Hamersly's *Encyclopedia*, pp. 502-03.

    Here Luce discusses the procedures in mooring a ship, a flying moor, mooring to a buoy, and unmooring.

62. "Naval Songs." Hamersly's *Encyclopedia*, pp. 515-16.

    In this long article Luce outlines the history of songs in men-of-war and points out the songs that came from American seamen in the early history of the U.S. Navy. He later used this entire piece as the preface for his anonymous collection of naval songs. See item 69.

63. "Naval Tactics." Hamersly's *Encyclopedia*, pp. 518-20.

    In this two-page article illustrated with a full-page diagram, Luce discusses the problems involved in fleet tactics and ship maneuvers, basic formations, and the order of battle.

64. "Naval Training Systems." Hamersly's *Encyclopedia*, pp. 520-22.

    This article outlines the history of naval training in the United States from the 1835 proposal made by John Goin through 19 October 1880, when this article was apparently written. He concludes,

    > The present system has been in operation about five years; just about the lifetime of the experiments of 1837 and 1864. It is yet to be seen whether it will meet with the fate of its predecessors, or justify the hope expressed by Mr. Secretary [James K.] Paulding in 1839, that it will be a great and lasting benefit to the navy.

65. "Organization." Hamersly's *Encyclopedia*, pp. 628-29.

    This article is devoted to the problem of organizing a ship's company and establishing a watch, quarter, and station bill.

66. "Our Naval Policy." *The United Service*, vol. VI, No. 5, May 1882, pp. 501-21.

    "A brief review of the history of our navy during the first century of its existence will show that the United States have never had what is commonly known as a naval policy." These are the opening lines of Luce's most comprehensive article to date on the subjects of naval administration and line officer direction within the Navy Department.

    The want of a naval policy, he held, was due to failure of Congress to heed the executive branch. Congress, on the other hand, never received a clear and coordinated presentation of the Navy's needs. Luce recommends an independent commission as the means for establishing a wise policy. He notes that France in 1847 and Great Britain in 1861 and 1870 had marked success in improving their maritime arms by this method.

    Luce concludes this piece with this statement, "The organic

laws on which our naval establishment rests require revision, and none more so than that on which our naval administration is based." In a copy in the Naval Historical Collection, Naval War College, Luce has added in his own hand, "Congress did *not* do so, thus adding one more illustration to the long list. L "

This piece, which was unsigned, has been identified as Luce's from a signed copy at the Naval War College and by an interesting exchange of letters between two of his friends, John N. Maffitt and George H. Preble.[1]

---

[1] Maffitt to Preble, 2 May 1882, Preble Papers, Massachusetts Historical Society, Boston. Preble to Maffitt, 7 May 1882, Maffitt Papers, Southern Historical Collection, University of North Carolina, Chapel Hill.

67. "Christian Ethics as an Element of Military Education," *The United Service,* vol. VIII, No. 1, January 1883, pp. 1-16.

"Religion and war are the two great central facts of history . . . Religion gave birth to education. War led the way to civilization."

With his usual historical approach, Luce explains how the ritual of ancient pagan worship necessitated an educated priesthood. Man's highest faculties were developed in doing homage to the Supreme Being whose presence was everywhere felt and whose wisdom and justice in ordering affairs were everywhere acknowledged in the known civilized world.

Next in scale of influence was the military or warrior caste. War was the school wherein men of intellect could cultivate their genius and gratify their ambition.

Cicero, Gibbon, and Carlyle, according to Luce, all agreed that the Romans singularly blended the warlike and the religious. He also discusses the amalgam of religion and war in the German, Hebrew, Arabic, and Chaldean cultures. Life, in all, was represented as a battle between good and evil.

Under the Christian dispensation, the central idea of Love was introduced. As a result, the word Duty assumed a wider and deeper significance, and Honor became one of the cardinal virtues of military ethics.

The remainder of the article is critical of the teaching of Christian ethics within the educational system of the United States, especially at the two national Academies. The naval officer held that while the Articles of War declared commanding officers should show in themselves good examples of virtue, honor, patriotism, and subordination, "We can find in the list of subjects taught at these academies no study which inculcates the practice of virtue, none in which a correct standard of honor is given; no instruction as to the nature and duties of patriotism, in the obligations of duty or the necessity of subordination."

The piece was unsigned when first published, but he added his name to the revised reprinting 24 years later. (See item 129.) In the revision he added several significant footnotes. One of these, concerning a recent hazing scandal, reflected on the Naval

Academy. It brought heated reaction from some faculty members and cadets.

68. "War Schools." U.S.N.I. *Proceedings*, vol. IX, No. 5, 1883, pp. 633-57.

   Luce here addressed the recently formed Newport Chapter of the U.S. Naval Institute on the subject of higher education for naval officers. He describes the several U.S. Army institutions devoted to that purpose, the Infantry and Cavalry School, Fort Leavenworth, Kans.; the Engineer Post and Depot of Willets Point, N.Y.; and, in particular, the U.S. Artillery School at Fortress Monroe, Hampton Roads. This school had become a model institution of higher learning in the military under the direction of the foremost artillery officer of the U.S. Army, William F. Barry, and later, under Luce's friend Emory Upton. Luce devotes over half the article to the details of its curriculum. He also remarks on the Infantry and Cavalry School at Fort Leavenworth and the school for the Engineer Corps at Willets Point, N.Y.

   This article gives evidence of being hurriedly put together. He does, however, get his chief point across near its end when he claims that the naval officer also should possess a knowledge of the science and practice of war.

   > He should be led into a philosophic study of naval history, that he may be enabled to examine the great naval battles of the world with the cold eye of professional criticism, and to recognize where the principles of the science have been illustrated, or where a disregard for the accepted rules of the art of war has led to defeat and disaster.

69. *Naval Songs: A Collection of Original, Selected and Traditional Sea Songs.* New York: Pond, 1883.

   This collection of 200 songs was published anonymously. The first portion of the preface was published earlier as part of Hamersly's *Encyclopedia.* See item 62. Luce states in the preface,

   > The sea victories achieved by the heroes of modern times have not lacked poets to celebrate them in verse, and the sailor, with all that pertains to his perilous life and to his home on the trackless deep, has been sung by minstrels of all degrees . . . .
   > This collection has been undertaken to revive the old songs which commemorate our early naval victories, and to cultivate in our young sailors not only a love for the sea, but also that devotion to their flag which distinguished those who laid the foundation of our naval reknown.

   Luce strongly believed that these songs were particularly valuable in training apprentices.

70. U.S. Congress. Senate. *Report of the Commission on Navy-Yards, 1 December 1883.* Executive Doc. No. 55, 48th Congress, 1st sess. Washington: U.S. Govt. Print. Off., 1884.

Under the authority of the act of Congress of 5 August 1882, a commission was appointed to investigate the condition of the navy yards. Commodore Luce was appointed President of the Commission with members Charles H. Loring and A.B. Mullett. In an interim report of 11 October 1883, the commission stated among its recommendations:

> To a proper understanding of the subject, it should be stated, that the present wasteful extravagance in employing so great an excess of non-producers, and the inefficient system of doing business which has for years past been steadily increasing in our navy-yards, is but the natural outgrowth of the constitution of the Navy Department itself. There can be no manner of doubt of this. . . .For what ever changes may be introduced now, and how beneficial soever they may be, still the same causes remaining in active operation must inevitably produce the same results. . . . Hence we conclude that to organize our navy yards on a just and permanent basis, to consolidate their several plants, to introduce thrift in the management and promptness in the methods of doing work, with a proper system of accountability; to secure in short, in each of our yards unification, method economy, and dispatch, with an administration of its affairs agreeable to the principles of business as understood in civil life, it is absolutely necessary to begin within the Navy Department itself. (p. 44)

This report was the basis for Luce's later article, "On Navy Yards and Their Defense," item 102.

71. *Text-Book of Seamanship. The Equipping and Handling of Vessels Under Sail or Steam. For the Use of the United States Naval Academy.* Revised and enlarged by Lt. Aaron Ward,[1] U.S. Navy, with illustrations by Lt. S. Seabury,[2] U.S. Navy. New York: Van Nostrand, 1884.

Because Luce was deeply involved in the Navy Yard Commission, the establishment of the Naval War College, and the acquisition of Coasters Harbor Island in Narragansett Bay for the Navy, he left the new edition of *Seamanship* largely up to Aaron Ward. In late October 1882, Luce sent out a circular letter to a number of officers in the Navy announcing his intention to issue a new edition of his textbook and soliciting information. He wrote that "the book as it now stands needs to be made fuller in all that relates to the handling of steamers and fore and aft sailing vessels. Information concerning various emergencies, accidents, etc. would be particularly valuable." Ward's revision of the book was the first substantial revision since the edition of 1866. (For earlier editions see items 11, 25, and 40.) Luce's preface is dated, "Training Squadron, Newport, R.I., Feb. 1883."

---

[1] Rear Adm. Aaron Ward (1851-1918) was graduated from the Naval Academy in 1871. He commanded *Wasp* in Cuban waters during the Spanish American War. Commended for gallantry at the Battle of Santiago, he was promoted to lieutenant commander. Ward commanded the Third Division, Atlantic Fleet, in 1911-12, and was Supervisor of New York Harbor until his retirement in 1913.

[2] Lt. Samuel Seabury joined the Navy as an apprentice in 1865. He was graduated from the Naval Academy in 1871. He served with Luce on the staff of Commander, Training Squadron, in 1883-84, and in 1887-88 in the flagship of the Commander in Chief, North Atlantic Squadron. He was retired for medical reasons, in 1896, as a lieutenant.

72. *Johnson's New Universal Aecyclopedia.* Davenport, Iowa: Brown, 1884.

    This is a new edition of item 45. Luce was naval editor for this edition.

73. "United States Naval War College," *The United Service,* vol. XII, No. 1, January 1885, pp. 79-90.

    Luce here outlines the aims of the new War College and describes the courses of study that will be undertaken. A sizable part of this article is devoted to reviewing and quoting from the report of the board from which resulted the founding of the institution by a general order of Secretary of the Navy William E. Chandler, dated 4 October 1884.

    Early in the essay, he listed Jomini's six branches of the Science of War:—Statesmanship, Strategy, Grand Tactics, Logistics, Engineering, and Minor or Elementary Tactics. He gives the naval application of each. "The naval student reading military history" he claims, "can hardly fail to be struck by the similarity between hostile operations on shore and those afloat."

    The plan of the first War College President was to have the naval students study military science with a parallel course in naval history so that they might formulate principles for the guidance of a sea-army preparatory to and during war. This was the comparative method of research. In closing, he quotes at length the board's report on what he believed naval students should study;

    > Campaigns that have depended for success upon the co-operation of a fleet; campaigns that have been frustrated through the interposition of a fleet; the transfer, by water, of a numerous Army to distant points and their landing on an enemy's coasts under the guns of a fleet; the various results of engagements between ships and shore batteries; naval expeditions that have ended in disasters that could have been foretold by an intelligent study of the problem beforehand; and the great naval battles of history, even from the earliest times, which illustrate and

enforce many of the most important and immutable principles of war should be carefully examined and rendered familiar to the naval student

74. U.S. Congress. Senate. *Report Upon the Comparative Merits of Anthracite and Bituminous Coal for Naval Use.* Executive Doc. No. 26, 48th Congress. 2d sess. Washington: U.S. Govt. Print. Off., 1885.

   Luce served as President of this Board with members Capt. D.B. Harmony, Chief Engineer Charles H. Baker, Chief Engineer Fred G. McKean, and Lt. Comdr. C.F. Goodrich. On 5 July 1884 Luce submitted a brief preliminary report of the Board, concluding that anthracite coal was better suited to naval use than bituminous coal. He went on to state that the Board felt that semibituminous coal was preferable to either of these types of coal, especially if a smokeless variety was available. Luce was detached from this duty shortly after the preliminary report was submitted and before the final report could be written. The job of completing the report fell to Captain Harmony as the next senior member, consequently the final report shows little of Luce's influence. The chart showing the location of coal deposits and repairing facilities may well have been something that Luce would have elaborated on had he written the final report.

75. U.S. Congress. Senate. *Letter from the Secretary of the Navy Reporting in Answer to Senate Resolution of the 4th Instant, the Steps Taken by Him to Establish an Advanced Course of Instruction of Naval Officers at Coaster's Harbor Island, Rhode Island.* Executive Doc. No. 68, 48th Congress, 2d sess. Washington: U.S. Govt. Print. Off., 1885.

   This document includes the "Report of Board on a Post-Graduate Course," dated 13 June 1883. The report was submitted by the Board headed by Luce and with members: Comdr. W.T. Sampson and Lt. Comdr. C.F. Goodrich. Written in Luce's flagship for the Training Squadron, U.S.S. *New Hampshire,* the report is divided into three sections: (1) reasons for establishing such a school, (2) outline for the proposed course and practical exercises, and (3) location. Very obviously written by Luce himself, the report states in the first section:

   > In the earnest prosecution of what is but a means to an end, the officer is too apt to lose sight of the ultimate object of all. Thus, electricity in its application to torpedoes, chemistry in application to explosives, metallurgy in relation to ordnance, and steam as a motive power, are only means to the end of which a navy may be said to exist—*success in war.* The establishment of the proposed school, by opening to officers the higher branches, will serve to correct any misapprehension on this point and to dissipate the haze, which, to a greater or

less extent, obscures the perception in regard to the true aim of naval education and the duties of naval officers.

76. U.S. Navy Dept. Bureau of Navigation. Office of Naval Intelligence. "Landing of the Naval Brigade of North Atlantic for Instruction on Gardiner's Island, August 1884." *Papers on Naval Operations During the Year Ending July, 1885.* Information from Abroad, General Information Series, No. IV. Washington: U.S. Govt. Print. Off., 1885, pp. 103-10.

    According to reports provided by S.B. Luce as Commander, North Atlantic Station, this exercise took place 11-13 August 1884 during the period of his first and temporary command of the North Atlantic Station, July to October 1884. Landing forces totaling 660 officers and men from *Tennessee* (flagship), *Vandalia, Swatara, Yantic,* and *Alliance* took part. The brigade landed comprised two battalions of infantry, one of them marines, the other seamen; an artillery battalion of six pieces; plus pioneers, commissary, medical, and signal personnel. No exercises other than normal drills were undertaken. Capt. J.N. Miller, commanding *Tennessee,* commanded the brigade ashore and was charged with all arrangements.

    The operation was a surprise movement. The order was issued while the squadron was en route to Newport. Two days were allowed for preparation. The report stated that such an exercise had never before been previously attempted in secrecy in the U.S. Navy, on such a large scale.

77. *Inauguration of the Perry Statue, September 10, A.D. 1885, with the Addresses of William P. Sheffield, and the Remarks in Receiving the Statue by Governor Wetmore and Mayor Franklin, with the Speeches at the Dinner of the Governor, Mayor, Hon. George Bancroft, Justices Blatchford and Durfee, Admirals Rodgers, Almy and Luce, the Letter of Col. William H. Potter, &c. with an Appendix.* Newport, R.I.: Sanborn, 1885, pp. 42-45.

    This volume is devoted to the dedication of the statue of Oliver Hazard Perry in Washington Square, Newport, R.I. Newport was the home of both Oliver Hazard and Matthew Calbraith Perry. The statue stands today in its original location in the center of town, nearly in front of O.H. Perry's former home.

    Luce was one of several speakers, and he restricted his remarks to the new Naval War College which was soon to have its first session. He praised the school of the quarterdeck which developed Lawrence and Perry, but the college, he said, had been called into existence by the necessity of keeping pace with the advancement of science and of keeping fresh the lessons of history. Luce then extols the sailors to whom Perry owed his victory and quotes two ballads about the Battle of Lake Erie. He does not forget to mention the Naval Apprentice Battalion which paraded on the occasion.

78. *Text-Book of Seamanship. The Equipping and Handling of Vessels Under Sail or Steam. For the Use of the United States Naval Academy,* New York: Van Nostrand, n.d. [1885?]. Revised and enlarged by Lt. Aaron Ward, U.S. Navy. With Illustrations drawn by Lt. S. Seabury, U.S. Navy.

   This is a reissue of item 71. When a copy was received by the Navy Department Library, Washington, D.C., in 1898, it was cataloged as the 1885 edition. There are a number of differences in typography, as well as the publisher's name, in this issue.

79. "On the Study of Naval Warfare as a Science." U.S.N.I. *Proceedings,* vol. XII, No. 2, 1886, pp. 527-46.

   Reprinted here with annotation in chapter III.

80. "Merchant Marine and Navy: Admiral Luce Mourns the Disappearance of the American Sailor." *New York Herald,* 9 January 1887, p. 15.

   This is a newspaper interview with Luce while he was serving as Commander in Chief of the North Atlantic Squadron. The interview clearly demonstrates Luce's flair for public relations. The interviewer notes that in his sailor talk, the accent is strong and the emphasis pronounced. The admiral told his interviewer that the *Herald* had pumped the subject of naval improvement and of coast defense, "as dry as a purser's biscuit." Then he goes on to inundate the reporter with the differences between the modern sailor and the tar of yesteryear, the relations as they should be between the merchant marine and the Navy but are not, on the importance of schoolships, and of sentiment and traditions in a military and naval service, and, above all, the difficulty in getting Americans to go to sea. This means the sad fact that the U.S. Navy must still depend on foreign seamen, despite years of effort with the naval training systems. "It is with sorrow that I say this, but the truth remains."

81. "On the Study of Naval History (Grand Tactics)." U.S.N.I. *Proceedings,* vol. XIII, No. 2, 1887, pp. 175-201.

   Reprinted here with annotation in chapter IV.

82. "Annual Address, 1888." U.S.N.I. *Proceedings,* vol. XIV, no. I, 1888, pp. 1-8.

   Luce was still on the active list, Commander North Atlantic Station, when elected president of the U.S. Naval Institute in 1888, an office he held for 11 years. He opens his address with congratulations on the organization's success but immediately counsels: "Let us look ahead."

   He is not long in introducing his recurring subject: the absence of proper naval administration by which a navy should be held together and its policy shaped. Bad as this is in time of peace, it would be intolerable in war. "We present to the world the extraordinary spectacle of having an organization confessedly unfit for war."

"Now the corner stone of the Institute," Luce reminded his listeners,

> is the "advancement of professional knowledge in the Navy," but of what use is the use of that knowledge if it cannot be applied? It is the application of knowledge that makes it valuable.... The question for the Institute to ask itself, then, is: Can we continue forever to disseminate useful knowledge without a hope of substantial benefits therefrom?

The Institute, he claimed, should be able to point to reforms and progressive steps which will keep the profession abreast, if not in advance, of the nautical world, but he warned that essays on reforms must be followed by action to effect them.

This article is similar in theme to his article in the *Army and Navy Journal,* 16 April 1864. See item 10.

83. U.S. Navy Dept. Bureau of Navigation, Office of Naval Intelligence. "Combined U.S. Naval and Military Manoeuvres, November, 1887." *Naval Reserves, Training, and Materiel June 1888.* General Information Series, No. VII. Washington: U.S. Govt. Print. Off., 1888, pp. 167-78.

The second major exercise of the North Atlantic Squadron under Luce's command received detailed reporting by the Office of Naval Intelligence. This information was based on Luce's official report and orders. The training exercise which took place 10 November 1887 consisted of (1) the passage of the warships through a minefield protected by the guns of Fort Adams, and (2) a landing on Coddington Point with a simulated advance, repulse, and reembarkation, covered by the guns of the fleet. Ships participating were *Richmond* (flagship), *Atlanta, Ossippee, Galena,* and *Dolphin.* The attacking party against Coddington Point consisted of 10 companies of seamen and a battery of artillery totaling 396 men. The defense comprised one army battalion, one seamen battalion, one marine battalion, a battalion of artillery, and a company of naval apprentices, totaling 396 men.

The attacking force comprised the five ships above plus four steam launches acting as torpedo boats. The harbor defense consisted of the Fort Adams battery, a line of submarine mines, and two steam launch torpedo boats.

Luce had made arrangements for ample newspaper coverage. Reporters embarked sent in long articles which appeared in *The New York Times* and *Herald* and the *Army and Navy Journal.* Editorial reaction was favorable. Numerous photographs were taken by E.H. Hart, the New York photographer who produced a beautiful pictorial volume, the first of several he was to do on the growing U.S. Navy of this period. E.H. Hart's *Squadron Evolutions, As Illustrated by the Combined Military and Naval Operations at Newport, R.I., November, 1887, North Atlantic Squadron, Rear Admiral S.B. Luce.* New York: Hart, n.d., is sometimes attributed to Luce since his name appeared on the title page. He undoubtedly approved its publication, but no documentary evidence has been found to indicate that he took an active part in compiling it. The only written portion in this volume of portraits and action photographs is an introductory chapter entitled, "Applied Tactics, as Illustrated by the Combined Military and Naval Operations at Newport, R.I., November, 1887." This chapter is a revision of an anonymous article, "The Sham Battle at Newport," *Army and Navy Journal*, vol. XXV, No. 17, 19 November 1887, p. 329.

A month previous, on 11 October, a torpedo exercise had been conducted in which a flotilla of steam launches from other vessels made a night attack on *Atlanta* while at anchor. However, *Atlanta's* searchlights proved so efficient that the boats of the attacking torpedo flotilla were all out of action within 15 minutes.

The report of the board of umpires for the 10 November exercises included the statement: "It is hoped that these maneuvers are only the beginning of what may, on a more comprehensive scale, give our service an equivalent of autumn maneuvers in Europe."

Such plans never came to pass. Luce prepared for more extensive joint exercises on Fisher's Island in Long Island Sound off New London in the fall of 1888. In this he had the hearty approval of Maj. Gen. John M. Schofield, commanding the Army's Department of the Atlantic. Gen. Philip H. Sheridan also gave his approval, and Secretary of the Navy Whitney appeared favorably inclined. Lt. Tasker H. Bliss, USA, and Comdr. Colby M. Chester made extensive preliminary plans. The plans failed, however, when Capt. W.S. Schley, Chief of the Bureau of Equipment and Recruiting, expressed the Navy's intention to charge the Army for transportation of the troops to be embarked at New England ports in the Navy's ships. This was an example of Luce's complaint that the power of the Bureau chiefs equaled that of the Secretary.

A successful landing operation of several days' duration, however, was held at Pensacola in April 1888, following the winter cruising in the Caribbean.

The innovation of such fleet exercises is a major contribution by Luce. They were part of his concept of a squadron of evolution which would be an adjunct to the Naval War College, testing the theory and practice of sea warfare being worked out there. These exercises were as close to this as he would get, a creditable accomplishment considering the ships with which he had to work.

Luce seemed fond of landing operations, perhaps because they involved so many men, were different from the drills on board ships, required good administration, and kept the crews involved and interested. Most importantly, joint exercises were more realistic training for actual combat. This kind of exercise paralleled the stress which Luce placed in promoting the comparative study of military and naval subjects at the Naval War College.

84. "Naval Administration." U.S.N.I. *Proceedings,* vol. XIV, No. 3, 1888, pp. 561-88.

> Government, in the abstract, is the operation of law, and law has been defined as a rule of action.
>
> Naval Government may be said to be the system of rules by virtue of which the affairs of the navy are regulated.
>
> Administration, signifying *Management,* means, in a political sense, to manage and direct the affairs of Government, and belongs to the Executive as distinguished from the Legislative Branch.

Thus, by defining the terms he is to use, Stephen B. Luce introduced his three published lectures on Naval Administration (see items 117 and 122) which formed the core of his efforts to reform the Navy Department. These efforts spanned a period of about 50 years. As indicated above, 15 years separated the composition of the first from the other two, yet all are closely knit. The second and third, published in 1902 and 1903, in some features repeat the first, but they mostly provide documentations for the principles of military management set down in the piece of 1888.

In 1885 Secretary of the Navy Whitney presented a report to the President, extracts from which Luce quoted in these papers. Whitney had pointed out that the separate executive responsibilities of the Bureau chiefs made it impossible for them to provide him with intelligent guidance on the "art of war." S.P. Huntington in his study on national security and civil-military relations, *The Soldier and the State,* wrote:

> His [Whitney's] statement touched off a debate on naval organization which continued for thirty years until the establishment of the Office of the Chief of Naval Operations in 1915. This debate took the form of an outpouring of articles, reports, discussions and proposals which may well be unique in the history of American public administration. The focus of the controversy was the role of the professional military chief in relation to the bureau heads and Secretary.[1]

Stephen B. Luce led off the debate with his "Naval Administration" and kept it going with two sequels and at least a half dozen more of the same sort.

Luce held that knowledge of the naval organization in England was necessary for intelligent understanding of the weaknesses of that in the United States. So the first part of his study explains the Office of the Lord High Admiral, which dates back to the 13th century, and the Board of Admiralty and the Navy Board, both established by King Henry VIII. He then discusses at length how well or poorly these offices had functioned in directing the military and civil affairs of the Royal

Navy. He praises the creditable organization of the French Navy.

Then comes his severe commentary on the U.S. Navy Department, starting with the inadequate naval government which from 1798 to 1815 poorly provided for the needs of the early American Navy. He follows with his favorite theme to which he would often return, the potential for good naval government inherent in the Board of Naval Commissioners. These senior officers, after the experiences of the War of 1812, were placed in the office of the Secretary in order that he might have military advice. But the wording of the Act of 1815 assigned them civil duties also and they became overburdened by the latter. Their military and civil functions were mixed instead of being kept apart.

The Board itself in 1839 advised a reorganization of the Department. "The obvious remedy," wrote Luce, "was to unburden the Commissioners of all but their military duties and place the civil functions in the hands of another set of persons." Instead, the Board was abolished and replaced by five bureaus, later increased to eight. The civil branch was thus provided for, but the Secretary was deprived of professional assistance and the Navy Department was without a truly military branch.

The rear admiral then condemns the bureau system in which each bureau chief managed his own share of the Navy independently of others. "While each individual bureau of the Navy Department is progressive in its character, the tendency of the Navy as a body has been retrogressive."

He pointed out that during the Civil War, Gustavus V. Fox, a former naval officer, as Assistant Secretary of the Navy, filled the gap between the Secretary and the bureaus, "the need of which had been felt for twenty years previous to the war and has wrought much evil during the twenty years following."

Luce concludes with a set of 15 rules that should obtain in the organization of a properly functioning naval government.

A discussion of this article by Rear Adm. E. Simpson and Lt. Richard Wainwright appeared in U.S.N.I. *Proceedings,* vol. XIV, No. 4, 1888, pp. 725-737.

---

[1]Samuel P. Huntington, *The Soldier and the State.* (New York: Belknap Press, 1957), p. 248.

CHAPTER X

ANNOTATED BIBLIOGRAPHY OF LUCE'S WRITINGS
THE RETIREMENT YEARS: 1889-1911

Editors' Introduction

A striking change can readily be detected in the writings of Stephen B. Luce after his retirement, an ease and maturity not found in the earlier material. They bore the mark of an accepted writer as they appeared in some of the foremost journals of the period: *The North American Review, The Critic,* and *The Youth's Companion.*

The pressure to find proper vehicles for both service and public expression was gone as was the need to gain legitimacy by writing for encyclopedias. More important, his literary efforts became increasingly less connected to the role of legislative lobbying. His special talent for the written word was no longer restricted by need within the service, and a wide variety of subjects could now be chosen on their own merit. Of course, he maintained his deep involvement in the affairs of the Navy and continued to apply pressure in those areas he felt necessary.

The series in *Youth's Companion* must have been a particular joy for him as were his book reviews. With these he was able to comment on the fine work being done by others and to share with the future sailors of the Nation the wealth of experience found in his career. For the first time, during the decade after 1889, he was able to vacation as he wished, make extended visits to Europe, and turn his attention to these subjects that he had hitherto been forced to put off.

After the Spanish-American War, however, he was recalled to active duty, first on the Board of Awards, then to the faculty of the Naval War College, and again his writing became linked to politics but toward one goal only—line officer direction of the Navy Department. The future infighting would be tough, but the lifetime goal would be achieved in 1909.

Two years of intense writing remained, eight long articles published in 2 years, a summation of a half century.

85. "Just the Boy That's Wanted for the Navy." *The Youth's Companion,* vol. LXII, No. 22, 30 May 1889, p. 285.
    The first piece that Luce wrote following his retirement from active service in February 1889 was one of a series published in this popular periodical during the first half of 1889 under the

Naval War College Class of 1896

Luce, in civilian clothes is seated on the far right. Standing to his left is Lieutenant Commander Richard Wainwright, Chief Intelligence Officer of the Navy, the future hero of Santiago and the first Aide for Operations. Seated on the steps, two men to the right of Luce, is the inventor and future Aide for Operations, Lieutenant Bradley A. Fiske. Directly above Fiske is the President of the War College, Captain Henry C. Taylor. Standing two rows directly above Taylor is Ensign William A. Moffett.

Photo: Naval Historical Collection, Naval War College

general title "Just the Boy That's Wanted..." All the articles were by distinguished men in their fields:—"... In the Law" by Judge Oliver Wendell Holmes; "... In the Army" by Gen. Nelson A. Miles; "... In Journalism" by E.L. Godkin, eminent editor of *The Nation* and the *New York Evening Post.*

Luce outlines the many requirements officers must fulfill in the new Navy. He stresses that, above all, a naval officer must have love for his profession, to keep him in its frontline, for he cannot advance his temporal fortune or hasten his way along the slow road of promotion. "If the aspirant for naval glory believes in himself, and is of a robust constitution, if he has a decided taste for the sea, and carries his heart in the right place, I should say he is 'just the boy that is wanted in the Navy.'"

86. "Our Future Navy." *The North American Review,* vol. CXLIX, No. 392, July 1889, pp. 53-65.

    The year 1889 saw Luce's retirement in February; the passing from the naval scene a few days later of his nemesis, Secretary of the Navy W.C. Whitney; his renewed hope of saving the War College with the new Secretary, Benjamin F. Tracy, assuming office; and his finally achieving a publishing vehicle with which to reach directly an opinion-forming segment of the American people. This was *The North American Review* to which he contributed often during the next two decades.

    Thirteen years before, when Henry Adams was its editor and Henry Cabot Lodge his assistant, Luce had tried unsuccessfully to get a piece on naval administration published in it. Shortly after, in 1878, *North American Review* acquired a new life under the editorship of Allen Thorndyke Rice, Lloyd Bryce, and William H. Rideing, also managing editor of *The Youth's Companion.* By 1889 Luce had become a colorful and prominent public figure, whose offerings to these periodicals and to *The Critic,* a weekly review of books, were welcomed.

    "Our Future Navy" was reprinted in the winter issue of the U.S.N.I. *Proceedings.* (See item 87.) Its theme was the pressing need for battleships in the new Navy which the United States had begun creating in 1881. Up to that time only cruisers had been built. However, Luce wrote, a navy of cruisers without the support of battleships would prove as ineffective in war as an army of cavalry without infantry.

    He gave a history of efforts to acquire battleships for the U.S. Navy, only four of which were ever placed in commission. He pointed out that Great Britain's program for 1889-1894 called for building 10 battleships, as well as 60 other types.

    A navy without battleships, he states, is no navy at all in the real sense. "A solitary American steel cruiser, with the delusive prefix, 'protected,' represents the latent possibility of a great country placidly awaiting some national disaster to generate its mighty force."

    The naval race between Great Britain and France and the growing power of a united Germany plus the strong economy but military weakness of the United States worried a small number of thoughtful naval officers like Luce, members of Congress like Representative Washington C. Whitthorne and Henry Cabot Lodge and some businessmen and industrialists, all with national rather than local viewpoints. Luce had been convinced by Mahan's deductions that a battle fleet was the foundation of seapower and the *sine qua non* of a maritime nation. The pragmatic Luce immediately related this to the United States, weak and exposed.

His letters of this period indicate his conviction that the way to correct this situation was to get Mahan's manuscript into print. On 5 August 1889, Luce wrote his good friend, wealthy John S. Barnes, endeavoring to enlist his help. He described Mahan's work in detail and related his own extensive efforts to find a publisher. As late as 21 September, Mahan did not have one and was about ready to give up. But on 16 October he wrote Luce that Little, Brown & Co. had "undertaken to publish the work."

Luce's prime concern at this time, however, was saving the War College. He had advanced his retirement a month to that purpose and on 14 March 1889, 10 days after the inauguration of President Harrison, he addressed a letter direct to Secretary Tracy in which he reviewed the entire subject of location and future existence of the Naval War College. This effort was successful.

Luce had always aimed his professional attention to personnel, not materiel—to officer education, enlisted training, and naval administration. He subsequently wrote extensively in these fields. The subject of the battle fleet, however, he hardly mentioned in his writings until the piece on naval bases of April 1911 (item 146) and then only to state "we had one." His essay "The Fleet," Chapter VII (item 138), is essentially a summation of his three articles on naval administration.

B.F. Cooling, in his *Benjamin Franklin Tracy, Father of the Modern American Fighting Navy* (Hamden, Conn.: Archon, 1973), states that the impact of "Our Future Navy" on the new Secretary was marked. Tracy without doubt was impressed by the unusual officer whose long letter of 14 March he had recently received. The Luce documents, however, indicate that the effort in *The North American Review* was a one-shot affair for Mahan. If it influenced Tracy, that was an added gain. This fine essay, on the other hand, may have had the reciprocal effect of inducing the new Secretary to accept Luce's recommendations on the Naval War College.

87. "Our Future Navy." U.S.N.I. *Proceedings,* vol. XV, No. 4, 1889, pp. 541-52.

This is a reprint of item 86. Pages 553-59, immediately following this article, contain a discussion of Luce's paper. Among the comments, Capt. A.T. Mahan notes,

If I am right in my opinion, which I understand to be that

of Admiral Luce as well, that a war against an enemy's commerce is an utterly insufficient instrument, regarded as the main operation of war, though doubtless valuable as a secondary operation, the United States and its people are committed to an erroneous and disastrous policy. No harm has been done in building the new cruisers, for new ships of that kind are wanted; but great harm has been done by the loss of so many years in which have not been built any battleships, which are undoubtedly the real strength of the navy.

To this Lt. Richard Wainwright added,

The great value of this article is that he [Luce] so clearly and interestingly exemplifies the point as to impress it upon the general public. All naval officers must be convinced that the real reason for their existence as such is to fight in case of need, and that while useful and ornamental in time of peace, they will be of little ornament and no use in time of war without battle-ships. The public have heard so much of the fine navy that has been building for some years past that they imagine the United States Navy has considerable fighting power. Admiral Luce's paper is well calculated to disenchant their minds of this fallacious impression.

88. "The Influence of Sea Power upon History." *The Critic*, vol. XVII, No. 343, 26 July 1890, pp. 41-42. (This book review of Mahan's work is reprinted in chapter V.)

89. "Naval Training." U.S.N.I. *Proceedings*, vol. XVI, No. 3, 1890, pp. 367-96.

Luce, in this long article, enlists the aid of psychology, strategy, and logistics to convince his brother naval officers that boys of the steam navy should be trained in sailing ships. He did not succeed, but his arguments were original, fascinating, and plausible.

He reminded them then that the best training for war was war itself. Readiness to face death ennobles the profession of soldier and sailor. The sailor's life is always attended by danger in battling the elements, hence his quality of reckless daring that is of inestimable value in war. Luce then argued that to retain these qualities in the seaman of the steel and steam navy, it will be necessary to train them in sailing ships.

He then took another tack, using strategy and logistics to prove the point that modern men-of-war men should be trained in sail. For the United States, with no overseas coal depots, cruisers must have full sail power in order to reach their stations with bunkers filled. Luce's arguments, however, were easily refuted by young officers who pointed out that chartered colliers, not sail power, provided the solution to the requirement of full bunkers.

Luce failed, in this instance, to prove logically what he knew intuitively. Time has sustained him, however, for today most foreign navies still train their prospective officers in sail as does the U.S. Coast Guard.

The discussion on sail power for modern cruisers was continued at length in *The New York Times* of 26 October 1890.

In the next quarterly issue of the *Proceedings,* Lt. William F. Fullam[1] in the title: "The System of Training and Discipline Required to Promote Efficiency and Attract Americans" held that a navy should not be formed of men less skillful and less trustworthy than soldiers. He claimed that when marines were withdrawn from warships, a better class of men, native-born Americans, would enter the service and discipline would markedly improve. As long as the Marine Guards remained, he believed that the officers would not learn to rely upon the sailor nor trust and develop the petty officer.

Fullam, of course, sent Luce a copy of the article. The older man answered,[2] but did not join in the public discussion which brought forth over 40 pages in the *Proceedings* from some 22 officers. Luce agreed with Fullam in regard to the Navy's lack of *esprit de corps* and the absence of native born, but he could not agree that the Marine Guards deterred Americans from entering or remaining in the Navy. It was rather the harsh treatment they received from officers and the lack of inducement to remain in the service. "It is the one great weaknesses of our naval organization that we cannot, or will not, keep American Seamen in the Navy."

---

[1] Rear Adm. William Freeland Fullam (1855-1926). According to Rear Adm. Richard W. Bates, USN (Ret.), who was a naval cadet under the strict regime of Fullam as Superintendent of the Naval Academy, 1915-1916, Fullam had wanted a commission in the Marine Corps when he graduated at the head of his class in 1873. The Navy Department would not allow this. The first Academy graduates commissioned in the Marine Corps were from the class of 1882.

[2] Luce to Fullam, 24 November 1890, Fullam Papers, LC.

90. "Introduction." *History of the United States Marine Corps* by Richard S. Collum, Maj., USMC, New York: Hamersly, 1890, pp. 14-21.

This introduction is a reprint of item 28. Luce adds one footnote to this edition. To the last sentence recommending the education of young Marine officers at West Point, he notes: "The officers of the Corps, since 1881 [sic], are appointed from the graduates of the Naval Academy, a course advocated by progressive members of the Corps many years before the passage of the law.—Author."

91. "High Praise for Captain Collum's History and the Marine Corps." *The Army-Navy Register,* vol. XII, No. 5, 31 January 1891, p. 74.

In this letter to the editor, Luce remarked on the book's

value as support for the corps against its detractors. He commented, "these periodical attacks on the Corps must be expected; but they never amount to much."

92. "How Shall We Man Our Ships?" *The North American Review,* vol. CLII, No. 410, January 1891, pp. 64-69.

    William H. Rideing, managing editor of the *Review,* had requested a short article on this subject from Luce since the public had been recently showing increasing interest in the new and growing Navy. The naval officer first reviewed how the problem was solved in Great Britain. During the Crimean War its Government, still depending on the volunteer system and the short-term enlistment of one cruise, had great difficulty providing their men-of-war with adequate crews. The solution adopted was a continuous service system; seamen were induced to serve for terms of 10 years with a liberal pension provided at the end of the second enlistment; boys were also enlisted, who, from early association, became attached to the service and formed the most valuable crewmembers in ships of the Royal Navy.

    The U.S. Navy had no such workable system for manning its ships. It still depended on short-term enlistments by nomads of the sea. All attempts at a permanent enlisted force had so far failed. Fifteen years after the naval apprentice system had been first organized, only 15 of 450 in the crew of the recently built U.S.S. *Trenton* had passed through the naval apprentice system, and only one-third were native born. The young American "seamen gunners" were trained as machinists, gunsmiths, and electricians in the Navy and could easily find civil employment at the end of their short-term enlistments.

    Luce offered no new solutions. He was still hopeful that the naval apprentice system would work with renewed effort. He felt that its achievements demonstrated that it would ultimately succeed. In his concluding paragraphs, Luce noted that the question of manning ships was divided into two distinct parts: providing a peacetime Navy and providing a reserve of seafaring people on which the Navy could draw in wartime. He encouraged congressional support of an American merchant marine and recommended that a Department of Commerce be added to the executive branch.

93. "The Powder Monkey." *The Youth's Companion,* vol. LXIV, No. 17, 23 April 1891, p. 248.

    For his second piece in this essentially boys' magazine, Luce chose to exalt the smallest and youngest members of the crew in a man-of-war. They were the ones who had one of the most dangerous jobs on board, carrying powder from the magazine to the gun. Monkey was a sailor term applied to any small object. It was derived from the little monkeys kept on board as pets. Luce recalled Farragut performing duties of powder boy, and he alluded to another powder monkey who was his shipmate in the line-of-battleship U.S.S. *Columbus.* He was a sailor who became a famous journalist and author, Charles Nordhoff (1830-1901).

In conclusion, Luce noted that the days of the powder monkey were gone. The heavy guns of the new Navy required charges of 250-425 pounds. The powder boy had been replaced by purchase and tackle.

94. "The Benefits of War." *The North American Review,* vol. CLIII, No. 421, December 1891, pp. 672-83.

This is one of the best, certainly the most heartfelt, of Luce's essays. Into it he poured both his religious feelings and his love and respect for his profession. His choice of the title was unfortunate, however, and it brought forth reactions in the press and in personal letters. When he republished this article some 13 years later (see item 124), he changed the title to what the piece was really about: "War and Its Prevention." He claimed,

> War was one of the great agencies by which human progress is affected. War is the malady of nations; the disease is terrible while it lasts but purifying in its results. There is a wisdom that comes only of suffering, whether to the family or to the aggregation of families, the nation.

The Battles of Marathon, Salamis, and Plataea were only so many steppingstones toward an ascendancy of Hellenic civilization, the influence of which on human affairs shall never die. "Without war, Greece would have lived on aestheticism and wasted its life in idle dreams."

Our own Civil War, he pointed out, furnished a notable example of the operation of this law of strife by which human progress is achieved.

Nevertheless, the continued existence of war was still charged as a failure of Christianity. Luce argued that, on the same grounds, dreadful railroad accidents might be charged to Christian failure or disease regarded as a reproach to human nature. Christianity, he reminded his readers, has to do with the regeneration of the human heart and not with changing the laws of nature.

It was by war and pestilence that the children of Israel were disciplined. Moses conducted his campaigns in accordance with instructions received from God. From the lowest and most abject state of Egyptian bondage, the children of Israel, trained by war, became a powerful race and, through the imperishable literature of the Bible, gave to all succeeding ages the principles of the highest civilization.

As a science, war should be cultivated by the few qualified to undertake it; as an art it should be constantly practiced by the entire body set apart for that purpose, with the implements to be used in war actually in hand. By a perfect state of preparedness, a collision of arms is avoided and the shedding of blood spared.

The United States, he said, is known not to be disposed to

utilize its abundant resources for military purposes. Ready as they are to wage commercial warfare, our people close their eyes to the possibilities of an actual collision of arms.

"Let practical Americans," he stated in conclusion, "recognize the truth that war is a calamity that may overtake the most peaceful nation, and that insurance against war by preparation for it is the most businesslike, the most humane, and the most in accordance with the teachings of the Christian religion."

95. "The Caravels of Columbus." *The Youth's Companion*, vol. LXV, No. 22, 21 June 1892, pp. 281-82.

In this centennial year of the discovery of America, it was proper to include a piece on the three ships that made the landfall on San Salvador Island, 12 October 1492. Models of these caravels were under construction at Cadiz, Spain, under the supervision of Lt. William McCarty Little, USN (Ret.)[1] Manned by Spanish sailors, they were to be part of the Columbian Exposition in Chicago.

Luce discusses the difficulty of constructing the models, as paintings of the caravels did not agree with the written descriptions in Columbus' journal and other trustworthy accounts.

Santa Maria had a lofty poop for the officers, a high prow for the crew, with four masts of which two were square rigged and two had lateen sails. She was 90 feet long at the keel and decked over. Luce includes description of the smaller ships, as well as an account of the voyage. Listing the ships in the U.S. Navy named for Columbus' ships, he mentions the line-of-battleship *Columbus* in which he had served and the sloop-of-war *St. Mary's*, named for the *Santa Maria* and which he himself had converted into a schoolship for the State of New York.

---

[1] Capt. William McCarty Little (1842-1915), who was retired for medical reasons in 1884, served with Luce in the training ship U.S.S. *Minnesota* and assisted with the early organization of the War College. He introduced the Naval War Game at the Naval War College, where he remained on the faculty until 1910. For additional information relating to Little and his work in Spain at this time, see W. McC. Little Papers, Naval Historical Collection, Naval War College.

96. "My First Ship." *The Youth's Companion*, vol. LXV, No. 51, 22 December 1892, pp. 673-74.

For his fourth article in *Youth's Companion*, Luce chose to describe the 74-gun line-of-battleship *North Carolina*, to which he reported as a newly appointed midshipman in October 1841. She was then anchored off the Battery, in New York's upper bay.

North Carolina, after 20 years service at sea, was serving as a receiving ship, on board which were assembled the crews that were to serve in ships being commissioned for active service. No Naval Academy existed in those days, and new midshipmen went directly to cruising vessels after a few months indoctrination on board the receiving ship.

Luce graphically describes such incidents as reporting on board, living in the semidarkness of the orlop deck, and his first duty as boat officer.

He goes on to briefly comment on the change to more modern naval education and refers to his own article in 1889 outlining the curriculum at the Naval Academy. (See item 85.) In conclusion, he notes that neither the old system nor the new would produce good results if it had poor quality to work with.

> Every boy has his own specific gravity,—if the figure be allowed,—which gives him his relative place among his associates. If he is very dense, and is determined to remain so, then the most learned professor and the best textbooks cannot float him above the plane where the laws of gravitation place him. If he is determined to rise, he will rise though he should have neither books nor professor to buoy him up. The best results flow from a combination of taste for a vocation with the opportunities for cultivating it.

97. "Captain Mahan's 'Admiral Farragut.'" *The Critic*, vol. XXI, No. 563, 3 December 1892, p. 309.

    This brief review of Mahan's biography of Farragut was written while Mahan was the President of the Naval War College.
    After summarizing the work, Luce concludes,
    > in a word, here is a model biography. It is the story of a sea-king told by a seaman to whom the pen is as familiar as the sword or rope. It will interest the young reader and the student of the great war, but it will be a delight to those who value also a fine gloss of style and a profound philosophy crystallized in simple language.

98. "England and France on the Sea." *The Critic*, vol. XXII, No. 569, 14 January 1893, p. 17. (This book review of Mahan, *The Influence of Sea Power upon the French Revolution and Empire: 1793-1812*, has been reprinted in chapter V.)

99. *A Standard Dictionary of the English Language: Upon Original Plans Designed to Give, in Complete and Accurate Statement, in the Light of the Most Recent Advances in Knowledge, and in the Readiest Form for Popular Use, the Meaning, Orthography, Pronunciation, and Etymology of All the Words, and the Idiomatic Phrases in the Speech and Literature of the English Speaking Peoples.* Prepared by more than 200 specialists and other scholars. Isaac L. Funk, Editor-in-Chief. New York and London: Funk and Wagnalls, 1893.

    In December 1890 Luce agreed to undertake editing the department of naval terms for this work edited by Isaac K. Funk. Luce was paid $3.00 per hour for this work.

Luce's name appeared also in the editions of 1895 and 1903 as the "naval and nautical terms editor." For the edition of 1913, he was succeeded by Rear Adm. John Elliott Pillsbury, USN, former Chief of the Bureau of Navigation, and Adm. Sir Cyprian Bridge.

100. "Orders and Signals of the Venetian Fleet. Commanded by Mr. James Dolfin, A.D. 1365," and "Ancient Naval Warfare," U.S.N.I. *Proceedings*, vol XX, Nos. 3 and 4, 1894, pp. 541-553 and 721-745.

The above essays were written by Rear Adm. Luigi Fincati of the Italian Navy whose avocation was naval archeology. Medical Director Philip Lansdale,[1] Luce's brother-in-law, translated both while Luce wrote their introductions and added footnotes and comments. Lt. Albert Gleaves, his future biographer, assisted.

The introduction to the first article explains Luce's interest in signaling around 1877. Sufficient material remained from his entry "Naval Signals" in *Johnson's New Universal Cyclopedia* for him to compose another article which appeared in *Potter's American Monthly* (items 43 and 46).

His research for these pieces had impressed on Luce the need for more published history of the medieval naval operations of Venice and Genoa. He sent a copy of the *Potter's* essay to a friend in the Italian Navy, a Captain Martinez, whom he had probably met during his *Juniata* cruise, 1869-1872. Martinez communicated the American's desires, with the copy of the article to Fincati. The latter wrote the two essays based on research in the Italian State Archives.

Luce in his introduction apologized for the delay in publication caused by translation difficulties and the press of other duties. But he also observed:

> Though written fifteen years ago, these articles have lost none of their value. On the contrary, with the dissipation of the false idea that modern naval science had nothing to learn from the past, there has been a decided tendency of late years towards what may be called the philosophical study of history.

In the second of his essays, Fincati mainly discussed naval tactics in ancient Greek and Roman wars. Excellent diagrams accompany this piece. He quotes the Greek historian Diodorus Siculus on the danger of offering a flank to attack and adds in italics: "So with us at Lissa!" See item 104.

No reference to the Fincati articles has been found in Vice Adm. William L. Rodgers, *Naval Warfare Under Oars* (Annapolis: Naval Institute, 1940, 1967).

---

[1] Philip Lansdale (1817-1894), physician and naval officer, was a graduate in medicine of the University of Pennsylvania, entered the U.S. Navy as an assistant surgeon, November 1846, was surgeon in *Hartford* at the Battle of Mobile Bay, and retired in 1879 as Medical Director with the relative rank of captain. He married Olivia, Stephen B. Luce's

next older sister, in September 1841. Their son, Philip Van Horn Lansdale, USN, was killed in action, 1 April 1899, at Apia, Samoa. Margaret Luce, the oldest sister married Capt. Andrew A. Harwood, USN, a widower. Jane, the youngest, never married. John, the oldest in the family, settled in Arkansas. William, the next, was killed in action in 1863. See the interesting, but not biographically dependable, *Two Colonial Families: the Lansdales of Maryland and the Luces of New England* by Maria Hornor Lansdale (Philadelphia: n.p., 1938).

101. *Commemoration of the Fourth Centenary of the Discovery of America. Columbian Historical Exposition, Madrid. History of the Participation of the United States in the Columbian Historical Exposition at Madrid.* Washington: U.S. Govt. Print. Off., 1895, pp. 7-15.

At the instigation of Secretary of State James G. Blaine, Secretary of the Navy B.F. Tracy, and Senator Henry Cabot Lodge, President Benjamin Harrison appointed Luce the Commissioner General of the United States to the Columbian Historical Exposition in Madrid. Luce served in this capacity from May 1892 until May 1893.

Luce reports in the form of a letter, undoubtedly written by himself, to Walter Q. Gresham, Secretary of State,[1] dated 2 May 1893, at Washington, D.C. As Commissioner General he first introduced the other members of the Commission which included James C. Wellings, President of Columbian University (later George Washington University), and the Assistant Secretary of the Smithsonian Institution, the noted naturalist George Brown Goode.

The American portion of the exposition in Madrid had the task of depicting the state of civilization in the New World in the period during which American history was most closely identified with Spain, that period from 1492, when the Spanish caravels first reached the New World, to 1620, when the *Mayflower* brought the English Puritans to New England.

Luce then described the extensive American exhibits. The exposition opened 30 October 1892 and closed 31 January 1893. The admiral regretted being excluded, because of lack of diplomatic status, from the most singular affair held, the unveiling of the monument at La Rabida[2] commemorating the fourth centenary of the discovery of America.

The Luce letters for this period indicate his friendly association with Adm. Pasqual Cervera y Topete, the Spanish Minister of Marine and later the Commander of the Spanish Squadron defeated at Santiago, 3 July 1898. Cervera was not the Minister of Marine during the Exposition, but when he succeeded to that position immediately afterward, he obtained for Luce the Grand Cross of the Order of Naval Merit (White Badge).

---

[1] Walter Quinton Gresham (1832-1895) served as a major general during the Civil War. He served as Postmaster General, 1883-84; Secretary of the Treasury, 1884; Judge of the U.S. Circuit Court, 1884-92; Secretary of State, 1893-95.

²The Franciscan monastery of Santa Maria de la Rabida, near Palos, Andalusia, on the Gulf of Cadiz. It was at this monastery that Columbus left his 5-year-old son, Diego, when he first came to Spain in 1485. The prior of the monastery, Fray Juan Perez, arranged for Columbus' first contacts at the court of Queen Isabella in 1491. The monument to which Luce refers is a large statue of Columbus. A replica of the monastery was in Chicago for the World's Columbian Exposition in 1893. See Samuel E. Morison, *Admiral of the Ocean Sea* (Boston: Little, Brown, 1942), pp. 80-81, 98-99, 158-59.

102. "As to Navy Yards and Their Defense." U.S.N.I. *Proceedings*, vol. XXI, No. 4, 1895, pp. 679-89.

Luce produced two articles based on his research and work in connection with the Commission on Navy Yards 1882-1883 of which he was the senior member. One of these, "The Navy and Its Needs," has been reprinted in chapter VIII. The second, abstracted here, is based upon the research he did among the naval records in Washington preparing himself for this duty.

This article is limited to the history of the location of the shipbuilding sites selected for the six frigates of the new Navy to be built under the Act of 27 March 1794. No expressed provision was made by Congress for the building of these six ships. Joshua Humphreys, the naval constructor who designed them, did visit possible sites along the Atlantic coast, and the Secretary of the Navy reported to Congress that ground had been purchased at Portsmouth, N.H., Charlestown (near Boston), Philadelphia, Washington, and Norfolk and would soon be obtained at New York. Nothing in the original act authorized the sum expended, $240,906, so the formation of a permanent Shore Establishment can be credited also to the executive department.

All navy yards, with the exception of that at Washington, were selected because of their availability, the Government taking over shipyard facilities already established. The best site for a naval base, however, is remote from the seaboard where it cannot be subject to attack. The Hudson beyond West Point was thus considered for New York and the James River for Norfolk. But it was eventually determined that the great centers of population on the coasts were the more suitable locations since the yards would be included within the protection required for such regions of wealth and commerce.

Luce concludes the article by discussing briefly the relationship between ships and bases. He discusses the terms "battleship" and "line-of-battle ship," and then goes on to state,

> The naval tactician of to-day requires that there shall be a certain measure of homogeneity in the ships that are to compose the main body of the fleet with which he may be called upon to guard our coasts and navy-yards. In other words, his line of battle must be composed of line-of-battle ships.

103. "A Fo'castle Court Martial." *The Youth's Companion*, vol. LXVIII, No. 3570, 24 October 1895, pp. 501-02.

Luce is at his storytelling best in presenting this most unusual of all his "yarns" published in this youth's magazine. He portrays also the men whose memories he cherished, the American sailors of his first ships.

He tells of an occasion one night aboard *Columbus* in the harbor of Monterey, Calif., in 1846 when virtually all officers were ashore and the best of the crew took discipline into their own hands. He represents the occasion as a case showing the aptitude of the Anglo-Saxon race for self-government in correcting abuses that the law has failed to reach.

What Luce tells with charm is how the Americans in the crew took the occasion to punish those of the large foreign element who had blatantly displayed their disrespect for the flag and for American institutions, especially after a return from a drunken liberty. These men were brought before a "mock" court-martial held on deck, tried in accordance with court procedures, found guilty, and made to swear allegiance and kiss the flag. The supreme penalty could have been disappearance over the side at night while underway.

104. "Naval Warfare Under Modern Conditions." *The North American Review*, vol. CLXII, No. 470, January 1896, pp. 70-77.

The defeat of the Italians by the Austrians at Lissa in the Adriatic Sea during 1866 offered painful lessons in the need for intelligent naval planning and for proper organization within a navy department.

This Italian defeat and the Japanese victory over the Chinese in 1894 at Yalu furnished striking illustrations, in Luce's opinion, of naval warfare under modern conditions. The victors proved how naval success may be assured by careful training of personnel during peace, by study of the operations of war as conducted by the great masters, and by applying immutable principles of naval strategy. The defeated demonstrated how a want of discipline and drills in tactics and gunnery and a disregard for elementary principles of the science of war lead to disaster.

An indispensable condition for the creation of an efficient navy is the creation of the power to use it intelligently. Developing his thought from the concepts of Jomini, Hamley, and Mahan, Luce states,

> Naval strategy is more comprehensive than military strategy. The latter is confined to the theater of the war, the former may embrace all the navigable waters of a continent. Military strategy is called into play only during war. Naval strategy adopts some of its most important measures during peace, in anticipation of war.

105. "Joe Hardy." *The Youth's Companion*, vol. LXIX, No. 22, 28 May 1896, p. 274.

This article recounts the true tale of a sailor in the U.S.S. *Wabash*, a topman and favorite of the crew, whose cap blew off as he descended from the yard. He jumped overboard to save it because in its brim was his sweetheart's picture. The boy was drowned or attacked by sharks, but not before Luce, the officer of the deck at the time, and the quartermaster of the watch jumped in the water to save him. The two would-be rescuers almost lost their lives.

Luce does not identify himself as one of the heroes, but he does state that after the man went down the two clung to the life buoy that had been thrown to them. It was not until they were in the rescue boat that the sharks were seen. This brought terrible dreams that night.

This story reached print in three different forms. James Barnes, the author and newspaper correspondent, published it in *Harper's Weekly*. He had evidently heard it from his father, Luce's old shipmate and friend, John Sanford Barnes. Another version appeared in a newspaper, the Albany N.Y., *Journal*, during one of Luce's visits to his birthplace while the Training Squadron was in the North River in the 1880's. An Albany policeman who in 1861 had been a member of the *Wabash* crew gave this story to a reporter. The true name of the drowned man was William Emmet.

106. "The Life of Nelson." *The Critic*, vol. XXVII, No. 789, 3 April 1897, p. 321.

In this review of A.T. Mahan's biography of Nelson, Luce observed that the author had made Nelson reveal himself. "... The hero stands before us in all his naked humanity." Mahan had produced "abundant evidence to show that the so-called 'dash' of Nelson, a term which, in such connection, carries a latent idea of recklessness, was in truth the result of plans carefully matured long in advance of the occasion."

After mentioning Emma Hamilton, their child Horatia, and the estrangement from Lady Nelson, Luce remarks, "All this sad phase of Nelson's life, including the execution of [Admiral] Caracciola, which bears the stigma of judicial murder, is treated with absolute impartiality by Capt. Mahan. He shows the duplicate nature of the man."

In a later edition of *The Critic*,[1] it was reported that Dr. Edward Everett Hale of Massachusetts had requested that Captain Mahan consider writing a history of the American Navy, now that his *Nelson* was completed. Mahan responded that an effort would depend on the interest of the American public. "So far as I can at present observe, that interest is not very great. There is no use of a man writing what he has no reason to believe that many will read."

Mahan also refused to have his War College lectures published in the *Proceedings* of the U.S. Naval Institute. His main reason was that readers of the *Proceedings* would not have the advantages of student listeners at the War College, freedom from all diversions, and with minds fresh and without preoccupation. Moreover, the rapport between lecturer and listener could not be created between author and reader. In the *Proceedings*, the lecturers on the art of war would be competing with all the articles on material phases of the naval profession which seemed to interest officers more.

"Why should I go to the College? I can read that which is taught there."[2] This was what Mahan feared—an end to the college.

---

[1] "Notes on Authors," *The Critic*, vol. XXVII, No. 799, 12 June 1897, p. 413.

[2] "Letter of Captain A.T. Mahan," U.S.N.I. *Proceedings*, vol. XV, No. 1, 1889, pp. 57-60.

107. "A History of the Royal Navy." *The Critic*, vol. XXVIII, No. 808, 14 August 1897, pp. 84-85.

Luce reviewed five of the seven volumes of this monumental work individually as they appeared over 6 years. (See items 110, 114, 115, 123.) In the review of the last two volumes which goes up to the death of Queen Victoria, he is able to congratulate the principal author on being selected for knighthood.

Luce is never altogether complimentary in his opinions of this work. In the review of the first volume, he lauds the style, but he takes the editor, William Laird Clowes, severely to task for the General Preface, which was carelessly prepared, inaccurate, controversial, and not in keeping with a work of this character.

In this first review Luce reveals his extensive knowledge of the literature of English naval history by comparing Clowes' work to that of Sir Harris Nicolas, Edward Pelham Brenton, and William James.

The structure in each volume was by chronological periods, three chapters devoted to each period, one dealing with civil history, a second with military history, and the third giving an account of maritime discoveries and scientific expeditions. This makes for ready reference, but does provide a distracting and disjointed story.

Illustrations are numerous, and the indexing leaves nothing to be desired. "We wish as much could be said for the style in which much of the valuable information is conveyed. In a number of chapters it lacks dignity and precision of expression."

108. "The Interest of America in Sea Power." *The Critic*, vol. XXIX, No. 831, 22 January 1898, pp. 55-56.

This is a book review of A.T. Mahan's *The Interest of America in Sea Power, Present and Future*. This book, a collection of detached papers published at intervals in periodicals during the previous several years, does constitute a definite part of Mahan's early seapower presentation before he turned from historian to pundit and prophet.

In this review Luce came to his first philosophical difference with Mahan. His argument was that while the author refers to ocean commerce, Mahan did not give it due prominence as a factor of seapower. In Luce's view he had allowed the views of the naval strategist to dominate those of the political economist. Seapower in its military sense is the offspring, not the parent, of commerce. Both from the military and the economic view, an extensive marine commerce is a necessity to a country aspiring to become a naval power.

109. "A False Alarm." *The Youth's Companion,* vol. LXXII, No. 7, 17 February 1898, p. 11.

In December 1863 the monitor *Nantucket* was stationed in Wassaw Sound, Ga., to watch for the coming out of an ironclad which the Confederates were reported to be building in Savannah.

On a bright Sunday morning, church services were being held on the berth deck, with Captain Luce reading the liturgy of the Protestant Episcopal Church. It was 11 o'clock. All nature seemed hushed; not even the note of a bird broke the stillness of the air. Overhead the sky was beautifully bright and clear; but on the quiet waters and on the low, marshy ground that lay between the river and the mainland, there hung a light mist that curiously distorted distant objects.

Suddenly a messenger came down from the deck and whispered in the captain's ear. "The officer of the deck told me to report that the rebel ram is coming down the river, Sir!"

The captain turned to the executive officer and told him to go on deck to verify the report. The executive, a cool, clearheaded officer, lost no time in getting there. Meanwhile, the captain was almost overcome with anxiety which he could not show, although the crew sensed that something was afoot.

The executive, on first looking, saw what appeared to be a rooflike structure, like the casemate of the *Merrimac* with broadside in full view. He was just about to sound "general quarters" when the character of the ram changed, with the roof separating and giving the appearance of two turrets. Keeping his glasses riveted on the object, it finally turned out to be a small boat with two refugees who used the misty weather to escape. Both refugees were white and declared themselves to be Union sympathizers.

A clipping of this signed article by Luce with magazine title, date, and page number is in the Luce papers in the Library of Congress. However, when checked against bound copies of the periodical at Brown University, it could not be found.

110. "The Royal Navy." *The Critic,* vol. XXIX, No. 848, 21 May 1898, pp. 342-43.

This is a review of Clowes, *A History of the Royal Navy,* volume II. (See items 107, 114, 115, and 123 for review of other volumes.)

111. "The Dawn of Naval History." U.S.N.I. *Proceedings,* vol. XXIV, No. 3, 1898, pp. 441-50.

In this article Luce defined a navy as designed primarily for the preservation of peace by the exercise of that wholesome moral influence inseparable from a judicious exhibition of adequate material force, also for policing the ocean highways, patrolling its own coasts, exploring distant seas for the benefit of commerce and navigation, sharing the labors in the field of science, standing guard on the frontiers of civilization, and for offensive and defensive operations of war.

Luce reached back to Homer's *Odyssey* and follows this by several quotations from the *Iliad* illustrating the accuracy of Homer's nautical descriptions. Then Luce describes the Biblical navies from the Ark of Noah, 525 feet long, 87½ feet beam, three decks, 19,000 tons, to the ships of Tarshish of the navies of Solomon and King Hiram of Tyre. The Phoenician Navy and that of Minos of Crete followed. These gave way to those of Carthage, Greece, and Rome after the dawn of naval history.

112. *Text-Book of Seamanship, the Equipping and Handling of Vessels Under Sail or Steam for the Use of the United States Naval Academy.* New York: Van Nostrand, 1898. By Rear Admiral S.B. Luce, USN. Rev. by Lt. W.S. Benson, USN, with illustrations drawn by Lt. S. Seabury, USN.

In this edition the general arrangement which had been established for this text in the revision by Aaron Ward was retained. (See item 71.) This last revision of *Seamanship* was undertaken by Lt. William S. Benson,[1] then an assistant instructor in the Department of Seamanship at the Naval Academy. In his preface to this edition, dated "Newport, R.I., August 5th, 1898," Luce commented that "Lieutenant Benson's labors have been attended with marked success, notwithstanding the distractions due to the breaking out of the war with Spain." In a reviser's note written on the receiving ship *Vermont* in New York, 27 September 1898, Benson states that an attempt has been made in this revision to eliminate all obsolete material and to introduce as much new information as time and space would permit. A chapter on storms was added with the latest information on sounding machines, patent logs, steam capstans, and steampower steering equipment. The chapter on shipboard organization was omitted since no system of organization had yet been given official sanction.

Although the preface to this edition is labeled "Fourth Edition," it is the fifth edition which makes substantial changes to the text and the ninth known issue since 1862. (See items 2, 3, 4, 11, 25, 40, 71, and 78.) This edition was reprinted in 1950 by Cornell Maritime Press, Cambridge, Md., with an introduction by M.V. Brewington.

---

[1] Adm. William Shepherd Benson (1855-1932) graduated from the Naval Academy in 1877. He commanded the *Albany* (CL-22), *Missouri* (BB-11), *Utah* (BB-31), and the Philadelphia Navy Yard. In 1915 he was appointed the first Chief of Naval Operations, an office which he held through World War One, until his retirement 25 September 1919.

113. "Stonewall Jackson and the American Civil War." *The Critic*, vol. XXXIV, No. 859, January 1899, pp. 65-67. (This review of G.F.R. Henderson's study has been reprinted in chapter V.)

114. "The Royal Navy." *The Critic*, vol. XXXV, No. 867, September 1899, pp. 856-58.

This piece is a review of Clowes, *History of the Royal Navy*, volume III.

Luce gives high praise to the chapter in this volume authored by Mahan, "by far, the most readable portion of the book." Luce concludes his review with the statement that, "the book contains much that is curious in the way of old naval customs, much that is very interesting; and to Americans, now that we have outlying colonies, much that is very instructive, from a political as well as from a naval and military point of view." (See items 107, 110, 115, and 123 for review of other volumes.)

115. "Privateers and Men-of-War." *The Critic*, vol. XXXVI, No. 4, April 1900, pp. 359-64.

This is a review article which comments on Edgar Stanton Maclay, *A History of American Privateers;* William Laird Clowes, *A History of the Royal Navy*, vol. IV, and Edward Kirk Rawson, *Twenty Famous Naval Battles—Salamis to Santiago*. (See items 107, 110, 114, and 123 for reviews of the other volumes in Clowes' multivolume study.)

In this article Luce disagrees with Maclay's assertion that privateering was being practiced by the United States in the Spanish-American War. He goes on to correct the erroneous impression given by Maclay in stating that *Olympia* and her class have taken the place of privateers in their roles as commerce destroyers.

In discussing Clowes' work, the reviewer singles out the fair treatment given the American Navy in this book. He agrees with Clowes that William James' *History* is notable for its accuracy up to the War of 1812 when it suddenly becomes biased and untrustworthy. This he traced to James' experience during that war when he was detained in Boston.

Luce gives the work by Rawson high praise, but strongly disagrees with him that the great Dutch admirals were fighting for the "honor" of their nation and to win fame for themselves. "Honor," he comments, "cut but a small figure in the business. It was the greed of commercial gain."

116. *Naval Songs: a Collection of Original, Selected, and Traditional Sea Songs, Songs of Sailors and Shanties.* 2d ed., rev. and corr. New York: Pond & Co., 1902.

   In this edition Luce rearranged the songs, made several deletions and additions. In his revised preface dated "Newport, R.I., June 17, 1902," Luce points out that

> this collection was originally undertaken with a view of the revival, as far as practicable, of the old Songs which commemorate our early naval victories, in hope that they would serve in no small degree, to cultivate in our young sailors, not only a love for their vocation as Seamen, but also that devotion to their flag, which distinguished those who laid the foundation of our Naval renown. The work has been only partially successful, however, owing to the fact that while many songs of the old navy were to be found, the airs to which they were sung have been lost. Some of the best were never published—they were handed down, words and music, from generation to generation till about the time of the Civil War, since when with few exceptions they have been hopelessly lost.

   As a midshipman in the 1840's, Luce had remembered some of these songs; his scrapbooks and journals for this period contain some of the songs that he later published. With the help of old sailors, he was able to rescue such songs as "Constitution and Guerriere," "Paul Jones' Victory," "Ye Parliament of England," "The Yankee Man of War," and "The Constellation and the Insurgente."

   Just before his death Luce arranged for another printing of this book. It appeared in 1918 without any change from this edition.

117. "Naval Administration, II." *U.S.N.I. Proceedings*, vol. XXVIII, No. 4, December 1902, pp. 839-49.

   This article was written as a sequel to his 1888 piece, "Naval Administration." (See item 84.) An early paragraph in this article summed up the dilemma as Luce saw it: "It was through the want of a Military Branch that the Navy Department has, on several notable occasions, in the not very remote past, been thrown into such states of panic as to fully demonstrate its incapacity to perform the very duties for which it was created." Several cases documenting this are offered.

   In 1812 Captains Charles Stewart and William Bainbridge had to protest vigorously to prevent the laying up the entire Navy as the administration feared it should be swept out of existence by English cruisers.

   The lessons of the Civil War outlined earlier went unheeded, and so in 1898 the Naval War Board or Strategy Board had to be formed to advise the President.

   In closing, Luce outlines the prompt action of First Lord

Barham and the British Admiralty in 1805 when notified by Nelson of the sailing of the French Fleet from the West Indies, which led to the successful campaign of Trafalgar. He compares this favorably with the dilatory action of our Navy Department in April 1898 in failing to send instructions to Adm. George Dewey until 3 days after war had been declared and after he had been forced to leave the harbor of Hong Kong by orders of the British Governor. Luce commented on the victory Dewey achieved:

> Had a Board of Navy Commissioners come down to us in an unbroken line, Admiral Dewey would not have been left so long in the isolated and trying position in which he found himself after the victory of May 1.
>
> The Navy Commissioners would have started re-enforcements from San Francisco, knowing that war was inevitable, and that, in any event, Dewey would need them. By the timely arrival of such re-enforcements, the Philippine insurrection would have been averted and much blood and treasure saved.

Another article was published the following year as part of the same series, "Naval Administration, III." (See item 122.)

118. "The Story of the *Monitor*." *Naval Actions and History 1799-1898, Massachusetts Military History Society Papers*. Boston: Griffith-Stillings Press, 1902, vol. XII, pp. 127-54.

Luce told this story many times and in many places, beginning in 1876 when in the U.S.S. *Hartford* he related it to the naval apprentices and other members of the crew. He stressed then and always the *moral* results of the battle. "Of every decisive battle fought on land or at sea, there may be said in general to be three results, viz., the strategic, the tactical, and the moral." To these the historian has added a fourth—the political.

In this action between the *Monitor* and the *Merrimac*, fought on the 9th of March 1862, all four results followed, but Luce was interested only in the moral effect. This battle, confined to two vessels and not at all decisive, nevertheless exercised an influence and importance far beyond our shores and to a degree that is hard to overestimate.

Great Britain feared the North as a growing commercial rival and so was favorable to the secession of the Confederacy as was France. The *Trent* affair all but precipitated war. A few months later, in the midst of preparations for the Union assault on the peninsula of Virginia, the Confederate ironclad appeared in Hampton Roads on 8 March and easily sank two warships with the indication that several more would be sunk the next day. Instead, the *Monitor* from New York arrived that night, and a drawn battle took place the next day. *Merrimac* eventually withdrew, leaving the scene of battle to *Monitor*.

The result of this action was a sensation abroad. Opinions on the military and naval efficiency of the United States immediately underwent a startling change. The London *Times* admitted that the Navy of England would have to be reconstructed on lines suggested by *Monitor*, especially the adoption of turrets. The Government of Great Britain also changed its attitude toward the type of maritime warfare the North had adopted. The blockade was accepted.

The *Monitor* story was given as a lecture to the Naval War College in September 1886, and the following January Luce delivered it at Cornell University, Ithaca, N.Y., and at Wells College for Women, Aurora, N.Y. It was presented in this article form to the Military Historical Society of Massachusetts on 7 January 1896.

After reading the published version, Harvard historian Albert Bushnell Hart wrote Luce, on 18 November 1902, commenting on the piece. Hart disagreed with Luce on Britain's attitude at the outbreak of the Civil War and on some points of international law. He wrote:

> My point is that the success of the Merrimac could not have meant the sweeping away of our blockading squadrons, and though it might have given cause for the recognition of the Confederacy, that is a different thing from breaking the blockade; and surely the destruction of the Monitor would hardly have been as conclusive evidence of the probable success of the south as the actual defeat of McClellan, Pope, practically McClellan again and Grant during the summer and fall of 1862. The Monitor-Merrimac struggle was undoubtedly a great turning point in naval warfare, and in the Civil War, and I hesitate to differ from the opinion of a renowned officer and authority. Is it a civilian's lack of humanity which makes me feel that when a nation goes to war, no matter how righteous its cause, it must accept the effects of war? I am not in favor of abolishing privateering or the capture of private property at sea, because I think these are two methods of bringing about peace; and the attitude of the United States towards captures of merchant vessels during the Civil War, is one which we may find turned against us in time of need.

119. "First Visit to Japan." *The Newport Mercury*, vol. CXLV, No. 35, 7 February 1903, p. 7.

> Luce's hometown newspaper reprints a long letter which he had written to the editor of the *Japan Daily Mail*. Dated 26 January 1903, the letter was contributed when he learned that a distinguished Japanese scholar proposed to write a history of modern Japan. In his letter Luce recounts his experiences as a midshipman on board U.S.S. *Columbus* when she visited Japan in 1846 under Commodore James Biddle. (See item 126.)

120. "Introduction." *History of the United States Marine Corps*, by Richard S. Collum, Maj., U.S.M.C. New York: Hamersly, 1903, pp. 13-20. (This is a reprint of items 28 and 90.)

121. "An Address Delivered at the United States Naval War College, Narragansett Bay, R.I., June Second, Nineteen Hundred and Three." U.S.N.I. *Proceedings,* vol. XXIX, No. 3, 1903, pp. 1-8. (This address has been reprinted in chapter II.)

122. "Naval Administration, III." U.S.N.I. *Proceedings,* vol. XXIX, No. 4, 1903, pp. 1-13.

    "Naval Administration, III" portrayed the failures of our naval administration during the Civil War, which as Luce puts it, was regarded with such scant respect as to border, at one critical period, on contempt.

    He describes the abortive attempt to relieve Fort Sumter in April 1861—which caused the opening of the war—and then he goes on to discuss other Navy Department administrative failures, to which he attributed the repulse of Du Pont's ironclad squadron at Charleston on 7 April 1863. Luce remarks, "there was no staff attached to the Secretary's office to prevent placing Admiral Du Pont and his command in the utterly false position of being called upon to solve an insoluble problem, viz.: the capture of Charleston without adequate co-operation by the Army."

    This series of three essays ends on a happy note for it is here that Luce told a delightful story of meeting Gen. William T. Sherman, in January 1865, when the general explained the Navy's strategic failures in a few pithy sentences and showed how he would bring about the fall of Charleston without a battle. "And that is just what actually came to pass."

    Luce concludes this study on naval administration with: "The Civil War demonstrated conclusively the necessity of a War College and of a General Staff. We have the one; let us now have the other without more ado." (See items 84 and 117 for the first two portions of this study.)

123. "The Queen's Navy." *The Critic,* vol. XLIII, No. 6, December 1903, p. 566.

    In this signed review of the last volume of Clowes' multivolume history of the Royal Navy, Luce comments that "it is very suggestive of change in feeling wrought by time that the names of two American authors [A.T. Mahan and Theodore Roosevelt] should be found among the collaborators in a work on the British Navy!" (See items 107, 110, 114, 115 for reviews of other volumes.)

124. "War and Its Prevention." U.S.N.I. *Proceedings,* vol. XXX, No. 3, 1904, pp. 611-22.

    This is a reprint of item 94. In a footnote to this article, Luce notes that it has been "reprinted, by permission, from *The North American Review* of December, 1891; where it appeared under the misleading caption of: 'The Benefits of War.'"

125. "The Department of the Navy." U.S.N.I. *Proceedings,* vol. XXXI, No. 1, March 1905, pp. 83-96.

Luce received an honorable mention for this article in the Naval Institute's prize essay contest of 1905, taking second place to Bradley Fiske's *American Naval Policy.* As he was almost 20 years before, Luce is again critical of the Naval Institute for not following up on its articles to insure what is recommended gets done. That meant the Department of the Navy must be reformed.

"There is something radically wrong with the Department," wrote Secretary of the Navy Whitney in his annual report to Congress, dated 30 November 1885. "The universal dissatisfaction is the conclusive proof of this." He then proceeded to dissect the bureau system and list a record of mismanagement, of wasteful expenditure, and of injudicious and ill-advised disposition of the public moneys.

Even with such overwhelming evidence, no reorganization was attempted during Whitney's tenure. So, in an annual report of November 1903, another Secretary, Charles Bonaparte, repeated what had been said 20 years before. President Theodore Roosevelt, shortly after, recommended that a Naval General Staff be provided who should control military affairs of the Navy and be the authorized advisers of the Secretary of the Navy. This recommendation met with violent opposition from those on whose support the President had every moral and legal right to count.

Luce then gives a review of the whole history of naval organization, including the English system on which ours was originally modeled. He concludes,

> What is needed is legislative action based on a liberal and enlightened consideration of the whole subject of naval organization, from both the military and the civil point of view, to the end that the several parts may be so evenly balanced and nicely adjusted that our naval administration may become a model of efficiency and economy.

126. "Commodore Biddle's Visit to Japan in 1846." U.S.N.I. *Proceedings,* vol. XXXI, No. 3, September 1905, pp. 555-63.

"The influence of the West upon the ancient civilization of Japan and the phenomenal progress made by that country toward becoming a formidable naval power, furnishes one of the most remarkable epochs of modern times." Luce then presented an entertaining and knowledgeable article on the first attempt of the United States to gain entry into Japan. It was written 59 years after this little-known event in which he had participated as a midshipman. The 50th anniversary of Matthew C. Perry's opening of that country to the West had been celebrated the year before. Biddle's visit with the line-of-battle ship *Columbus* and sloop-of-war *Vincennes* had been from 20 to 29 July 1846.

Luce's claim was that the total absence of display of any hostile intentions by Commodore Biddle and his officers impressed the Japanese officials and disposed them to receive with favor the demanding overtures of Perry. He retained a vivid recollection of these events and in his research learned of three enlisted men of the *Columbus* crew still alive. He discovered as well two etchings, originally created by two enlisted men, of *Columbus* and her consort *Vincennes* in Tokyo Bay. Both prints were published with the article, and copies were furnished the Japanese Government. (See item 119.)

In this article Luce recounts his reunion with Charles Nordhoff, a famous author and newspaper editor, who had served in the *Columbus* at this time, serving as a powder boy in Lt. Percival Drayton's division. Nordhoff's first book was about this voyage, and in it he favorably commented on the Japanese. "There was not one, old or young, whose appearance would not command respect in any society."[1]

On Nordhoff, Luce comments with his characteristic modesty: "Of the midshipman and the powder boy, the latter was by far, the more apt scholar."

---

[1] Charles Nordhoff, *Man-of-War Life: A Boy's Experience in the U.S. Navy.* (New York: n.p., 1855).

127. "A Plea for an Engineer Corps in the Navy." *The North American Review*, vol. CLXXXII, No. 590, January 1906, pp. 74-83.

    This article considers one aspect of the problem of officer specialization in the Navy. Luce had long been interested in engineering education for naval officers, and as early as 1875 he endeavored to get Professor William B. Rogers of the Massachusetts Institute of Technology to establish a school of naval architecture and marine engineering. He did not believe, however, that study of the technical sciences and the art of war were compatible. For this reason he was against training naval engineers at the Naval Academy and the amalgamation in 1899 of the Engineer Corps with the line.

    This amalgamation brought many able engineer officers into the line but few line officers to engineering duty. In July 1905 a boiler explosion in the gunboat *Bennington* at San Diego killed over 60 men. This accident prompted Luce to consider the question of whether a man can simultaneously master two professions; an officer of the Navy and a marine engineer.

    George Melville, Chief Engineer of the Navy, at first saw the amalgamation as a way to end the historical fight between line and staff, but later disavowed it.[1] Other officers, especially Lt. Comdr. L.H. Chandler, in a Naval Institute *Proceedings* article, considered amalgamation a success and claimed Luce had no extensive experience with steam engineering qualifying him to be a judge in this case.

    A compromise in this controversy was finally achieved in

1908 with the creation of the "engineering duty only" designation and the establishment of the postgraduate school to provide education for those officers.

---

[1] George W. Melville to Luce, 20 October 1905, Luce Papers, LC.

128. "A Powerful Navy Not Dangerous To Civil Liberty." U.S.N.I. Proceedings, vol. XXXII, No. 3, October 1906, pp. 1069-75.

This is a reprint of item 53 which appeared in The United Service in January 1880. Luce has made some minor changes in this publication in order to bring it up to date. The major changes from the original article occur in the last three paragraphs of the 1880 piece. He deleted the final paragraph quoting Secretary Robeson, updated the figures for customs revenues, and removed the sentence stating that one of the Navy's primary source of recruits was the merchant marine.

129. "Christian Ethics an Element of Military Education." U.S.N.I. Proceedings, vol. XXXII, No. 4, November 1906, pp. 1367-86.

This is a reprint of item 67 which appeared in The United Service in January 1883.

130. "Calhoun's Opinion of the Navy." The Newport Mercury, vol. CXLIX, No. 10, 18 August 1906, p. 4.

Written by Luce, unsigned of course, this editorial appeared in the oldest Rhode Island newspaper whose manager and editor was his friend J.P. Sanborn. The pieces are identified as having been composed by Luce from initialed copies in his papers at the Library of Congress.

The above article was on John C. Calhoun's advocacy, in 1816, of a strong navy for the United States. In a speech as U.S. Senator from South Carolina, he stated that a navy was "the most safe, most effective and cheapest means of defense." Luce then mentioned Calhoun's effective reorganization of the U.S. Army while Secretary of War in President Monroe's administration. Later Mercury editorials, written almost a year apart, were part of the admiral's efforts at this time to get drydocks in the Narragansett Bay area. (See items 133, 134, 137.)

131. "Narragansett Bay as a Naval Base." Newport Daily News, Wednesday, 31 October 1906, p. 4.

The second group of editorials were in the other local newspaper, the Newport Daily News. The subject of all was the same, the prospects of a naval base and dockyard in the Rhode Island area. In the first editorial Luce lauded the policy of concentrating our naval strength in home waters with a force of 12 battleships and accompanying cruisers and destroyers. Of course, the proper place to have that fleet based was Narragansett Bay.

132. "Dangerous Dry Docks." *Newport Daily News*, Friday, 2 November 1906, p. 3.

In this article Luce called attention to the troubles experienced with building the drydocks at the Brooklyn Navy Yard in New York. He noted that similar problems with other drydocks which had been built in wet soil had occurred at Charleston and Port Royal, S.C. He concludes, "On the shores of Narragansett bay may be found sites for half a dozen dry docks, where the soil is in every respect suitable and where the money spent will not be thrown away."

133. "Great Naval Depot." *Newport Mercury*, vol. CXLIX, No. 21, 3 November 1906, p. 1.

This front-page story was in the form of a well-prepared article in the usual Luce form of presenting historical evidence first. He discussed the extensive survey that British engineers had made in 1773-4 and their favorable report on a base in Narragansett Bay—centrally located, near the West Indies, deep water, little ice; a whole fleet might go from anchorage to sea area on one tack and in not more than 1 hour. Defense was feasible and worth the cost.

A similar favorable report was submitted in 1817 by a mixed commission of officers of the U.S. Navy and Corps of Engineers, stating Narragansett Bay was the best site for a naval base north of Chesapeake Bay. The time was ripe, Luce claimed, to start this base with its defensive works now completed. See chapter VIII for an expanded version of this same data.

134. "Navy and Dock Yards." *Newport Mercury*, vol. CXLIX, No. 22, 10 November 1906, p. 1.

In this short article which appeared on the front page of the *Mercury*, Luce discussed the Navy's need for a dockyard and drydocks. Noting that for the first time in American history the United States had "a fleet that is a fleet," it must be properly maintained. He pointed out the requisites for a good dockyard and concluded that "all these requirements are to be found in an eminent degree in Narragansett Bay."

135. "Up-To-Date Dock Yards." *Newport Daily News*, Monday, 19 November 1906, p. 4.

Luce starts this article with the shocking statement, "Japanese battleship Satsuma, 19,000 tons was launched last week. Her tonnage exceeds that of the English Dreadnought by about 1,000 tons." He goes on to warn that Japan, as well as England and Germany, were building suitable docks for their dreadnoughts. Great Britain already had 5 government and 10 private docks that could handle them. The United States would soon have ships of that type, and it takes as long to build a dock as it does the ship it will serve. Congress should appropriate funds for the construction of such a dock as soon as possible. For ships drawing 28-30 feet of water, Narragansett Bay is the only place on the coast where all the requirements for a dockyard are available.

136. "An American Dreadnought." *Newport Daily News,* Tuesday, 4 December 1906, p. 4.

   In his last article for the *Daily News,* Luce discusses the new large ships under construction, the *Connecticut*-class battleships, the *Invincible*-class of armored English cruisers, merchant ships like the White Star Line's *Baltic* and *Adriatic,* Cunard's *Lusitania,* and the German *Kaiserin Auguste Victoria.*

   In view of these figures it behooves us to see that our new dockyard shall be built to meet all possible contingencies, and that the site shall have all the advantages demanded by its importance. Narragansett bay possesses all those advantages in a marked degree. To build a dry dock today, of given size only to increase that size tomorrow in order to meet new conditions, is to throw away money. We have had already too much of that policy.

137. "The Value of the Dry Dock." *Newport Mercury,* vol. CL, No. 24, 23 November 1907, p. 4.

   The final article on the subject of drydocks appeared in the *Mercury* almost a year after the others. Like the previous editorials in that weekly, it was well thought out and ably presented. "We cannot close with the enemy" had been the cry of British seamen in the 18th century when French ships were sheathed and the British not. Copper sheathing for iron ships had proved infeasible, and so the only remedy for their heavy bottom fouling was frequent docking in order to scrape, clean, and paint. Luce explains how fouling affects speed and coal consumption as well as the special need for frequent docking in wartime. His final editorial again invited interest in Narragansett Bay and pointed out the fallacy of the drydock at Brooklyn.

138. "The Fleet." *The North American Review,* vol. CLXXXVIII, No. 635, October 1908, pp. 564-76. (This article is reprinted with annotation in chapter VI.)

139. "Wanted—an Admiralty Staff." *Army and Navy Life,*[1] vol. XIV, No. 1, January 1909, pp. 13-19.

   This presentation with an appropriate title represents Luce's final effort to bring the defects of the Navy at this time to public notice. It forms a succinct summary, but without repetition, of his several articles on naval administration, including "The Department of the Navy."

   He begins, as usual, with early administrative history. The Navy Department, at the behest of Secretary William Jones, was properly organized with a military and a civil side only after the War of 1812. Its primary feature was the inclusion of three post captains appointed as commissioners to advise the Secretary. The defect in this organization was that no provision was made for a similar staff on the civil side.

The result was that the three commissioners had to perform these duties. This became a heavy burden, so in 1842 the Bureau system was adopted. But this had the effect of separating the senior officers in the Department from the Secretary and also from each other. The Secretary was without counsel. An outstanding Navy declined to such a discreditable state that by 1889 the country was without any form of naval defense.

Luce sums up: . . . naval administration includes two separate and distinct parts, each one indispensable to the other, the military and the civil. The *employment* of vessels of war should be under the military head; *construction, armament,* and *equipment* belongs to the civil branch.

The Secretary should be chosen from civil life. And there must be a small but select board of naval officers to act as advisers to him on policy and on all questions relating to the employment of vessels of war. The senior officer of this board should be one of high rank and wide experience. This board would form an admiralty staff and be a part of the secretariat.

---

[1]*Army and Navy Life* was the successor to *The United Service* and *The Bluejacket*. The former had been sold in late 1905 to W.D. Walker, who founded *Army and Navy Life*. The new periodical was well illustrated, contained news of all armed services, and advocated increased armaments. Its "big navy" policy attracted both abuse and praise from newspapers. The magazine was not a financial success, and in August 1909 Walker abandoned it.

140. "Naval Strategy." U.S.N.I. *Proceedings*, vol. XXXV, No. 1, 1909, pp. 93-112. (This article is reprinted with annotation in chapter VII.)

141. "Naval Training, II." U.S.N.I. *Proceedings*, vol. XXXVI, No. 1, 1910, pp. 103-23.

This article was delivered as a lecture at the Naval War College in October 1910. It was the fourth Luce had delivered on the subject since the one printed in the *Proceedings* in 1874, and it was designed as a sequel to item 89 published in 1890. Despite these efforts, the Navy was still plagued with enlistment problems. Luce had recommended industrial education methods in 1874, and he had put them into effect in the Training Squadron. The Spanish War and the expansion of the Navy after the war had forced the abandonment of the Training Squadron and the naval apprentice system. Instead, men of from 21 to 25 were being trained in barracks or camps ashore in a manner that did about everything, in Luce's opinion, to make them unfit for life on board ship.

A movement to supplement industrial education for general

education was being adopted at this time, and Luce supported this strongly in his article.

The desertion situation at this time was deplorable with 5,000 missing annually from an enlisted strength of 38,500. The Department's methods for correcting this were (1) making service in the Navy more attractive; and (2) increasing punishments. This was the carrot and stick technique, but Luce claimed a third way had more merit: naturalizing youths to ship life during their formative years with enlistments at age 14 to 17 years. Older recruits with fixed habits and social affiliations can never adjust to life on board ship, whereas for the young naval apprentice "that little warlike world" within the ship, with all its privations, becomes to him a second nature.

Luce's program for providing the Navy with skilled seamen remained always the same:

1. Get boys inured early to ship life.
2. Provide advancement for ability, efficiency, and good conduct.
3. Seek legislation for liberal pensions and retirement.

142. "The U.S. Naval War College." U.S.N.I. *Proceedings,* vol. XXXVI, No. 2, 1910, pp. 559-86.

During the period from September 1910 to September 1911, Stephen B. Luce published his swan song on the Naval War College in the form of three articles in the *Proceedings:* first, a long piece in two parts on its history (items 142 and 143) and two shorter articles (items 144 and 145) on what he believed should be the relations between the War College and the Navy Department and between it and the line officers of the Navy.

In the first part of the historical piece, Luce recounts the early stages, and especially the early difficulties, of the institution. He gives a summary of the 10 sessions held between the first in 1885 and that of 1897. He goes into considerable detail on the efforts of Secretary William C. Whitney in 1888 to close the institution by wrongly joining it with the Torpedo School. Secretary Benjamin F. Tracy, in 1889, reversed the Whitney closing orders. The next Secretary, Hilary A. Herbert, at first held that if the War College should be allowed to exist at all, it should be at the Naval Academy. He changed his views after reading Captain Mahan's *Influence of Sea Power upon History, 1660-1783* and became an ardent supporter. But the man who, in fact, put the War College on a permanent basis was Capt. Henry C. Taylor, President of the Naval War College, 1893 to 1897.

143. "The U.S. Naval War College. (concluded)." U.S.N.I. *Proceedings,* vol. XXXVI, No. 3, 1910, pp. 683-96.

This piece is a continuation of item 142. The second part paid tribute to Capt. William McCarty Little and his Naval War

Game; Luce discussed American Kriegsspiel at some length. He reviewed the numerous war colleges that had followed the American naval institution, including the U.S. Army War College at Washington.

He quotes from the writings of Maj. W.R. Livermore, the U.S. Army expert on war gaming who had served on the staff of the Naval War College. In discussing the Royal Naval War College, Luce quotes extensively from Sir Julian Corbett's articles in the London *Times*[1] in which he points out the value of the "War Course" and mentions that it was designed broadly on the lines of the American War College when it was established in 1901. Luce then goes on to discuss the French and German Naval War Colleges.

However, this section in the main was devoted to the success at Newport of the study of marine international law under Rear Adm. C.H. Stockton, Professor John B. Moore of Columbia University, and Georg G. Wilson of Brown. The recognition of the work of the Naval War College in international law had by 1910 become worldwide, and the *International Law Situation* volumes, the "blue books" published annually, have become authoritative texts in this field of study.

Luce went on to discuss the curriculum of the college in detail. He noted that the study of international law had momentarily outstripped the study of the art and science of warfare, the subject that should be the principal branch of study at the college. Speaking about the methods of teaching used at the college, Luce noted,

> The value of lectures on professional subjects must not be underrated. They are indispensable. But it is one of the principles of the Science of Education that throughout youth and in maturity the process in the acquisition of knowledge shall be one of self-instruction. Knowledge which the student has himself acquired, a problem which he has himself solved, becomes by virtue of the conquest much more thoroughly his own than it could otherwise be.

For this reason, Luce always encouraged independent study which did not rely on the lecture method of instruction. He quoted from Herbert Spencer to support his thesis and then pointed to Mahan as an example of a scholar who achieved his position by individual application.

Turning to the field of naval history itself, Luce observed that for the most part it was a collection of isolated and independent facts. While the story of engagements was fascinating in itself and worthy of study, the student must go on and discover the relationship between these apparently isolated facts.

> What then had appeared to him as a series of independent, unrelated facts, he finds out to be phenomena which fall within the province of law. In short he has, by

self effort, gained knowledge, and has worked out for himself the science of Naval Strategy. "Science is organized knowledge."

Of course this was not all that Luce saw to the study of strategy. "There is a still higher field of inquiry. Why were those two nations at war?"

In his final words, Luce expressed the hope that there would be a few officers who were willing and anxious to specialize along the lines that Mahan had laid down. "To such the War College extends a cordial welcome."

---

[1] J.S. Corbett, "Naval War Course," *The Times,* Tuesday, 5 June 1906, p. 6, and "Naval War Course, No. II," *The Times*, Saturday, 9 June 1906, p. 6.

144. "On the True Relations Between the Department of the Navy and the Naval War College." U.S.N.I. *Proceedings,* vol. XXXVII, No. 1, 1911, pp. 83-86.

    1. The sole reason for the existence of the Navy Department is the probability of war.

    2. The most important office in the Navy Department (after that of the Secretary of the Navy) is the office of naval operations.

    3. All other offices in the navy are merely subsidiary to that one particular office—the Office for the Conduct of War.

There follows in this 4-page article 20 more numbered paragraphs which give a striking summation of the relationships that should exist between these two pillars of naval preparation for war.

The last summary paragraph states flatly that the purpose of the Naval War College is *educational,* not functional, that it is neither a war board nor a naval general staff. Herein is the difference, still existent today, between the Naval War College's approach to higher education and that of many other service schools.

145. "On the Relations Between the U.S. Naval War College and the Line Officers of the U.S. Navy. U.S.N.I. *Proceedings,* vol. XXXVII, No. 3, 1911, pp. 787-99.

This article embraces the last address that Luce made before the institution he founded. It was presented at the Naval and Military Conference on 2 June 1911, in the presence of Secretary of the Navy George von L. Meyer, the man who transformed the report of the Moody Board into the reality that, by 1915, became the Office of the Chief of Naval Operations.

Luce was now 84 years old, and he had returned to inactive duty the previous year. He could have taken this as an opportunity to reminisce historically, as he loved to do.

Instead, he chose to make a fighting speech about the future of the Navy.

He was frankly worried because there was so much interest in the new postgraduate school of engineering and still so little in the War College, showing that the majority of officers still cared little about the main purpose of their profession.

Instead of 4 months, Luce wanted a course of 2 years.[1]

> Let officers who have completed their terms of sea-service in their respective grades, come here for a two-year course of *study;* not for discussion, *but for study.* On the completion of such a course they will then be eligible as conferees to discuss intelligently questions relating to naval warfare—and not before.

He cites the dangers of the crude views of bright, but untrained minds that go forth with the imprimatur of the college.

"Your profession is the art of war and nature will be avenged if you violate one of its laws in undertaking to make a part greater than the whole."

---

[1] In 1911 the War College Course was extended to 1 year from a course of several months.

146. "The Navy and Its Needs." *The North American Review,* vol. CXCIII, No. 665, April 1911, pp. 494-507. (This article is reprinted with annotation in chapter VIII.)

147. "The Spanish-American War." *The North American Review,* vol. CXCIV, No. 671, October 1911, pp. 612-27.

Presumably a book review of Rear Adm. French E. Chadwick, *The Spanish-American War* (New York: Scribner, 1911), this piece was actually a tribute to and defense of Luce's good friend, Rear Adm. William T. Sampson, commander of North Atlantic Squadron that engaged the Spanish Squadron off Santiago de Cuba on 3 July 1898. Chadwick was commander of the flagship *New York* and acted as chief of staff for Sampson.

Luce in the review confined himself to the Battles of Manila Bay and Santiago; Chadwick, in his two volumes, devoted himself to the history of hostilities only and did not discuss the unfortunate Schley-Sampson controversy after it. Luce confined himself to arguing the point of whether Sampson had control during the battle or whether it was a "Captain's fight," with the issue determined by the actions of the ships' commanders on their own volition. In this case, however, Luce showed that Sampson had planned the method of attack, everything was done as he had ordered, and the situation at all times was the same as if he had been there.

Luce gives examples of soldiers' fights on land such as Missionary Ridge in the Civil War and the battles of British naval history. He mentions the Battle of the Nile where victory was achieved by the individual actions of Nelson's four leading captains "without stripping one leaf from Nelson's laurels."

The country that Sampson had served well paid him no mark of honor. He died without receiving the thanks of Congress or promotion in rank. He became instead the victim of a controversy for which he was in no way responsible and in which he took no part.

148. "The Board of Navy Commissioners. Commissioners for Executing the Office of Constitutional Commander-in-Chief of the Navy of the United States." U.S.N.I. *Proceedings,* vol. XXXVII, No. 4, 1911, pp. 1113-35.

It must be left to conjecture whether or not this last published article of Stephen B. Luce was so by intent or accident. There can be no doubt that the subject of this article was among his favorites, and it can be justifiably surmised that he wanted to have this piece presented in indisputable form before the end of his writing career. His prolific output suddenly ends in December of 1911, a year in which he published two articles in *The North American Review* and four in the *Proceedings.* The previous year he had published his "Naval Training II."

The subject of this article, "The Board of Navy Commissioners," was discussed in virtually every piece of writing on naval administration that Luce did in over 30 years of endeavoring to get military direction in naval affairs. At only one period in our history did the Navy have this form of direction, from 1815 to 1842.

What made his last treatment of this subject novel was his placing of an examination of the organization of the Navy with his recommendations regarding it into an easily understood tabular form. For purposes of analysis, he divides the naval administrative functions into two columns. On the left side are the executive and military branches charged with the employment of vessels of war. On the right are the civil and industrial branches for the procurement of naval stores and materials, construction, armament, and equipment for vessels of war.

The first table is that showing that the Act of 1789 which created the organization of the Navy Department failed to provide for its military or civil direction, except by the Secretary of the Navy. The second table, dated 1815, however, does show a provision for the Board of Commissioners and for military direction. The third table shows the impact of the Act of 1842, which transferred direction, providing for the civil but not military direction. As Luce put it, "The Act supplied the left arm of the militant body; *but cut off the right arm.*"

Luce then offered a table that would provide both right and left arms; "a scheme of naval administration based on sound military and business principles." He proposed the following:

The President (Commander in Chief)
The Secretary of the Navy
The Assistant Secretary of the Navy

Military and Executive Branch:	Civil and Industrial Branch:
Navy Commissioners. The chairman of the board to be "the one responsible Adviser to the Secretary."	Bureau of Yards and Docks. Bureau of Navigation. Bureau of Ordnance. Bureau of Construction and Repair Bureau of Steam Engineering. Bureau of Supplies and Accounts. Bureau of Medicine and Surgery. Without executive authority

This is followed by three pages, extracted from the *Moody Board Report* of 1909 entitled "General Principles Governing Naval Organization." This had been written by Mahan, but its ideas had come from Luce.

The conclusion states:

... It should be distinctly laid down as a cardinal principle that no scheme of naval organization can possibly be effective which does not recognize that the requirement of war is the true standard of efficiency in an administrative military system; that success in war and victory in battle can be assured only by that constant preparedness and that superior fighting efficiency which logically result from placing the control and responsibility in time of peace upon the same individuals and the same agencies that must control in time of war.

"We have fashioned the instrument—the fleet;" concluded Luce, "but we have failed to provide the power to wield it as a weapon of war."

This power was finally acquired in 1915. But no reaction was to come from Stephen B. Luce. He had laid down his pen; he had "written himself out."

U.S.S. *Minnesota*

Luce commanded the training ship *Minnesota* from 1877 until 1881. He wrote his article "United States Naval Training Ships" and contributed to *Johnson's Encyclopedia* during this time.

Photo: Naval History Division

CHAPTER XI

CHRONOLOGY OF LIFE AND WRITINGS

1827	March 25	Born Albany, N.Y., third son and fifth child to reach adulthood of Vinal and Charlotte Bleecker Luce.
1835		Vinal Luce, a druggist, obtained employment as a clerk in the new independent Treasury Department, and the family moved to Washington, D.C.
1841	Oct. 19	Appointed midshipman by President Martin Van Buren.
1841	Nov. 4	Ordered to U.S.S. *North Carolina*, receiving ship at New York.
1842	April 2	Ordered to new 50-gun frigate *Congress* at Portsmouth, N.H. Reported 20 April. Ship commissioned 7 May, sailed 15 July for Mediterranean. Transferred to South Atlantic Station, December 1843, serving there until January 1845.
1843	May 3	Warranted midshipman after an 18 months probationary period.
1845	March 14	*Congress* decommissioned at Norfolk. Luce granted 3-months leave.
1845	May 26	Ordered to report without delay to 92-gun ship-of-the-line *Columbus* at New York. Reported 28 May. Ship departed 3 June on 3-year cruise around the world.
1846	July 20	*Columbus* in Yeddo (Tokyo) Bay, Japan. Departed 29 July for Honolulu and California.
1847	March 3	*Columbus* arrived Monterey Bay; at San Francisco 23 June, departed for Norfolk, Va., 25 July.

1848	March 13	*Columbus* decommissioned at Navy Yard, Norfolk. Luce to report to Naval Academy, 1 April.
1848	June 22	Summer leave from Naval Academy until 10 October.
1849	March 6	Involved in a disturbance at the Academy, punished by loss of 72 numbers in a class of 135. Position on active list restored in January 1862.
1849	Aug. 20	Ordered to 20-gun sloop of war *Vandalia*, Pacific Squadron.
1849	Sep. 29	Warranted as passed midshipman from 10 August 1847.
1851	April 30	Requested furlough of 1 year to enter merchant service, repeating a similar request made in June 1850. Refused because only lieutenants were allowed this privilege.
1852	Oct. 12	Detached *Vandalia* at New York with 3 months leave.
1852	Dec. 31	Ordered to duty with Lt. James M. Gillis, astronomer, at Navy Yard, Washington, assisting with calculations connected with his observations of Venus and Mars, 1849-1852.
1853	May 9	Ordered to steamer *Vixen*, Home Squadron.
1854	Feb. 4	Detached *Vixen* with 3 months leave, suffering from yellow fever.
1854	May 18	Ordered to Coast Survey serving along Atlantic Coast in *Madison*, *Crawford*, and *Bibb* under Lts. John N. Maffitt and C.R.P. Rodgers.
1854	Dec. 7	Married childhood friend Eliza Henley of Washington, D.C., youngest daughter of Commodore John D. Henley. She was a grandniece of Martha Washington.

1855	Sep. 15 Sep. 16	Promoted to master and lieutenant on succeeding days due to large number of officers retired or separated by the Naval Efficiency Act.
1857	Nov. 16	Ordered to sloop of war *Jamestown*, 20 guns, Home Squadron, stationed on east coast of Central America.
1860	March 2	Detached *Jamestown* and reported to Naval Academy, assigned as instructor of Seamanship.
1861	May 2	Ordered without delay to steam frigate *Wabash*. Orders were received while Luce family was being transported to Newport, R.I., where Naval Academy was located during the Civil War.
1861	Oct. 10	Ordered back to Naval Academy but delivery of orders delayed until 11 January 1862 to allow Luce to take part in Port Royal campaign.
1862	March 29	Revised W.H. Parker's *Instructions for Light Artillery, Afloat and Ashore*. Second edition published under Luce's name in New York by Van Nostrand.
1862	May 12	First edition of *Seamanship* text prepared and published at Newport, R.I. Third printing by Van Nostrand under Luce's name appeared in 1863.
1862	Aug. 5	Promoted to lieutenant commander from 16 July.
1863	June 4	Ordered to command frigate *Macedonian* for cruise with midshipmen to England and France.
1863	Sep. 29	Report submitted on practice cruise, forwarded to Navy Department.

1863	Oct. 13	Ordered to command monitor *Nantucket* of South Atlantic Blockading Squadron.
1863	Oct. 24	Earliest published article appeared in *Army and Navy Journal,* first of a series of five entitled "Training Ships."
1864	Sep. 2	Assumed command of double-ender gunboat *Pontiac,* SAB Squadron.
1865	Jan. 13	Luce with *Pontiac* ordered to report to Gen. W.T. Sherman to guard crossing of Savannah River by left wing of his army, moving north.
1865	June 9	*Pontiac* placed out of commission at Navy Yard, N.Y.
1865	July 26	Request for leave of absence to enter merchant service disapproved.
1865	Sep. 26	Ordered to Naval Academy, reestablished at Annapolis, Md., as Commandant of Midshipmen.
1866	July 25	Promoted to commander.
1866	Nov. 17	Circular letter from Luce sent to prominent citizens proposing establishment of nautical colleges.
1868	Sep. 30	Detached from Naval Academy to command double-ender *Mohongo,* Pacific Fleet. Traveled to Mare Island, Calif. via Pacific Mail Steamer. Took command 10 November. Cruised in Gulf of California.
1869	May 26	Detached from *Mohongo;* returned from Pacific coast by railroad.
1869	July 1	Took command of steam sloop-of-war *Juniata,* commissioned 19 July at Philadelphia for duty in Mediterranean Squadron.

1870	Aug. 26	*Juniata* ordered to Helgoland Island, North Sea, to observe French naval blockade of Germany during Franco-Prussian War.
1871	July 22	First of seven articles on "Naval Tactics" by Vice Adm. Jean Pierre Edmond Jurien de la Gravière, translated by Luce and published in *Army and Navy Journal*. Last appeared 2 September.
1871	Oct. 24	Letter in *London Times* from Griffen and Co., publishers of G.S. Nares' text on *Seamanship* accused Van Nostrand, and Luce indirectly, of plagiarism.
1872	May 1	Essay, "Regina dal Chin" published in *The Galaxy*, vol. XIII.
1872	July 1	Detached *Juniata*. Assumed duty as Equipment Officer, Boston Navy Yard, 14 September 1872.
1872	Dec. 28	Promoted to captain.
1873	July 11	Ordered to consult with Board of Education, City of New York, on establishment of a nautical school.
1873	Nov. 13	Lecture, "The Manning of the Navy and Mercantile Marine," before Annapolis Chapter of Naval Institute, published as first article in U.S.N.I. *Proceedings*, vol. I, No. 1 (1874).
1874	June 20	Prepared bill which became law authorizing loan of naval vessels to a state for purposes of nautical schoolships and the detail of officers as instructors. *St. Mary's* so fitted out by Luce, ready January 1875.
1874	Dec. 20	Wrote Introduction to *History of the United States Marine Corps* by Capt. Richard S. Collum, USMC, published 1875, 1890, and 1903.

1875	Oct. 15	Detached Navy Yard, Boston, and on 26 October assumed command of *Hartford* at Hampton Roads.
1876	Feb. 7	Met Representative Washington C. Whitthorne of Tennessee, Democratic Chairman of House Naval Affairs Committee.
1876	April 20	Lecture "Fleets of the World" before U.S. Naval Academy Chapter of Naval Institute. Published in U.S.N.I. *Proceedings*, vol. III (1877).
1876	Aug. 12	First of six articles on "Modern Navies" published in *Army and Navy Journal*. Last appeared 7 October 1876.
1876	Nov. 1	First of three articles that appeared in *Potter's American Monthly*.
1877	Feb. 1	Essay, "The Modern Pythia," *The Galaxy*, vol. XXIII.
1877	May 1	Book review, *Fleets of the World* by Commodore F.A. Parker, *The Galaxy*, vol. XXIII.
1877	Aug. 21	Detached *Hartford* for temporary duty in connection with training ships. Assumed command 31 December 1877 of steam frigate *Minnesota*, training ship.
1879	July 1	Essay, "United States Naval Training Ships," *The United Service*, vol. I.
1879	Oct. 21	Bailey Medal, established by Luce, first awarded to the outstanding naval apprentice. Medal endowed in honor of Commodore Theodorus Bailey.
1880	Jan. 1	Essay, "A Powerful Navy Not Dangerous to Civil Liberty," *The United Service*, vol. II. Reprinted in U.S.N.I. *Proceedings*, vol. XXXII (September 1906).

1880	Dec. 18	Board of which Luce is a member selects Coasters Harbor Island, Newport, as permanent base for naval training.
1881	Feb. 15	Detached from command of *Minnesota*, 11 April 1881; took command of newly formed Training Squadron.
1881	Nov. 25	Promoted to commodore.
1882	May 1	Essay, "Our Naval Policy," *The United Service*, vol. VI.
1882	April 17	Departed on naval apprentice training cruise to Europe on board *Portsmouth* accompanied by *Saratoga*. Returned to Narragansett Bay, 8 October 1882.
1882	Aug. 5	Appointed senior member, Commission to Investigate Navy Yards. Final report submitted 1 December 1883.
1883	Jan. 1	Essay, "Christian Ethics as an Element of Military Education," *The United Service*, vol. VIII. Reprinted in U.S.N.I. *Proceedings* (December 1906).
1883	April 4	Lecture "War Schools," to Newport branch of U.S. Naval Institute. Published in U.S.N.I. *Proceedings*, vol. IX.
1883	June 17	*Naval Songs*, compiled by and with an introduction by Luce, published. First edition reprinted in 1888, second edition 1902, with reprintings in 1908 and 1918.
1884	July 16	Detached from command of Training Squadron and took temporary command of North Atlantic Station 27 July 1884. Appointed acting rear admiral 23 July 1884.
1884	Sep. 20	Assumed duty as President, Naval War College.

1885	Jan. 1	Essay, "United States Naval War College," *The United Service*, vol. XII.
1885	Sep. 4	Introductory lecture, "On the Study of Naval Warfare as a Science," at opening session Naval War College. Repeated 6 September 1886 and published in U.S.N.I. *Proceedings*, vol. XII (1886).
1885	Sep. 5	Lecture, "On the Study of Naval History (Grand Tactics)," Naval War College. Repeated 7 September 1886 and published in U.S.N.I. *Proceedings*, vol. XIII (1887).
1886	Jan. 30	Commissioned rear admiral with date of rank 5 October 1885.
1886	June 18	Detached as President, Naval War College, to command North Atlantic Station.
1887	Aug. 6	Canadian fisheries dispute. Secretary of the Navy W.C. Whitney ordered Luce to withdraw his instructions to American fishermen on basis that it reflected Canadian and not U.S. interpretation of treaty on fishing rights.
1888	March 1	Presidential Address to U.S. Naval Institute, published in U.S.N.I. *Proceedings*, vol. XIV.
1888	June 6	Lecture "Naval Administration," published in U.S.N.I. *Proceedings*, vol. XIV (September 1888).
1888	Sep. 11	Passage through inland waterways from New York to Norfolk in Herreshoff steam launch *Vixen*. Reached Annapolis 14 September and Norfolk 18 September 1888. Delayed by bad weather which damaged launch to extent that continuation to Ferandina, Fla., had to be abandoned.
1888	Dec. 8	Luce in *Galena* with *Yantic* ordered to Port au Prince, Haiti, to obtain surrender of American

steamer, *Haytian Republic*, charged with running a blockade by government forces during a recent rebellion. Luce commended by State Department for conducting negotiations with tact, judgment, and discretion.

1889 Jan. 18　Letter about retirement to Mrs. Luce from *Galena* en route to Key West: "I will then have done with the Navy for the rest of my natural life."

The Retired Years

1889 Feb. 1　Relieved all active duty. Transferred to the retired list 25 March 1889.

1889 March 14　Letter to Secretary Benjamin F. Tracy, giving the reasons why the proposed plan for amalgamating the Naval War College with the Torpedo School should be reviewed. Thirteen typescript pages.

1889 May 30　Article, "Just the Boy That's Wanted for the Navy," the first of seven that appeared in *The Youth's Companion*, 1889-1898.

1889 July 1　Essay, "Our Future Navy," the first published in *The North American Review*. Reprinted in U.S.N.I. *Proceedings*, vol. XV (December 1889).

1890 March 1　Lecture, "Naval Training," to Naval Institute, published in U.S.N.I. *Proceedings*, vol. XVI (September 1890).

1890 June 26　Book review of A.T. Mahan's *Influence of Sea Power Upon History, 1660-1783* in *The Critic*, beginning a 16-year period of reviewing in that periodical, including all Mahan's works, G.F.R. Henderson, *Stonewall Jackson and the American Civil War* (1898), and William L. Clowes, *A History of the Royal Navy*, seven volumes, 1897-1903.

1890	Sep. 22	Letter to Secretary opposing amalgamation of the Revenue Marine with the Navy.
1890	Dec. 15	Accepted position of naval editor of Funk and Wagnalls, *Standard Dictionary of the English Language,* first edition, 1894.
1891	May 1	Essay, "How Shall We Man Our Ships," *North American Review,* vol. CLII.
1891	Dec. 1	Essay, "The Benefits of War," published in *North American Review.* Reprinted under title "War and Its Prevention," U.S.N.I. *Proceedings,* vol. XXX (September 1904).
1892	May 13	Appointed Commissioner General of the United States Commission for the Columbian Historical Exposition at Madrid, Spain, 11 November 1892 to 31 January 1893.
1893	May 27	Permission granted to leave the United States for 1 year.
1895	Dec. 1	Essay, "As to Navy-Yards and Their Defense," U.S.N.I. *Proceedings,* vol. XXI.
1896	Jan. 1	Essay, "Naval Warfare Under Modern Conditions," *North American Review,* vol. CLXII.
1896	Jan. 7	Lecture, "The Story of the Monitor," before the Military History Society of Massachusetts, published in the Society *Papers,* vol. XII (1902). This lecture had been delivered many times, the first to the apprentice boys and crew of *Hartford* in 1876.
1898	Sep. 1	"The Dawn of Naval History," U.S.N.I. *Proceedings,* vol. XXIV.
1901	Aug. 13	Ordered to active duty, U.S. Naval War College, Newport, R.I.

1902	Dec. 1	Essay, "Naval Administration II," published in U.S.N.I. *Proceedings*, vol. XXVIII, a sequel to "Naval Administration" in vol. XIV (1888). "Naval Administration III" appeared in vol. XXIX (December 1903) having been given as a lecture 11 June 1903.
1903	June 2	Address delivered at the Naval War College, published in U.S.N.I. *Proceedings*, vol. XXIX (September 1903).
1904	April 11 April 26	First efforts by Navy Department to get a naval general staff enacted into law fails.
1904	July 26	Death of Henry C. Taylor in Toronto, Canada.
1905	March 1	Essay, "The Department of the Navy," won honorable mention in U.S. Naval Institute's prize essay contest. Published in U.S.N.I. *Proceedings*, vol. XXXI.
1905	Sep. 1	Narrative essay, "Commodore Biddle's Visit to Japan in 1846," published in U.S.N.I. *Proceedings*, vol. XXXI. A shorter version appeared in the Newport, R.I. *Mercury*, 7 February 1903.
1906	Jan.	Essay, "A Plea for an Engineer Corps in the Navy." *North American Review*, vol. CLXXXII.
1906	Nov. 17	First letter to W.S. Sims, relating to his article, "The Inherent Tactical Qualities of All-Big Gun, One Caliber Battleships of High Speed, Large Displacement and Gunpower," which was to appear in the U.S.N.I. *Proceedings*, vol. XXXII (December 1906).
1907	April 30	Submitted to Secretary T.H. Metcalfe, a plan for naval administration reform which included his unpublished "Memorandum on Naval Efficiency" of 25 March 1907.

1907	Oct. 1	Lecture, "The Fleet" delivered at the Naval War College and published in *North American Review*, vol. CLXXXVIII (October 1908).
1907	Oct. 1	George H. Putnam expressed a desire to publish Luce's autobiography or reminiscences. Putnam eventually published Gleaves' biography of Luce.
1907	Dec. 10	Dinner given by W.C. Church at the Union League Club to surviving male contributors to *The Galaxy*. Luce did not attend.
1908	April 30	Luce sent W.S. Sims a copy of "The Fleet" and also unpublished "Circular for Naval Officers," 1904, relating to the attempt to get Congress that year to establish a general staff for the Navy.
1909	Jan. 1	Essay, "Wanted-An Admiralty Staff," published in *Army and Navy Life*, vol. XIV.
1909	Jan. 7	Appointed to Board of Naval Reorganization, which was reinstituted 27 January 1909, by President Roosevelt, independent of Secretary Truman H. Newberry, as the Moody Commission to recommend how best to emphasize the military character of the Navy Department.
1909	Feb. 26	At Luce's suggestion, Moody Commission Report was submitted so as to reach Congress before adjournment.
1909	March	Lecture, "Naval Strategy," published in U.S.N.I. *Proceedings*, vol. XXXV.
1909	March 4	George V.L. Meyer appointed Secretary of the Navy by President Taft.
1909	Oct. 6	Lecture, "Naval Training II," delivered at Naval War College and published in U.S.N.I. *Proceedings*, vol. XXXVI (March 1910).

1909	Dec. 1	Moody Commission recommendations implemented by Secretary Meyer's appointment of Naval Aides for Operations, Personnel, Material, and Inspections.
1910	March 1	Essay, "The Naval War College," published in two parts in U.S.N.I. *Proceedings*, vol. XXXVI.
1910	Nov. 20	Released from active duty, on the insistence of Senator Eugene Hale of the Naval Affairs Committee.
1911	March 1	Essay, "On the True Relations Between the Department of the Navy and the Naval War College," U.S.N.I. *Proceedings*, vol. XXXVII.
1911	April 1	Essay, "The Navy and Its Needs," *North American Review*, vol. CXCIII.
1911	June 2	Lecture, "On the Relations Between the U.S. Naval War College and the Line Officers of the U.S. Navy," published in U.S.N.I. *Proceedings*, vol. XXXVII (September 1911).
1911	Oct. 1	Book review, "The Spanish American War," *North American Review*, vol. CXCIV.
1911	Dec. 1	Essay, "The Board of Navy Commissioners," U.S.N.I. *Proceedings*, vol. XXXVII.
1917	July 28	Died, 15 Francis St., Newport, R.I. Age 90. Buried, St. Mary's Episcopal Church graveyard, Portsmouth, R.I.
1917	Aug. 11	Obituary by Frank W. Hackett in *Army and Navy Journal* included the sentence: "A writer equal to the task may well take up betimes the work of giving to his countrymen a complete story of the character, and of the great achievements of Admiral Luce."

APPENDIX

CATEGORY LISTING OF SIGNIFICANT ARTICLES

CITED IN CHAPTERS IX AND X

Naval Organization and Administration: Items 10, 37, 38, 39, 66, 70, 84, 102, 117, 122, 125, 138, 139, 144, 146, 148.

Naval Warfare: Items 16-22, 53, 79, 81, 86, 87, 102, 104, 140.

Maritime and Naval History: Items 28, 30-35, 36, 41, 43, 111, 118, 119, 126, 130, 147.

Officer Education: Items 1, 3, 68, 73, 75, 121, 127, 142-143, 144, 145.

Sea Training: Items 5-9, 13, 24, 27, 29, 50, 51, 89, 92, 141.

Interesting Youths in the Sea Life: Items 85, 93, 95, 96, 103, 105, 109.

Military Ethics: Items 53, 67, 94.

General Subjects: Items 23, 42, 101.

Book Reviews: Items 44, 88, 97, 98, 106, 107, 108, 110, 113, 114, 115, 123, 147.

Encyclopedias and Dictionaries: Items 45-49, 54-65, 99.

Textbooks: Items 1, 3, 29, 69, 71, 112, 116.

Public Relations: Items 10, 50, 80, 82.

INDEX

A

Achilles 129
Actium, battle of 62,76
Adams, Brooks 29,33
Adams, Charles F. 180,181n
Adams, Henry 203
administration, Naval see Naval administration and government
Agamemnon 43
Agassiz, Jean L.R. 55
Agrippa, Marcus V. 75
Ahab, King 43
Albemarle, *Duke of see* Monk 58n,77,89
Aldrich, Almy 174
Aldrich, Nelson W. 15
Alexander the Great 50,62,63,76,101, 129-30
Alger, Philip R. xi
Almanza, battle of 130,130n
American frontier 2
Amherst, Jeffrey, *Baron* Amherst 103
anchoring 170,171,188
Anson, George, *Baron* Anson 91
arbitration, international 150
Arbuthnot, Mariot 82,82n
Aristobulus of Cassandreia 129
Army schools 11,47,49,49n,191
Arrian, Flavius A. 129
art of war 38,44,76,101,106,134-40,216, 233
astronomy 6,52-53

B

Bainbridge, William 159,220
Bainbridge-Hoff, William 95,95n
Baker, Charles H. 194
Bancroft, George *SecNav* 180,181n,195
Bannerman, *Sir* Henry C. 113
Barham, *Baron see* Middleton 137,138, 140
Barnard, Frederick A.P. 185
Barnard, Henry 170
Barnes, John S. 204-215
    comment on Luce 24-25
Barnette, William J. 110
Barras, *Comte* Louis de 86,87,134
Barry, William F. 191
Bartlett, Samuel C. 65
Basseterre Road, St. Kitt 61
Bates, Arthur L. 146
Bates, Richard W. 206n
battle, the moral effect of 54
battleships 16,112-16,124,148,150,203-05,228
Benson, William S. 218-19
Bettesworth, George E.B. 137
Bidder, Friedrich H. 55

Biddle, James 222,224
Bigot, Sebastien F. 85,85n. *See* Morogues
Blaine, James G. 212
Blake, George S. 165
Blake, Robert 58,58n,77
Bliss, Cornelius N. 143
Bliss, Tasker 32,47,67,67n
blockade 9,76-77,85,137-38,177,222
Boer War 122
Bolingbroke, *Viscount* 74n. *See* St. John
Bonaparte, Charles J. *SecNav* 22,122,224
Bonaparte, Napoleon 50,61,62,63,87,101, 104,105,107,129,130,131,132,136, 137,138,139
Boscawen, Edward 91,103
Bouet-Willaumez, *Comte* Louis E. 59,67, 67n,71
Bowles, *Sir* William 59,59n
Brahe, Tycho 52,52n,54
Brenton, Edward P. 216
Brewington, M.V. 218
British Navy *see* Navy, British
Brooklyn Navy yard 227
Brown-Sequard, Charles E. 55
Bryce, Lloyd 33,203
Buckle, Thomas H. 46,51n,53n,55
Bureaus, Naval *see* Naval Bureaus
Burrows, Montagu 88n,93n
Byng, John 61,78,79,82,83,90
Byron, George G., *Baron* Byron 139,183
Byron, John 82,82n

C

Caesar, Julius 50,62,63,101,107,130,131
Calder, *Sir* Robert 137,138
Calhoun, John C. 226
Camara, Manuel de la 136
Canadian fisheries question 13-14
Canadian Navy 148,148n
Cannae, battle of 75,75n
Cannon, Joseph G. 114
Caroline and Ladrone Islands 19
Cass, Lewis 176
Cervera y Topete, Pasqual 120,123,135, 212
Chadwick, French E. 32,233
Chandler, Lloyd H. 225
Chandler, William E. *SecNav* 11,12,47n, 49,193
Charnock, John 89
Chatham, *Earl of see* Pitt 103,105
Chesapeake Bay 156-57,159,227
Chesney, Cornwallis 106
Chiefs of Naval Bureaus *see* Naval Bureaus, Chiefs of
China—Open Door Policy 42,42n
Christian ethics 29,43,190,226
Church, Francis P. 172

Church, William C. 11,33,166,168, 170,172,180,184,185
Churchill, John 50,101. *See* Marlborough
civil liberty 187-88,226
Civil War 1-2,107,108,132,133,140,141, 142,144,160,208,220,222,223
civilization 40,42,190
Clausewitz, Karl von 107,123
Clemens, Samuel (Mark Twain) 172
Clerk, John 59,59n,69,75,81,81n,82,83, 87,88,89
Clinton, *Sir* Henry 86,86n
Clive, Robert, *Baron* Clive 10,103
Clowes, William L. 216,219,223
Coal report 194
Coasters Harbor Island 14,15,49,148,194
Coligny, Gaspard 58,58n
Collingwood, Cuthbert, *Baron* Collingwood 93,93n,104
Collum, Richard S. 174-75
Colomb, Philip H. 46,66,66n,69,222
Columbian Historical Exposition, Madrid 16,212
Columbus, ships of 209
commercial ports vs. military ports 154
comparative method 27,54-57,60,65
compass, magnetic (Mariner's) 40,40n,41
competition, need for in Navy 168
Contentin, Anne H. de 84n. *See* Tourville
Cooling, Benjamin F. 204
Copernicus, Nicolas 52,52n
copper sheathing of ships 53,228
Corbett, Julian S. 73n,231,232n
Cornwallis, Charles, *Earl* and *Marquis* Cornwallis 85,85n,86,134
Cornwallis, *Sir* William 134,137,138,139
court-martial, a fo'castle 214
Cowles, William S. 23
Creasy, *Sir* Edward S. 129
Creswell, John 73n
Crimean War 76,76n,122
Crowninshield, Arent S. 142-43,143n
Cullen, Charles W. 126n
Cuvier, George L.C.F.D. 52,52n,54,55

D

Dahlgren, John A.B. 59,59n,165
Dalton, John C. 54,54n
Davis, Charles H. 33
Davis, Cushman K. 143
Day, William R. 143
Dayton, Alston G. 23
Deane, Richard 77
De Barras, *Comte* Louis *see* Barras
De Forest, John W. 172
De Grasse, Francois J.P.M. *see* Grasse
Demosthenes 183
Desertions, Naval *see* Naval personnel
Dewey, George 21,117n,118,135,141, 142,143,144,148,221
Digby, Robert 87

Dillingham, Benjamin F. 145
Diodorus Siculus 211
dock, dry *see* drydocks
Douglas, *Sir* Howard 28,46,59n,61,88, 165
Dover, artificial harbor 153
Drake, *Sir* Francis 91
Drayton, Percival 3
drydocks
　European 152-53,227
　in Narragansett Bay 226
　in Brooklyn Navy yard and Narragansett Bay 227
　Japan 153
　value of 228
Dreux, battle of 58
Duncan, Adam, *Viscount* Duncan 88,92
DuPont, Samuel F. 29,123,166,173,223
Dutch Navy *see* Navy, Dutch

E

education of officers
　Christian ethics as an element 190
　courses at Naval War College 193-94
　an engineer corps 225,233
　failures in Naval administration 223
　purpose of the War College 37-41
　same regulations for all crews 7
　texts Luce wrote at Academy 164-65
　training ships 167
　War College and line officers 232-33
　war gaming at War College 230-31
Edward III, King 77
Effingham, *Baron* of *see* Howard 58n,91
Ekins, *Sir* Charles 69,83,83n,90,91-92
Elchingen, battle of 62
elements of a balanced Navy 151
Emmet, William 215
Engineer Corps, Naval 225,233
Epibatae, The 175
d'Estrees, *Comte* Jean 88
ethics, Christian 29,43,190,226
Eugene, Prince of Savoy 101,107
Evans, Robley D. 23,25,32
Evans, Samuel 159
extrasensory perception *see* Luce—on extrasensory perception

F

Fabius, Quintus 108
Fairfax, Donald McN. 119
Falconer, William 182,182n
Farragut, David G. 108,140n,148,173, 207,210
Fincati, Luigi 211
Fiske, Bradley A. 24,32,134,224
　comment on Luce 25
Fiske, John 29
Flodden, battle of 57,57n
Folger, William M. 23

Forbes, Robert B. 169
Fox, Gustavus V. 168
Foy, Maximilian S. 129
Frederick the Great 50,62,63,101,107, 131
Fremantle *Sir* Edmund R. 66,66n,69,94n
French colonies in America 105
French Navy *see* Navy, French
Frobisher, *Sir* Martin 91
Fullam, William F. 206
Funk and Wagnall's Dictionary 32,210
Fyffe, Charles A. 104

G

Galileo 52,52n
Galway, *Earl* of *see* Ruvigny 130
Gardiner, Arthur 90
General Board, The 20,21,119-20,223, 224
General Order #325 12,49,49n
General Staff, Navy *see* General Board
German General Staff 126
German Navy *see* Navy, German
Gibbon, Edward 132
Gilder, Joseph B. ix,33,99
Giron, *Vicomte* de *see* Grenier
  tactics 85,85n
Glorious First of June, battle of 73,73n
Goin, Thomas 172-73
Goodrich, Caspar 12,47n,48,194
Goschen, George J. *Viscount* Goschen 170
government, Naval *see* Naval administration and government
Grand tactics *see* Naval tactics
Grant, Ulysses S. *Pres.* 107,108,133,179
Grasse, Francois J.P.M. de 85,85n,86-87, 92,134. *See* Tilly
Graves, Thomas 82,82n,86-87,134
Graviere, Jurien de la 71,170-71,180, 181n
Great White Fleet 22
Grenier, Jacques R. 85,85n. *See* Giron
Gresham, Walter Q. 212
Griggs, John W. 143
Guantanamo Bay, Cuba 157
Guibert, *Comte* Jacques A.H. de 61,61n, 64
Guillot, Louis 81,81n,84n. *See* Orvilliers, de
Gunnery *see* Naval Light Artillery
Gunzburg, battle of 62
Gustavus, King 107
Guyot, Arnold 185
Guzman, Perez de 62. *See* Medina-Sidonia

H

Hale, Edward E. 215
Hale, Eugene 143
Halleck, Henry W. 179n

Hamersly's Encyclopedia 32,188-89
Hamilcar 68
Hamilton, Emma 215
Hamilton, *Sir* William 51n
Hamley, Edward B. 31,107,135
Hannibal 50,62,63,68,101,107,129-30
Harmony, D.B. 193
Harrison, Benjamin F. *Pres.* 15,212
Hart, Albert B. 222
Harte, Francis B. 172
Harvey, William 55
Hattendorf, John B. 126n
Hawaii 41,145-46,160
Hawke, *Lord* Edward 81,88,90,94,103
Hawkins, *Sir* John 91
Hayes, John D. 163n
Henderson, G.F.R. 28,100,105-06,132, 219
Herbert, Hilary O. *SecNav* 10,32,230
Herodotus 75
Hipparchus 52,52n
Hiram of Tyre 218
Hobson, Richmond P. 24
Holmes, Oliver W. 203
Hood, Samuel, *Viscount* Hood 61,82,82n, 83,92
Hoste, Paul 59,59n,69,75,78,84,88,96, 181
Howard, Charles 58,58n,91. *See* Effingham
Howe, Richard, *Earl* Howe 72,73,88
Hughes, *Sir* Edward 88,90
Humphreys, Joshua 158,159
Hunt, William H. *SecNav* 115
Huntington, Samuel P. 200

I

Imperial Naval College at Yeddo 177
The Influence of Sea Power upon History 1660-1783 by Alfred T. Mahan 99, 101-103
The Influence of Sea Power upon the French Revolution and Empire 1793-1812 by Alfred T. Mahan 100,104-108,210
international law
  maritime 39,178,179n,231
  Naval War College "blue books" 231
  study of 16,47,231

J

Jackson, Thomas J. (Stonewall) 105-06
  professor at V.M.I. 108,219
James, *Duke* of York 88
James, Henry 172
James, William 216,219
Japan 123,177,222,224-25
Jaques, William H. 102
Jarnac, battle of 57,57n,58
Johnson's New Universal Cyclopedia 32, 185,193,211

Jomini, *Baron* Henri 68,75,75n,107,133
Jones, William *SecNav* 228-29

K

Kent, James 180
Kepler, Johann 52,52n,54
Keppel, Augustus, *Viscount* Keppel 80,80n,81,82,84,85,90
Key, Albert L. 23
Knox, Dudley W. 25
Kray von Krajova, Paul 135-36
Key West, Florida 15,157

L

Ladrone Island *see* Caroline and Ladrone Islands
Lake Erie, battle of 76,76n
Lake Champlain, battle of 76,76n
Land and Naval warfare
  and military science 64-68
  fleet evolutions 59-61
  German General Staff 126
  military character of 132
  rules of the art of war 132-40
  a study needed 31
  tactics and strategy 96-97
  to learn Naval history 131
Lanier, Sidney 172
Lansdale, Philip 211
Laughton, *Sir* John K. 71,84,84n,91,99,178
Lavoisier, Antoine L. 52,52n
LeConte, Joseph 55
Lee, Robert E. 131,131n
Leibrich, Karl M. von 136
Lepanto, battle of 58,77,174,181
Lestock, Richard 79
Lieber, Francis 51,51n
Lima Bay, Panama 157
Lincoln, Abraham *Pres.* 107,132-33
Lissa, battle of 170,211,214
Little, William McC. 32,209
  war gaming 13,47,230-31
Livermore, W.R.
  on war gaming 231
Lodge, Henry C. 10,20,31,33,203,204,212
Long, John D. *SecNav* 143,144
Loring, Charles H. 192
Louis XV King of France 103
Luce, Stephen B.
  The Luce family
    Caroline(daughter) 6n
    Charlotte(daughter) 6n
    Eliza Henly(wife) 6,238
    Jane(sister) 212n
    John(brother) 212n
    John Dandridge Henly(son) 6n
    Margaret(sister) 212n
    Olivia(sister) 212n
    William(brother) 212n

Life of Luce Chronology 237-249
  born(1827) 3
  midshipman(1841) 1,3
  giftbook on Greece(1848) 5
  2d class of Naval Academy(1848) 5
  in Coast Survey(1850-53) 6
  married(1854) 6,238
  to Newport with Academy (1860) 8
  visited English and French developing navies(1863) 9
  Commandant of Academy (1865) 10,240
  President of Commission on Navy Yards(1882) 11,192
  appointed to head a Board to enlarge Naval War College plans (1884) 11-12
  established Naval War College in March 1884—became first President 11-13
  North Atlantic Squadron (1885) 13,45
  President of U.S. Naval Institute (1888) 196,244
  retired February 1889 1,15,203
  ordered to Naval War College faculty(1890) 16
  Commissioner-General of the United States at Columbian Historical Exposition, Madrid (1892-93) 16,212
  Revenue Cutter Service(1893) 16-18,246
  personal contacts outside of the Navy 33
  home in Newport(1911)—became ill—wrote no more 24
  died July 1917 1,24
  obituary by Bradley A. Fiske 25
  photographs 4,127,162, cover
Influence of Luce on the Navy
  acknowledged leader of intellectuals in the Service 32
  avant-garde ideas from European military thought 34
  breadth of Naval officer outlook 37
  breadth of reading 46
  catalyst for new ideas on the Navy 35
  chooses Naval War College faculty 12
  commended for exercises in North Atlantic Squadron 14
  contributions to the Navy 24
  influence in Navy's new age 2,3
  influence on American Naval thought 1
  influences on tactics and strategy in history 31

opposition to Navy reform 34
reform of the merchant training system 9
relationship to Mahan 17
reliance on Mahan 126
suggested "chief of naval operations" 21
a teacher 27
uniform rules for all ships 7
Writings of Luce
  categories of writings 26,251
  enduring quality of writing 163
  literary critic 98-108
  on extrasensory perception 182-83
  on land and Naval tactics 28
  on military ethics 187-88
  on Naval education see education of officers
  on Naval organization and administration 28,115-16
  on Naval organization in tabular form 234-35
  on Naval science 51-52
  on Naval training for seamen see Naval personnel
  on Naval War College see Naval War College
  on preferred anthracite coal 194
  on religion and war 29,190,208-09
  on rope-making 186
  on youths into the sea life 26-27, 201-02,207-08,209-10,214,215, 217
  pugnacious quality of writing 34
  Seamanship(text) 8,10,26,163,165-66,168-69,173,176,181,192, 196,218
  spiritualism 29,30
  writing becomes diversified 201
  writings reflect intellectual foundation of the 20th century U.S. Navy 35
  writings for *Youth Companion* 26
  Young Seaman's Manual 10,26

M

Macaulay, Thomas B. 57,84
Maclay, Edgar S. 219
Maffitt, John N. 190
Maguire, Edward 64
Mahan, Alfred T.
  Admiral Farragut article 210
  August 1886 at Naval War College 45
  became president of War College 13
  chapter in Clowes' *History of the Royal Navy* 219-223
  first to reach fame 47
  footnotes to 137,139
  historical data for Luce 126
  importance of base at Pearl Harbor 145-46
  Laughton to be his British critic 71
  Luce's review of his first book 99-105
  Luce's review of Nelson's biography 215-17
  Luce suggested *Naval Strategy* 21-22
  Moody Board report 125,235
  the "Naval Jomini" 68n
  need of battleships 204-05
  on the Moody Board 23
  photograph 98
  publisher for Mahan 204
  a scholar 231
  Secretary Herbert influenced by 230
  tactics, strategy and national power in lectures 29
Manila, battle of 142,233
Marines, Greek and Roman 175
maritime international law, see international law
Marjoribanks, Edward 113. See Tweedmouth
Marlborough, Duke of see Churchill 50,101
Martin, William A.P. 114
Martinique, ceding of 148
Marvin, Winthrop L. 19
Massachusetts Military Historical Society 221-22
Mathews, Thomas. 78,79,80,83,90
Matteucci, Carlo 55
Matthews, Edward O. 165
Maury, Matthew F. 179
McArthur, John 83,83n,84,84n
McCulloch, Hugh 169
McDonough, Thomas 76n
McKean, Fred G. 194
McKinley, William Pres.
  dispatch to Admiral Dewey 19,143-44
Meade, Richard W. 179-80
Medina-Sidonia, Duke of see Guzman 62
Mercantile Marine see Merchant Marine
Mercantile Marine Commission 19
Merchant Marine
  officers of 9,173
  personnel training 173,174,196
  shipping interests 41
Merrimac see *Monitor*
Metcalf, Victor SecNav 22
Meyer, George von L. SecNav 23,128,232
Middleton, Charles 137,138,140. See Barham
Miles, Nelson A. 203
Military and Naval operations at Newport, R.I. 197-98
Military and Naval tactics, ancient 57
Military art and education, Greece 67-68
Military science and art 54,101. See also land and Naval warfare
Miller, J.N. 195
Missionary Ridge, battle of 233
Mississippi River 140-41

Mobile Bay, battle of 211n
Mobility 62-63
Moltke, Helmuth J.L. von 153
Moltke System 108
Moncontour, battle of 57,57n
Monitor and the *Merrimac* 1-2,221-22
Monk, George 58,77n,89. *See* Albemarle
Monroe Doctrine 41,114,115
Montague, Edward 89,89n. *See* Sandwich
Montecuccoli, *Count* Raimondo 50,50n
Montojo y Pasaron, *Don* Patricio 136
Moody Board 11,110,125,181,232,235
Moody, William H. *SecNav* 20,21,23,32, 33,110,118
Moore, John B.
   on international law 231
Morison, Samuel E. 213n
Morogues, *Vicomte* de *see* Bigot 85,85n
Morrill Act, 1862 9,10
Morton, Paul *SecNav* 23
Muller, Friedrich M. 46,56,56n
Mullett, A.B. 192

N

Narragansett Bay, R.I.
   best site for Naval base 148,156
   British engineers survey 157-58
   drydocks in 226,228
   U.S. engineers in favor of 159-60,227
Nautical schools 169,172,189
Naval Academy at Newport, R.I. 148, 190-91,210
Naval administration and government
   the future Navy 203-04
   Hamersly's on administration 188
   Luce devoted major writings to 28
   Luce duty on Moody Board 110
   Naval base on Hawaii 145
   Navy yards 213
   need for Board of Admiralty 167-68, 228-29
   recommendation for Naval reform in table form 234-35
   reorganization of Navy 179-80
   report of Commission on Navy yards 192
   to reform Navy Department 199,220, 223,224
Naval archeology 104,185,211
Naval artillery 164-65
Naval bases
   British bases 153
   Chesapeake Bay 156
   eleven components of 155
   German bases 154
   in China 153-54
   in the Caribbean 18
   Narragansett Bay 148,149,159-60, 226-28
   need for 147
   Newport, R.I. best Atlantic site 148
   on Pearl Harbor 145-46
   summary on 161
Naval Bureaus, Chiefs of 19,20,49,116-19,121-23,125,142,161
Naval customs 219
Naval efficiency 109,112-18,124,138
Naval encyclopedia *see* Hamersly's Encyclopedia
Naval government *see* Naval administration and government
Naval history
   History of the United States Marine Corps 174-75
   Naval actions and history 1799-1898 221-22
   the Navy and Japan 224-25
   Navy to preserve peace 218
   of Naval fleets 171-82
   of Naval signalling 184
   of wars 128-140
   review of Mahan's *Influence of Sea Power upon History 1660-1783* 101-03
   Spanish-American war 233-34
   summary of "modern" navies 176-78
Naval Light Artillery, Afloat and Ashore by Luce 164-65
Naval officers
   as a profession 58-59
   as engineers 225
   condition of Naval officers 7
   contribution of Naval War College to 37-41
   promotion of 168
   requirements to be filled 203
Naval officers *see also* education of officers
Naval Operations, Chief of 21
   first "chief of" realized 232
   proposed office of 23-24
Naval personnel
   apprentice system 10,207
   desertions 230
   enlisted men's training 7,174
   training schools 186
   training ships 166,167,186,205-06
   training squadron 10,148,186,187,229
Naval policy 112-13,114-15,116,189-90
Naval safety 188
Naval science *see* science
Naval Signal Book (British) 38,72,74,88, 94-95,96 refers to *Manual of Fleet Evolutions* 73
Naval Signal Book of the United States of America 170,182,184,185
Naval Songs by Luce 10,163,189,191,220
Naval strategy
   and Naval bases 161
   applied by G.F.R. Henderson 100
   at the War College 39
   needs aid of a fleet 76

"one must serve a long apprenticeship in" 107
strategic plans 144
strategy and narrow seas 178
strategy during peace 214
triumph of 135-46
Naval tactics 182,185,189
fleet and military tactics 56
fleet tactics under steam 50,60
Grand tactics 69,73-76,92,95,96,196
Naval and land tactics 64
"Naval Tactics" by Luce 71-97
speed as an element 63
tactics as an art 38-39
under sail 90-91
Naval tactics, British 63,65,71-79,83,84, 91,92,93,94,95
Naval tactics, French 63,87-91,92, 170-71,172
Naval War Board 120,122,142,144,220-21
Naval War College
consolidated with Torpedo Station 15-16
employs no teachers 38
established by General Order #325 under Luce 11-13,194
extension of courses to one year 233
history of 230-33
"is educational not functional" 16, 232
Luce appointed to faculty 201,246
Luce Hall 36
mission 38-40
Narragansett Bay site for 148
photographs 36,70,202
review of Mahan's lectures 101
statement of intellectual concept 46-47,193-94
use of war gaming boards 14-15
Naval War College, French 231
Naval War College, German 231
Naval warfare, study of
battleships essential to Naval warfare 203-05
during peace, anticipating war 214
French Naval tactics 170-72
Naval warfare and Naval tactics 88
Naval warfare as a science 54-56
Navy yards are essential 213
similarity of land and Naval tactics 28
some history of Naval warfare 101-03
Naval warfare under steam 59,65-67,165, 196
Navy, British
battle in broad oceans with the Dutch and French 79-82
Board of Admiralty and Navy Board 199
British Admiralty and ironclad fleet 177
British battleship 203

British schoolships 166-67
during U.S. Civil War 221-22
England and France on the sea 104-08
government, Naval 188-89
history of Royal Navy 216,218,219, 223
interchange of Naval and Army officers in command 57-58
Naval policy of England 113,114
practical training of crew and officers 77-78
"The Queen's Navy" 223
system of tactics needed 65-67
volunteer system for crew 207
William Pitt defeats French 103
Navy Commissioners, Board of 234
Navy, Department see U.S. Navy Department
Navy, Dutch 78-79
Navy, French
Corvette 188
efficiency of British and French navies 174
Luce praises organization of 200
Naval policy of France 113n-114n
Naval race between Great Britain and France 203-04
Navy of France 177
policy of manoeuvre 79-87
ships are sheathed 58,228
Navy, German 124,148,177,203-04
Navy, Greece 177,181
Navy yards 152,175,192,213,227
Nebuchadnezzar 183
Nelson, Horatio, Viscount Nelson 61,62, 63,72,73,74,88,89,92,93,94,102, 103,104,105,108,132,136,137, 139,215,221,233-34
Newberry, Truman SecNav 110
New Orleans, battle of 140-41, 173
Newton, Sir Isaac 52,52n
Nicolas, Sir Harris 216
Nordhoff, Charles 208,225
North Atlantic Squadron see North Atlantic Station
North Atlantic Station 13,32,45,195, 197,233

O

Onslow, Sir Richard 93,93n
Orford, Earl of see Russell 75,75n,90
Orvilliers, Comte de see Guillot 81,81n, 84n
Osbon, Bradley S. 173

P

Paine, Alfred C. 173
Palliser, Sir Hugh 80,80n
Panama Canal 41,41n,115,157,181
Parker, Foxhall A. 60,60n,174,181,184, 185

260

Parker, William A. 164-65
Paulding, James K. SecNav 189
Pearl Harbor, Hawaii 145,146,160
Pemberton, John C. 133
Periodicals
   Periodicals of Reference
      American Journal of Education 170
      Atheneum 99
      Atlantic Monthly, The 99,172
      Blackwood's Magazine 132n
      Century Magazine 133n
      Congressional Record 145n
      Edinburgh Review 65n,71
      Fortnightly Review 178
      Forum 65n,145n
      Journal of the History of Ideas 51n
      Journal of the Royal United Service Institution 66n,71n,94n
      London Times, The 231
      Mariner's Mirror 53n
      McClure's Magazine 22
      Military Affairs 163n
      Nautical Gazette 172,173
      Naval Chronicle 83n
      Naval War College Review 126n
      New York Times, The 99,116n, 157,206
      Pall Mall Gazette 154n
      Past and Present 77n
      Revue Maritime et Coloniale 171n
      Rhode Island Historical Magazine 158n
      Southern Literary Messenger 179
   Periodicals—published Luce's writings
      Army and Navy Journal 9,32,33, 121n,164,166,167,168,169,170, 172,174,176,177,179,180
      Army and Navy Life 228,229n
      Army-Navy Register, The 206
      Brentano's Aquatic Monthly and Sporting Gazetteer 186
      Critic, The 32,33,99,101n,104n,105n 201,205,210,215,216,219,223
      Galaxy, The 33,172,182,184
      Harper's New Monthly Magazine 33
      Harper's Weekly 215
      Japan Daily Mail 222
      Magazine of American History 33
      Newport Daily News 226,227,228
      Newport Mercury, The 222,226, 227,228
      New York Herald 196
      North American Review 23,32,33, 60,109n,147n,201,203,207,208, 213,214,223,225,228,233,234
      Potter's American Monthly 177, 178n,179,184,211
      Record(U.S. Naval Institute) 77n, 78n

United Service Magazine, The 32, 90n,186,187,189,193,226
U.S. Naval Institute Proceedings 32, 37,45,55n,69,77n,78n,117n, 125n,168,174,181,191,196,199, 203,205,206,211,213,215,218, 220,223,224,226,229,230,231-32,234-35
Youth's Companion 26,32,33,201, 202,208,214,215,217
Perkins, George C. 146
Perry, Matthew C. 224
Perry, Oliver H. 75,75n,159,195
Pharsalia, battle of 75,75n
Philippines, The 41
Phoenician Navy 218
Phormio 75,75n
Phythia, Robert L. 10
Pillsbury, John E. 211
Pitt, William 103,105. See Chatham
Pocock, Sir George 82,82n,85
Popham, Edward 77
Port Arthur, battle of 117,123
Port Royal, battle of 54,54n,166,173
Porter, David D. 3,108,180
   comment on Luce 25
Porto Praya, battle of 63
Posnett, Hutcheson M. 57
Potter, John E. 178n
Potter, William H. 195
powder monkey 207-08
Preble, George H. 190
Privateers 177,219
Ptolemaeus, Claudius 52,52n
Ptolmey I (Soter) 129

Q

Quiberon, battle of 91

R

Raleigh, Sir Walter 58
Ramatuelle, Audibert 85,85n
Randolph, Sir George C. 69,95n
Rawson, Edward K. 219
reasoning, inductive and deductive 46, 52,53
Reuterdahl, Henry 22
Revenue Cutter Service see U.S. Coast Guard
Rice, Allen T. 203
Rideing, William H. 33,203
Robeson, George M. SecNav 170,179,226
Rodgers, Christopher R.P. 195
Rodney, George B., Baron Rodney 62, 82,82n,83,88,89
Rogers, William B. 225
Roosevelt, Theodore Pres. 20,31,33,109, 110,115,117,121,123,141,150,223
Root, Elihu 150
Royal Marines of Great Britain 175

Royal Naval War College 231
Royal Navy see Navy, British
Rozhdestvenski, Zinovi P. 123
Russell, Edward 75,75n,90. See Orford
Russell, William C. 102
Rupert, Prince, Count Blatine of Rhine 58,58n,77,88,89
Ruvigny, Henri de Massue de 130. See Galway
Ruyter, Michiel A. de 89

S

safety in ships 169
sailing ship training see Naval personnel
St. John, Henry 74n. See Bolingbroke
Salamis, battle of 40,62,76,139,186,208, 219
Sampson William T. 12,47n,48,136n,194, 233
Sanborn, John P. 226
Sandwich, Earl of see Montague 89,89n
Santiago, Battle of 219,233
Saxe, Comte Hermann de 62
Schmidt, Carl 55
science
    and art of war 38,146,232
    and technology growth 2-3,46,51-52
    of Naval warfare 30,31,53-54,68
    of war 38,93-94,100,101,128-31,177, 182
    scientific method 55-56
Scipio Africanus, Cornelius 108,130
Seabury, Samuel 193,196,218
seamanship see Luce—Writings of—Seamanship(text)
sea power 17,22,115,145,155
Secretaries of the Navy
    1801 Smith, Robert 158-59
    1838 Paulding, James K. 189
    1845 Bancroft, George 180,181n,195
    1861 Welles, Gideon 140,172
    1869 Robeson, George M. 170,179, 226
    1881 Hunt, William H. 115
    1882 Chandler, William E. 11,12,47n, 49,193
    1885 Whitney, William C. 14,32,199, 203,224,230
    1889 Tracy, Benjamin F. 15,32,203, 204,212,230
    1893 Herbert, Hilary O. 10,32,203
    1897 Long, John D. 143,144
    1902 Moody, William H. 20,21,23,32, 33,110,118
    1904 Morton, Paul 23
    1905 Bonaparte, Charles J. 22,122,224
    1906 Metcalf, Victor 22
    1908 Newberry, Truman 110
    1909 Meyer, George von L. 22,128, 232
Seven Years War 89,103
Shepard, Henry L. 174-75

Sherman, William T. 108,133,134,139, 223
Ships, U.S.
    Adams(frigate) 151-52
    Bennington(gunboat) 225
    Brutus(collier) 142
    Columbus(line-of-battleship) 3,208, 213,222,224-25
    Congress(frigate) 3,5
    Delaware(battleship) 124n
    Evening Star(coastal steamer) 169
    Galena 15
    Hartford 10,184,211n,221
    Jamestown(sloop-of-war) 6
    Juniata(sloop-of-war) 170,177,187,211
    Macedonian(midshipman practice ship) 9,166
    Maine(battleship) 14
    Mercury(schoolship) 33
    Merrimac(steam frigate) 1,164,217, 221,222
    Minnesota(frigate) 128n,186,187n.236
    Monitor(steam frigate) 1-2,221-22
    Monterey(monitor) 142
    Nantucket (monitor) 9,166,167,217
    New Hampshire(ship-of-the-line) 48, 194
    New York(flagship) 233
    North Carolina(line-of-battleship) 3, 209-10
    North Dakota(battleship) 23,124n
    Patrick Henry(CSS) 164
    St. Marys(schoolship) 10,33
    Tennessee(flagship) 45,195
    Vandalia(sloop-of-war) 6
    Vermont(receiving ship) 218
    Vincennes(sloop-of-war) 224-25
    Wabash 215
Shipyards became Navy yards 152
Shufelt, Robert W. 187
Signal Book see Naval Signal Book
Simpson, Edward 200
Sims, William S. 22,23,32,109,110
    on Luce's contribution 128-29
    photograph 111
Sluys, battle of 77,77n
Smith, Adam 134-35
Smith, Robert SecNav 158-59
Smollett, Tobias 84
Soley, James R. 16,47
South Atlantic Blockading Squadron 8, 166
Spanish-American War 41-43,120,122, 141,144,161,201,229,233-34
speed, a necessity in war 62-64
Sperry, Charles S. 19
Stevens, John A. 33
Stewart, Charles 220
Stockton, Charles H. 231
Stolypin, Petr A. 123
Stonewall Jackson and the American Civil War by G.F.R. Henderson 105-06

acceptance compared to the acceptance of Mahan's writing 100
Storey, Joseph 180
strategy *see* Naval strategy
Suffren, Pierre A., de 63,85,85n,88,90
Sumner, Charles 169
Swift, Joseph 159
Swift, William 23

T

tactics, Grand *see* Naval tactics
Taft, William H. *Pres.* 23,150,156,157
Taylor, Bayard 172
Taylor, Henry C. 20,33,230
Taylor, Zachary, *Pres.* 166
Technology *see* science
Texel, battle of 181
Themistocles 38,183
Thucydides 75,129
Tilly, *Comte* de *see* Grasse 85,85n,86-87, 92,134
Togo, *Count* Heihachiro 123
Torpedo Station at Newport, R.I. 15,49
Tracy, Benjamin F. *SecNav* 15,32,203, 204,212,230
Trafalgar, battle of 62,76,88,89,92,93, 104,134,135,136-37,221
training ships *see* Naval personnel
Trinity Church, Newport, R.I. 24
Trollope, Anthony 172
Tromp, Maarteen H. 89
Tourville, *Comte* de *see* Contentin 84,84n
Turenne, Henri de la T. d'A. 50,50n,58, 107,130
Tweedmouth, *Baron see* Marjoribanks 113
Tyndall, John 54
Tyre, Siege of 76,76n

U

U.S. Army War College 47,67n,231
U.S. Artillery School 191
U.S. Coast Guard
  Letter by Luce to Secretary opposing Revenue Marine with the Navy 246
  Revenue Cutter Service 16-18
U.S. Marine Corps 168,174,175,176,165, 206,222
U.S. Naval Signal Book *see* Naval Signal Book of the United States of America
U.S. Navy Department, reorganization
  administration reform—the fleet 109-10,112-124
  an Admiralty staff 228-29
  Board of Navy Commissioners 200

Luce cautious in writing about 164
Luce's plea for reform 224
need of centralized direction 20-24
"outlook for reform" 126,128
reforming Navy Department 10-11
reorganization of Navy 179-80
tabular form of reorganization 234-35
Upton, Emory 11,28,31,191

V

Van Nostrand, Daniel 33
Velpeau, Alfred A.L.M. 55
Villaret de Joyeuse, Louis 73
Villehuet, Bourdé de 166
Villeneuve, Pierre C.J.B.S. 123,137-39

W

Wagram, battle of 75,75n
Wainwright, Richard 32,200,205
war
  effects of 42
  preparation for 43
  prevention of 208,223
  study of 47
war gaming *see* Little
War of 1812 219,220
Ward, Aaron 192,192n,196,218
Ward, James H. 61,61n
Watson, John C. 136
Welles, Gideon *SecNav* 140,172
Wellesley, Arthur 50,101,106,108. *See* Wellington
Wellings, James C. 212
Wellington, Duke of *see* Wellesley 50, 101,106,108
Wheaton, Henry 179n
Whitman, Walt 172
Whitney, William C. *SecNav* 14,32,199, 203,224,230
Whittlesey, Humes H. 142,143
Whitthorne, Washington C. 10,180,181n, 204
Wilson, Georg G. 231
Wolfe, James 103
Wolseley, *Viscount* Garnet J. 132
Woods, *Sir* Henry F. (Pasha) 60,60n
Woolsey, Theodore W. 179n,187-88

X

Xenophon 129,183

Y

Young Seaman's Manual see Luce— writings of